the food of the world

450 classic recipes from around the world

the food of
the world

450 classic recipes from around the world

bay books

Many towns have a market selling local, seasonal produce. On this page bread is sold at a market in Provence, France, and vegetable and potatoes in a a Paris market. Honfleur is one of France's many fishing ports.

CONTENTS

Tuscany's hills are covered with Chianti vines, while Siena's Duomo dominates a town famed for its panforte. Italian produce includes cherries from Emilia-Romagna, figs eaten with the Parma ham, and peaches from Le Marche. Bologna's streets are full of restaurants serving many local dishes.

The flavors of Southern Italy: ripe tomatoes, citrus fruit, olives from twisted groves and fresh herbs. Palermo is home to both the Vucciria market, set in its backstreets, and a busy fish market, where the bellies of Sicily's famous tuna are cut out for export to Asia. Seafood is prepared simply, while marzipan fruit has been elevated to art.

7

A man hurls his fish onto the Sassoon Docks in Mumbai (Bombay) and poppadoms are made on the rooftops in the shadow of Delhi's Moghul architecture. Women plant rice in Kerala; Indian cooking makes great use of pulses and spices.

India is a very complex country from a culinary point of view. Cooking styles vary from suburb to suburb. Fish are popular in Bengal and Maharashtra. Tea is grown in Assam. On the west coast in Mumbai (Bombay), people gather on Chowpatty beach at sunset to walk, talk and eat chaat. Bhajis are fried on request. In Hyderabad the selection of pickles is incomparable.

9

Visitors climb the steps to the Temple of Heaven despite the cold of a Beijing winter. Steaming hot buns are a staple of Northern China, along with cabbage, huge winter melons, red carrots and pickled vegetables. Barbecued skewers of lamb and the ubiquitous pot noodles are sold as warming street snacks.

China has one of the great cuisines of the world. Bean curd and chives are used in many dishes, while fried fish rolls served at a banquet and fried bread sold in the market both use the same cooking technique.

Bananas are seen growing all over Thailand. Young monks ride on river boats along the Chaophraya in Bangkok. Delicious street food is available at night markets. Ornate architecture on Wat Saen Fang in Chiang Mai, Thailand.

Reserved for monks

Vegetables on sale at Aw
Taw Kaw market, Bangkok,
Thailand. Frantic Bangkok,
Thailand's capital, contrasts
with the serenity of transport
boats used around the quiet
khlongs of Damnoen
Saduak.

SNACKS

CHICKEN WRAPPED IN PANDANUS LEAF

PANDANUS LEAVES ACT AS BOTH A WRAPPING AND A FLAVOURING IN THIS DISH. LEAVING A LONG TAIL ON THE PARCELS WILL MAKE THEM PRETTIER AND EASIER TO HANDLE SO DON'T TRIM THE LEAVES. TO EAT, CAREFULLY UNWRAP THE PARCELS AND DIP THE CHICKEN IN THE SAUCE.

5 coriander (cilantro) roots, cleaned and roughly chopped
4–5 garlic cloves
1 teaspoon ground white pepper
¼ teaspoon salt
600 g (1 lb 5 oz) skinless chicken breast fillets, cut into 25 cubes
2 tablespoons oyster sauce
1½ tablespoons sesame oil
1 tablespoon plain (all-purpose) flour
25 pandanus leaves, cleaned and dried
vegetable oil, for deep-frying
plum sauce (page 562) or a chilli sauce, to serve

MAKES 25

USING a pestle and mortar or a small blender, pound or blend the coriander roots, garlic, white pepper and salt into a paste. In a bowl, combine the paste with the chicken, oyster sauce, sesame oil and flour. Cover with plastic wrap and marinate in the refrigerator for at least 3 hours, or overnight.

FOLD one of the pandanus leaves, bringing the base up in front of the tip, making a cup. Put a piece of chicken in the fold and, moving the bottom of the leaf, wrap it around to create a tie and enclose the chicken. Repeat until you have used all the chicken.

HEAT the oil in a wok or deep frying pan over a medium heat.

WHEN the oil seems hot, drop a small piece of leaf into it. If it sizzles immediately, the oil is ready. Lower some parcels into the oil and deep-fry for 7–10 minutes or until the parcels feel firm. Lift out with a slotted spoon and drain on paper towels. Keep the cooked ones warm while deep-frying the rest. Transfer to a serving plate. Serve with plum sauce or a chilli sauce.

Pandanus leaves are used to enclose the chicken in an attractive tie shape.

Luk Yu Tea House,
Hong Kong

Gather in the tops of the buns as
neatly as you can to make round
balls. Bear in mind that they will
open slightly as they cook to
show their filling.

CHAR SIU BAU

MANTOU, OR STEAMED BUNS, ARE A FILLING STAPLE EATEN ALL OVER CHINA, BUT ESPECIALLY IN THE
NORTH. HOWEVER, THESE FILLED, SLIGHTLY SWEET BUNS MADE WITH BARBECUE PORK (CHAR SIU)
ARE A CANTONESE SPECIALITY, ENJOYED IN EVERY DIM SUM RESTAURANT.

1 teaspoon oil
250 g (9 oz) barbecue pork
   (char siu), diced
3 teaspoons Shaoxing rice wine
1 teaspoon roasted sesame oil
2 tablespoons oyster sauce
2 teaspoons light soy sauce
3 teaspoons sugar
1 quantity basic yeast dough
   (page 570)
chilli sauce

MAKES 12 LARGE OR
24 SMALL

HEAT the oil in a wok. Add the pork, rice wine,
sesame oil, oyster sauce, soy sauce and sugar
and cook for 1 minute. Leave to cool.

DIVIDE the dough into 12 or 24 portions,
depending on how large you want your buns
to be, and cover with a tea towel. Working with
one portion at a time, press the dough into circles
with the edges thinner than the centre. Place
1 teaspoon of filling on the dough for a small bun
or 3 teaspoons for a large bun. Draw the sides in
to enclose the filling. Pinch the top together and
put each bun on a square of greaseproof paper.
When you get more proficient at making these,
you may be able to get more filling into the buns,
which will make them less doughy. Ensure that
you seal them properly. The buns can also be
turned over, then cooked the other way up so
they look like round balls.

PLACE the buns well apart in 3 steamers. Cover
and steam over simmering water in a wok,
reversing the steamers halfway through, for
15 minutes, or until the buns are well risen and
a skewer inserted into the centre comes out hot.
Serve with some chilli sauce.

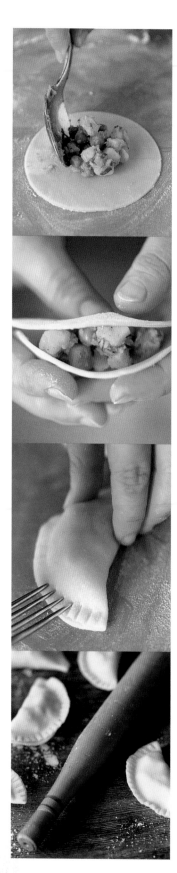

Don't over-stuff the samosas or they will burst when cooked. Seal them and use a fork to press the edges together firmly.

SAMOSAS

THESE CRISP, DEEP-FRIED PASTRIES ARE THE MOST POPULAR SAVOURY SNACK IN INDIA. THIS RECIPE HAS A DELICIOUS SPICY VEGETABLE FILLING BUT VARIOUS COMBINATIONS OF MEAT AND VEGETABLES EXIST. SAMOSAS ARE USUALLY SERVED WITH CHUTNEY.

PASTRY
450 g (1 lb) maida or plain flour
1 teaspoon salt
4 tablespoons oil or ghee

FILLING
400 g (14 oz) potatoes, cut into
    quarters
80 g (3 oz) peas
1 1/2 teaspoons cumin seeds
1/2 teaspoon coriander (cilantro)
    seeds
2 tablespoons oil
1/2 onion, finely chopped
1/4 teaspoon ground turmeric
1/2 teaspoon garam masala
    (page 556)
2 green chillies, chopped
3 cm (1 1/4 inch) piece of ginger,
    chopped
1 1/2 tablespoons lemon juice
2 tablespoons chopped coriander
    (cilantro) leaves

oil for deep-frying

MAKES 30

TO MAKE the pastry, sift the maida and salt into a bowl, then rub in the oil or ghee until the mixture resembles breadcrumbs. Add 180–200 ml (2/3 cup) warm water, a little at a time, to make a pliable dough. Turn out onto a floured surface and knead for 5 minutes, or until smooth. Cover and set aside for 15 minutes. Don't refrigerate or the oil will harden.

TO MAKE the filling, cook the potato in simmering water until tender. Drain and cut into small cubes. Cook the peas in simmering water for 2 minutes. Drain and refresh in cold water.

PLACE a small frying pan over low heat, dry-roast the cumin seeds until aromatic, then remove. Dry-roast the coriander seeds. Grind 1/2 teaspoon of the cumin and all the coriander to a fine powder in a spice grinder or pestle and mortar.

HEAT the oil in a heavy-based saucepan over low heat and fry the onion until light brown. Stir in all the cumin, the coriander, turmeric and garam masala. Add the potato, chilli, ginger and and stir for 1 minute. Mix in the lemon juice and coriander leaves and salt, to taste, then leave to cool.

ON a floured surface, roll out one-third of the pastry to a 28 cm (11 inch) circle, about 3 mm (1/8 inch) thick. Cut 10 circles with an 8 cm (3 1/4 inch) cutter and spoon 1/2 tablespoon of filling onto the centre of each. Moisten the edges with a little water, then fold over and seal with a fork into a semicircle. Repeat to use all the filling and pastry. Cover until ready to fry.

FILL a karhai or heavy-based saucepan one-third full with oil and heat to 180°C/350°F. Fry a few samosas at a time until lightly browned. Turn them over and brown them on the other side. Drain on a wire rack for 5 minutes before draining on paper towels. Serve warm or cold.

FRIED FISH CAKES WITH GREEN BEANS

FISH CAKES ARE JUST ONE OF MANY DELICIOUS SNACKS SOLD AS STREET FOOD IN THAILAND. BATCHES ARE FRIED ON REQUEST AND SERVED IN A PLASTIC BAG, ALONG WITH A BAMBOO SKEWER FOR EATING THEM AND A SMALL BAG OF SAUCE FOR ADDITIONAL FLAVOUR.

450 g (1 lb) firm white fish fillets
1 tablespoon red curry paste
    (page 558) or bought paste
1 tablespoon fish sauce
1 egg
50 g (2 oz) snake beans,
    finely sliced
5 makrut (kaffir) lime leaves,
    finely shredded
peanut oil, for deep-frying
sweet chilli sauce (page 562),
    to serve
cucumber relish (page 563),
    to serve

MAKES 30

REMOVE any skin and bone from the fish and roughly chop the flesh. In a food processor or a blender, mince the fish fillets until smooth. Add the curry paste, fish sauce and egg, then blend briefly until smooth. Spoon into a bowl and mix in the beans and makrut lime leaves. Use wet hands to shape the fish paste into thin, flat cakes, about 5 cm (2 inches) across, using about a tablespoon of mixture for each.

HEAT 5 cm (2 inches) oil in a wok or deep frying pan over a medium heat. When the oil seems hot, drop a small piece of fish cake into it. If it sizzles immediately, the oil is ready.

LOWER five or six of the fish cakes into the oil and deep-fry them until they are golden brown on both sides and very puffy. Remove with a slotted spoon and drain on paper towels. Keep the cooked fish cakes warm while deep-frying the rest. Serve hot with sweet chilli sauce and cucumber relish.

FOR a variation make up another batch of the fish mixture but leave out the curry paste. Cook as above and serve both types together.

Using wet hands makes the fish mixture less likely to stick to your hands and also easier to handle.

PIZZETTE

½ quantity pizza dough (page 577)
cornmeal
1 tablespoon olive oil
250 g (9 oz) mozzarella, grated

GARLIC AND ROSEMARY PIZZETTE
4 garlic cloves, crushed
2 teaspoons chopped rosemary
1½ tablespoons olive oil
55 g (2 oz) Parmesan, grated
3 garlic cloves, thinly sliced

TOMATO AND OLIVE PIZZETTE
200 g (7 oz) pitted black olives, diced
400 g (14 oz) plum tomatoes, diced
3 garlic cloves, crushed
2 tablespoons finely shredded basil
3 tablespoons olive oil
5 small basil sprigs

MAKES 10 PIZZETTE

PREHEAT the oven to 240°C (475°C/Gas 9). Form the pizza dough into ten bases. Place the pizza bases on two baking trays dusted with cornmeal. Brush with the oil, then sprinkle the bases with mozzarella. Make five garlic and rosemary pizzette and five tomato and olive pizzette.

TO MAKE the garlic and rosemary pizzette, scatter five bases with the crushed garlic and rosemary and drizzle the oil over the top. Sprinkle with Parmesan and garnish with some slices of garlic.

TO MAKE the tomato and olive pizzette, mix together the olives, tomato, garlic and shredded basil and spoon over the remaining bases. Drizzle over the oil and garnish with the basil sprigs.

BAKE the pizzette for 10 minutes, or until the bases are crisp and golden.

An old olive oil press at the Ravida estate in Menfi in Sicily. This stone was turned by a donkey who walked around it in a circle. Olives were ground between the two stones before being pressed to extract the oil.

GRISSINI

1 tablespoon malt syrup
2 teaspoons dried yeast or 15 g
 (½ oz) fresh yeast
500 g (1 lb 2 oz) plain flour
1½ teaspoons salt
2 tablespoons olive oil
fine semolina

MAKES 20

PUT 310 ml (1¼ cups) warm water in a bowl and stir in the malt and yeast. Leave until the yeast foams. Sift the flour and salt into a bowl, add the yeast and the oil and mix until the dough clumps together.

FORM into a ball and knead on a lightly floured surface until smooth and elastic. Put the dough on a lightly oiled tray and squash out to fill the shape of the tray. Brush with oil. Slide into a plastic bag and leave for 1 hour, or until doubled in size.

PREHEAT the oven to 230°C (450°F/Gas 8) and lightly oil two baking trays. Sprinkle the dough with semolina. Cut into four portions along its length, then slice each one into five strips. Pick up each strip by both ends and stretch out to 20 cm (8 inches) long. Place on the trays, 5 cm (2 inches) apart. Bake for 20 minutes, or until crisp and golden. Cool slightly on the trays and then on wire racks.

GRISSINI

VEGETABLE BHAJI

THESE DEEP-FRIED VEGETABLES MAKE AN EXCELLENT SNACK OR STARTER. IN INDIA, STREET VENDORS LINE THE STREETS ALL DAY, DUCKING BETWEEN BICYCLES, CARS AND PEDESTRIANS WHILE SETTING UP STALLS SELLING SUCH ITEMS. USUALLY THE BUSIER THE STALL, THE TASTIER THE SNACK.

240 g (8 oz) besan flour
1 teaspoon chilli powder
1 teaspoon ground turmeric
1/4 teaspoon asafoetida
100 g (3 oz) carrots, cut into thin
   sticks
100 g (3 oz) mangetout, cut into
   thin sticks
50 g (2 oz) thin eggplant
   (aubergines), cut into thin sticks
6 curry leaves
oil for deep-frying

MAKES 20

MIX together the besan flour, chilli powder, turmeric, asafoetida and a pinch of salt. Add enough water to make a thick batter which will hold the vegetables together. Mix the vegetables and curry leaves into the batter.

FILL a karhai or heavy-based saucepan one-third full with oil and heat to 180°C/350°F (a cube of bread will brown in 15 seconds). Lift clumps of vegetables out of the batter and lower carefully into the oil. Fry until golden all over and cooked through, then drain on paper towels. Sprinkle with salt and serve hot with chutney or raita.

Fry the vegetable sticks in clumps. The batter will help them stick to each other and will set around them as they cook.

MASALA VADA

100 g (3 oz) urad dal
120 g (4 oz) chana dal
2 green chillies, seeded and
   finely chopped
8 curry leaves, roughly chopped
1/2 teaspoon fennel seeds, crushed
1 red onion, finely chopped
1/2 teaspoon garam masala
   (page 556)
3 tablespoons grated coconut
   (page 555)
3 cm (1 1/4 inch) piece of ginger,
   grated
4 tablespoons chopped coriander
   (cilantro) leaves
3 tablespoons rice flour or
   urad dal flour
pinch of baking powder (optional)
oil for deep-frying

MAKES 18

SOAK the dal in cold water for 4 hours, then drain. Reserve 2 tablespoons of the soaked dal and coarsely grind the remainder in a food processor or pestle and mortar. Add the reserved dal to the ground dal for texture. Add the chopped chillies, curry leaves, fennel, onion, garam masala, coconut, ginger and coriander leaves. Mix well and season with salt. Add the flour and baking powder, if using (it gives a crisper texture), then mix until the texture is soft but the dough can be shaped (you may need to add a little water). Divide the mixture into 18 portions and form each into a ball. Slightly flatten each ball to form a patty.

FILL a karhai or heavy-based saucepan one-third full with oil and heat to 180°C/350°F (a cube of bread will brown in 15 seconds). Fry the patties in the hot oil, in batches of four or five, until golden brown and crisp. Drain well on paper towels and serve hot with a chutney.

MASALA VADA

HAR GAU

HAR GAU ARE THE BENCHMARK DIM SUM BY WHICH CHINESE RESTAURANTS ARE MEASURED AND THEY ARE NOT EASY TO MAKE. THE WHEAT STARCH DOUGH IS HARD TO HANDLE AND NEEDS TO BE KEPT WARM WHILE YOU WORK WITH IT, BUT THE RESULTS ARE VERY SATISFYING.

FILLING
500 g (1 lb 2 oz) prawns
45 g (1½ oz) pork or bacon fat (rind removed), finely chopped
40 g (1 oz) fresh or tinned bamboo shoots, rinsed, drained and finely chopped
1 spring onion (scallion), finely chopped
1 teaspoon sugar
3 teaspoons light soy sauce
½ teaspoon roasted sesame oil
1 egg white, lightly beaten
1 teaspoon salt
1 tablespoon cornflour

WRAPPER DOUGH
170 g (6 oz) wheat starch
3 teaspoons cornflour
2 teaspoons oil

soy sauce, chilli sauce or a dipping sauce (page 564)

MAKES 24

PEEL and devein the prawns and cut half of them into 1 cm (½ inch) chunks. Chop the remaining prawns until finely minced. Combine all the prawns in a large bowl. Add the pork or bacon fat, bamboo shoots, spring onion, sugar, soy sauce, sesame oil, egg white, salt and cornflour. Mix well and drain off any excess liquid.

TO MAKE the dough, put the wheat starch, cornflour and oil in a small bowl. Add 250 ml (1 cup) boiling water and mix until well combined. Add a little extra wheat starch if the dough is too sticky. Roll the dough into a long cylinder, divide it into 24 pieces and cover with a hot damp tea towel. Working with one portion at a time, roll out the dough using a rolling pin or a well-oiled cleaver. If using a rolling pin, roll the dough into a 10 cm (4 inch) round between two pieces of oiled clingfilm. If using a cleaver, place the blade facing away from you and gently press down on the flat side of the blade with your palm, squashing the dough while twisting the handle at the same time to form a round shape. Fill each wrapper as you make it.

PLACE a heaped teaspoon of the filling in the centre of each wrapper. Spread a little water along the edge of the wrapper and fold the wrapper over to make a half-moon shape. Use your thumb and index finger to form small pleats along the top edge. Press the two opposite edges together to seal. Place the har gau in four steamers lined with greaseproof paper punched with holes. Cover the har gau as you make them to prevent them drying out.

COVER and steam the har gau over simmering water in a wok, reversing the steamers halfway through, for 6–8 minutes, or until the wrappers are translucent. Serve with soy sauce, chilli sauce or a dipping sauce.

Har gau pastry is more delicate to handle than noodle-type wrappers. To make it easier, keep the pastry warm and pliable while you are working with it.

GOLD BAGS

THIS DELICATE STARTER OR SNACK LOOKS EXACTLY AS IT IS DESCRIBED—A TINY GOLD BAG. BLANCHED CHIVES WILL ALSO WORK AS TIES FOR THE TOPS OF THE BAGS. IF YOU LIKE YOU CAN USE HALF PRAWNS AND HALF CHICKEN OR PORK FOR THE FILLING.

280 g (10 oz) raw prawns (shrimp),
  peeled, deveined and roughly
  chopped, or skinless chicken
  or pork fillet, roughly chopped
225 g (8 oz) tin water chestnuts,
  drained and roughly chopped
3–4 garlic cloves, finely chopped
3 spring onions (scallions),
  finely sliced
1 tablespoon oyster sauce
1 teaspoon ground white pepper
1 teaspoon salt
2–3 bunches of spring onions
  (scallions), or 40 chives, for ties
2 tablespoons plain (all-purpose)
  flour
40 spring roll sheets 13 cm
  (5 inches) square
peanut oil, for deep-frying
a chilli sauce, to serve

MAKES 40

USING a food processor or blender, whiz the prawns, chicken or pork to a fine paste. In a bowl, combine the minced prawn or meat, water chestnuts, garlic, spring onions, oyster sauce, white pepper and salt.

TO MAKE spring onion ties, cut each into 4 to 6 strips, using only the longest green parts, then soak them in boiling water for 5 minutes or until soft. Drain, then dry on paper towels.

MIX the flour and 8 tablespoons cold water in a small saucepan until smooth. Stir and cook over a medium heat for 1–2 minutes or until thick.

PLACE 3 spring roll sheets in front of you and keep the remaining sheets in the plastic bag to prevent them drying out. Spoon 2 teaspoons of filling into the middle of each sheet. Brush around the filling with flour paste, then pull up into a bag and pinch together to enclose the filling. Place on a tray that is lightly dusted with plain (all-purpose) flour. Repeat until you have used all the filling and sheets. Tie a piece of spring onion twice around each bag and tie in a knot. Use chives if you prefer.

HEAT 7.5 cm (3 inches) oil in a wok or deep frying pan over a medium heat. When the oil seems hot, drop a small piece of spring roll sheet into it. If it sizzles immediately, the oil is ready. It is important not to have the oil too hot or the gold bags will cook too quickly and brown. Lower four bags into the oil and deep-fry for 2–3 minutes until they start to go hard. Lower another three or four bags into the oil and deep-fry them all together. To help cook the tops, splash the oil over the tops and deep-fry for 7–10 minutes or until golden and crispy. As each batch is cooked, lift the bags out with a slotted spoon and add another batch. Drain on paper towels. Keep the gold bags warm while deep-frying the rest. Serve with a chilli sauce.

Traditionally, Thais use spring onion greens for tying these bags but you may find it easier to use chives.

STEAMED GLUTINOUS RICE IN LOTUS LEAVES

LOR MAI GAI ARE A DIM SUM CLASSIC THAT ALSO MAKE GOOD SNACKS. WHEN STEAMED, THE RICE TAKES ON THE FLAVOURS OF THE OTHER INGREDIENTS AND FROM THE LOTUS LEAVES THEMSELVES. THE PARCELS CAN BE MADE AHEAD AND FROZEN, THEN STEAMED FROM FROZEN FOR 40 MINUTES.

600 g (1 lb 5 oz) glutinous rice
4 large lotus leaves

FILLING
2 tablespoons dried shrimp
4 dried Chinese mushrooms
2 tablespoons oil
360 g (13 oz) skinless chicken
    breast fillet, cut into 1 cm (½ inch)
    cubes
1 garlic clove, crushed
2 Chinese sausages (lap cheong),
    thinly sliced
2 spring onions (scallions), thinly
    sliced
1 tablespoon oyster sauce
3 teaspoons light soy sauce
3 teaspoons sugar
1 teaspoon roasted sesame oil
1 tablespoon cornflour
chilli sauce

MAKES 8

PLACE the rice in a bowl, cover with cold water and leave to soak overnight. Drain in a colander and place the rice in a bamboo steamer lined with a tea towel. Steam, covered, over simmering water in a wok for 30–40 minutes, or until the rice is cooked. Cool slightly before using.

SOAK the lotus leaves in boiling water for 1 hour, or until softened. Shake dry and cut the leaves in half to give eight equal pieces.

TO MAKE the filling, soak the dried shrimp in boiling water for 1 hour, then drain. Soak the dried mushrooms in boiling water for 30 minutes, then drain and squeeze out any excess water. Remove and discard the stems and finely chop the caps.

HEAT a wok over high heat, add half the oil and heat until very hot. Stir-fry the chicken for 2–3 minutes, or until browned. Add the shrimp, mushrooms, garlic, sausage and spring onion. Stir-fry for another 1–2 minutes, or until aromatic. Add the oyster sauce, soy sauce, sugar and sesame oil and toss well. Combine the cornflour with 200 ml (¾ cup) water, add to the sauce and simmer until thickened.

WITH WET hands, divide the rice into 16 balls. Place the lotus leaves on a work surface, put a ball of rice in the centre of each leaf and flatten the ball slightly, making a slight indentation in the middle. Spoon one eighth of the filling onto each rice ball, top with another slightly flattened rice ball and smooth into one ball. Wrap up firmly by folding the leaves over to form an envelope.

PLACE the parcels in 3 steamers. Cover and steam over simmering water in a wok, reversing the steamers halfway through, for 30 minutes. To serve, open up each leaf and eat straight from the leaf while hot with some chilli sauce.

Enclose the filling in the rice as much as possible, then neatly fold over the leaves. The leaves seal in the flavour and hold the rice in shape while cooking.

33

PRAWN PAKORAS

PAKORAS, ALSO KNOWN AS BHAJIS, ARE VERSATILE SNACKS THAT CAN BE MADE USING PRAWNS, FISH PIECES OR CHOPPED VEGETABLES. THE BESAN FLOUR AND POMEGRANATE SEEDS MAKE A TANGY FLAVOURSOME BATTER. MANGO CHUTNEY AND MINT CHUTNEY GO WELL WITH PAKORAS.

600 g (1 lb 5 oz) prawns
50 g (2 oz) besan flour
1 large red onion, finely chopped
1 teaspoon dried pomegranate
    seeds
4 green chillies, seeded and
    finely chopped
2 tablespoons finely chopped
    coriander (cilantro) leaves
pinch of bicarbonate of soda
ghee or oil for deep-frying

MAKES 30

PEEL and devein the prawns, then cut into small pieces. Put the besan flour in a bowl and add 2 tablespoons of water, or enough to make a thick batter, mixing with a fork to beat out any lumps. Add the remaining ingredients, except the oil, to the batter, season with salt and mix well.

FILL a karhai or heavy-based saucepan one-third full with ghee or oil and heat to 180°C/350°F (a cube of bread will brown in 15 seconds). Drop 1 heaped teaspoon of batter at a time into the ghee or oil and deep-fry in lots of six or eight pakoras until they are brown all over. Remove and drain on paper towels. Serve hot.

Deep-fry the pakoras in batches of six or eight so that the temperature of the oil remains constant. Cooking too many at once will cool the oil.

GOLL BHAJI

THESE ARE DEEP-FRIED NIBBLES ENJOYED AS TEA TIME SNACKS IN INDIA. THEY ARE KNOWN BY DIFFERENT NAMES IN DIFFERENT AREAS AND HAVE REGIONAL IDIOSYNCRASIES INCLUDING THEIR SHAPE AND THE TYPES OF FLOUR AND FLAVOURINGS USED IN THE BATTER. SERVE WITH A CHUTNEY.

90 g (3 oz) rice flour
50 g (2 oz) cashew nuts
75 g (2½ oz) besan flour
pinch of bicarbonate of soda
10 curry leaves, chopped
4 green chillies, seeded and
    finely chopped
2 cm (¾ inch) piece of ginger, finely
    chopped
1 red onion, finely chopped
1 tablespoon ghee
oil for deep-frying

MAKES 20

PLACE a small frying pan over low heat and dry-roast the rice flour until it turns light brown. Dry-roast the cashew nuts in the same pan until they brown, then finely chop them. Mix the rice flour with the besan flour, then add the bicarbonate of soda and a pinch of salt. Add the cashew nuts, curry leaves, green chilli, ginger, onion and ghee. Mix together well, adding a few drops of water, if necessary, to make a stiff dough. Form into 20 small balls.

FILL a karhai or heavy-based saucepan one-third full with ghee or oil and heat to 180°C/350°F (a cube of bread will brown in 15 seconds). Fry five or six balls at a time until golden brown, then drain each batch on paper towels.

GOLL BHAJI

Travelling by truck in Yunnan.

STEAMED RICE NOODLE ROLLS

A DIM SUM FAVOURITE, THESE SILKY RICE NOODLES CAN BE FILLED WITH BARBECUE PORK (CHAR SIU), PRAWNS OR VEGETABLES. THE NOODLES ARE SOLD AS A LONG SHEET FOLDED INTO A ROLL. DO NOT REFRIGERATE THEM—THEY MUST BE USED AT ROOM TEMPERATURE OR THEY WILL BREAK.

PORK FILLING

350 g (12 oz) barbecue pork (char siu), chopped

3 spring onions (scallions), finely chopped

2 tablespoons chopped coriander (cilantro)

OR

PRAWN FILLING

250 g (9 oz) small prawns

1 tablespoon oil

3 spring onions (scallions), finely chopped

2 tablespoons chopped coriander (cilantro)

OR

VEGETABLE FILLING

300 g (10 oz) Chinese broccoli (gai lan)

1 teaspoon light soy sauce

1 teaspoon roasted sesame oil

2 spring onions (scallions), chopped

4 fresh rice noodle rolls

oyster sauce

MAKES 4

TO MAKE the pork filling, combine the pork with the spring onion and coriander.

TO MAKE the prawn filling, peel and devein the prawns. Heat a wok over high heat, add the oil and heat until very hot. Stir-fry the prawns for 1 minute, or until they are pink and cooked through. Season with salt and white pepper. Add the spring onion and coriander and mix well.

TO MAKE the vegetable filling, wash the broccoli well. Discard any tough-looking stems and chop the rest of the stems. Put on a plate in a steamer, cover and steam over simmering water in a wok for 3 minutes, or until the stems and leaves are just tender. Combine the Chinese broccoli with the soy sauce, sesame oil and spring onion.

CAREFULLY UNROLL the rice noodle rolls (don't worry if they crack or tear a little at the sides). Trim each one into a neat rectangle about 15 x 18 cm (6 x 7 inches) (you may be able to get two out of one roll if they are very large). Divide the filling among the rolls, then re-roll the noodles. Put the rolls on a plate in a large steamer, cover and steam over simmering water in a wok for 5 minutes. Serve the rolls cut into pieces and drizzled with the oyster sauce.

Put the filling on the piece of noodle roll closest to you. Roll up carefully so you don't tear it, keeping the filling tucked inside.

SON-IN-LAW EGGS

A TRADITIONAL CELEBRATION DISH, THESE EGGS ARE ENJOYED ON NEW YEAR'S DAY OR AT WEDDING FEASTS, AND ARE TAKEN AS AN OFFERING TO THE MONKS WHEN THAI PEOPLE VISIT THEIR LOCAL TEMPLE. THEY MAKE GOOD SNACKS. DEEP-FRYING GIVES THE SKINS A UNIQUE TEXTURE.

2 dried long red chillies, about
   13 cm (5 inches) long
vegetable oil, for deep-frying
110 g (4 oz) Asian shallots,
   finely sliced
6 large hard-boiled eggs, shelled
2 tablespoons fish sauce
3 tablespoons tamarind purée
5 tablespoons palm sugar

SERVES 4

CUT the chillies into 5 mm (¼ inch) pieces with scissors or a knife and discard the seeds. Heat 5 cm (2 inches) oil in a wok or deep frying pan over a medium heat. When the oil seems hot, drop a slice of the Asian shallot into the oil. If it sizzles straight away, the oil is ready. Deep-fry the chillies for a few seconds, being careful not to burn them, to bring out the flavour. Remove them with a slotted spoon, then drain on paper towels.

IN the same wok, deep-fry the Asian shallots for 3–4 minutes until golden brown. Be careful not to burn them. Remove with a slotted spoon, then drain on paper towels. Use a spoon to slide one egg at a time into the same hot oil. Be careful as the oil may splash. Deep-fry for 10–15 minutes or until the whole of each egg is golden brown. Remove with a slotted spoon, then drain on paper towels. Keep warm.

IN a saucepan over a medium heat, stir the fish sauce, tamarind purée and sugar for 5–7 minutes or until all the sugar has dissolved.

HALVE the eggs lengthways and arrange them with the yolk upwards on a serving plate. Drizzle the tamarind sauce over the eggs and sprinkle the crispy chillies and shallots over them.

When the eggs are golden, they are ready. Carefully remove with a slotted spoon and drain on paper towels.

SALTED SOYA BEAN PODS

300 g (10 oz) fresh soya bean pods
1 tablespoon coarse sea salt
4 star anise

SERVES 4 AS A SNACK

TOP and tail the soya bean pods, then place in a bowl with the salt and rub some of the fuzz off the skin. Rinse the pods. Place in a saucepan of salted water with the star anise and bring to the boil. Reduce the heat and simmer for 20 minutes, or until tender. Drain and leave to cool.

TO EAT, suck the beans out of the pods and throw the pods away. Serve as a snack.

SALTED SOYA BEAN PODS

FRIED PEANUTS

1 tablespoon Sichuan peppercorns
4 star anise
1 tablespoon sugar
1 teaspoon salt
450 g (1 lb) shelled peanuts with
  skins on
3 tablespoons roasted sesame oil

SERVES 8 AS A SNACK

PUT 750 ml (3 cups) water in a saucepan with the spices, sugar and salt and bring to the boil. Add the peanuts and simmer for 5 minutes. Turn off the heat and leave the peanuts to cool in the liquid.

DRAIN and dry the peanuts, removing the whole spices. Heat the sesame oil in a wok and fry the peanuts until brown. Serve warm or cold as a snack.

CANDIED WALNUTS

250 g (9 oz) sugar
450 g (1 lb) shelled walnut halves
oil for deep-frying

SERVES 8 AS A SNACK

DISSOLVE the sugar in 100 ml (⅓ cup) water, then bring to the boil and cook for 2 minutes.

BLANCH the walnuts in a pan of boiling water briefly, then drain. Tip immediately into the syrup, stirring to coat. Cool for 5 minutes, then drain.

FILL a wok one quarter full of oil. Heat the oil to 190°C (375°F), or until a piece of bread fries golden brown in 10 seconds when dropped in the oil. Add the walnuts in batches, stirring to brown evenly. As soon as they brown, remove with a wire sieve or slotted spoon and put on some foil, making sure they are well spaced. Do not touch as they will be hot. When cool, drain on paper towels. Serve as a snack or at the start of a meal.

FRIED PEANUTS

CANDIED WALNUTS

The pork is threaded onto skewers using a sewing action.

PORK ON STICKS

PORK ON STICKS IS A POPULAR SNACK, AN EXCELLENT PARTY FOOD AND IS IDEAL FOR INFORMAL OCCASIONS SUCH AS BARBECUES. IT CAN BE SERVED WITH RICE OR STICKY RICE. NO ADDITIONAL SAUCE IS NECESSARY WITH THIS RECIPE.

1 kg (2 lb 4 oz) fillet of pork
250 ml (1 cup) coconut milk
   (page 551)
2 tablespoons coconut sugar
2 tablespoons light soy sauce
2 tablespoons oyster sauce
110 g (4 oz) Asian shallots,
   roughly chopped
4 garlic cloves, roughly chopped
5 coriander (cilantro) roots,
   finely chopped
2.5 cm (1 inch) piece of ginger,
   sliced
1½ teaspoons ground turmeric
¼ teaspoon ground white pepper
25 bamboo skewers, 18–20 cm
   (7–8 inches) long

MAKES 25

CUT the pork into pieces 4 cm (1½ inches) wide x 8 cm (3 inches) long x 5 mm (¼ inch) thick and put them in a bowl.

MIX the coconut milk, sugar, light soy sauce, oyster sauce, shallots, garlic, coriander roots, ginger, turmeric and pepper in a bowl until the sugar has dissolved. Pour over the meat and mix using your fingers or a spoon. Cover with plastic wrap and refrigerate for at least 5 hours, or overnight, turning occasionally.

SOAK the bamboo skewers in water for 1 hour to help prevent them from burning during cooking.

THREAD a piece of the marinated pork onto each skewer as if you were sewing a piece of material. If some pieces are small, thread two pieces onto each stick. Heat a barbecue or grill (broiler) to high heat. If using a grill, line the grill tray with foil.

BARBECUE for 5–7 minutes on each side, or grill (broil) the pork for 10 minutes on each side, until cooked through and slightly charred. Turn frequently and brush the marinade sauce over the meat during the cooking. If using the grill, cook a good distance below the heat. Serve hot or warm.

Selling souvenirs in Mae Tang.

BHEL PURI

BHEL PURI IS A MIXTURE OF SAVOURY MORSELS, INCLUDING CRISP PUFFED RICE, POTATOES AND GREEN MANGO, TOSSED WITH TART CHUTNEYS. SERVED FRESHLY MADE IN BOWLS, IT IS A FAVOURITE SNACK AT SUNSET ON CHOWPATTY BEACH IN MUMBAI (BOMBAY), INDIA.

A bhel puri seller prepares potatoes on Chowpatty beach.

MINT CHUTNEY
50 g (2 oz) coriander (cilantro)
    leaves
50 g (2 oz) mint leaves
6 garlic cloves, chopped
3 red chillies, chopped
1/2 red onion, chopped
3 tablespoons lemon juice

TAMARIND CHUTNEY
60 g (2 oz) fennel seeds
450 ml (1¾ cups) tamarind purée
    (page 554)
100 g (3 oz) ginger, sliced
300 g (10 oz) jaggery or soft brown
    sugar
1 teaspoon chilli powder
1 tablespoon ground cumin
1 tablespoon chaat masala
    (page 556)
1 teaspoon black salt

3 potatoes
1 tomato
120 g (4 oz) puffed rice
60 g (2 oz) sev noodles
1 green unripe mango, sliced
    into thin slivers
1 onion, finely chopped
4 tablespoons finely chopped
    coriander (cilantro) or mint leaves
1 teaspoon chaat masala
    (page 556)
12 crushed puri crisps

coriander (cilantro) leaves

SERVES 6

TO MAKE the mint chutney, blend the ingredients together in a food processor or pestle and mortar. Transfer to a saucepan and bring to the boil. Remove from the heat, leave to cool, then season with salt.

TO MAKE the tamarind chutney, place a small frying pan over low heat and dry-roast the fennel seeds until aromatic. Mix together the tamarind, ginger and sugar with 250 ml (1 cup) water in a saucepan. Cook over low heat until the tamarind blends into the mixture and the sugar completely dissolves.

STRAIN OUT the ginger and cook the remaining mixture to a thick pulp. Add the fennel seeds, chilli powder, cumin, chaat masala and black salt. Season with salt and reduce, stirring occasionally, over medium heat until thickened to a dropping consistency (it will fall in sheets off the spoon). Leave to cool.

TO MAKE the bhel puri, cook the potatoes in boiling water for 10 minutes or until tender, then cut into small cubes. Score a cross in the top of the tomato. Plunge into boiling water for 20 seconds, then drain and peel. Roughly chop the tomato, discarding the core and seeds and reserving any juices.

PUT the puffed rice, noodles, mango, onion, chopped coriander, chaat masala and puri crisps in a large bowl and toss them together. When well mixed, stir in a little of each chutney. Vary the chutney amounts depending on the flavour you want to achieve. The tamarind chutney has a tart flavour and the mint chutney is hot. Serve in small bowls and garnish with coriander leaves.

LEFTOVER mint chutney can be eaten with samosas (page 20) or pakoras (page 56) but cannot be stored. Store unused tamarind chutney in a jar in the fridge. It will keep for several weeks.

BEAN CURD ROLLS

THESE DELICATE ROLLS MAKE A CHANGE TO SPRING ROLLS AND ARE OFTEN SERVED AS DIM SUM.
BEAN CURD SKINS CAN BE PURCHASED EITHER VACUUM-PACKED AND READY TO USE, OR DRIED. THE
DRIED BEAN CURD SKINS NEED TO BE HANDLED CAREFULLY AS THEY BREAK EASILY.

4 dried Chinese mushrooms
100 g (3 oz) fresh or tinned
   bamboo shoots, rinsed and
   drained
1 small carrot
3 tablespoons oil
300 g (10 oz) firm bean curd,
   drained and diced
200 g (7 oz) bean sprouts
1/2 teaspoon salt
1/2 teaspoon sugar
2 spring onions (scallions), finely
   shredded
1 tablespoon light soy sauce
1 teaspoon roasted sesame oil
1 tablespoon plain flour
12 sheets soft or dried bean curd
   skins
oil for deep-frying
red rice vinegar, soy sauce or a
   dipping sauce (page 564)

MAKES 12

SOAK the dried mushrooms in boiling water for
30 minutes, then drain and squeeze out any excess
water. Remove and discard the stems and finely
shred the caps. Cut the bamboo shoots and carrot
into thin strips about the size of the bean sprouts.

HEAT a wok over high heat, add the oil and heat
until very hot. Stir-fry the carrot, bean curd and
bean sprouts for 1 minute. Add the mushrooms
and bamboo shoots, toss, then add the salt,
sugar and spring onion. Stir-fry for 1 minute, then
add the soy sauce and sesame oil, and blend
well. Remove the mixture from the wok and drain
off the excess liquid. Leave to cool. Combine the
flour with a little cold water to make a paste.

IF YOU are using dried bean curd skins, soak
them in cold water until they are soft. Peel off a
sheet of bean curd skin and trim to a 15 x 18 cm
(6 x 7 inch) rectangle. Place about 2 tablespoons of
the filling at one end of the skin, and roll up to
make a neat parcel, folding the sides in as you
roll. Brush the skin with some of the flour paste to
seal the flap firmly. Repeat with the remaining
bean curd skins and filling.

FILL a wok one quarter full of oil. Heat the oil to
180°C (350°F), or until a piece of bread fries
golden brown in 15 seconds when dropped in the
oil. Cook the rolls in batches for 3–4 minutes, or
until golden. Serve with some red rice vinegar, soy
sauce or a dipping sauce.

As the bean curd skins are rather
thin, spread them out well before
you roll them up.

SWEET CORN CAKES

400 g (14 oz) corn kernels
1 egg
3 tablespoons rice flour
1 tablespoon yellow curry paste
 (page 559)
2 tablespoons chopped Asian
 shallots
1 tablespoon fish sauce
25 g (½ cup) roughly chopped
 coriander (cilantro)
1 large red chilli, chopped
peanut oil, for shallow-frying
cucumber relish (page 563), to serve

MAKES 8

COMBINE the corn kernels, egg, rice flour, curry paste, shallots, fish sauce, coriander and chilli in a bowl. Shape the mixture into small patties, adding more rice flour, if necessary, to combine into a soft mixture.

HEAT the oil and fry the corn cakes for 3–4 minutes, turning once, until golden brown. Serve hot with cucumber relish.

Akah girl.

SESAME PRAWNS ON TOASTS

280 g (10 oz) raw prawns (shrimp),
 peeled and deveined
2 teaspoons light soy sauce
1 egg
4–5 large garlic cloves,
 roughly chopped
7–8 coriander (cilantro) roots,
 roughly chopped
¼ teaspoon ground white pepper
½ teaspoon salt
7 slices day-old white bread,
 crusts removed, each slice
 cut into two triangles
3 tablespoons sesame seeds
peanut oil, for deep-frying
cucumber relish (page 563), to serve

MAKES 14

USING a food processor or blender, whiz the prawns into a smooth paste. Transfer to a bowl, add the light soy sauce and egg and mix well. Leave for about 30 minutes to firm.

USING a pestle and mortar, pound the garlic, coriander roots, white pepper and salt into a smooth paste. Add to the prawns. (Using a pestle and mortar gives the best texture but you can also whiz the garlic, coriander roots, pepper, light soy sauce and egg with the prawns.) Heat the grill (broiler) to medium. Spread the bread on a baking tray and put under the grill for 3–4 minutes or until the bread is dry and slightly crisp. Spread the prawn paste thickly on one side of each piece. Sprinkle with sesame seeds and press on firmly. Refrigerate for 30 minutes.

HEAT the oil in a wok or deep frying pan over a medium heat. Drop in a small cube of bread. If it sizzles immediately, the oil is ready. Deep-fry a few toasts at a time, paste-side down, for 3 minutes or until golden. Turn with a slotted spoon. Drain paste-side up on paper towels. Serve with relish.

SESAME PRAWNS ON TOASTS

SPRING ONION PANCAKES

ONE OF THE MOST POPULAR SNACKS IN NORTHERN CHINA IS CRISP SPRING ONION PANCAKES EATEN STRAIGHT FROM THE HOT OIL. SOME RESTAURANTS ALSO MAKE BIG, THICK ONES THAT THEY CUT INTO WEDGES AND SERVE AS AN ACCOMPANIMENT TO A MEAL.

250 g (9 oz) plain flour
1/2 teaspoon salt
1 tablespoon oil
3 tablespoons roasted sesame oil
2 spring onions (scallions), green part only, finely chopped
oil for frying

MAKES 24

PLACE the flour and salt in a mixing bowl and stir to combine. Add the oil and 220 ml (¾ cup) boiling water and, using a wooden spoon, mix to a rough dough. Turn the dough out onto a lightly floured surface and knead for 5 minutes, or until smooth and elastic. If the dough is very sticky, knead in a little more flour. Cover the dough with a cloth and let it rest for 20 minutes.

ON a lightly floured surface, use your hands to roll the dough into a long roll. Divide the dough into 24 pieces. Working with one portion of dough at a time, place the dough, cut edge down, on the work surface. Using a small rolling pin, roll it out to a 10 cm (4 inch) circle. Brush the surface generously with the sesame oil and sprinkle with some spring onion. Starting with the edge closest to you, roll up the dough and pinch the ends to seal in the spring onion and sesame oil. Lightly flatten the roll, then roll it up again from one end like a snail, pinching the end to seal it. Repeat with the remaining dough, sesame oil and spring onion. Let the rolls rest for 20 minutes.

PLACE each roll flat on the work surface and press down with the palm of your hand. Roll out to a 10 cm (4 inch) circle and place on a lightly floured tray. Stack the pancakes between lightly floured sheets of baking paper and leave to rest for 20 minutes.

HEAT a frying pan over medium heat, brush the surface with oil, and add two or three of the pancakes at a time. Cook for 2–3 minutes on each side, turning once, until the pancakes are light golden brown and crisp. Remove and drain on paper towels. Serve immediately.

YOU CAN reheat the pancakes, wrapped in foil, in a 180°C (350°F/Gas 4) oven for 15 minutes.

Spread the spring onion through the dough by first rolling up the pancake and spring onion, then rolling this into a snail shape, and finally by rolling the snail into a pancake again.

APPETISERS
AND ANTIPASTO

BRUSCHETTA

4 large slices of 'country-style'
  bread, such as ciabatta
1 garlic clove
drizzle of extra virgin olive oil

MAKES 4

GRILL (broil), chargrill or toast the bread until it is crisp. Cut the garlic clove in half and rub the cut edge over both sides of each bread slice. Drizzle a little olive oil over each bread slice.

TOMATO AND BASIL BRUSCHETTA

4 ripe tomatoes
1 tablespoon shredded basil
4 pieces basic bruschetta

SERVES 4

ROUGHLY chop the tomatoes and mix with the basil. Season well and pile onto the bruschetta.

Bruschetta is a traditional Italian antipasto. Use slightly stale bread (this is an excellent dish for using up leftovers) that is dense enough to stop the olive oil seeping through. Technically speaking, real bruschetta is just plain grilled bread, rubbed with garlic while it is still hot and then drizzled with good quality olive oil.

WILD MUSHROOM BRUSCHETTA

2 tablespoons olive oil
400 g (14 oz) selection of wild
  mushrooms, particularly fresh
  porcini, sliced if large or chestnut
  mushrooms
2 garlic cloves, crushed
1 heaped tablespoon chopped
  thyme
4 pieces basic bruschetta

SERVES 4

HEAT the olive oil in a large saucepan or frying pan. When the oil is hot, add just enough mushrooms to cover the base of the pan and cook over high heat, stirring frequently. Season with salt and pepper. (Sometimes the mushrooms can become watery when cooked. Continue cooking until all the liquid has evaporated.)

ADD a little crushed garlic and thyme and cook for a further minute. Remove from the pan and repeat with the remaining mushrooms. Spoon over the bruschetta and serve immediately.

EGGPLANT BRUSCHETTA

2 large eggplants (aubergine), sliced
2 garlic cloves, crushed
150 ml (⅔ cup) extra virgin olive oil
juice of 1 small lemon
3 tablespoons roughly chopped mint
4 pieces basic bruschetta

SERVES 4

HEAT a griddle on the stove. Place a few eggplant slices on the griddle and cook over moderately high heat, turning once, until the eggplant is soft and cooked.

MIX together the garlic, oil, lemon juice and mint and season well. Put the eggplant in a dish with the marinade and leave for 30 minutes. Place a couple of eggplant pieces on each bruschetta and spoon the marinade over the top.

EGGPLANT BRUSCHETTA

PORK RILLETTES

OFTEN KNOWN AS *RILLETTES DE TOURS*, THIS SPECIALITY OF THE LOIRE VALLEY IS THE FRENCH VERSION OF POTTED MEAT. SPREAD ON TOAST OR BREAD AND SERVE WITH A GLASS OF WINE, OR STIR A SPOONFUL INTO SOUPS AND STEWS TO ADD FLAVOUR.

750 g (1 lb 10 oz) pork neck or
  belly, rind and bones removed
150 g (5 oz) pork back fat
100 ml (⅓ cup) dry white wine
3 juniper berries, lightly crushed
1 teaspoon sea salt
2 teaspoons dried thyme
½ teaspoon ground nutmeg
¼ teaspoon ground allspice
pinch of ground cloves
1 large garlic clove, crushed

SERVES 8

PREHEAT the oven to 140°C (275°F/Gas 1). Cut the meat and fat into short strips and put in a casserole dish with the rest of the ingredients. Mix together thoroughly and cover with a lid. Bake for 4 hours, by which time the pork should be soft and surrounded by liquid fat.

TIP the meat and fat into a sieve placed over a bowl to collect the fat. Shred the warm meat with two forks. Season if necessary. Pack the meat into a 750 ml (3 cups) dish or terrine and leave until cold. Strain the hot fat through a sieve lined with damp muslin.

ONCE the pork is cold, pour the fat over it (you may need to melt the fat first, if it has solidified as it cooled). Cover and refrigerate for up to a week. Serve at room temperature.

PORK RILLETTES

DUCK RILLETTES

600 g (1 lb 5 oz) pork belly, rind
  and bones removed
800 g (1 lb 12 oz) duck legs
100 ml (⅓ cup) dry white wine
1 teaspoon sea salt
¼ teaspoon black pepper
½ teaspoon ground nutmeg
¼ teaspoon ground allspice
1 large garlic clove, crushed

SERVES 8

PREHEAT the oven to 140°C (275°F/Gas 1). Cut the pork belly into small pieces and put in a casserole dish with the rest of the ingredients and 200 ml (¾ cup) water. Mix together thoroughly and cover with a lid. Bake for 4 hours. The meat should be soft and surrounded by liquid fat.

TIP the meat and fat into a sieve placed over a bowl to collect the fat. Remove the meat from the duck legs and shred the meat with two forks. Season if necessary. Pack the meat into a 750 ml (3 cup) dish or terrine and leave until cold. Strain the hot fat through a sieve lined with damp muslin.

ONCE the meat is cold, pour the fat over it (you may need to melt the fat first, if it has solidified as it cooled). Cover and refrigerate for up to a week. Serve at room temperature.

Use two forks to shred the meat.

DUCK RILLETTES

The risotto made for the arancini must be thick enough for the balls to hold their shape while they are being fried.

ARANCINI

ARANCINI—THE NAME MEANS 'LITTLE ORANGES'—ARE A SPECIALITY OF SICILY. THE SAFFRON RISOTTO IS TRADITIONAL. IF YOU CAN FIND IT, USE VIALONE NANO OR ANOTHER SEMI-FINE RICE—THE GLUTINOUS TEXTURE KEEPS THE GRAINS OF RICE TOGETHER.

large pinch of saffron threads
250 ml (1 cup) white wine
100 g (3 oz) butter
1 onion, finely chopped
1 large garlic clove, crushed
750 ml (3 cups) chicken stock
2 tablespoons thyme
225 g (8 oz) risotto rice (vialone
    nano, arborio or carnaroli)
50 g (2 oz) Parmesan, grated

100 g (3 oz) mozzarella or fontina,
    cut into cubes
75 g (2½ oz) dried breadcrumbs
oil for deep-frying

MAKES 20

LEAVE the saffron to soak in the wine while you prepare the risotto. Melt the butter in a large saucepan. Add the onion and garlic and cook over low heat for 3–4 minutes until softened but not browned. Heat the stock to simmering point in another saucepan.

ADD the thyme and rice to the onion and cook, stirring, for 1 minute to seal the rice. Add the wine and saffron and stir until the wine is all absorbed. Add several ladles of the hot stock, stirring continuously so that the rice cooks evenly. Keep adding enough stock to just cover the rice, stirring frequently. Continue in this way for about 20 minutes, or until the rice is creamy.

FOR ARANCINI it is not so essential to keep the rice *al dente*. Add more water or chicken stock if the rice is not fully cooked. Make sure all this liquid is absorbed. Remove from the heat and stir in the Parmesan, then spread out onto a tray covered with clingfilm. Leave to cool and, if possible, leave in the fridge overnight.

TO MAKE the arancini, roll a small amount of risotto into a walnut-sized ball. Press a hole in the middle with your thumb, place a small piece of cheese inside and press the risotto around it to enclose in a ball. Repeat with the rest of the risotto. Roll each ball in the breadcrumbs, pressing down to coat well.

HEAT enough oil in a deep-fat fryer or deep frying pan to fully cover the arancini. Heat the oil to 180°C (350°F), or until a piece of bread fries golden brown in 15 seconds when dropped in the oil. Deep-fry the arancini in batches, without crowding, for 3–4 minutes. Drain on paper towels and leave for a couple of minutes before eating. Serve hot or at room temperature.

Gently fry the onion and garlic before adding the chicken livers and thyme. Once the livers have changed colour, add the brandy.

CHICKEN LIVER PÂTÉ

500 g (1 lb 2 oz) chicken livers
80 ml (⅓ cup) brandy
90 g (3 oz) unsalted butter
1 onion, finely chopped
1 garlic clove, crushed
1 teaspoon chopped thyme
60 ml (¼ cup) double cream
4 slices white bread

SERVES 6

TRIM the chicken livers, cutting away any discoloured bits and veins. Rinse them, pat dry with paper towels and cut in half. Place in a small bowl with the brandy, cover and leave for a couple of hours. Drain the livers, reserving the brandy.

MELT half of the butter in a frying pan, add the onion and garlic and cook over low heat until the onion is soft and transparent. Add the livers and thyme and stir over moderate heat until the livers change colour. Add the reserved brandy and simmer for 2 minutes. Cool for 5 minutes.

PLACE the livers and liquid in a food processor and whiz until smooth. Add the remaining butter, chopped, and process again until smooth. (Alternatively, roughly mash the livers with a fork, then push them through a sieve and mix with the melted butter.) Pour in the cream and process until just incorporated.

SEASON the pâté and spoon into an earthenware dish or terrine, smoothing the surface. Cover and refrigerate until firm. If the pâté is to be kept for more than a day, chill it and then pour clarified butter over the surface to seal.

TO MAKE Melba toasts, preheat the grill (broiler) and cut the crusts off the bread. Toast the bread on both sides and then slice horizontally with a sharp serrated knife, to give you eight pieces. Carefully toast the uncooked side of each slice and then cut it into two triangles. Serve with the

SEAFOOD ANTIPASTI

THE GOLDEN RULE FOR COOKING SEAFOOD IS THAT ALL YOUR INGREDIENTS MUST BE ABSOLUTELY STRAIGHT-FROM-THE-SEA FRESH. BUY LIVING SHELLFISH FROM THE FISHMONGER AND BE ADVISED AS TO WHAT IS IN SEASON, A REGIONAL SPECIALITY, OR A GOOD CATCH OF THE DAY.

500 g (1 lb 2 oz) mussels
500 g (1 lb 2 oz) clams
250 g (9 oz) octopus
250 g (9 oz) small squid
250 g (9 oz) prawns
100 ml (⅓ cup) olive oil
juice of 2 lemons
2 tablespoons finely chopped
    parsley
lemon wedges

SERVES 6

CLEAN the mussels and clams by scrubbing them thoroughly and scraping off any barnacles. Pull off the beards from the mussels and rinse well under running water. Discard any mussels or clams that are broken or open and do not close when tapped on the work surface.

CLEAN the octopus by slitting the head and pulling out the innards. Cut out the eyes and hard beak and rinse. If the flesh is still springy and has not been tenderized, beat with a mallet until soft.

PREPARE the squid by pulling the heads and tentacles out of the bodies along with any innards. Cut the heads off below the eyes, just leaving the tentacles. Discard the heads and set the tentacles aside. Rinse the bodies, pulling out the clear quills, then cut the bodies into rings. Peel and devein the prawns, leaving the tails intact.

BRING a large pan of water to the boil and add the octopus. Reduce the heat and simmer for about 20 minutes or until tender. Add the squid and prawns. Cook for about 2 minutes, or until the prawns turn pink. Drain well.

PUT the mussels and clams in an even layer in a steamer. Steam over boiling water for 2 minutes or until the shells have just opened (discard any that stay closed). Pull the top shell off each mussel and clam. Arrange on a platter.

IF YOU have one octopus, cut it into pieces; if you have baby ones then leave them whole. Arrange the octopus, squid and prawns on the platter and sprinkle with sea salt and black pepper. Mix the olive oil with the lemon juice and drizzle over the seafood. Cover with clingfilm and leave to marinate in the fridge for at least 2 hours. Before serving, sprinkle with parsley. Serve with lemon wedges and bread to mop up the juices.

Spoon the choux pastry around the edge of the baking dish and bake until well risen. To remove the bone from the trout, simply lift off the top fillet and then lift the bone away cleanly.

SMOKED TROUT GOUGÈRE

FOR A GOUGÈRE, CHOUX PASTRY IS TRADITIONALLY PIPED INTO A CIRCULAR OR OVAL SHAPE AND FILLED WITH A SAVOURY MIXTURE. IF YOU PREFER, THE PASTRY CAN ALSO BE MADE INTO SMALL CHOUX BUNS, SPLIT OPEN AND THE FILLING SPOONED INTO THE CENTRES.

75 g (2½ oz) butter
120 g (4 oz) plain flour, sifted twice
¼ teaspoon paprika
3 large eggs, beaten
100 g (3 oz) Gruyère, grated

FILLING
400 g (14 oz) smoked trout
100 g (3 oz) watercress, trimmed
30 g (1 oz) butter
20 g (⅔ oz) plain flour
300 ml (1¼ cups) milk

SERVES 4

PREHEAT the oven to 200°C (400°F/Gas 6) and put a baking tray on the top shelf to heat up.

MELT the butter with 185 ml (⅔ cup) water in a saucepan, then bring it to a rolling boil. Remove from the heat and sift in all the flour and the paprika. Return to the heat and beat continuously with a wooden spoon to make a smooth shiny paste that comes away from the side of the pan. Cool for a few minutes. Beat in the eggs one at a time, until shiny and smooth—the mixture should drop off the spoon but not be too runny. Stir in two-thirds of the cheese.

SPOON the dough round the edge of a shallow, lightly greased baking dish. Put this in the oven on the hot tray and cook for 45–50 minutes, or until the choux is well risen and browned.

MEANWHILE, to make the filling, peel the skin off the trout and lift off the top fillet. Pull out the bone. Break the trout into large flakes. Wash the watercress and put in a large saucepan with just the water clinging to the leaves. Cover the pan and steam the watercress for 2 minutes, or until just wilted. Drain, cool and squeeze with your hands to get rid of the excess liquid. Roughly chop the watercress.

MELT the butter in a saucepan, stir in the flour to make a roux and cook, stirring, for 3 minutes over very low heat without allowing the roux to brown. Remove from the heat and add the milk gradually, stirring after each addition until smooth. Return to the heat and simmer for 3 minutes. Stir in the smoked trout and watercress and season well.

SPOON the trout filling into the centre of the cooked choux pastry and return to the oven for 10 minutes, then serve immediately.

Fresh tuna has a dark meaty flesh that is delicious both raw and cooked. Tuna is fished off the coasts of Sicily and Calabria where the fish come to spawn. The better-tasting red flesh indicates that the tuna was caught by hand, killed and bled quickly, while muddy-brown flesh means the fish drowned and so probably was caught by net.

CARPACCIO

CARPACCIO IS NAMED AFTER THE RENAISSANCE PAINTER WHOSE USE OF REDS IS REFLECTED IN THE DISH. IT WAS CREATED IN HARRY'S BAR IN VENICE FOR A FAVOURITE CUSTOMER WHOSE DOCTOR HAD PLACED HER ON A DIET FORBIDDING COOKED MEAT.

700 g (1 lb 9 oz) good-quality beef fillet
1 egg yolk
3 teaspoons Dijon mustard
3 tablespoons lemon juice
2 drops Tabasco
75 ml (⅓ cup) olive oil
1 tablespoon single cream
2–3 tablespoons capers, rinsed

SERVES 6

PLACE the beef in the freezer for about half an hour, or until it is firm. Using a sharp knife or mandolin, cut the beef into paper-thin slices. Cover six serving plates with the beef in an even layer.

BLEND together the egg yolk, mustard, lemon juice and Tabasco in a bowl or food processor. Add the olive oil in a thin stream, whisking or processing continuously until the mayonnaise thickens. Whisk in the cream. Season to taste with salt and pepper. Drizzle over the beef slices and sprinkle with capers.

TUNA CARPACCIO

400 g (14 oz) sashimi-quality tuna
50 g (2 oz) basil leaves
1 garlic clove
80 ml (⅓ cup) extra virgin olive oil
1 teaspoon lemon juice

SERVES 4

PLACE the tuna in the freezer for about half an hour, or until it is firm. Using a sharp knife or a mandolin, cut the tuna into paper-thin slices. Cover four serving plates with the slices in a thin even layer.

BLANCH the basil leaves in salted boiling water for 10 seconds, then drain well. Place the leaves in a food processor or blender with the garlic, olive oil and lemon juice and mix well. Season with salt and pepper. Drizzle over the tuna and serve with bread.

TUNA CARPACCIO

AÏOLI

OFTEN REFERRED TO AS 'PROVENCE BUTTER', AÏOLI IS A SIMPLE BUT SUPERB GARLIC-FLAVOURED

MAYONNAISE. IT IS SERVED WITH A SELECTION OF CRUDITÉS OR HOT VEGETABLES, POACHED CHICKEN,

SNAILS OR FISH, AND IT CAN ALSO BE ADDED TO FISH SOUPS.

4 egg yolks
8 garlic cloves, crushed
1/2 teaspoon salt
2 tablespoons lemon juice
500 ml (2 cups) olive oil

CRUDITÉS
6 baby carrots, trimmed with stalks
    left on
6 asparagus spears, trimmed and
    blanched
6 French beans, trimmed and
    blanched
6 button mushrooms, halved
1 yellow capsicum (pepper),
    seeded and cut into batons
1 red capsicum (pepper), seeded
    and cut into batons
6 cauliflower florets
1 fennel bulb, cut into batons

SERVES 6

A mortar and pestle is ideal for making tapenade, which should be a fairly rough paste. The name comes from *tapenado*, the Provençal word for caper.

PUT the egg yolks, garlic, salt and half the lemon juice in a mortar and pestle or food processor and pound or mix until light and creamy. Add the oil, drop by drop from the tip of a teaspoon, whisking constantly until it begins to thicken, then add the oil in a very thin stream. (If you're using a processor, pour in the oil in a thin stream with the motor running.) Season, add the remaining lemon juice and, if necessary, thin with a little warm water.

ARRANGE the crudités around a large platter and serve the aïoli in a bowl in the centre. You can keep aïoli sealed in a sterilized jar in the fridge. It will last for up to 3 weeks.

TAPENADE

300 g (10 oz) black olives, pitted
3 tablespoons capers, rinsed
8 anchovies
1 garlic clove, crushed
180 ml (6 oz) olive oil
1 tablespoon lemon juice
2 teaspoons Dijon mustard
1 teaspoon chopped thyme
1 tablespoon chopped parsley

SERVES 6

POUND TOGETHER the olives, capers, anchovies and garlic, either using a mortar and pestle or a food processor. Add the olive oil, lemon juice, mustard and herbs and pound or process again until you have a fairly rough paste.

SERVE with bread or crudités for dipping. Can be kept, covered, in the fridge for several days.

TAPENADE

STUFFED MUSHROOMS

8 large flat mushrooms
1 1/2 tablespoons lemon juice
12 button mushrooms
20 g (2/3 oz) butter
1 shallot, finely chopped
1 garlic clove, crushed
2 tablespoons white wine
100 g (3 oz) Parmesan, grated, plus
    1 tablespoon to serve
50 g (2 oz) fresh breadcrumbs
1 egg, lightly beaten
3 tablespoons double cream
1 tablespoon chopped tarragon
1 tablespoon chopped parsley

SERVES 4

PREHEAT the oven to 150°C (300°F/Gas 2).
Wipe the large mushrooms with a damp cloth,
remove and discard the stalks and rub the caps
with a little lemon juice to keep them white. Wipe
the button mushrooms and chop them finely, then
mix with the remaining lemon juice.

HEAT the butter in a small frying pan, add the
shallot and garlic and cook, stirring, for 4 minutes.
Add the chopped mushroom and the wine and
cook, stirring, for another 4 minutes. Remove
from the heat and stir in the Parmesan,
breadcrumbs, egg, cream and tarragon. Season.

PLACE the mushroom caps on a lightly oiled
baking tray and stuff with the filling. Bake for
12 minutes. Sprinkle with the Parmesan and
parsley and serve either warm or cold.

STUFFED MUSHROOMS

CHARGRILLED ASPARAGUS

24 asparagus spears
1 tablespoon extra virgin olive oil
2 tablespoons balsamic vinegar
Parmesan shavings

SERVES 4

WASH the asparagus and remove the woody
ends (hold each spear at both ends and bend it
gently—it will snap at its natural breaking point).

PUT the asparagus in a bowl, add the olive oil
and toss well. Heat a griddle or barbecue and
cook the asparagus for about 10 minutes, or
until *al dente*. Drizzle with balsamic vinegar and
sprinkle with the Parmesan to serve.

(IF YOU DON'T have a griddle or barbecue, you
can steam the asparagus or boil in salted water
for 6–8 minutes until *al dente*. Drain and mix with
the olive oil, balsamic and Parmesan.)

CHARGRILLED ASPARAGUS

RAW OYSTERS

RAW OYSTERS

24 oysters in their shells
1 shallot, finely chopped
2 tablespoons red wine vinegar
1 lemon, cut into wedges

SERVES 4

SHUCK the oysters by holding each one, rounded side down, in a cloth in your left hand. Using an oyster knife, carefully wiggle the point of the knife between the two shells and, keeping the blade flat, run the knife across the top shell to sever the muscle. Pull off the top shell and loosen the oyster from the bottom shell, being careful not to lose any liquid. Nestle the opened oysters on a bed of crushed ice or rock salt on a large platter (this will keep them steady).

MIX the shallot with the red wine vinegar and some black pepper in a small bowl. Put this in the centre of the platter and arrange the lemon wedges around the oysters. Serve with slices of rye bread and butter.

OYSTERS MORNAY

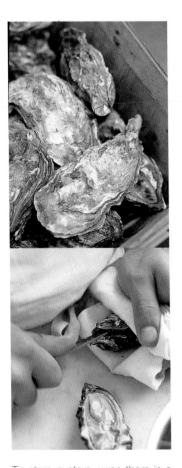

To store oysters, wrap them in a damp cloth and refrigerate in the salad compartment for up to 3 days. Eat oysters that have been shucked immediately.

24 oysters in their shells
50 g (2 oz) butter
1 shallot, finely chopped
30 g (1 oz) plain flour
375 ml (1½ cups) milk
pinch of nutmeg
½ bay leaf
20 g (⅔ oz) Gruyère, grated
20 g (⅔ oz) Parmesan, grated, plus
  a little extra for grilling

SERVES 6

SHUCK the oysters, reserving all the liquid. Strain the liquid into a saucepan. Rinse the oysters to remove any bits of shell. Wash and dry the shells.

MELT 30 g (1 oz) of the butter in another saucepan, add the shallot and cook, stirring, for 3 minutes. Stir in the flour to make a roux and stir over very low heat for 3 minutes without allowing the roux to brown. Remove from the heat and add the milk gradually, stirring after each addition until smooth. Return to the heat, add the nutmeg and bay leaf and simmer for 5 minutes. Strain through a fine sieve into a clean pan.

HEAT the oyster liquid in the saucepan to a simmer (add a little water if you need more liquid). Add the oysters and poach for 30 seconds, then lift them out with a slotted spoon and place them back into their shells. Stir the cooking liquid into the sauce. Add the cheeses and remaining butter and stir until they have melted into the sauce. Season with salt and pepper. Preheat the grill (broiler).

SPOON a little sauce over each oyster, sprinkle with Parmesan and place under the hot grill for a couple of minutes, or until golden.

ARTICHOKES VINAIGRETTE

ONLY SMALL YOUNG ARTICHOKES OF A FEW VARIETIES, SUCH AS VIOLETTO TOSCANO, ARE TENDER ENOUGH TO BE EATEN RAW. IF THEY ARE UNAVAILABLE, USE COOKED HEARTS, EITHER FRESH OR CANNED. ALLOW ONE HEART PER PERSON AS PART OF AN ANTIPASTO, TWO EACH AS A FIRST COURSE.

There are three different sizes of artichoke. The largest are the first to appear on the plant and are known as *la mamma* (the mother). Next to grow are the *figli* (children), which are smaller and more tender. Finally, the *nipoti* (nephews) appear further down the plant, the smallest and most

2 tablespoons lemon juice
4 young Romanesco or Violetto Toscano artichokes
1 quantity vinaigrette (page 568)

SERVES 4

MIX the lemon juice in a large bowl with 1 litre (4 cups) cold water. Using kitchen scissors or a sharp knife, cut off and discard the top third of each artichoke. Discard the tough outer leaves and snip off any spikes from the remaining leaves. Chop off and discard all but 2–3 cm (1 inch) of the stem and peel this with a potato peeler.

SLICE each artichoke in half from top to bottom, including the stem. Scrape out the furry choke and discard it. As each artichoke is prepared, place it straight into the bowl of lemon water to avoid discolouring.

SHAKE each artichoke half dry and arrange on a serving platter. Spoon the vinaigrette over the top and leave for at least 30 minutes before serving.

WARM ARTICHOKES VINAIGRETTE

4 x 350 g artichokes
juice of 1 lemon
1 quantity vinaigrette (page 568)

SERVES 4

BRING a large pan of salted water to the boil. Cut off the artichoke stalks at the base so the artichokes stand upright. Put them in the boiling water and add the lemon juice. Boil gently for 30–40 minutes or until a leaf from the base comes away easily. Cool quickly under cold running water and drain upside down on a tray.

TO SERVE, put each artichoke on a serving plate and gently prise it open a little. Spoon the vinaigrette over the top, letting it drizzle into the artichoke and around the plate.

(TO EAT the artichokes, scrape off the flesh from the leaves between your teeth, then remove and discard the furry choke at the base with a spoon. You can now eat the tender base or 'heart'.)

WARM ARTICHOKES
VINAIGRETTE

SALMON TERRINE

IF YOU CAN FIND WILD SALMON IT WILL GIVE YOU A MUCH BETTER FLAVOUR THAN FARMED. A MILD SMOKED SALMON IS BETTER THAN A REALLY SMOKY ONE—SOME SMOKED SALMON VARIETIES CAN BE SO STRONG THEY MAKE THEIR PRESENCE FELT THROUGHOUT THE WHOLE TERRINE.

700 g (1 lb 9 oz) salmon fillet, skinned and all small bones removed
4 eggs
550 ml (2¼ cups) double cream
10 g (⅓ oz) finely chopped chervil
250 g (9 oz) button mushrooms
1 teaspoon lemon juice
30 g (1 oz) butter
1 tablespoon grated onion
2 tablespoons white wine
10 large spinach leaves
300 g (10 oz) smoked salmon, thinly sliced

LEMON MAYONNAISE
1 tablespoon lemon juice
grated zest of 1 lemon
250 ml (1 cup) mayonnaise (page 566)

SERVES 8

Line the terrine with smoked salmon, leaving the slices hanging over the sides. Once the terrine is filled, fold the smoked salmon over to cover the top.

PREHEAT the oven to 170°C (325°F/Gas 3). Purée the salmon fillet and eggs in a food processor until smooth. Push through a fine sieve into a glass bowl. (Alternatively, mash with a fork and push through a fine sieve.) Place over iced water and gradually mix in the cream. Stir in the chervil and season. Cover and leave in the fridge.

DICE the mushrooms and toss with the lemon juice to prevent discolouring. Melt the butter in a frying pan and cook the onion, stirring, for 2 minutes. Add the mushrooms and cook for 4 minutes. Add the wine and cook until it has evaporated. Season and remove from the heat.

DIP the spinach leaves in boiling water, then remove them carefully with a slotted spoon and lay them flat on paper towels. Brush a 20 x 7 x 9 cm (8 x 2¾ x 3½ inch) terrine or loaf tin with oil and line the base with baking paper. Line the base and sides with the smoked salmon, leaving enough hanging over the sides to cover the top. Spoon in enough salmon mixture to half-fill the terrine. Lay half the spinach over the salmon mixture, then spread with the mushrooms and another layer of spinach. Cover with the remaining salmon mixture, fold over the smoked salmon and cover with a piece of buttered baking paper.

PLACE the terrine in a large baking dish and pour water into the baking dish to come halfway up the side of the terrine. Bake in this bain-marie for 45–50 minutes, or until a skewer inserted into the terrine comes out clean. Leave for 5 minutes before unmoulding onto a serving plate. Peel off the baking paper, cover and chill the terrine.

TO MAKE the lemon mayonnaise, stir the lemon juice and zest through the mayonnaise and serve with slices of salmon terrine.

ARTICHOKE FRITTATA

ALMOST AN OMELETTE, BUT FLASHED UNDER THE GRILL (BROILER) TO FINISH OFF THE COOKING, THE FRITTATA VARIES FROM THIN AND PANCAKE-LIKE, TO THICKER, WITH A GOLDEN CRUST AND CREAMY CENTRE. IT IS A FAVOURITE THROUGHOUT ITALY.

175 g (6 oz) broad beans, fresh or frozen
1 onion
400 g (14 oz) tin artichoke hearts, drained
3 tablespoons olive oil
6 eggs
2 tablespoons chopped parsley
45 g (1½ oz) pecorino, grated
pinch of nutmeg

SERVES 4

BRING a small saucepan of water to the boil and add a large pinch of salt and the broad beans. Boil for 2 minutes, then drain and rinse under cold water. Peel off the skins from the beans.

HALVE the onion and slice thinly. Cut the artichoke hearts from bottom to top into slices about 5 mm (¼ inch) wide. Discard any slices that contain the tough central choke.

HEAT the oil in a 30 cm (12 inch) frying pan and fry the onion over low heat for 6–8 minutes, without allowing it to brown. Add the artichoke slices and cook for 1–2 minutes. Stir in the broad beans.

PREHEAT the grill (broiler). Lightly beat together the eggs, parsley, pecorino and nutmeg and season well with salt and pepper. Pour into the frying pan and cook over low heat until three-quarters set, shaking the pan often to stop the frittata sticking. Finish the top off under the grill and leave to cool before serving in wedges.

Preparing artichokes by hand at the Rialto market in Venice.

RED CAPSICUM (PEPPER) AND ZUCCHINI FRITTATA

1 tablespoon olive oil
1 onion, sliced
1 red capsicum (pepper), sliced
2 zucchinis, sliced
6 eggs
1 tablespoon chopped basil
45 g (1½ oz) Parmesan, grated

SERVES 4

HEAT the olive oil in a 30 cm (12 inch) frying pan and cook the onion until soft. Add the red capsicum and zucchini and fry until soft. Preheat the grill (broiler).

LIGHTLY beat the eggs, basil and Parmesan and season well. Pour into the frying pan and cook over low heat until three-quarters set, shaking the pan to stop the frittata sticking. Finish the top off under the grill (broiler) and leave to cool before serving in wedges.

The zucchini (courgette) is one of Italy's favourite vegetables. In the north it is baked in béchamel, in the south fried with tomatoes and basil. These long ones are from Sicily.

ARTICHOKE FRITTATA WITH RED CAPSICUM AND COURGETTE FRITTATA

SOUPS

A pavement café in Marseille.

Basil is more usually associated with Italy than France but, in fact, the herb originated not in Italy, but in India. It was introduced to Europe in the sixteenth century and is often used in southern French cooking as a perfect match for Provençal tomatoes and olive oil. It can be bought in pots or as bunches.

SOUPE AU PISTOU

PISTOU IS A PROVENÇAL MIXTURE OF GARLIC, BASIL AND PARMESAN MIXED TOGETHER WITH OLIVE OIL FROM THE SOUTH OF FRANCE. SIMILAR TO ITALIAN PESTO, IT IS THE TRADITIONAL ACCOMPANIMENT TO THIS SPRING VEGETABLE SOUP AND IS ADDED AT THE TABLE.

250 g (9 oz) dried haricot beans
2 teaspoons olive oil
1 onion, finely chopped
2 garlic cloves, crushed
1 celery stalk, chopped
3 carrots, diced
bouquet garni
4 potatoes, diced
150 g (5 oz) small green beans, chopped
500 ml (2 cups) chicken stock
3 tomatoes
4 zucchinis, diced
150 g (5 oz) vermicelli, broken into pieces
150 g (5 oz) peas, fresh or frozen

PISTOU
6 garlic cloves
80 g (3 oz) basil leaves
100 g (3½ oz) Parmesan, grated
200 ml (¾ cup) olive oil

SERVES 4

SOAK the haricot beans in cold water overnight, then drain, put in a saucepan and cover with cold water. Bring to the boil, then lower the heat and simmer for 1 hour, or until the beans are tender. Drain well.

TO MAKE the pistou, put the garlic, basil and Parmesan in a food processor or a mortar and pestle and process or pound until finely chopped. Slowly add the olive oil, with the motor running if you are using the food processor or pounding constantly with the mortar and pestle, and mix thoroughly. Cover with clingfilm and set aside.

HEAT the olive oil in a large saucepan, add the onion and garlic and cook over low heat for 5 minutes until softened but not browned. Add the celery, carrot and bouquet garni and cook for 10 minutes, stirring occasionally. Add the potato, green beans, chicken stock and 1.75 litres (7 cups) water and simmer for 10 minutes.

SCORE a cross in the top of each tomato. Plunge into boiling water for 20 seconds, then drain and peel the skin away from the cross. Chop the tomatoes finely, discarding the cores. Add to the soup with the zucchinis, haricot beans, vermicelli and peas and cook for 10 minutes or until tender (if you are using frozen peas, add them at the last minute just to heat through). Season and serve with pistou on top.

Soup flavourings are often sold ready-made in bundles.

It is best to carefully measure ingredients such as fish sauce as the flavour is quite strong.

CHICKEN, COCONUT AND GALANGAL SOUP

THIS IS ONE OF THE CLASSIC SOUPS OF THAILAND. ALTHOUGH USUALLY MADE WITH CHICKEN, YOU CAN MAKE THIS RECIPE USING PRAWNS, FISH OR VEGETABLES. DON'T WORRY WHEN THE COCONUT MILK SPLITS — IT IS SUPPOSED TO.

750 ml (3 cups) coconut milk
  (page 555)
2 lemon grass stalks, white part
  only, each cut into a tassel
  or bruised
5 cm (2 inch) piece of galangal,
  cut into several pieces
4 Asian shallots, smashed with
  the flat side of a cleaver
400 g (14 oz) skinless chicken
  breast fillets, cut into slices
2 tablespoons fish sauce
1 tablespoon palm sugar
200 g (7 oz) baby tomatoes, cut
  into bite-sized pieces if large
150 g (5 oz) straw mushrooms
  or button mushrooms
3 tablespoons lime juice
6 makrut (kaffir) lime leaves,
  torn in half
3–5 bird's eye chillies, stems
  removed, bruised, or 2 long red
  chillies, seeded and finely sliced
a few coriander (cilantro) leaves,
  for garnish

SERVES 4

PUT the coconut milk, lemon grass, galangal and shallots in a saucepan or wok over a medium heat and bring to a boil.

ADD the chicken, fish sauce and palm sugar and simmer, stirring constantly for 5 minutes or until the chicken is cooked through.

ADD the tomatoes and mushrooms and simmer for 2–3 minutes. Add the lime juice, makrut lime leaves and chillies in the last few seconds, taking care not to let the tomatoes lose their shape. Taste, then adjust the seasoning if necessary. This dish is not meant to be overwhelmingly hot, but to have a sweet, salty, sour taste. Serve garnished with coriander leaves.

The soup base is called a *soffritto*, which means 'underfried'. The slow-cooked mixture of onion, garlic, pancetta and herbs gives the soup its base flavour. Other types of minestrone simmer the vegetables in stock without frying them first, then add olive oil towards the end for flavour.

MINESTRONE ALLA GENOVESE

JUST ABOUT EVERY REGION OF ITALY HAS ITS OWN MINESTRONE. THIS VERSION HAS A SPOONFUL OF PESTO STIRRED THROUGH AT THE END; OTHERS HAVE RICE INSTEAD OF PASTA. FOR *MINESTRONE ALLA MILANESE*, ADD 200 GRAMS (7 OUNCES) ARBORIO RICE INSTEAD OF THE PASTA.

220 g (8 oz) dried borlotti beans
50 g (2 oz) lard or butter
1 large onion, finely chopped
1 garlic clove, finely chopped
15 g (½ oz) parsley, finely chopped
2 sage leaves
100 g (3 oz) pancetta, cubed
2 celery stalks, halved then sliced
2 carrots, sliced
3 potatoes, peeled but left whole
1 teaspoon tomato purée
400 g (14 oz) tin chopped tomatoes
8 basil leaves
3 litres (12 cups) chicken or
    vegetable stock
2 zucchinis, sliced
220 g (8 oz) shelled peas
120 g (4 oz) runner beans, cut into
    4 cm (1½ inch) lengths
¼ cabbage, shredded
150 g (5 oz) ditalini, avemarie or
    other small pasta
1 quantity pesto (page 569)
grated Parmesan

SERVES 6

PUT the dried beans in a large bowl, cover with cold water and leave to soak overnight. Drain and rinse under cold water.

TO MAKE the *soffritto*, melt the lard in a large saucepan and add the onion, garlic, parsley, sage and pancetta. Cook over low heat, stirring once or twice, for about 10 minutes, or until the onion is soft and golden.

ADD the celery, carrot and potatoes and cook for 5 minutes. Stir in the tomato purée, tomatoes, basil and borlotti beans. Season with plenty of pepper. Add the stock and bring slowly to the boil. Cover and leave to simmer for 2 hours, stirring once or twice.

IF the potatoes haven't already broken up, roughly break them up with a fork against the side of the pan. Taste for seasoning and add the zucchini, peas, runner beans, cabbage and pasta. Simmer until the pasta is *al dente*. Serve with a dollop of pesto and the Parmesan.

Stripping corn cobs in Yunnan.

CHICKEN AND
MUSHROOM SOUP

CANTONESE CORN SOUP

THIS DELECTABLE SOUP IS A CANTONESE CLASSIC. YOU NEED TO USE A GOOD QUALITY TIN OF CREAMED CORN WITH A SMOOTH TEXTURE, OR ALTERNATIVELY, IF IT IS QUITE COARSE, QUICKLY BLEND YOUR CREAMED CORN IN A BLENDER OR FOOD PROCESSOR TO MAKE IT EXTRA SMOOTH.

250 g (9 oz) skinless chicken breast
  fillet, minced
150 ml (⅔ cup) Shaoxing rice wine
400 g (14 oz) tinned creamed corn
1.5 litres (6 cups) chicken stock
  (page 565)
1 teaspoon salt
2¹/₂ tablespoons cornflour
2 egg whites, lightly beaten
1 teaspoon roasted sesame oil

SERVES 6

PLACE the chicken in a bowl, add 3 tablespoons of the rice wine and stir to combine. In a large clay pot or saucepan, combine the creamed corn, stock, remaining rice wine and salt. Bring to the boil, stirring. Add the chicken and stir to separate the meat. Return to the boil and skim any scum from the surface.

COMBINE the cornflour with enough water to make a paste, add to the soup and simmer until thickened. Remove from the heat. Mix 2 tablespoons water into the egg white, then slowly add to the clay pot or saucepan in a thin stream around the edge of the pan. Stir once or twice, then add the sesame oil. Check the seasoning, adding more salt if necessary. Serve immediately.

CHICKEN AND MUSHROOM SOUP

FOR THIS SOUP YOU CAN USE EITHER BUTTON OR CHINESE MUSHROOMS. CHINESE MUSHROOMS ARE USUALLY LABELLED SHIITAKE (THE JAPANESE NAME FOR THEM) WHEN FRESH AND WILL ADD MORE FLAVOUR TO THE FINISHED SOUP.

2 tablespoons cornflour
3–4 egg whites, beaten
1 teaspoon salt
100 g (3 oz) skinless chicken breast
  fillet, thinly sliced
750 ml (3 cups) chicken and meat
  stock (page 281)
100 g (3 oz) fresh button or
  Chinese (shiitake) mushrooms,
  thinly sliced
1 teaspoon roasted sesame oil
chopped spring onion (scallion)

SERVES 4

COMBINE the cornflour with enough water to make a paste. Mix 1 teaspoon each of the egg white and cornflour paste and a pinch of salt with the chicken. Blend the remaining egg white and cornflour mixture to a smooth paste.

BRING the stock to a rolling boil in a large clay pot or saucepan. Add the chicken and return to the boil, then add the mushrooms and salt. Return to the boil then, very slowly, pour in the egg white and cornflour mixture, stirring constantly. As soon as the soup has thickened, add the sesame oil. Serve sprinkled with the spring onion.

FRENCH ONION SOUP

THE ORIGINS OF THIS ONION SOUP ARE UNCLEAR, SOME CLAIMING IT TO BE A LYONNAISE INVENTION AND OTHERS CREDITING IT TO PARIS. THERE IS ALSO MUCH DISPUTE OVER HOW THE DISH SHOULD BE MADE: WHEN TO ADD THE BREAD AND WHETHER THE ONIONS ARE COARSELY SLICED OR PURÉED?

Lyon is certainly the area of France most associated with the onion: 'à la lyonnaise' means a dish containing onions.

50 g (2 oz) butter
750 g (1 lb 10 oz) onions, finely sliced
2 garlic cloves, finely chopped
45 g (1½ oz) plain flour
2 litres beef or chicken stock
250 ml (1 cup) white wine
1 bay leaf
2 thyme sprigs
12 slices stale baguette
100 g (3 oz) Gruyère, finely grated

SERVES 6

MELT the butter in a heavy-based saucepan and add the onion. Cook over low heat, stirring occasionally, for 25 minutes, or until the onion is deep golden brown and beginning to caramelize.

ADD the garlic and flour and stir continuously for 2 minutes. Gradually blend in the stock and the wine, stirring all the time, and bring to the boil. Add the bay leaf and thyme and season. Cover the pan and simmer for 25 minutes. Remove the bay leaf and thyme and check the seasoning. Preheat the grill (broiler).

TOAST the baguette slices, then divide among six warmed soup bowls and ladle the soup over the top. Sprinkle with the grated cheese and grill until the cheese melts and turns light golden brown. Serve immediately.

CAULIFLOWER SOUP

30 g (1 oz) butter
1 onion, finely chopped
½ celery stalk, finely chopped
600 g (1 lb 5 oz) cauliflower, broken into florets
440 ml (1¾ cups) chicken stock
315 ml (1¼ cups) milk
1 bay leaf
1 thyme sprig
125 ml (½ cup) single cream
freshly grated nutmeg
2 tablespoons chopped chives

SERVES 4

MELT the butter in a large saucepan and add the onion and celery. Cook over low heat until the vegetables are softened but not browned. Add the cauliflower, stock, milk, bay leaf and thyme and bring to the boil. Cover the pan, reduce the heat and simmer for 20 minutes, or until the cauliflower is tender.

LEAVE the soup to cool, then remove the bay leaf and thyme. Purée the soup until smooth in a blender or food processor and return to the clean saucepan. Bring to the boil, stirring constantly, add the cream and reheat without boiling. Season with salt, white pepper and nutmeg. Serve garnished with chives.

CAULIFLOWER SOUP

STUFFED TOFU SOUP WITH PRAWNS

THIS RECIPE IS QUITE FIDDLY BUT WELL WORTH THE EFFORT. DON'T OVERSTUFF THE TOFU OR IT MIGHT EXPLODE OUT AS IT COOKS. AS WITH OTHER 'BLAND' SOUPS, USE A GOOD QUALITY STOCK. THE STUFFED TOFU CAN ALSO BE FRIED AND EATEN ON ITS OWN.

275 g (10 oz) raw prawns (shrimp)
2–3 coriander (cilantro) roots, roughly chopped
2 garlic cloves, roughly chopped
¼ teaspoon salt
1 tablespoon cornflour (cornstarch)
¼ teaspoon ground white pepper
320 g (11 oz) firm tofu (bean curd)
1.5 litres (6 cups) vegetable stock
2.5 cm (1 inch) piece of ginger, sliced
4 tablespoons light soy sauce
1 tablespoon preserved radish
5 spring onions (scallions), cut into slivers, for garnish

SERVES 4

PEEL and devein the prawns. Set aside about 80 g (3 oz) of the prawns and cut the rest of them along their backs so they open like a butterfly (leave each prawn joined along the base and at the tail).

USING a food processor or blender, whiz the coriander roots and garlic until as smooth as possible. Add the prawns that are not butterflied, along with the salt, cornflour and white pepper, then blend until as smooth as possible. If you prefer, you can use a pestle and mortar to pound the coriander roots and garlic into a paste before processing with the prawns. This gives a slightly better flavour.

DRAIN the tofu and cut it into 16 triangles. Cut a pocket into the long side of each piece of tofu with a knife. Spoon some prawn mixture into each pocket and gently press down on top. Repeat until you have used all the tofu and the mixture.

HEAT the stock to boiling point in a saucepan. Reduce the heat to low and add the ginger, light soy sauce and preserved radish. Lower the tofu envelopes into the stock and cook for 4–5 minutes or until cooked. Add the butterflied prawns and cook for another 1–2 minutes or until the prawns open and turn pink. Taste, then adjust the seasoning if necessary. Serve garnished with spring onions.

Spoon some of the prepared prawn mixture into each tofu pocket, then carefully lower them into the stock.

A spirit house in Damnoen Saduak.

WON TON SOUP

WON TON LITERALLY TRANSLATED MEANS 'SWALLOWING A CLOUD'. WON TONS, KNOWN AS HUN TUN OUTSIDE OF GUANGZHOU, ARE CATEGORIZED AS NOODLES AS THEY USE THE SAME DOUGH AS EGG NOODLES. WON TON SOUP CAN ALSO INCLUDE EGG NOODLES—ADD SOME IF YOU LIKE.

250 g (9 oz) prawns
80 g (3 oz) peeled water chestnuts
250 g (9 oz) lean minced pork
3¹/₂ tablepoons light soy sauce
3¹/₂ tablespoons Shaoxing rice wine
1¹/₂ teaspoons salt
1¹/₂ teaspoons roasted sesame oil
¹/₂ teaspoon freshly ground black pepper
1 teaspoon finely chopped ginger
1¹/₂ tablespoons cornflour
30 square or round won ton wrappers
1.5 litres (6 cups) chicken stock (page 565)
450 g (1 lb) spinach, trimmed (optional)
2 spring onions (scallions), green part only, finely chopped

SERVES 6

PEEL and devein the prawns. Place in a tea towel and squeeze out as much moisture as possible. Mince the prawns to a coarse paste using a sharp knife or in a food processor.

BLANCH the water chestnuts in boiling water for 1 minute, then refresh in cold water. Drain, pat dry and roughly chop them. Place the prawns, water chestnuts, pork, 2 teaspoons of the soy sauce, 2 teaspoons of the rice wine, ¹/₂ teaspoon of the salt, ¹/₂ teaspoon of the sesame oil, the black pepper, ginger and cornflour in a mixing bowl. Stir vigorously to combine.

PLACE a teaspoon of filling in the centre of one won ton wrapper. Brush the edge of the wrapper with a little water, fold in half and then bring the two folded corners together and press firmly. Place the won tons on a cornflour-dusted tray.

BRING a saucepan of water to the boil. Cook the won tons, covered, for 5–6 minutes, or until they have risen to the surface. Using a wire sieve or slotted spoon, remove the won tons and divide them among six bowls.

PLACE the stock in a saucepan with the remaining soy sauce, rice wine, salt and sesame oil, and bring to the boil. Add the spinach and cook until just wilted. Pour the hot stock over the won tons and sprinkle with the spring onion.

The easiest way to make the won tons is to shape them in the same way as tortellini.

Leaving the skin on the fish is traditional as originally whole fish would have been used for this dish. The skin also helps the pieces hold together while the soup is cooking.

Fishermen selling their morning's catch on the Quai des Belges, in the old port of Marseille.

BOUILLABAISSE

BOUILLABAISSE IS THE MOST FAMOUS FRENCH FISH SOUP AND IS ASSOCIATED WITH THE SOUTH OF THE COUNTRY, PARTICULARLY MARSEILLE. AS A FISHERMAN'S MEAL IT IS OFTEN MADE WITH WHOLE FISH, ESPECIALLY *RASCASSE* (SCORPION FISH). USING FILLETS IS MUCH SIMPLER.

ROUILLE
1 small red capsicum (pepper)
1 slice white bread, crusts removed
1 red chilli
2 garlic cloves
1 egg yolk
80 ml (⅓ cup) olive oil

SOUP
18 (3 lb 5 oz) mussels
1.5 kg firm white fish fillets such
　as red mullet, bass, snapper,
　monkfish, rascasse, John Dory
　or eel, skin on
2 tablespoons oil
1 fennel bulb, thinly sliced
1 onion, chopped
750 g (1 lb 10 oz) ripe tomatoes
1.25 litres (5 cups) fish stock or
　water
pinch of saffron threads
bouquet garni
5 cm (2 inch) piece of orange zest

SERVES 6

TO MAKE the rouille, preheat the grill (broiler). Cut the capsicum in half, remove the seeds and membrane and place, skin side up, under the hot grill until the skin blackens. Leave to cool before peeling away the skin. Roughly chop the capsicum.

SOAK the bread in 3 tablespoons of water, then squeeze dry with your hands. Put the capsicum, chilli, bread, garlic and egg yolk in a mortar and pestle or food processor and pound or mix together. Gradually add the oil in a thin stream, pounding or mixing until the rouille is smooth and has the texture of thick mayonnaise. Cover and refrigerate the rouille until needed.

TO MAKE the soup, scrub the mussels and remove their beards. Discard any mussels that are already open and don't close when tapped on the work surface. Cut the fish into bite-sized pieces.

HEAT the oil in a large saucepan and cook the fennel and onion over medium heat for 5 minutes, or until golden.

SCORE a cross in the top of each tomato. Plunge into boiling water for 20 seconds, then drain and peel the skin away from the cross. Chop the tomatoes, discarding the cores. Add to the pan and cook for 3 minutes. Stir in the stock, saffron, bouquet garni and orange zest, bring to the boil and boil for 10 minutes. Remove the bouquet garni and either push the soup through a sieve or purée in a blender. Return to the cleaned pan, season well and bring back to the boil.

REDUCE the heat to simmer and add the fish and mussels. Cook for 5 minutes or until the fish is tender and the mussels have opened. Throw out any mussels that haven't opened in this time. Serve the soup with rouille and bread. Or lift out the fish and mussels and serve separately.

CHESTNUT, PANCETTA AND CABBAGE SOUP

100 g (3 oz) cavolo nero or savoy
   cabbage, roughly chopped
2 tablespoons olive oil
1 large onion, finely chopped
185 g (6 oz) pancetta, diced
3 garlic cloves, crushed
10 g (1/3 oz) rosemary, chopped
300 g (10 oz) cooked peeled
   chestnuts
150 ml (2/3 cup) red wine
drizzle of extra virgin olive oil

SERVES 4

COOK the cabbage in 1.5 litres boiling salted water for about 10 minutes. Drain, reserving the water. Rinse the cabbage in cold water if too hot to handle, and chop more finely.

HEAT the olive oil in a large saucepan and cook the onion and pancetta over moderately high heat until the onion is soft and the pancetta lightly browned. Add the garlic and rosemary and cook for a few minutes. Break up the chestnuts a little and add to the pan with the cabbage. Stir to infuse the flavours, season, then add the wine. Bring to the boil and cook for a couple of minutes. Finally add the cabbage water and simmer for about 15 minutes.

PUREE half of the soup, leaving the remainder unpuréed to create a little texture. Serve hot with a drizzle of extra virgin olive oil over each bowl.

Spoleto town centre.

Farro is a grain also known as 'spelt'. It was widely used by the Romans to make porridge, soups and, in its ground form, bread.

MINESTRA DI FARRO

200 g (7 oz) dried borlotti beans
2 tablespoons olive oil
1 small onion, thinly sliced
2 garlic cloves, crushed
1.5 litres (6 cups) chicken stock
8 mint leaves, roughly torn
200 g (7 oz) farro (spelt)
100 g (3 oz) Parmesan, grated
1 tablespoon finely chopped mint
4 teaspoons extra virgin olive oil

SERVES 4

SOAK the borlotti beans in cold water overnight. Drain and place in a large saucepan with plenty of cold water. Bring to the boil and simmer until tender (about 1 1/2 hours, depending on the age of the beans). Drain.

HEAT the olive oil in a large saucepan and cook the onion over low heat for 6 minutes, or until soft. Season. Add the garlic and cook without browning for 20–30 seconds. Add the stock and torn mint and bring to the boil.

STIR in the farro a little at a time so that the stock continues to boil, then lower the heat and simmer for 15 minutes. Add the borlotti beans and simmer for 30 minutes, or until the farro is tender and the soup thick. Purée half the soup. Return to the pan and stir in the Parmesan and chopped mint. Season and stir in 125–250 ml (1/2–1 cup) hot water to give a spoonable consistency. Serve immediately, with a teaspoon of extra virgin olive oil stirred through each bowl.

MINESTRA DI FARRO

CRAB BISQUE

ORIGINALLY BISQUES WERE MADE WITH POULTRY AND GAME BIRDS (IN PARTICULAR PIGEONS) AND
WERE MORE OF A STEW. TODAY THEY HAVE EVOLVED INTO RICH VELVETY SOUPS AND TEND TO USE
CRUSTACEANS. YOU CAN RESERVE SOME OF THE CRAB MEAT OR CLAWS FOR A GARNISH.

You will need a large saucepan or stockpot for making crab bisque—the crab shells take up a lot of room in the pan.

1 kg (2 lb 3 oz) live crabs
50 g (2 oz) butter
1/2 carrot, finely chopped
1/2 onion, finely chopped
1 celery stalk, finely chopped
1 bay leaf
2 thyme sprigs
2 tablespoons tomato purée
2 tablespoons brandy
150 ml (2/3 cup) dry white wine
1 litre (4 cups) fish stock
60 g (2 oz) rice
60 ml (1/4 cup) double cream
1/4 teaspoon cayenne pepper

SERVES 4

PUT the crabs in the freezer for 1 hour. Remove the top shell and bony tail flap from the underside of each crab, then remove the gills from both sides of the crab and the grit sac. Detach the claws and legs.

HEAT the butter in a large saucepan. Add the vegetables, bay leaf and thyme and cook over moderate heat for 3 minutes, without allowing the vegetables to colour. Add the crab claws, legs and body and cook for 5 minutes, or until the crab shells turn red. Add the tomato purée, brandy and white wine and simmer for 2 minutes, or until reduced by half.

ADD the stock and 500 ml (2 cups) water and bring to the boil. Reduce the heat and simmer for 5 minutes. Remove the shells and reserve the claws. Finely crush the shells with a pestle and mortar (or in a food processor with a little of the soup).

RETURN the crushed shells to the soup with the rice. Bring to the boil, reduce the heat, cover the pan and simmer for 30 minutes, or until the rice is very soft.

STRAIN the bisque into a clean saucepan through a fine sieve lined with damp muslin, pressing down firmly on the solids to extract all the cooking liquid. Add the cream and season with salt and cayenne, then gently reheat to serve. Ladle into warmed soup bowls and garnish, if you like, with the crab claws or some of the meat.

TEN-TREASURE SOUP

THIS MEAL-IN-ONE SOUP IS ALMOST A KIND OF STEW, WHERE THE INGREDIENTS SIMMER TOGETHER SO THAT THE FLAVOURS MIX. TRADITIONALLY THIS SOUP HAS TEN MAIN INGREDIENTS, BUT THE EXACT NUMBER DOES NOT MATTER AND YOU CAN VARY THE INGREDIENTS DEPENDING ON WHAT'S AVAILABLE.

400 g (14 oz) Chinese cabbage
2 tablespoons oil
4 garlic cloves, smashed with the
    flat side of a cleaver
130 ml (½ cup) Shaoxing rice wine
1.5 litres (6 cups) chicken stock
    (page 565)
1 teaspoon salt
250 g (9 oz) centre-cut pork loin,
    trimmed
2 teaspoons light soy sauce
½ teaspoon roasted sesame oil
450 g (1 lb) prawns
3 slices ginger, smashed with the
    flat side of a cleaver
30 g (1 oz) bean thread noodles
6 dried Chinese mushrooms
450 g (1 lb) firm bean curd, drained
    and cut into 2.5 cm squares
2 carrots, cut into 2 cm (1 inch)
    pieces
200 g (7 oz) baby spinach leaves
3 spring onions (scallions), green
    part only, cut diagonally into 1 cm
    (6 inch) lengths

SERVES 6

REMOVE the stems from the cabbage and cut the leaves into 5 cm (2 inch) squares. Separate the hard cabbage pieces from the leafy ones. Heat a wok over high heat, add the oil and heat until very hot. Add the hard cabbage pieces and the garlic. Toss lightly over high heat, adding 1 tablespoon of the rice wine. Stir-fry for several minutes, then add the leafy cabbage pieces. Stir-fry for 1 minute, then add 4 tablespoons of the rice wine, the stock and half of the salt. Bring to the boil, then reduce the heat to low and cook for 30 minutes. Transfer to a clay pot or saucepan.

CUT the pork across the grain into slices about 2 mm (⅛ inch) thick. Place the pork in a bowl, add the soy sauce and sesame oil, and toss lightly. Marinate in the fridge for 20 minutes.

PEEL and devein the prawns, then place in a bowl with the ginger, remaining rice wine and salt and toss lightly. Marinate in the fridge for 20 minutes. Remove and discard the ginger.

SOAK the bean thread noodles in hot water for 10 minutes, then drain and cut into 15 cm (6 inch) lengths. Soak the dried mushrooms in boiling water for 30 minutes, then drain and squeeze out any excess water. Remove and discard the stems.

ARRANGE the pork slices, bean curd, mushrooms, noodles and carrot in separate piles on top of the cabbage in the casserole, leaving some space in the centre for the prawns and spinach. Cover and cook over medium heat for 20 minutes. Arrange the prawns and spinach in the centre and sprinkle with the spring onion. Cover and cook for 5 minutes, or until the prawns are pink and cooked through. Season with salt if necessary. Serve directly from the pot.

Use the flat side of a cleaver to smash the garlic cloves and the blade for cutting the carrots.

Pepper, shown here in its fresh form, is indigenous to India.

TAMATAR SHORBA

RASAM

THIS SOUP-LIKE DISH WAS ORIGINALLY KNOWN AS 'MULLIGA THANNI', LITERALLY TRANSLATED AS 'PEPPER WATER'. IN AN INDIAN SETTING, IT IS SERVED SPOONED OVER RICE AS PART OF THE MAIN MEAL. THE BRITISH VERSION IS CALLED MULLIGATAWNY.

3 tablespoons tamarind purée
  (page 554)
1¹/₂ tablespoons coriander (cilantro)
  seeds
2 tablespoons cumin seeds
1 tablespoon black peppercorns
1 tablespoon oil
5 garlic cloves, skins on,
  roughly pounded
1 red onion, thinly sliced
2–3 dried chillies, torn into pieces
2 stalks curry leaves
200 g (7 oz) skinless, boneless
  chicken thighs, cut into small
  pieces

SERVES 4

MIX the tamarind purée with 750 ml (3 cups) water. Place a small frying pan over low heat and dry-roast the coriander seeds until aromatic. Remove, then dry-roast the cumin seeds, followed by the black peppercorns. Grind them together using a spice grinder or a pestle and mortar.

HEAT the oil in a large, heavy-based saucepan over low heat, add the garlic and onion and fry until golden. Add the chilli and the curry leaves and fry for 2 minutes, or until they are aromatic. Add the tamarind water, the ground spices and season with salt. Bring to the boil, reduce the heat and simmer for 10 minutes.

ADD the chicken to the saucepan with 250 ml (1 cup) water and simmer for 20 minutes, gradually adding another 250 ml (1 cup) water as the soup reduces. Remove any garlic skin which has floated to the top. Season with salt, to taste. Serve with rice (page 552).

TAMATAR SHORBA

2 tablespoons oil
1 onion, finely chopped
3 Indian bay leaves (cassia leaves)
5 cm (2 inch) piece of cinnamon
  stick
12 peppercorns
2 teaspoons ground cumin
2 teaspoons garam masala
  (page 556)
2 x 400 g (14 oz) tins chopped
  tomatoes
1 teaspoon sugar
250 ml (1 cup) chicken or vegetable
  stock
coriander (cilantro) leaves

SERVES 2

HEAT the oil over low heat in a heavy-based saucepan and fry the onion, bay leaves, cinnamon and peppercorns until the onion is soft. Add the cumin, garam masala and the tomato, mashing the tomatoes with a fork to break them up. Add the sugar and stock and slowly bring to the boil. Simmer over low heat for 30 minutes.

STRAIN the soup by pushing it through a sieve, using the back of a metal spoon to push against the solids and extract as much of the liquid as possible. Discard what's left in the sieve. Reheat, then season with salt, to taste, and garnish with the coriander leaves before serving.

ZUPPA DI PESCE

FOR A COUNTRY WHERE ALMOST EVERY REGION HAS A SEA COAST, IT IS HARDLY SURPRISING THAT
ITALY HAS ALMOST AS MANY VERSIONS OF THIS SOUP AS THERE ARE FISH IN THE SEA. THIS RECIPE
INCLUDES SUGGESTIONS FOR FISH VARIETIES, BUT ASK YOUR FISHMONGER WHAT'S BEST ON THE DAY.

Score a criss-cross pattern into the squid to make it curl.

FISH STOCK

300 g (10 oz) firm white fish fillets,
  such as monkfish, red mullet,
  cod, deep sea perch, skinned
  and cut into large cubes, bones
  reserved
12 prawns
1 small onion, roughly chopped
1 carrot, roughly chopped
15 g (½ oz) parsley, roughly
  chopped, stalks reserved

200 g (7 oz) squid tubes
4 tablespoons olive oil
1 onion, finely chopped
1 celery stalk, finely chopped
1 carrot, finely chopped
2 garlic cloves, finely chopped
pinch of cayenne pepper
1 fennel bulb, trimmed and thinly
  sliced
125 ml (½ cup) dry white wine
400 g (14 oz) tin chopped tomatoes
250 g (9 oz) scallops, cleaned

CROSTINI

3 tablespoons extra virgin olive oil
2 garlic cloves, crushed
4 slices 'country-style' bread, such
  as ciabatta

SERVES 4

TO MAKE the fish stock, rinse the fish bones in
cold water, removing any blood or intestines. Peel
and devein the prawns and put the fish bones
and prawn shells in a large saucepan with just
enough water to cover. Bring slowly to a simmer,
skimming any froth from the surface. Add the
onion, carrot and the stalks from the parsley, then
simmer gently for 20 minutes. Strain through a
fine colander and measure 1.5 litres (6 cups)
stock. If there is less than this, add a little water; if
there is more than this, put the strained stock
back into the saucepan and simmer until reduced
to 1.5 litres (6 cups).

LIE the squid out flat, skin side up, and score a
criss-cross pattern into the flesh, being careful not
to cut all the way through. Slice diagonally into
bite-sized strips.

HEAT the oil in a large saucepan and cook the
onion, celery, carrot, garlic and chopped parsley
over moderately low heat for 5–6 minutes, or until
softened but not browned. Add the cayenne
pepper and season well. Stir in the fennel and
cook for 2–3 minutes. Add the white wine,
increase the heat and cook until it has been
absorbed. Stir in the tomatoes, then add the fish
stock and bring to the boil. Reduce the heat and
simmer for 20 minutes.

ADD the squid to the pan with the fish pieces
and simmer for 1 minute. Add the scallops and
prawns and simmer for a further 2 minutes.
Taste and add more seasoning if necessary.

TO MAKE the crostini, heat the olive oil and
crushed garlic in a large frying pan over
moderately low heat. Add the slices of bread and
fry on both sides until golden. Place a slice of
bread into each of four warmed serving bowls.
Ladle the soup on top and serve immediately.

SLICED FISH AND CORIANDER SOUP

THE CHINESE OFTEN USE A CHICKEN AND MEAT STOCK WHEN COOKING SEAFOOD. HOWEVER, IF YOU

PREFER, YOU CAN USE A VEGETABLE OR FISH STOCK FOR THIS RECIPE.

250 g (9 oz) firm white fish fillets,
   such as cod, halibut or monkfish,
   skin removed
2 teaspoons egg white, beaten
1 teaspoon Shaoxing rice wine
2 teaspoons cornflour
750 ml (3 cups) chicken and meat
   stock (page 565)
1 tablespoon light soy sauce
40 g (1 oz) coriander (cilantro)
   leaves

SERVES 4

CUT the fish into 2 x 3 cm (¾ x 1¼ inch) slices.
Blend the egg white, rice wine and cornflour to
make a smooth paste, and use it to coat each fish
slice.

BRING the stock to a rolling boil in a large clay
pot or saucepan. Add the fish slices one by one,
stir gently and return to the boil. Reduce the heat
and simmer for 1 minute, then add the soy sauce
and coriander leaves. Return to the boil, season
with salt and white pepper and serve immediately.

Using a cornflour mixture to coat
seafood before cooking is called
'velveting'. The coating adds a
silky texture to the cooked food
as well as protecting it and
keeping it moist.

WEST LAKE BEEF SOUP

THERE IS A WEST LAKE (AND OFTEN A NORTH, SOUTH OR EAST LAKE) IN MOST CITIES IN CHINA, SO

THIS SOUP IS MORE LIKELY NAMED AFTER A LAKE IN ITS PROVINCE OF ORIGIN, GUANGZHOU, THAN THE

FAMOUS WEST LAKE OF HANGZHOU.

150 g (5 oz) rump or fillet steak
1 teaspoon salt
1 teaspoon sugar
1 tablespoon light soy sauce
1 tablespoon Shaoxing rice wine
2 tablespoons cornflour
½ teaspoon roasted sesame oil
750 ml (3 cups) chicken and meat
   stock (page 565)
100 g (3 oz) peas, fresh or frozen
1 egg, lightly beaten
chopped spring onion (scallion)

SERVES 4

TRIM the fat off the steak and cut the steak into
small pieces, about the size of the peas. Combine
the beef with a pinch of the salt, about half the
sugar, 1 teaspoon each of the soy sauce, rice
wine and cornflour and the sesame oil. Marinate
in the fridge for at least 20 minutes.

BRING the stock to a rolling boil in a large clay
pot or saucepan. Add the beef and stir to
separate the meat, then add the peas and the
remaining salt, sugar, soy sauce and rice wine.
Return to the boil, then stir in the egg. Combine
the remaining cornflour with enough water to
make a paste, add to the soup and simmer until
thickened. Garnish with the spring onion.

WEST LAKE BEEF SOUP

LEEK AND POTATO SOUP

LEEK AND POTATO SOUP CAN BE SERVED HOT OR CHILLED. IN ITS HOT FORM THE DISH IS TRADITIONALLY FRENCH. THE CHILLED VERSION, VICHYSSOISE, WAS THOUGHT TO HAVE BEEN FIRST SERVED AT THE RITZ-CARLTON HOTEL IN NEW YORK BY A FRENCH CHEF FROM VICHY.

50 g (2 oz) butter
1 onion, finely chopped
3 leeks, white part only, sliced
1 celery stalk, finely chopped
1 garlic clove, finely chopped
200 g (7 oz) potatoes, chopped
750 ml (3 cups) chicken stock
220 ml (¾ cup) single cream
2 tablespoons chopped chives

SERVES 6

MELT the butter in a large saucepan and add the onion, leek, celery and garlic. Cover the pan and cook, stirring occasionally, over low heat for 15 minutes, or until the vegetables are softened but not browned. Add the potato and stock and bring to the boil.

REDUCE the heat and leave to simmer, covered, for 20 minutes. Allow to cool a little before puréeing in a blender or food processor. Return to the clean saucepan.

BRING the soup gently back to the boil and stir in the cream. Season with salt and white pepper and reheat without boiling. Serve hot or well chilled, garnished with chives.

Do not hurry the initial cooking of the leeks. The long cooking time over low heat is what gives them their sweet flavour.

WATERCRESS SOUP

30 g (1 oz) butter
1 onion, finely chopped
250 g (9 oz) potatoes, diced
600 ml (2½ cups) chicken stock
1 kg (2 lb 3 oz) watercress, trimmed
  and chopped
125 ml (½ cup) single cream
125 ml (½ cup) milk
freshly grated nutmeg
2 tablespoons chopped chives

SERVES 4

MELT the butter in a large saucepan and add the onion. Cover the pan and cook over low heat until the onion is softened but not browned. Add the potato and chicken stock and simmer for 12 minutes, or until the potato is tender. Add the watercress and cook for 1 minute.

REMOVE from the heat and leave the soup to cool a little before pouring into a blender or food processor. Blend until smooth and return to the clean saucepan.

BRING the soup gently back to the boil and stir in the cream and milk. Season with nutmeg, salt and pepper and reheat without boiling. Serve garnished with chives.

WATERCRESS SOUP

HOT AND SOUR PRAWN SOUP

THIS SOUP IS PROBABLY THE MOST WELL KNOWN THAI DISH OF ALL. ALTHOUGH IT IS USUALLY MADE WITH PRAWNS, IT WORKS EQUALLY WELL WITH FISH. TO ACHIEVE THE FAMOUS DISTINCTIVE AROMA AND FLAVOURS, USE ONLY THE FRESHEST GOOD QUALITY INGREDIENTS.

350 g (12 oz) raw prawns (shrimp)
1 tablespoon oil
3 lemon grass stalks, white part
   only, bruised
3 thin slices of galangal
2 litres (8 cups) chicken stock
   or water
5–7 bird's eye chillies, stems
   removed, bruised
5 makrut (kaffir) lime leaves, torn
2 tablespoons fish sauce
70 g (2 oz) straw mushrooms,
   or quartered button mushrooms
2 spring onions (scallions), sliced
3 tablespoons lime juice
a few coriander (cilantro) leaves,
   for garnish

SERVES 4

PEEL and devein the prawns, leaving the tails intact and reserving the heads and shells. Heat the oil in a large stockpot or wok and add the prawn heads and shells. Cook for 5 minutes or until the shells turn bright orange.

ADD one stalk of lemon grass to the pan with the galangal and stock or water. Bring to the boil, then reduce the heat and simmer for 20 minutes. Strain the stock and return to the pan. Discard the shells and flavourings.

FINELY slice the remaining lemon grass and add it to the liquid with the chillies, lime leaves, fish sauce, mushrooms and spring onions. Cook gently for 2 minutes.

ADD the prawns and cook for 3 minutes or until the prawns are firm and pink. Take off the heat and add the lime juice. Taste, then adjust the seasoning with extra lime juice or fish sauce if necessary. Garnish with coriander leaves.

SALADS

PRAWN AND POMELO SALAD

THIS NORTHERN THAI SALAD USES POMELO TO GIVE IT A SWEET/TART FLAVOUR. DIFFERENT VARIETIES OF POMELO ARE AVAILABLE IN THAILAND: SOME HAVE PINK FLESH AND OTHERS HAVE YELLOW. SERVE THE SALAD WITH STICKY RICE AND EAT IT AS SOON AS IT IS READY.

Slice off a section from the top of the pomelo before cutting it into sections and segmenting it.

1 large pomelo
1 tablespoon fish sauce
1 tablespoon lime juice
1 teaspoon sugar
1 tablespoon chilli jam (page 561)
300 g (10 oz) raw medium prawns (shrimp), peeled and deveined, tails intact
3 tablespoons shredded fresh coconut, lightly toasted until golden (if fresh unavailable, use shredded desiccated)
3 Asian shallots, finely sliced
5 bird's eye chillies, bruised
20 g (1 cup) mint leaves
10 g (⅓ cup) coriander (cilantro) leaves
1 tablespoon fried Asian shallots

SERVES 4

TO PEEL a pomelo, first, slice a circular patch off the top of the fruit, about 2 cm (¾ inch) deep (roughly the thickness of the skin). Next, score four deep lines from top to bottom, dividing the skin into four segments. Peel away the skin, one quarter at a time. Remove any remaining pith and separate the segments of the fruit. Peel the segments and remove any seeds. Crumble the segments into their component parts, without squashing them or releasing the juice.

TO MAKE the dressing, combine the fish sauce, lime juice, sugar and chilli jam in a small bowl and stir.

BRING a large saucepan of water to the boil. Add the prawns and cook for 2 minutes. Drain and allow the prawns to cool.

IN a large bowl, gently combine the pomelo, prawns, toasted coconut, shallots, chillies, mint and coriander. Just before serving, add the dressing and toss gently to combine all the ingredients. Serve sprinkled with fried shallots.

Peeling pomelo in Pattaya.

INSALATA CAPRESE

INSALATA CAPRESE IS TRADITIONALLY SERVED WITH NO OTHER DRESSING THAN A DRIZZLE OF EXTRA
VIRGIN OLIVE OIL. HOWEVER, IF YOU'RE NOT ABSOLUTELY CONFIDENT THAT YOUR TOMATOES HAVE THE
BEST FLAVOUR, A LITTLE BALSAMIC VINEGAR WILL HELP THEM ALONG.

6 ripe plum tomatoes
3–4 balls mozzarella
2 tablespoons extra virgin olive oil
15 young basil leaves
1/2 teaspoon balsamic vinegar
   (optional)

SERVES 4

SLICE the tomatoes, pouring off any excess
juice, and cut the mozzarella into slices of a
similar thickness.

ARRANGE alternating rows of tomato and
mozzarella on a serving plate. Sprinkle with salt
and pepper and drizzle the olive oil over the top.
Tear the basil leaves into pieces and scatter over
the oil. To serve, take to the table and sprinkle
with the balsamic vinegar, if you're using it.

INSALATA DI RINFORZO

Caprese is also known as *insalata
tricolore*—the mozzarella, ripe
tomatoes and basil reflect the
colours of the Italian flag.

250 g (9 oz) carrots
150 g (5 oz) green beans
1/2 red onion
600 ml (2 1/2 cups) white wine
   vinegar
1 tablespoon sea salt
1 tablespoon sugar
1 bay leaf
300 g (10 oz) cauliflower florets

DRESSING
80 ml (1/3 cup) extra virgin olive oil
2 tablespoons lemon juice
1 tablespoon finely chopped parsley
1 tablespoon chopped capers
1 garlic clove, halved

4 anchovy fillets, halved lengthways
85 g (3 oz) small black olives, such
   as Ligurian
1 tablespoon roughly chopped
   parsley
1–2 tablespoons extra virgin olive oil

SERVES 4

CUT the carrots into lengths the size of your little
finger, slice the beans into similar lengths and slice
the onion into rings.

COMBINE the vinegar, salt, sugar and bay leaf in
a saucepan with 500 ml (2 cups) water and bring
to the boil. Cook the carrots for about 3 minutes
until just tender. Transfer to a bowl with a slotted
spoon. Add the beans to the pan and cook for
about 2 minutes until similarly done. Add to the
carrots in the bowl. Add the onion and cauliflower
to the pan and cook for about 3 minutes until the
cauliflower just starts to soften. Drain, add to the
bowl and cool.

TO MAKE the dressing, mix together the olive oil,
lemon juice, parsley, capers and garlic and season
well. Pour over the cooled vegetables and toss
gently. The salad can be stored in an airtight
container for up to 2 weeks at this stage.

TO SERVE toss through the anchovy fillets, olives,
parsley and oil.

INSALATA DI RINFORZO

GREEN PAPAYA SALAD

THIS DISH FROM NORTH-EAST THAILAND IS NOW POPULAR THROUGHOUT THE COUNTRY. MULTIPLY THE INGREDIENTS BY THE NUMBER OF PORTIONS BUT MAKE JUST ONE SERVE AT A TIME OTHERWISE IT WON'T FIT IN YOUR MORTAR.

120 g (4 oz) small hard, green, unripe papaya
1½ tablespoons palm sugar
1 tablespoon fish sauce
1–2 garlic cloves
25 g (1 oz) roasted peanuts
25 g (1 oz) snake beans cut into 2.5 cm (1 inch) pieces
1 tablespoon ground dried shrimp
2–6 bird's eye chillies, stems removed (6 will give a very hot result)
50 g (2 oz) cherry tomatoes, left whole, or 2 medium tomatoes, cut into 6 wedges
half a lime
sticky rice (page 550), to serve

SERVES 1

PEEL the green papaya with a vegetable peeler and cut the papaya into long, thin shreds. If you have a mandolin, use the grater attachment.

MIX the palm sugar with the fish sauce until the sugar has dissolved.

USING a large, deep pestle and mortar, pound the garlic into a paste. Add the roasted peanuts and pound roughly together with the garlic. Add the papaya and pound softly, using a spoon to scrape down the sides, and turning and mixing well.

ADD the beans, dried shrimp and chillies and keep pounding and turning to bruise these ingredients. Add the sugar mixture and tomatoes, squeeze in the lime juice and add the lime skin to the mixture. Lightly pound together for another minute until thoroughly mixed. As the juice comes out, pound more gently so the liquid doesn't splash. Discard the lime skin. Taste the sauce in the bottom of the mortar and adjust the seasoning if necessary. It should be a balance of sweet and sour with a hot and salty taste.

SPOON the papaya salad and all the juices onto a serving plate. Serve with sticky rice.

Only one portion of the salad at a time will fit into your mortar.

121

SALADE AU CHÈVRE

50 g (2 oz) walnuts, broken into
pieces
1 teaspoon flaked sea salt
8 slices baguette
1 large garlic clove, cut in half
125 g (4 oz) chèvre, cut into 8
slices
50 g (2 oz) mesclun (mixed salad
leaves and herbs)
1 small red onion, thinly sliced

DRESSING
2 tablespoons olive oil
1 tablespoon walnut oil
1 1/2 tablespoons tarragon vinegar
1 garlic clove, crushed

SERVES 4 AS A STARTER

PREHEAT the grill (broiler) to hot. Put the walnuts
in a bowl and cover with boiling water. Leave for
1 minute, then drain and shake dry. Toast under
the grill for 3–4 minutes until golden. Sprinkle sea
salt over the top, toss lightly and leave to cool.

PUT the baguette under the grill and toast one
side until lightly golden. Remove from the heat
and rub the toasted side with the cut garlic. Leave
for a few minutes to cool and crisp, then turn over
and place a slice of chèvre on each one. Grill for
2–3 minutes, or until the cheese browns.

TO MAKE the dressing, mix together the olive oil,
walnut oil, vinegar and garlic and season well.

TOSS the mesclun, onion and toasted walnuts
together on a large platter. Arrange the chèvre
croutons on top and drizzle with the dressing.
Serve while the croutons are still warm.

For the salade au foie gras, cut
the foie gras terrine into eight
slices. Slice the truffle as finely as
you can and place a slice on top
of each piece of foie gras.

SALADE AU FOIE GRAS

100 g (3 oz) salad potatoes, thickly
sliced
12 asparagus spears, cut into short
lengths
1 small black truffle, very thinly
sliced into at least 8 pieces
120 g (4 oz) foie gras terrine, sliced
into 8 pieces
1 tablespoon butter
50 g (2 oz) mesclun (mixed salad
leaves and herbs)

DRESSING
2 tablespoons olive oil
1 tablespoon walnut oil
1 tablespoon Armagnac
1 1/2 tablespoons red wine vinegar

SERVES 4 AS A STARTER

SIMMER the potatoes in boiling salted water for
15 minutes until tender. Remove with a slotted
spoon, rinse in cold water and cool. Simmer the
asparagus in the water for 3–4 minutes until
tender. Drain, rinse under cold water and chill.

TO MAKE the dressing, mix together the olive oil,
walnut oil, Armagnac and vinegar. Season well.

PLACE a slice of truffle on the centre of each slice
of foie gras and press it in gently. Melt the butter
in a frying pan, add the foie gras to the pan and
brown lightly, turning after 30 seconds. The foie
gras becomes quite soft as it heats, so use a
spatula to turn and lift it out. Drain on paper
towels and keep warm.

PUT the potatoes, asparagus and mesclun in a
bowl. Add the dressing and toss lightly. Top with
the foie gras, truffle side up, and sprinkle with any
leftover truffle slices. Serve at once.

SALADE AU FOIE GRAS

CRISPY FISH SALAD

THE FISH (TRADITIONALLY CATFISH) IN THIS RECIPE IS TURNED INTO AN ALMOST UNRECOGNIZABLE FLUFFY, CRUNCHY AFFAIR THAT IS THEN FLAVOURED WITH A SWEET, HOT AND SOUR DRESSING. PINK SALMON IS SUITABLE TO USE AS A SUBSTITUTE FOR THE WHITE FISH.

DRESSING
1 lemon grass stalk, white part
   only, roughly chopped
4 bird's eye chillies,
   stems removed
1 garlic clove, chopped
1 tablespoon fish sauce
2 tablespoons lime juice
2 teaspoons palm sugar
¼ teaspoon ground turmeric

300 g (10 oz) skinless firm white
   fish fillets
1 tablespoon sea salt
peanut oil, for deep-frying
3 tomatoes or large cherry
   tomatoes, each cut into
   4 or 6 wedges
2 Asian shallots, thinly sliced
1 small red onion, sliced into
   thin wedges
15 g (½ cup) coriander (cilantro)
   leaves
18–24 mint leaves
2 tablespoons roasted peanuts,
   roughly chopped

SERVES 4

TO MAKE the dressing, use a pestle and mortar or food processor to pound or blend the lemon grass, chillies and garlic to a paste. Transfer to a bowl and add the fish sauce, lime juice, sugar and turmeric. Stir until the sugar dissolves.

PREHEAT the oven to 180°C/350°F/Gas 4. Pat dry the fish fillets, then toss them in the sea salt. Place them on a rack in a baking tray and bake for 20 minutes. Remove, allow to cool, then transfer to a food processor and chop until the fish resembles large breadcrumbs.

HALF fill a wok with oil and heat over a high heat. Drop a small piece of fish into the oil. If it sizzles immediately, the oil is ready. Drop a large handful of the chopped fish into the hot oil. The fish will puff up and turn crisp. Cook for 30 seconds and carefully stir a little. Cook for another 30 seconds until golden brown. Remove with a slotted spoon and drain on paper towels. Repeat to cook all the fish.

PUT the tomatoes, shallots, red onion, coriander leaves, mint leaves and peanuts in a bowl with about half of the dressing. Transfer the salad to a serving plate. Break the fish into smaller pieces if you wish and place on the salad. To ensure that the fish stays crispy, pour the remaining dressing over the salad just before serving.

This tasty salad is made using a colourful combination with flavours that contrast well.

RADISH SALAD

USE THE SMALLEST RADISHES THAT YOU CAN FIND FOR THIS SALAD. COMBINING THE RADISHES WITH PEANUTS GIVES A CRUNCHY TEXTURE AND HOT FLAVOUR. IT SERVES AS A FRESH-TASTING ACCOMPANIMENT TO MOST COOKED DISHES.

200 g (7 oz) small radishes
1 tablespoon oil
$1/4$ teaspoon cumin seeds
$1/4$ teaspoon black mustard seeds
pinch of asafoetida
$1/4$ teaspoon ground turmeric
$1/4$ teaspoon salt
1 tablespoon lemon juice
100 g (3 oz) roasted peanuts,
  roughly chopped

SERVES 4

WASH the radishes and top and tail them. Cut each radish into four or eight pieces.

HEAT the oil in a small saucepan over medium heat, add the cumin and mustard seeds, then cover and shake the pan until the seeds start to pop.

ADD the asafoetida, turmeric and salt to the pan, then remove from the heat, add the lemon juice and leave to cool. Just before serving, arrange the radishes and the peanuts in a bowl, pour the dressing over the top and mix thoroughly.

CARROT SALAD

CARROT SALAD

CARROT SALADS ARE POPULAR THROUGHOUT INDIA. IN THIS ONE, THE SPICES ARE HEATED IN THE OIL IN ORDER FOR THEIR FLAVOUR TO PERMEATE THE DRESSING. THIS SALAD GETS MORE FLAVOURSOME IF IT IS ALLOWED TO STAND FOR HALF AN HOUR BEFORE SERVING.

1 tablespoon oil
$1/4$ teaspoon black mustard seeds
$1/4$ teaspoon cumin seeds
pinch of ground turmeric
$1/4$ teaspoon salt
$1/4$ teaspoon caster sugar
$1 1/2$ tablespoons lemon juice
500 g (1 lb 2 oz) carrots, finely
  grated
coriander (cilantro) leaves

SERVES 4

HEAT the oil in a small saucepan over medium heat, add the mustard and cumin seeds, then cover and shake the pan until the seeds start to pop.

ADD the turmeric, salt and sugar to the pan, then remove the pan from the heat and leave the spices to cool for 5 minutes. Mix in the lemon juice, then toss the carrot through. Cover and leave for 30 minutes. Garnish with coriander leaves just before serving.

CRAB AND GREEN MANGO SALAD

2 tablespoons fish sauce

2 tablespoons lime juice

2 teaspoons palm sugar

2 green bird's eye chillies, chopped

2 red bird's eye chillies, chopped

1 teaspoon ground dried shrimp

300 g (10 oz) fresh crab meat

30 g (⅔ cup) chopped mint leaves

20 g (⅓ cup) chopped coriander
   (cilantro) leaves

4 Asian shallots, finely sliced

1 green mango, flesh finely shredded

1 tomato, cut in half lengthways and
   thinly sliced

1 large green chilli, thinly sliced on
   an angle

SERVES 4

TO make a dressing, put the fish sauce, lime juice, palm sugar, bird's eye chillies and dried shrimp in a small bowl and stir to dissolve the sugar.

JUST before serving, put the crab meat, mint and coriander leaves, shallots, mango and tomato in a large bowl and toss gently.

POUR the dressing over the salad, then toss to combine and serve with the sliced chilli on top.

YAM PLAA YAANG

HOT AND SOUR GRILLED FISH SALAD

2 mackerel or whiting (about
   400 g/14 oz each fish), cleaned
   and gutted, with or without head,
   or firm white fish fillets

2 lemon grass stalks, white part
   only, finely sliced

2 Asian shallots, finely sliced

1 spring onion (scallion), finely sliced

2.5 cm (1 inch) piece of ginger,
   finely sliced

5 makrut (kaffir) lime leaves,
   finely sliced

20 g (1 cup) mint leaves

5 tablespoons lime juice

1 tablespoon fish sauce

4–5 bird's eye chillies, finely sliced

a few lettuce leaves

1 long red chilli, seeded and finely
   sliced, for garnish

SERVES 4

HEAT a barbecue or grill (broiler) to medium. If using a grill, line the tray with foil. Cook the fish for about 20 minutes on each side or until the fish is cooked and light brown. You can use a special fish-shaped griddle that opens out like tongs to make it easier to lift and turn on the barbecue.

USE your hands to remove the fish heads, backbone and other bones. Break all the fish, including the skin, into bite-sized chunks and put them in a bowl.

ADD the lemon grass, shallots, spring onion, ginger, makrut lime leaves, mint leaves, lime juice, fish sauce and chillies to the fish. Mix well, then taste and adjust the seasoning if necessary.

LINE a serving plate with lettuce leaves, then spoon the salad over the leaves. Sprinkle with chilli slices.

HOT AND SOUR GRILLED
FISH SALAD

CRAB AND GREEN MANGO SALAD

SALADE AUX NOIX

4 thin slices baguette

1 garlic clove, cut in half

75 ml (⅓ cup) olive oil

1 large crisp green lettuce or a
   selection of mixed lettuce leaves

1 tablespoon walnut oil

1 tablespoon red wine vinegar

1 teaspoon Dijon mustard

70 g (2½ oz) walnuts, broken into
   pieces

150 g (5 oz) streaky bacon, cut into
   small pieces

SERVES 4 AS A STARTER

PREHEAT the grill (broiler) and rub the bread with
the cut garlic to give it flavour. Drizzle a little of the
olive oil on each side of the bread and then grill
until golden brown. Leave to cool.

TEAR the lettuce leaves into pieces and arrange
on a large platter. Mix together the remaining olive
oil, walnut oil, vinegar and mustard and season to
make a dressing.

PUT the walnuts in a bowl and cover with boiling
water. Leave for 1 minute, drain and shake dry.

COOK the bacon in a frying pan until crisp, then
lift out of the pan with a slotted spoon and
sprinkle over the lettuce. Add the walnuts to the
pan and cook for a couple of minutes until
browned, then add to the salad. Pour the
dressing into the pan and heat through.

POUR the dressing over the salad and toss well.
Add the garlic croutons to serve.

Frying the sweetbreads before
adding the creamy dressing
gives them a crisp outer layer
while the centre stays soft.

SWEETBREADS SALAD

225 g (8 oz) sweetbreads (lambs
   or calves)

1 batavia lettuce or a selection of
   mixed lettuce leaves

1 tablespoon butter

1 shallot, finely chopped

2 tablespoons red wine vinegar

1 tablespoon Dijon mustard

100 ml (⅓ cup) olive oil

2 tablespoons single cream

SERVES 4 AS A STARTER

SOAK the sweetbreads in cold water for 2 hours,
changing the water every 30 minutes, or
whenever it turns pink. Put the sweetbreads in a
saucepan of cold water and bring them to the
boil. Simmer for 2 minutes, then drain and refresh
under cold water. Pull off any skin and membrane
and divide into bite-sized pieces.

TEAR the lettuce leaves into pieces and arrange
on a plate. Melt the butter in a frying pan and fry
the shallot until tender. Add the sweetbreads and
fry until browned and cooked through. Add the
vinegar, mustard, oil and cream to the pan and
stir well. Spoon over the salad leaves and serve.

SWEETBREADS SALAD

SALADE AUX NOIX

SHREDDED CHICKEN AND BANANA BLOSSOM

BANANA BLOSSOMS LOOK LIKE VERY LARGE PURPLE FLOWER BUDS. MOST OF THE BLOSSOM IS DISCARDED DURING PREPARATION AND ONLY THE SLIGHTLY BITTER CORE IS EATEN. THEY DISCOLOUR IN SECONDS SO WORK QUICKLY OR YOU WILL END UP WITH BLACKENED SHREDS.

3 tablespoons lime juice
1 large banana blossom
250 ml (1 cup) coconut cream
   (page 551)
200 g (7 oz) skinless chicken breast
   fillet, trimmed
1 tablespoon chilli jam (page 561)
1 tablespoon fish sauce
1 tablespoon palm sugar
2 teaspoons lime juice
12 cherry tomatoes, cut in halves
20 g (1 cup) mint leaves
10 g (⅓ cup) coriander (cilantro)
   leaves
1 makrut (kaffir) lime leaf, finely
   shredded, for garnish

SERVES 4

PUT the lime juice in a large bowl of cold water. Using a stainless steel knife, remove the outer leaves of the banana blossom until you reach the creamy pale centre. Cut the heart or centre into quarters and remove the hard cores and stamens from each. Finely slice the fleshy heart on an angle and place the slices in the lime water until ready to use.

RESERVE 2 tablespoons of the coconut cream and pour the rest into a small saucepan and bring to a boil. Add the chicken breast, return to a boil, then reduce the heat and simmer for 5 minutes. Remove from the heat and cover the pan with a tight lid for 20 minutes. Remove the chicken from the pan and discard the cream. Allow the chicken to cool, then shred it into bite-sized pieces.

IN a small bowl, combine the reserved coconut cream with the chilli jam, fish sauce, palm sugar and lime juice.

JUST before serving, drain the banana blossom and put it in a large bowl with the shredded chicken, tomato halves, and mint and coriander leaves. Add the dressing and gently toss to combine the ingredients. Garnish with the shredded makrut lime leaf.

Remove the outer leaves of the banana blossom until you come to the pale centre.

CHARGRILLED EGGPLANT SALAD

2 large eggplants (aubergines),
   thinly sliced lengthways
2 garlic cloves, crushed
150 ml (⅔ cup) extra virgin olive oil
juice of 1 small lemon
½ red chilli, finely chopped
15 g (½ oz) basil or mint leaves,
   roughly chopped

SERVES 4

HEAT a griddle on the stove and cook the eggplant, a few slices at a time, over moderately high heat, turning once until it is soft and cooked. (There is no need to add oil or to salt the eggplant first.) As you remove the eggplant slices from the griddle, put them on a plate on top of each other—this helps them to steam a little and soften further.

IF you do not have a griddle, preheat the oven to 200°C (400°F/Gas 6). Drizzle a couple of tablespoons of olive oil over a baking tray and place the eggplant slices on top. Drizzle with a little more oil and cook the eggplant until soft.

MIX TOGETHER the garlic, olive oil, lemon juice, chilli and herbs. (If you have baked the eggplant, use a little less oil.) Place the eggplant in a flat dish and pour over the marinade. Mix briefly without breaking up the eggplant and marinate for at least 30 minutes before serving.

CHARGRILLED VEGETABLE SALAD

4 long thin eggplants
4 zucchini
4 plum tomatoes
1 small red capsicum (pepper)
1 small green capsicum (pepper)
1 small yellow capsicum (pepper)
60 ml (¼ cup) olive oil
2 garlic cloves, halved

DRESSING
60 ml (¼ cup) extra virgin olive oil
1 tablespoon balsamic vinegar
1 garlic clove, crushed
3 tablespoons chopped parsley
¼ teaspoon caster sugar

SERVES 4

SLICE the eggplants and zucchinis diagonally into 1 cm (½ inch) thick pieces. Halve the tomatoes lengthways and slice the capsicums into short strips. Place all the vegetables in a bowl and add the olive oil and the garlic. Toss well.

PREHEAT a griddle and brush with oil. Cook the eggplant and zucchini for 2–4 minutes on each side, or until browned. Transfer to a shallow serving dish. Cook the tomatoes and capsicums for 1–2 minutes on each side, or until the capsicums start to smell sweet and their skins blister. Transfer to the serving dish and set aside to cool.

TO MAKE the dressing, mix together all the ingredients and then season. Drizzle the dressing over the vegetables and toss lightly. Serve at room temperature.

CHARGRILLED
VEGETABLE SALAD

SLICED STEAK WITH HOT AND SOUR SAUCE

THIS THAI SALAD IS OFTEN EATEN WITH STICKY RICE AND IS PERFECT WITH BEER, THAI WHISKY OR
WINE. SERVE THE SALAD WITH RAW VEGETABLES SUCH AS GREEN CABBAGE.

Heat the barbecue to medium before adding the meat.

350 g (12 oz) lean sirloin, rump
    or fillet steak
2 tablespoons fish sauce
4 tablespoons lime juice
1 teaspoon sugar
¼ teaspoon roasted chilli powder
3–4 Asian shallots, finely sliced
a few lettuce leaves, to serve
20 g (⅓ cup) roughly chopped
    coriander (cilantro) leaves,
    for garnish
15 g (¼ cup) roughly chopped mint
    leaves, for garnish

SERVES 4

HEAT a barbecue or grill (broiler) to medium. If
using a grill, line the tray with foil. Put the beef on
the grill rack and sprinkle both sides with salt and
pepper. Cook for 5–7 minutes on each side,
turning occasionally. Fat should drip off the meat
and the meat should cook slowly enough to
remain juicy and not burn. Using a sharp knife,
slice the cooked beef crossways into strips.

MIX the fish sauce, lime juice, sugar and chilli
powder in a bowl. Add the Asian shallots and
the slices of beef. Taste, then adjust the seasoning
if necessary.

LINE a serving plate with lettuce leaves, then
spoon the mixture over the leaves. Sprinkle with
coriander and mint leaves.

Paddy fields in Phetchaburi.

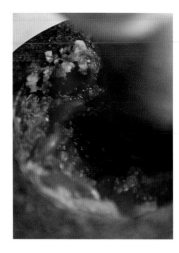

CHICKEN AND PAPAYA SALAD

THIS HOT AND TANGY SALAD, HAS COCONUT RICE INCLUDED, BUT YOU COULD SERVE IT ON ITS OWN IF YOU PREFER. MAKE SURE THE PAPAYA IS GREEN, AND NOT RIPE, OR THE SALAD WON'T TASTE AT ALL RIGHT.

250 ml (1 cup) coconut cream
  (page 551)
200 g (7 oz) skinless chicken breast
  fillet, trimmed
200 g (1 cup) jasmine rice
350 ml (1⅓ cups) coconut milk
  (page 551)
2 garlic cloves, chopped
3 Asian shallots, chopped
3 small red chillies
1 teaspoon small dried shrimp
2 tablespoons fish sauce
8 cherry tomatoes, cut in halves
150 g (5 oz) green papaya,
  grated
2 tablespoons lime juice
30 g (1½ cups) mint leaves,
  roughly chopped
20 g (⅔ cup) coriander (cilantro)
  leaves, roughly chopped

SERVES 4

BRING the coconut cream to a boil in a small saucepan. Add the chicken breast and simmer over a low heat for 5 minutes. Turn off the heat and cover the pan for 20 minutes. Remove the chicken from the pan and shred it.

WASH the rice under cold running water until the water runs clear. Put the rice and coconut milk in a small saucepan and bring to the boil. Reduce the heat to low, cover the pan with a tight-fitting lid and simmer for 20 minutes. Remove from the heat and leave the lid on until ready to serve.

USING a pestle and mortar or blender, pound or blend the garlic, shallots and chillies together. Add the shrimp and fish sauce and pound to break up the dried shrimp. Add the tomatoes and pound all the ingredients together to form a rough paste.

IN a bowl, combine the shredded chicken and chilli paste mixture with the grated papaya, lime juice, mint and coriander leaves. Serve with the hot coconut rice.

Pound the chilli paste ingredients together in a pestle and mortar, or if you prefer, use a blender.

FISH, SHELLFISH AND SEAFOOD

Cut down each side of the underside of the lobster tail and peel back the shell.

A busy Provence port.

POACHED SEAFOOD WITH HERB AÏOLI

THE BEST WAY TO APPROACH THIS RECIPE IS AS A GUIDE—AS WITH ALL SEAFOOD COOKING, YOU SHOULD ALWAYS ASK YOUR FISHMONGER'S ADVICE AS TO WHAT'S THE BEST CATCH THAT DAY. DON'T FORGET TO PROVIDE FINGERBOWLS.

2 raw lobster tails
12 mussels
250 g (9 oz) scallops on their shells
500 g (1 lb 2 oz) prawns
250 ml (1 cup) dry white wine
250 ml (1 cup) fish stock
pinch of saffron threads
1 bay leaf
4 black peppercorns
4 x 50 g (2 oz) salmon fillets

HERB AÏOLI
4 egg yolks
4 garlic cloves, crushed
1 tablespoon chopped basil
4 tablespoons chopped flat-leaf
  parsley
1 tablespoon lemon juice
200 ml (¾ cup) olive oil

lemon wedges

SERVES 4

REMOVE the lobster meat from the tail by cutting down each side of the underside with scissors and peeling back the middle piece of shell. Scrub the mussels and remove their beards, discarding any that are open and don't close when tapped on the work surface. Remove the scallops from their shells and pull away the white muscle and digestive tract around each one, leaving the roes intact. Clean the scallop shells and keep them for serving. Peel and devein the prawns, leaving the tails intact, and butterfly them by cutting them open down the backs.

TO MAKE the herb aïoli, put the egg yolks, garlic, basil, parsley and lemon juice in a mortar and pestle or food processor and pound or mix until light and creamy. Add the oil, drop by drop from the tip of a teaspoon, pounding constantly until the mixture begins to thicken, then add the oil in a very thin stream. (If you're using a processor, pour in the oil in a thin stream with the motor running.)

PUT the wine, stock, saffron, bay leaf and peppercorns in a frying pan and bring to a very slow simmer. Add the lobster and poach for 5 minutes then remove, cover and keep warm.

POACH the remaining seafood in batches: the mussels and scallops will take about 2 minutes to cook and open (discard any mussels that have not opened after this time). The prawns will take 3 minutes and the salmon a little longer, depending on the thickness. (Keep the poaching liquid to use as soup stock.) Cut the lobster into thick medallions, put the scallops back on their shells and arrange the seafood on a large platter with the aïoli in a bowl in the centre. Serve with lemon wedges.

Whether you are using chillies or capsicums, remove all the seeds and membrane.

Fishing in Phang-nga.

CURRIED FISH STEAMED IN BANANA CHILLIES

A SMOOTH CURRIED CUSTARD WITH FISH FILLS THESE CHILLIES. CHOOSE A SELECTION OF COLOURS FOR A VERY STRIKING DISH. RED, YELLOW AND ORANGE CHILLIES KEEP THEIR COLOUR BETTER THAN GREEN ONES. YOU CAN ALSO USE SMALL CAPSICUMS OF VARIOUS COLOURS.

FISH FILLING
4–5 dried long red chillies
3 garlic cloves, roughly chopped
1–2 Asian shallots, roughly chopped
4 coriander (cilantro) roots,
   roughly chopped
1 lemon grass stalk, white part only,
   finely sliced
1 cm (½ inch) piece of galangal,
   finely chopped
1 teaspoon makrut (kaffir) lime zest
   or 2 makrut (kaffir) lime leaves,
   finely sliced
1 teaspoon shrimp paste
¼ teaspoon salt
275 g (10 oz) firm white fish fillets,
   cut into 1 cm (½ inch) pieces,
   or small raw prawns (shrimp)
   or small scallops
400 ml (1⅔ cups) coconut milk
   (page 551)
2 eggs
2 tablespoons fish sauce

10 banana chillies,
   or small capsicums (peppers),
   preferably elongated ones
2 handfuls of Thai sweet basil
   leaves
2 tablespoons coconut cream
3–4 makrut (kaffir) lime leaves,
   finely sliced, for garnish
1 long red chilli, seeded, finely
   sliced, for garnish

SERVES 4

TO MAKE the fish filling, using a pestle and mortar or blender, pound or blend the chillies, garlic, shallots and coriander roots together. Add the lemon grass, galangal, makrut lime zest, shrimp paste and salt, one ingredient at a time, until the mixture forms a curry paste.

IN a bowl, combine the curry paste, fish, coconut milk, eggs and fish sauce. Keep stirring in the same direction for 10 minutes, then cover and refrigerate for 30 minutes to set slightly.

IF USING chillies, or if the capsicums are the long ones, make a long cut with a sharp knife, or if they are the round ones, cut a small round slice from the tops. Remove the seeds and membrane, then clean the chillies or capsicums and pat them dry. Place a few basil leaves in the bottom of each. Spoon in the fish mixture until it nearly reaches the top edge.

FILL a wok or a steamer pan with water, cover and bring to a rolling boil over a high heat. Place the chillies or capsicums on a plate. Use a plate that will fit on the rack of a traditional bamboo steamer basket or on a steamer rack inside the wok or pan. Taking care not to burn your hands, set the basket or rack over the water and put the plate on the rack. Reduce the heat to a simmer. Cover and cook for 15–20 minutes. Check and replenish the water after 10 minutes.

TURN off the heat and transfer the chillies or capsicums to a serving plate. Spoon the coconut cream on top and sprinkle with makrut lime leaves and sliced chilli.

STIR-FRIED SCALLOPS WITH CHINESE GREENS

THIS DISH EMPHASIZES THE FRESHNESS AND DELICATE SEASONING THAT GIVE CANTONESE CUISINE ITS REPUTATION, WHILE A HIGH HEAT AND SHORT COOKING TIME ARE ALSO ESSENTIAL TO ITS SUCCESS. CHINESE BROCCOLI OR BOK CHOY IS TRADITIONALLY USED, BUT YOU COULD USE REGULAR BROCCOLI.

350 g (12 oz) scallops, roe removed
2 tablespoons Shaoxing rice wine
1 tablespoon roasted sesame oil
1 teaspoon finely chopped ginger
1/2 spring onion (scallion), finely chopped
200 g (7 oz) Chinese broccoli (gai lan) or bok choy
80 ml (1/3 cup) chicken stock (page 565)
1/2 teaspoon salt
1/4 teaspoon sugar
1/4 teaspoon freshly ground white pepper
1 teaspoon cornflour
1 tablespoon oil
1 tablespoon finely shredded ginger
1 spring onion (scallion), finely shredded
1 garlic clove, very thinly sliced

SERVES 6

SLICE the small, hard white muscle off the side of each scallop and pull off any membrane. Rinse the scallops and drain. Holding a knife blade parallel to the cutting surface, slice each scallop in half horizontally. Place the scallops in a bowl with 1 tablespoon of the rice wine, 1/4 teaspoon of the sesame oil and the chopped ginger and spring onion. Toss lightly, then leave to marinate for 20 minutes.

WASH the broccoli well. Discard any tough-looking stems and diagonally cut into 2 cm pieces through the stem and the leaf. Blanch the broccoli in a pan of boiling water for 2 minutes, or until the stems and leaves are just tender, then refresh in cold water and dry thoroughly.

COMBINE the chicken stock, salt, sugar, white pepper, cornflour and the remaining rice wine and sesame oil.

HEAT a wok over high heat, add the oil and heat until very hot. Add the scallops and stir-fry for 30 seconds, then remove. Add the shredded ginger, spring onion and garlic and stir-fry for 10 seconds. Add the stock mixture and cook, stirring constantly, until the sauce thickens. Add the Chinese broccoli and scallops. Toss lightly to coat with the sauce.

Slice the white muscle off the side of each scallop—these will be hard and rubbery if left on and cooked. Stir-fry the scallops in the sauce for only a few seconds just to heat them through; if they overcook they can be tough.

PATRA NI MACCHI

THIS IS A DISH FROM THE PARSI PEOPLE, DESCENDANTS OF PERSIANS WHO MIGRATED TO THE WEST COAST OF INDIA, WHICH IS TYPICALLY SERVED AT WEDDINGS. THE LITTLE PARCELS ARE QUITE AROMATIC WHEN OPENED AND LOOK VERY APPEALING. YOU CAN USE ANY FIRM, WHITE FISH FOR THE RECIPE.

500 g (1 lb 2 oz) pomfret, sole or
    leatherjacket fillets, skinned
young banana leaves
1 teaspoon ground cumin
1/2 teaspoon sugar
150 g (5 oz) grated coconut
    (page 555)
4 green chillies, seeded and
    chopped
4 tablespoons chopped coriander
    (cilantro) leaves
a few mint leaves
6 garlic cloves, chopped
1 green unripe mango, diced
3 tablespoons oil or ghee
3 tablespoons lime or lemon juice
mint leaves
whole green chillies

SERVES 4

WASH the fish fillets, pat dry and cut into 8 cm pieces. Cut the banana leaves into as many 22–24 cm (9–10 inch) squares as there are pieces of fish (you should have about six to eight) and soften the banana leaves by dipping them into a pan of very hot water. Wipe the pieces dry as they become pliant. If you can't get banana leaves, use foil.

GRIND the cumin, sugar, coconut, chilli, coriander, mint, garlic and green mango to a paste in a food processor, blender or pestle and mortar. Heat 1 tablespoon of the oil or ghee in a frying pan and cook the paste over low heat until aromatic. Season with salt.

PLACE the banana leaf squares on a work surface. Apply the paste liberally to both sides of each piece of fish. Sprinkle some lime or lemon juice on the fish. Place a piece of fish on each banana leaf and wrap up like a parcel, tying them firmly with kitchen string.

USING a large, heavy-based frying pan which has a lid, heat the remaining oil or ghee and shallow-fry the fish parcels together on one side. After about 5 minutes, turn the parcels over and fry for another 5 minutes. The leaves will darken and shrink. Cover the pan and cook the fish for a few more minutes.

OPEN out each fish parcel on its plate. Garnish with mint leaves and green chilli 'flowers' (do this by making slits down into the chilli from the top towards the stem so you form strips which fan out).

Wrap each piece of fish in banana leaf and then use pieces of string to tie up the parcels so they don't spring open.

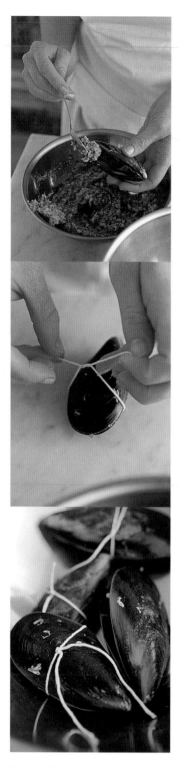

STUFFED MUSSELS

MUSSELS ARE ESPECIALLY POPULAR IN THE PUGLIA REGION—THE HEEL OF ITALY'S 'BOOT'. THIS DISH, FLAVOURED WITH OLIVE OIL, GARLIC, TOMATO AND BASIL, EPITOMISES THE FLAVOURS OF THAT STRETCH OF MEDITERRANEAN COAST.

24 mussels
3 tablespoons olive oil
4 garlic cloves, crushed
500 ml (2 cups) tomato passata
1 1/2 tablespoons roughly chopped
  basil
15 g (1/2 oz) parsley, finely chopped
40 g (1 oz) fresh white breadcrumbs
2 eggs, beaten
pinch of cayenne pepper

SERVES 4

CLEAN the mussels by scrubbing them thoroughly. Discard any that are broken or cracked or do not close when tapped on the work surface. Insert a sharp knife at the point where the beard protrudes and prise the shell open, leaving the mussel intact inside and keeping the two shells attached. Pull out the beard and discard. Rinse the mussels.

HEAT the oil in a large saucepan and gently cook half the garlic for 15–20 seconds, without browning. Add the passata and basil, season lightly with salt and pepper and bring to the boil. Reduce the heat and simmer for 5 minutes, then add 300 ml (1 1/4 cups) cold water. Return to the boil, cover and keep at a low simmer until needed.

COMBINE the parsley, breadcrumbs and the remaining garlic, then blend in the eggs. Add the cayenne pepper and season. Using a teaspoon, fill each mussel with a little of this mixture. Tie the mussels closed with kitchen string as you go, to prevent the filling escaping.

WHEN the mussels have all been stuffed, place them in the tomato sauce and simmer, covered, for 10 minutes.

LIFT OUT the mussels with a slotted spoon and remove the string. Pile on a warm platter and serve with the tomato sauce, bread and finger bowls.

The stuffing of parsley, breadcrumbs and garlic is bound together with beaten egg. The mussels are filled with the stuffing and tied with lengths of kitchen string, then simmered in tomato sauce. Remove the string before you serve.

Test if the flesh of the fish is cooked by pressing it to see if it feels or looks flaky—you can either use a pair of chopsticks or your fingers.

CANTONESE-STYLE STEAMED FISH

ALL CHINESE COOKS, BUT PARTICULARLY THE CANTONESE, DEMAND THE FRESHEST INGREDIENTS. THE LUSH LAND OF GUANGZHOU PROVIDES FRESH VEGETABLES, AND SINCE THE REGION IS BORDERED BY THE SEA AND HAS MANY RIVERS AND LAKES, FISH IS SOLD LIVE AND KILLED JUST BEFORE COOKING.

750 g–1 kg (2 lb) whole fish, such as carp, bream, grouper or sea bass
2 tablespoons Shaoxing rice wine
1 1/2 tablespoons light soy sauce
1 tablespoon finely chopped ginger
1 teaspoon roasted sesame oil
2 tablespoons oil
2 spring onions (scallions), finely shredded
3 tablespoons finely shredded ginger
1/4 teaspoon freshly ground black pepper

SERVES 4

IF YOU do manage to buy a swimming (live) fish, then ask the fishmonger to gut it through the gills. This is harder than gutting through the stomach, but leaves the fish looking whole. If you are gutting the fish yourself, make a cut from the throat to the tail and pull out the guts through the stomach. Remove any scales with a fish scaler or the back of a knife. Check that the gills have been cut out, then rinse the fish under cold, running water and drain thoroughly in a colander.

PLACE the fish in a large bowl. Add the rice wine, soy sauce, chopped ginger and sesame oil, and toss lightly to coat. Cover with clingfilm and leave to marinate in the fridge for 10 minutes.

ARRANGE the fish on a heatproof plate, with the marinade, and place in a steamer. Steam over simmering water in a covered wok for 5–8 minutes, or until the fish flakes when the skin is pressed firmly or the dorsal fin pulls out easily. Remove the fish from the steamer and place on a heatproof platter.

HEAT a wok over high heat, add the oil and heat until smoking. Sprinkle the steamed fish with the spring onion, shredded ginger and pepper, and slowly pour the hot oil over the fish. This will cause the skin to crisp, and cook the garnish.

153

The Quai des Belges, Marseille.

COQUILLES SAINT JACQUES MORNAY

SCALLOPS IN FRANCE ARE NAMED AFTER SAINT JAMES. THEIR SHELLS WERE ONCE WORN BY PILGRIMS WHO FOUND THEM AS THEY WALKED ALONG THE SPANISH COAST ON THEIR PILGRIMAGE TO A CATHEDRAL IN SPAIN DEDICATED TO THE SAINT.

COURT BOUILLON
250 ml (1 cup) white wine
1 onion, sliced
1 carrot, sliced
1 bay leaf
4 black peppercorns

24 scallops on their shells
50 g (2 oz) butter
3 shallots, finely chopped
3 tablespoons plain flour
400 ml (1½ cups) milk
125 g (4 oz) Gruyère, grated

SERVES 6

TO MAKE the court bouillon, put the wine, onion, carrot, bay leaf, peppercorns and 500 ml (2 cups) water into a deep frying pan, bring to the boil and simmer for 20 minutes. Strain the court bouillon and return to the clean frying pan.

REMOVE the scallops from their shells and pull away the white muscle and digestive tract from each one, leaving the roes intact. Clean the shells and keep for serving.

BRING the court bouillon to a gentle simmer, add the scallops and poach over low heat for 2 minutes. Remove the scallops from the court bouillon, drain and return to their shells. Pour away the court bouillon.

MELT the butter in a heavy-based saucepan, add the shallot and cook, stirring, for 3 minutes. Stir in the flour to make a roux and cook, stirring, for 3 minutes over low heat without allowing the roux to brown.

REMOVE from the heat and add the milk gradually, stirring after each addition until smooth. Return to the heat and simmer, stirring, for about 3 minutes, until the sauce has thickened. Remove from the heat and stir in the cheese until melted. Season with salt and pepper. Preheat the grill (broiler). Spoon the sauce over the scallops and place under the grill until golden brown. Serve immediately.

Poach the scallops in court bouillon first, so that they are thoroughly cooked before grilling. The heat of the grill alone isn't enough to cook them.

CRACKED CRAB WITH CURRY POWDER

THIS CRAB RECIPE IS ONE OF THE FEW THAI DISHES TO USE CURRY POWDER AS A MAIN FLAVOURING. BOUGHT CURRY POWDER (LOOK FOR A THAI BRAND) IS USUALLY VERY GOOD AND THIS IS WHAT THAI COOKS WOULD USE BUT THERE IS A RECIPE ON PAGE 563 IF YOU NEED TO MAKE YOUR OWN.

Cut the crab into quarters, leaving the legs attached. Add the coconut milk mixture and onion after 5 minutes.

1 live crab, 500 g (1 lb 2 oz)
170 ml (⅔ cup) coconut milk (page 551)
1 tablespoon light soy sauce
½ tablespoon oyster sauce
2 teaspoons Thai curry powder (page 563) or bought Thai curry powder
¼ teaspoon sugar
2 tablespoons vegetable oil
3–4 garlic cloves, finely chopped
1 small onion, cut into 3 wedges
2 spring onions (scallions), finely sliced
½ long red chilli, seeded and finely sliced, for garnish
a few coriander (cilantro) leaves, for garnish

SERVES 4

PUT the crabs in the freezer for 1 hour. Leaving the legs attached, cut the crab in half through the centre of the shell from head to rear. Cut in half again from left to right (quartering the crab), with legs attached to each quarter. Twist off and remove the upper shell pieces. Discard the stomach sac and the soft gill tissue. Using crackers or the back of a heavy knife, crack the crab claws to make them easier to eat. If the claws are too big, cut them in half.

MIX the coconut milk, light soy sauce, oyster sauce, curry powder and sugar in a bowl.

HEAT the oil in a wok or frying pan. Stir-fry the garlic over a medium heat until light brown. Add the crab and stir-fry for about 4–5 minutes. Add the coconut mixture and onion and continue stir-frying for another 5–7 minutes or until the crab meat is cooked through and the sauce is reduced and very thick. Add the spring onions. Taste, then adjust the seasoning if necessary. Spoon onto a serving plate and sprinkle with sliced chilli and coriander leaves.

Snack seller in Bangkok.

SWEET-AND-SOUR FISH FILLETS

THIS SWEET-AND-SOUR DISH IS SUBTLY VINEGARY AND HAS JUST A FAINT TOUCH OF SWEETNESS.
SWEET-AND-SOUR FISH IS EATEN ALL OVER CHINA, OFTEN USING A WHOLE DEEP-FRIED FISH, BUT
THIS RECIPE COMES FROM SOUTH-EAST CHINA AND IS A GREAT WAY TO COOK FISH FILLETS.

450 g (1 lb) firm white fish fillets,
  such as haddock, monkfish or
  sea bass, skin removed
1/2 teaspoon salt
1 1/2 tablespoons Shaoxing rice
  wine
1 egg, beaten
3–4 tablespoons plain flour
oil for deep-frying
1/2 teaspoon chopped ginger
1 spring onion (scallion), finely
  chopped
100 ml (1/3 cup) chicken and meat
  stock (page 565)
2 tablespoons light soy sauce
1 tablespoon sugar
2 tablespoons clear rice vinegar
1 red chilli, finely chopped (optional)
1 tablespoon cornflour
1/2 teaspoon roasted sesame oil
coriander (cilantro) leaves

SERVES 4

PAT DRY the fish, cut into 3 cm (1 1/4 inch) cubes
and marinate with the salt and 2 teaspoons of the
rice wine for about 15–20 minutes.

MEANWHILE, blend the egg and flour with a little
water to form a smooth batter the consistency of
double cream. Coat the fish cubes with the batter.

FILL a wok one quarter full of oil. Heat the oil to
180°C (350°F), or until a piece of bread fries
golden brown in 15 seconds when dropped in the
oil. Carefully lower the pieces of fish, one by one,
into the hot oil and stir gently to make sure they
do not stick together. Cook for about 3 minutes,
or until golden. Remove and drain well on
crumpled paper towels. Pour off the oil, leaving
1 tablespoon, and wipe out the wok.

REHEAT the reserved oil over high heat until very
hot and add the ginger, spring onion, stock, soy
sauce, remaining rice wine, sugar and half the rice
vinegar. Bring to the boil, then reduce the heat
and simmer for 30 seconds. Add the fish pieces
and cook for 2 minutes. Add the chilli, if using,
and the remaining rice vinegar. Combine the
cornflour with enough water to make a paste, add
to the sauce and simmer until thickened.

SPRINKLE the fish with the sesame oil and the
coriander leaves to serve.

You can use your wok for deep-
frying, but make sure that it is
really steady on the wok burner.
A wire sieve drains away far
more oil than a slotted spoon
leaving the batter less greasy.

159

RED MULLET WITH FENNEL

2 fennel bulbs
2 tablespoons butter
2 tablespoons olive oil
1 onion, chopped
1 garlic clove, crushed
4 red mullet, gutted and scaled
extra virgin olive oil
1 lemon, quartered
2 teaspoons chopped oregano,
    or 1/2 teaspoon dried oregano
lemon wedges

SERVES 4

PREHEAT the oven to 190°C (375°F/Gas 5) and grease a large shallow ovenproof dish. Finely slice the fennel, keeping the green fronds.

HEAT the butter and olive oil in a large frying pan and gently cook the fennel, onion and garlic for 12–15 minutes until softened but not browned. Season with salt and pepper.

STUFF each fish with a heaped tablespoon of the fennel mixture and a quarter of the fennel fronds. Brush with extra virgin olive oil, squeeze a lemon quarter over each one and season well.

SPOON the remainder of the cooked fennel into the dish and sprinkle with half of the oregano. Arrange the fish, side by side, on top. Sprinkle the remaining oregano over the fish and cover the dish loosely with foil. Bake for 25 minutes, or until just cooked through. Serve with lemon wedges.

Brushing the fish with oil prevents the skin from drying out while it bakes and helps the seasoning to stick to the fish skin.

BAKED SWORDFISH SICILIANA

IN ITALY SWORDFISH IS FISHED MAINLY OFF THE COAST OF SICILY. WHILE MANY MORE DELICATE FISH WOULD BE OVERPOWERED BY THE STRONG MEDITERRANEAN FLAVOURS OF THIS DISH, THE MORE ROBUST FLESH OF THE SWORDFISH CAN HOLD ITS OWN. YOU CAN ALSO USE TUNA.

80 ml (1/3 cup) olive oil
2 tablespoons lemon juice
2 1/2 tablespoons finely chopped
    basil
4 swordfish steaks
60 g (2 oz) pitted black olives,
    chopped
1 tablespoon baby capers
1/2 teaspoon finely chopped
    anchovies in olive oil
400 g (14 oz) tomatoes, peeled,
    seeded and chopped
2 tablespoons dried breadcrumbs

SERVES 4

MIX half the olive oil with the lemon juice and 1 tablespoon of the basil. Season and pour into a shallow ovenproof dish, large enough to hold the swordfish in a single layer. Arrange the swordfish in the dish and leave to marinate for 15 minutes, turning once. Preheat the oven to 230°C (450°F/Gas 8) and preheat the grill (broiler).

COMBINE the olives, capers, anchovies and tomatoes with the remaining olive oil and basil and season well. Spread over the swordfish and sprinkle the breadcrumbs over the top. Bake for about 20 minutes, or until the fish is just opaque. Finish off by placing briefly under the hot grill until the breadcrumbs are crisp. Serve with bread to soak up the juices.

BAKED SWORDFISH SICILIANA

DEEP-FRIED SQUID FLOWERS WITH SPICY SALT

500 g (1 lb 2 oz) squid tubes
1 teaspoon ginger juice (page 554)
1 tablespoon Shaoxing rice wine
oil for deep-frying
2 teaspoons spicy salt and pepper
  (page 557)
coriander (cilantro) leaves

SERVES 4

Score the inside of the squid with fine lines in a crisscross pattern before cutting into pieces.

OPEN UP the squid tubes and scrub off any soft jelly-like substance, then score the inside of the flesh with a fine crisscross pattern, making sure you do not cut all the way through. Cut the squid into 3 x 5 cm (1¼–2 inch) pieces.

BLANCH the squid in a pan of boiling water for 25–30 seconds—each piece will curl up and the crisscross pattern will open out, hence the name 'squid flower'. Remove and refresh in cold water, then drain and dry well. Marinate the squid in the ginger juice and rice wine for 25–30 minutes.

FILL a wok one quarter full of oil. Heat the oil to 180°C (350°F), or until a piece of bread fries golden brown in 15 seconds when dropped in the oil. Cook the squid for 35–40 seconds, then remove and drain well. Sprinkle with the spicy salt and pepper and toss to coat. Serve sprinkled with the coriander.

STIR-FRIED SQUID FLOWERS WITH CAPSICUM

STIR-FRIED SQUID FLOWERS
WITH CAPSICUM

400 g (14 oz) squid tubes
3 tablespoons oil
2 tablespoons salted, fermented
  black beans, rinsed and mashed
1 small onion, cut into small cubes
1 small green capsicum (pepper),
  cut into small cubes
3–4 small slices ginger
1 spring onion (scallion), cut into
  short lengths
1 small red chilli, chopped
1 tablespoon Shaoxing rice wine
½ teaspoon roasted sesame oil

SERVES 4

OPEN UP the squid tubes and scrub off any soft jelly-like substance, then score the inside of the flesh with a fine crisscross pattern, making sure you do not cut all the way through. Cut the squid into 3 x 5 cm (1¼–2 inch) pieces.

BLANCH the squid in a pan of boiling water for 25–30 seconds—each piece will curl up and the crisscross pattern will open out, hence the name 'squid flower'. Remove and refresh in cold water, then drain and dry well.

HEAT a wok over high heat, add the oil and heat until very hot. Stir-fry the black beans, onion, green capsicum, ginger, spring onion and chilli for 1 minute. Add the squid and rice wine, mix together and stir for 1 minute. Sprinkle with the sesame oil.

SALMON CURRY

THERE ARE SEVERAL STAGES TO THE MAKING OF THIS GOAN-STYLE DISH AND IT TAKES A LITTLE TIME

TO PREPARE THE SPICES AND THE SAUCE. THE END RESULT IS A DRY TYPE OF CURRY WITH A FAIRLY

THICK SAUCE THAT WORKS WELL WITH THE RICH FLESH OF THE SALMON CUTLETS.

SPICE MIX
6 dried chillies
1 tablespoon cumin seeds
1 teaspoon coriander (cilantro)
  seeds
1 teaspoon mustard seeds
1/4 teaspoon garam masala
  (page 556)
1/2 teaspoon ground turmeric

3 tablespoons oil
1 onion, finely sliced
1 ripe tomato, chopped
2 onions, finely chopped
8 garlic cloves, chopped
6 green chillies, chopped
5 cm (2 inch) piece of ginger,
  grated
100 ml (1/3 cup) tamarind purée
  (page 554)
3 tablespoons coconut milk powder
  or coconut cream (page 551)
1 kg (2 lb 3 oz) salmon cutlets

SERVES 6

PREPARE the spice mix by grinding the chillies, cumin, coriander and mustard seeds to a fine powder using a spice grinder or pestle and mortar, then mixing with the garam masala and turmeric.

HEAT the oil over low heat in a heavy-based frying pan large enough to hold the pieces of fish in a single layer. Add the sliced onion and fry until golden. Add the tomato, chopped onion, garlic, green chilli and ginger and fry, stirring occasionally, for 20 minutes, or until the oil separates from the sauce.

ADD the spice mix and the tamarind to the pan and bring to the boil. Add the coconut milk powder or coconut cream and stir until well mixed. Season with salt, to taste. Add the fish and bring slowly to the boil. The sauce is not very liquid but it needs to be made very hot in order to cook the fish. Simmer for 5 minutes, then turn the pieces of fish over and simmer for another 5 minutes, or until the fish is cooked through and the sauce is thick.

Flesh being extracted from semi-dried coconuts in Kerala. The dried flesh is called copra.

SPICY LOBSTER AND PINEAPPLE CURRY

EVEN THOUGH THIS RED CURRY IS EXPENSIVE BECAUSE OF THE LOBSTER, IT IS EXCELLENT FOR SPECIAL OCCASIONS. YOU CAN USE LARGE PRAWNS OR CRAB HALVES INSTEAD IF YOU LIKE. ALSO, YOU CAN MAKE THE SAUCE AND SERVE IT WITH BARBECUED LOBSTER HALVES.

60 ml (¼ cup) coconut cream
  (page 551)
2 tablespoons red curry paste
  (page 558) or bought paste
1 tablespoon fish sauce
1 tablespoon palm sugar
250 ml (1 cup) coconut milk
  (page 551)
200 g (7 oz) fresh pineapple,
  cut into bite-sized wedges
300 g (10 oz) lobster tail meat
3 makrut (kaffir) lime leaves,
  2 roughly torn and 1 shredded
1 tablespoon tamarind purée
  (page 554)
50 g (1 cup) Thai sweet basil
  leaves, for garnish
1 large red chilli, finely sliced,
  for garnish

SERVES 4

PUT the coconut cream in a wok or saucepan and simmer over a medium heat for about 5 minutes, or until the cream separates and a layer of oil forms on the surface. Stir the cream if it starts to brown around the edges.

ADD the curry paste, stir well to combine and cook until fragrant. Add the fish sauce and sugar and stir to combine. Cook for 4–5 minutes, stirring constantly. The mixture should darken.

STIR in the coconut milk and the pineapple. Simmer for 6–8 minutes to soften the pineapple. Add the lobster tail meat, makrut lime leaves, tamarind purée and basil leaves. Cook for another 5–6 minutes until the lobster is firm. Serve with basil leaves and sliced chilli on top.

When the mixture has darkened, stir in the pineapple pieces.

Beaches in Khao Sok National Park.

Salt cod on sale in a Paris market.

BRANDADE DE MORUE

THIS RICH GARLICKY PURÉE IS TRADITIONALLY MADE WITH *MORUE*, SALT COD PRESERVED BY THE SALT RATHER THAN BY DRYING. SALT COD IS ALSO SOLD AS BACALAO, ITS SPANISH NAME. YOU WILL HAVE TO PREPARE TWO DAYS IN ADVANCE, BECAUSE OF THE TIME NEEDED TO SOAK THE COD.

750 g (1 lb 10 oz) piece salt cod
  (also known as *morue*)
310 ml (1¼ cups) olive oil
2 garlic cloves, crushed
300 ml (1¼ cups) single cream
2 tablespoons lemon juice

SERVES 4

PUT the salt cod in a shallow bowl and cover with cold water. Refrigerate for 1 or 2 days, changing the water every 8 hours, to soak the salt out of the fish.

DRAIN the cod and rinse again. Put in a saucepan and cover with 2 litres (8 cups) water. Bring to a simmer and cook for 10 minutes (do not boil or the salt cod will toughen). Drain and rinse again.

REMOVE the skin and bones from the cod. Use a fork to flake the cod into small pieces. Make sure there are no small bones left in the cod, then finely chop in a food processor or with a sharp knife. (It will have a fibrous texture.)

HEAT 60 ml (¼ cup) of the oil in a heavy-based frying pan and cook the garlic over low heat for 3 minutes without colouring. Add the cod and stir in a spoonful of the remaining oil. Beat in a spoonful of cream and continue adding the oil and cream alternately, beating until the mixture is smooth and has the consistency of fluffy mashed potato. Add the lemon juice and season with pepper (you won't need to add any salt). Serve warm or cold with bread or toast. Keep in the fridge for up to 3 days and warm through with a little extra cream before serving.

Add the cream and oil alternately, beating until the brandade has the consistency of fluffy mash.

PRAWNS WITH GREEN MANGO

250 g (9 oz) tiger prawns
1½ teaspoons chilli powder
1 teaspoon ground turmeric
½ teaspoon cumin seeds
½ teaspoon yellow mustard seeds
4 garlic cloves, roughly chopped
4 cm (1½ inch) piece of ginger,
   roughly chopped
1 red onion, roughly chopped
4 tablespoons oil
1 red onion, thinly sliced
1 green unripe mango, finely
   chopped

SERVES 4

PEEL and devein the prawns, leaving the tails intact. Put the chilli powder, turmeric, cumin, mustard, garlic, ginger and chopped red onion in a blender, food processor or pestle and mortar and process to form a paste. If necessary, add a little water.

HEAT the oil in a karhai or heavy-based frying pan and fry the sliced onion. When it starts to brown, add the curry paste and fry until aromatic.

ADD the prawns and 200 ml (¾ cup) water to the pan, then cover and simmer for about 3–4 minutes, until the prawns are cooked and start to curl up. Add the mango and cook for another minute or two to thicken the curry. Season with salt, to taste.

Green unripe mangoes, often used in Indian cookery, have a firm flesh and are used to give a tart flavour to recipes.

CREAMY PRAWN CURRY

THIS COCONUT-FLAVOURED PRAWN CURRY IS A SPECIALITY OF BENGAL. TRADITIONALLY, THE PRAWNS ARE COOKED INSIDE A PARTIALLY MATURED COCONUT. CARE SHOULD BE TAKEN NOT TO OVERCOOK THE PRAWNS OR THEY WILL BECOME RUBBERY.

CREAMY PRAWN CURRY

500 g (1 lb 2 oz) tiger prawns
1½ tablespoons lemon juice
3 tablespoons oil
½ onion, finely chopped
½ teaspoon ground turmeric
5 cm (2 inch) piece of cinnamon
   stick
4 cloves
7 cardamom pods
5 Indian bay leaves (cassia leaves)
2 cm (¾ inch) piece of ginger,
   grated
3 garlic cloves, chopped
1 teaspoon chilli powder
50 g (2 oz) creamed coconut mixed
   with 150 ml (⅔ cup) water, or
   150 ml (⅔ cup) coconut milk
   (page 551)

SERVES 4

PEEL and devein the prawns, leaving the tails intact. Put them in a bowl, add the lemon juice, then toss together and leave them for 5 minutes. Rinse the prawns under running cold water and pat dry with paper towels.

HEAT the oil in a karhai or heavy-based frying pan and fry the onion until lightly browned. Add the turmeric, cinnamon, cloves, cardamom, bay leaves, ginger and garlic, and fry for 1 minute. Add the chilli powder, creamed coconut or coconut milk, and salt, to taste, and slowly bring to the boil. Reduce the heat and simmer for 2 minutes. Add the prawns, return to the boil, then reduce the heat and simmer for 5 minutes, or until the prawns are cooked through and the sauce is thick.

LOBSTER FU RONG

THE WORDS 'FU RONG' MEAN EGG WHITES AND IN RECIPES DENOTE A CLASSIC CANTONESE COOKING
METHOD, THOUGH THE TERM IS OFTEN ASSOCIATED WITH THE QUITE DIFFERENT EGG FOO YOUNG OF
WESTERN CHINESE RESTAURANTS. THIS DISH CAN BE MADE WITH ANY KIND OF SEAFOOD.

450 g (1 lb) lobster meat
3 tablespoons Shaoxing rice wine
3 teaspoons finely chopped ginger
1¹/₂ teaspoons salt
12 egg whites
¹/₂ teaspoon cream of tartar
oil for deep-frying
125 ml (¹/₂ cup) chicken stock
　　(page 565)
¹/₄ teaspoon freshly ground white
　　pepper
1 teaspoon roasted sesame oil
1 teaspoon cornflour
2 spring onions (scallions), finely
　　chopped
2 spring onions (scallions), green
　　part only, sliced

SERVES 6

CUT the lobster meat into pieces, put in a bowl
with 1 tablespoon of the rice wine, 1 teaspoon of
the ginger and ¹/₂ teaspoon of the salt and toss
lightly to coat. Beat the egg whites and cream of
tartar using a balloon whisk or electric beaters until
stiff. Fold the lobster into the egg white mixture.

FILL a wok one quarter full of oil. Heat the oil to
190°C (375°F), or until a piece of bread fries
golden brown in 10 seconds when dropped in the
oil. Pour the lobster into the wok in batches—do
not stir, otherwise it will scatter, but gently stir the
oil from the bottom of the wok so that the 'fu
rong' rises to the surface. Remove each batch as
soon as it is set, without letting it go too brown,
and drain well. Pour the oil from the wok, leaving
2 tablespoons.

COMBINE the chicken stock, remaining rice wine
and salt, white pepper, sesame oil and cornflour.

REHEAT the reserved oil over high heat until very
hot and stir-fry the finely chopped spring onion
and the remaining ginger for 10 seconds, or until
fragrant. Add the stock mixture and cook, stirring
constantly to prevent lumps, until thickened. Add
the cooked lobster mixture and carefully toss it in
the sauce. Transfer to a serving platter, sprinkle
with the sliced spring onion and serve.

MOULES MARINIÈRE

GROWN ALL ALONG THE COAST OF FRANCE ON WOODEN POSTS, MUSSELS ARE REGIONAL TO MANY AREAS BUT ARE PARTICULARLY ASSOCIATED WITH BRITTANY, NORMANDY AND THE NORTHEAST. THIS IS ONE OF THE SIMPLEST WAYS TO SERVE THEM.

2 kg (4 lb 7 oz) mussels
45 g (1½ oz) butter
1 large onion, chopped
½ celery stalk, chopped
2 garlic cloves, crushed
410 ml (1½ cups) white wine
1 bay leaf
2 thyme sprigs
220 ml (¾ cup) double cream
2 tablespoons chopped parsley

SERVES 4

SCRUB the mussels and remove their beards. Discard any that are open already and don't close when tapped on the work surface. Melt the butter in a large saucepan and cook the onion, celery and garlic, stirring occasionally, over moderate heat until the onion is softened but not browned.

ADD the wine, bay leaf and thyme to the saucepan and bring to the boil. Add the mussels, cover the pan tightly and simmer over low heat for 2–3 minutes, shaking the pan occasionally. Use tongs to lift out the mussels as they open, putting them into a warm dish. Throw away any mussels that haven't opened after 3 minutes.

STRAIN the liquid through a fine sieve into a clean saucepan, leaving behind any grit or sand. Bring to the boil and boil for 2 minutes. Add the cream and reheat the sauce without boiling. Season well. Serve the mussels in individual bowls with the liquid poured over. Sprinkle with the parsley and serve with plenty of bread.

Wash the mussels, taking care to discard any that are already open and don't close when tapped.

GRILLED SARDINES

8 sardines
2 tablespoons olive oil
3 tablespoons lemon juice
½ lemon, halved and thinly sliced
lemon wedges

SERVES 4

SLIT the sardines along their bellies and remove the guts. Rinse well and pat dry. Use scissors to cut out the gills.

MIX TOGETHER the oil and lemon juice and season generously with salt and black pepper. Brush the inside and outside of each fish with the oil, then place a few lemon slices into each cavity.

PUT the sardines onto a preheated griddle and cook, basting frequently with the remaining oil, for about 2–3 minutes each side until cooked through. They can also be cooked under a very hot grill (broiler). Serve with lemon wedges.

GRILLED SARDINES

MOULES MARINIÈRE WITH GRILLED SARDINES

CALAMARI RIPIENI

IF YOUR FISHMONGER HAS HAD A CATCH OF SMALL TENDER SQUID, SNAP THEM UP—THIS IS THE PERFECT RECIPE FOR THEM. IF YOU ARE HAVING TO MAKE DO WITH LARGER SQUID, YOU MIGHT NEED TO INCREASE THE COOKING TIME AND TAKE CARE THAT THE LIQUID DOES NOT EVAPORATE.

TOMATO SAUCE
800 g (1 lb 12 oz) tin tomatoes
100 ml (⅓ cup) red wine
2 tablespoons chopped flat-leaf
    parsley
pinch of sugar

STUFFING
600 g (1 lb 5 oz) small squid
100 ml (⅓ cup) olive oil
1 small onion, finely chopped
1 small fennel bulb, finely chopped
2 garlic cloves, crushed
75 g (2½ oz) risotto rice (arborio,
    vialone nano or carnaroli)
large pinch of saffron threads
½ large red chilli, chopped
150 ml (⅔ cup) white wine
2 tablespoons chopped flat-leaf
    parsley

SERVES 4

TO MAKE the sauce, put the tomatoes, red wine, parsley and sugar in a saucepan. Season and simmer until some of the liquid has evaporated.

TO MAKE the stuffing, prepare the squid by pulling the heads and tentacles out of the bodies with any innards. Cut the heads off below the eyes, just leaving the tentacles. Rinse the bodies, pulling out the transparent quills. Finely chop the tentacles and set aside with the squid bodies.

HEAT the oil in a saucepan, add the onion, fennel and garlic and cook gently for 10 minutes until soft. Add the rice, saffron, chilli and chopped tentacles and cook for a few minutes, stirring frequently until the tentacles are opaque. Season and add the white wine and 6 tablespoons of the tomato sauce. Cook, stirring frequently, until the tomato and wine has reduced into the rice. Add 150 ml (⅔ cup) water and continue cooking until the rice is tender and all the liquid has been absorbed. Add the parsley and cool for a few minutes.

STUFF the squid with the filling, using a teaspoon to push the filling down to the bottom of the squid sacks. Do not overfill—you need to close the tops of the sacks easily without any filling squeezing out. Seal the tops with cocktail sticks.

PUT the remaining tomato sauce in a saucepan with 200 ml (¾ cup) water. Cook for 2 minutes, then add the stuffed squid, cover the pan and simmer gently for 30–45 minutes, depending on the size of the squid, until soft and tender. Don't stir, or the filling may fall out (if a little filling does fall out it will merely add flavour to the sauce). Shake the pan a little if you are worried about sticking.

REMOVE the cocktail sticks before serving, preferably with a salad and some bread.

Don't overfill the squid with stuffing or you'll find it leaking out into the tomato sauce.

DEEP-FRIED FISH WITH GINGER

ALTHOUGH THAI FISH ARE NOT TRADITIONALLY COATED IN FLOUR BEFORE BEING FRIED, IT WILL HELP GIVE A CRISPER SKIN. MAKE SURE THE FISH IS REALLY WELL COOKED AND CRISP OR THE SAUCE WILL MAKE IT SOGGY. IF YOU CAN'T GET ONE LARGE FISH, USE SEVERAL SMALLER ONES INSTEAD.

15 g (½ oz) dried black fungus
    (about half a handful)
1 large or 2 smaller red snapper,
    grey mullet, sea bass or grouper
    (total weight about 1 kg/2 lb 4 oz)
3 tablespoons plain (all-purpose)
    flour
pinch of ground black pepper
1 tablespoon oyster sauce
1 tablespoon light soy sauce
¼ teaspoon sugar
vegetable oil, for deep-frying
1½ tablespoons vegetable oil
4 garlic cloves, roughly chopped
1 small carrot, cut into matchsticks
2 cm (¾ inch) piece of ginger, cut
    into matchsticks
2 spring onions (scallions), finely
    sliced, for garnish

SERVES 4

SOAK the black fungus in hot water for 2–3 minutes until soft, then drain the fungus and finely chop.

CLEAN and gut the fish, leaving the head/s on. Dry the fish thoroughly. Score the fish three or four times on both sides with a sharp knife. Rub the fish inside and out with a pinch of salt. Put the flour and ground pepper on a plate and lightly press the fish into it until it is coated all over. Shake off any excess flour.

MIX the oyster sauce, light soy sauce, sugar and 2 tablespoons water in a small bowl.

HEAT 10 cm (4 inches) oil in a large wok or saucepan big enough to deep-fry the whole fish. When the oil seems hot, drop a small piece of spring onion into the oil. If it sizzles straight away, the oil is ready. Lower the heat to medium and gently slide the fish into the oil. Be careful as the hot oil may splash. Deep-fry the fish on just one side (but make sure the oil covers the whole fish) for about 5–10 minutes or until the fish is cooked and light brown (if you cook the fish until it is very brown, the fish will be too dry). Drain on paper towels before transferring to a warm plate. Keep warm. Drain off the oil.

HEAT 1½ tablespoons clean oil in the same wok and stir-fry the garlic over a medium heat until light brown. Add the carrot, ginger, mushrooms and the sauce mixture and stir-fry for 1–2 minutes. Taste, then adjust the seasoning if necessary. Pour over the warm fish and sprinkle with spring onions.

Cut the ginger into thin slices before cutting it into matchsticks.

Dried fish on sale.

STEAMED PRAWN CUSTARDS

4 eggs
300 ml (1¼ cups) chicken stock
    (page 565)
16 prawns
1 spring onion (scallion), finely
    chopped
1 tablespoon light soy sauce
1 tablespoon oil

SERVES 4

BEAT the eggs and chicken stock together and season with salt and white pepper. Peel and devein the prawns, then roughly chop the prawn meat.

DIVIDE the prawns among four small heatproof bowls. Pour the egg and stock mixture over the prawns. Put the bowls in a steamer, and steam over simmering water in a covered wok for 10 minutes. The custards should be just set. Shake them gently to see if the centre is set. If you overcook them they will be rubbery.

SPRINKLE the custards with the spring onion and soy sauce. Heat the oil in a wok until very hot and pour a little over each custard (it will spit as it hits the surface). Serve immediately.

STEAMED MUSSEL CUSTARDS

450 g (1 lb) mussels
2 tablespoons Shaoxing rice wine
1 tablespoon finely chopped ginger
6 eggs
1 teaspoon salt

SERVES 6

SCRUB the mussels, remove any beards, and throw away any that do not close when tapped on the work surface. Put the mussels in a wok with 250 ml (1 cup) water, the rice wine and ginger. Cook, covered, over high heat for 1 minute, or until the mixture is boiling. Reduce the heat to low and cook, covered, for 2 minutes, or until the mussels have opened, shaking the pan so that they cook evenly. Discard any that do not open after 2 minutes.

REMOVE the mussels with a wire sieve or slotted spoon, reserving the liquid, and allow to cool. Remove the mussels from their shells and divide among six small heatproof bowls. Lightly beat the eggs, salt and 250 ml (1 cup) of the reserved liquid, then pour over the mussels.

PUT the bowls in a steamer and steam over simmering water in a covered wok for 10 minutes. The custards should be just set. Shake them gently to see if the centre is set. If you overcook them they will be rubbery. Serve immediately.

STEAMED MUSSEL CUSTARDS

STEAMED PRAWN CUSTARDS

A fish stall at Fort Kochi (Cochin), Kerala.

Fish is sold fresh off the boats in the early hours of the morning all along India's coast.

FISH TIKKA

TIKKA IS THE HINDI WORD FOR CHUNK. HERE, FISH CHUNKS ARE MARINATED IN A BLEND OF SPICES AND YOGHURT AND COOKED. IN INDIA, A TANDOOR, A CHARCOAL-FIRED CLAY OVEN, WOULD BE USED. HOWEVER, BARBECUING IS A GOOD SUBSTITUTE AS IT ALSO IMPARTS A SMOKY FLAVOUR.

MARINADE
500 ml (2 cups) thick natural
    yoghurt (page 554)
1/2 onion, finely chopped
2 cm (3/4 inch) piece of ginger,
    grated
4 garlic cloves, crushed
1 teaspoon ground coriander
    (cilantro)
2 tablespoons lemon juice
1 1/2 tablespoons garam masala
    (page 556)
1 teaspoon paprika
1 teaspoon chilli powder
2 tablespoons tomato purée
1 teaspoon salt

500 g (1 lb 2 oz) skinless firm white
    fish such as halibut, monkfish or
    blue-eye
2 onions, each cut into 8 chunks
2 small green or red capsicum
    (peppers), each cut into 8 chunks

50 g (2 oz) cucumber, peeled and
    diced
1 tablespoon chopped coriander
    (cilantro)
lemon wedges

SERVES 8

TO MAKE the marinade, mix half the yoghurt with all the other marinade ingredients in a shallow dish that is long enough and deep enough to take the prepared skewers. You will need eight metal skewers.

CUT the fish into about 24–32 bite-sized chunks. On each metal skewer, thread three or four pieces of fish and chunks of onion and capsicum, alternating them as you go. Put the skewers in the marinade and turn them so that all the fish and vegetables are well coated. Cover and marinate in the fridge for at least 1 hour, or until you are ready to cook.

PREHEAT the barbecue or grill (broiler). Lift the skewers out of the marinade. Cook on the barbecue, or under a grill on a wire rack set above a baking tray, for 5–6 minutes, turning once, or until the fish is cooked and firm and both the fish and the vegetables are slightly charred.

MEANWHILE, stir the cucumber and coriander into the other half of the yoghurt. Serve the fish with the yoghurt and lemon wedges.

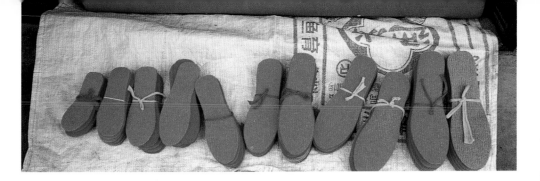

JELLYFISH AND CHICKEN SALAD

JELLYFISH ARE ONLY EVER EATEN ONCE THEY HAVE BEEN PRESERVED AND DRIED. THEY HAVE A CRUNCHY TEXTURE AND ARE NOT LIKE JELLY. YOU CAN BUY THEM DRIED, CUT INTO STRIPS OR WHOLE, AND ALSO ALREADY RECONSTITUTED IN VACUUM PACKS. THE LATTER ARE MUCH EASIER TO USE.

375 g (13 oz) dried or ready-prepared jellyfish
1.3 kg (2 lb 14 oz) chicken
2 celery stalks, cut into 5 cm (2 inch) lengths and finely shredded
1 carrot, cut into 5 cm (2 inch) lengths and finely shredded
1 tablespoon oyster sauce
2 teaspoons light soy sauce
2 teaspoons roasted sesame oil
25 g (1 oz) coriander leaves
3 teaspoons sesame seeds

DRESSING
185 ml (⅔ cup) clear rice vinegar
60 g (2 oz) sugar
1 tablespoon finely chopped ginger
3 spring onions (scallions), thinly sliced

SERVES 8

TO PREPARE dried jellyfish, remove from the packet, cover with tepid water and soak overnight. Drain, then rinse to remove any sand and sediment. Drain well. Cut into strands using a pair of scissors, then cut any long strands into shorter lengths. If you are using ready-prepared jellyfish, remove it from the packet and rinse.

RINSE the chicken, drain, and remove any fat from the cavity opening and around the neck. Cut off and discard the parson's nose. Bring a large saucepan of water to the boil. Add the chicken and bring the water to a gentle simmer. Cook, covered, for 25–30 minutes, or until the chicken is cooked through. Remove the chicken from the saucepan and plunge into cold water. When cool enough to handle, remove the skin and bones from the chicken and finely shred the meat.

PLACE the chicken in a large bowl and add the jellyfish, celery, carrot, oyster sauce, soy sauce, sesame oil and coriander. Mix well to combine.

TO MAKE the dressing, place the vinegar and sugar in a bowl and stir until dissolved. Stir in the ginger and spring onion.

TOAST the sesame seeds by dry-frying in a pan until brown and popping. Sprinkle the salad with the sesame seeds and serve cold with the dressing alongside.

It is easiest to cut the jellyfish using a pair of scissors. Make sure you keep the strands roughly the same width.

BAKED TROUT WITH FENNEL AND CAPERS

PURISTS LIKE THEIR TROUT COOKED WITH THE MINIMUM OF FUSS, PERHAPS DRESSED WITH A LITTLE BUTTER AND LEMON. THE FENNEL AND CAPERS, HOWEVER, COMPLEMENT THE TROUT PERFECTLY, THEIR FLAVOUR PERMEATING THE DELICATE FLESH OF THE FISH DURING BAKING.

Stuffing the trout allows the flavours to permeate the flesh. Use the vegetables as a rack for the fish to lie on.

2 fennel bulbs, with fronds
1 leek, white part only, thickly sliced
1 large carrot, cut into batons
2 tablespoons olive oil
2 tablespoons capers, rinsed and patted dry
1 shallot, finely chopped
1 x 1.3 kg (2 lb 14 oz) brown or rainbow trout, or 4 x 300 g (10 oz) trout, gutted and fins removed
1 or 2 bay leaves
25 g (1 oz) butter, cut into 4 cubes
4 slices lemon
200 ml (¾ cup) fish stock
50 ml (¼ cup) dry vermouth
2 tablespoons double cream
2 tablespoons chopped chervil

SERVES 4

PREHEAT the oven to 200°C (400°F/Gas 6). Cut off the fronds from the fennel bulbs and finely chop them. Thinly slice the bulbs and place in a roasting tin with the leek and carrot. Drizzle a tablespoon of olive oil over the vegetables, add salt and pepper and then toss well to coat them in the oil and seasoning. Bake on the middle shelf of the oven for 20 minutes.

MEANWHILE, mix the chopped fennel fronds with the capers and shallot. Season the inside of the trout and fill with the fennel and caper stuffing. Put the bay leaf, cubes of butter and the lemon slices inside the fish too. Mix together the fish stock and vermouth.

REMOVE the vegetables from the oven, stir well and reduce the oven temperature to 140°C (275°F/Gas 1). Lay the trout over the vegetables and pour the stock and vermouth over the fish. Season the trout and drizzle with the remaining tablespoon of olive oil. Cover the top of the tin with foil and return to the oven for 1 hour 15 minutes or until the fish is cooked through. The flesh should feel flaky through the skin and the inside will look opaque and cooked. Lift the fish onto a large serving platter.

TRANSFER the roasting tin of vegetables to the stove top and heat for a couple of minutes, until the juices bubble and reduce. Now add the cream and cook for 1 minute, then stir in the chervil and season to taste. Spoon the vegetables around the fish on the platter, pour over a little of the juice and hand around the rest separately in a jug.

Marseille fish market buildings.

The fish markets at Sassoon Dock, Mumbai (Bombay).

CHILLI CRAB

THIS RECIPE COMBINES SWEET-TASTING CRAB MEAT WITH AROMATIC SPICES AND THE HEAT FROM CHILLIES. PROVIDE YOUR GUESTS WITH A CRAB CRACKER, PICKS, FINGER BOWLS AND PIECES OF ROTI TO MOP UP THE WONDERFUL JUICES. YOU CAN USE ANY KIND OF CRAB FOR THIS RECIPE.

4 x 250 g (9 oz) small live crabs
   or 2 x 500 g (1 lb 2 oz) live crabs
120 ml (½ cup) oil
2 garlic cloves, crushed
4 cm (1½ inch) piece of ginger,
   grated
½ teaspoon ground cumin
½ teaspoon ground coriander
   (cilantro)
¼ teaspoon ground turmeric
¼ teaspoon cayenne pepper
1 tablespoon tamarind purée
   (page 554)
1 teaspoon sugar
2 small red chillies, finely chopped
2 tablespoons chopped coriander
   (cilantro) leaves

SERVES 4

PUT the crabs in the freezer for 2 hours to immobilize them. Using a large, heavy-bladed knife or cleaver, cut off the large front claws from each crab, then twist off the remaining claws. Turn each body over and pull off each apron piece, then pull out the spongy grey gills and discard them. Cut each crab body in half (quarters if you are using the large crabs). Crack the large front claws with the handle of a cleaver or a rolling pin. Rinse off any chips of shell under cold running water and pat dry with paper towels.

MIX half the oil with the garlic, ginger, cumin, coriander, turmeric, cayenne pepper, tamarind, sugar, chilli and a generous pinch of salt until they form a paste. Heat the remaining oil in a karhai or large, heavy-based, deep frying pan over medium heat. Add the spice paste and stir for 30 seconds, or until aromatic.

ADD the crab portions to the pan and cook, stirring for 2 minutes, making sure the spice mix gets rubbed into the cut edges of the crab. Add 50 ml (¼ cup) water, cover and steam the crabs, tossing them a couple of times during cooking, for another 5–6 minutes, or until cooked through. The crabs will turn pink or red when they are ready and the flesh will go opaque (make sure the large front claws are well cooked). Drizzle a little of the liquid from the pan over the crabs, scatter with the coriander leaves and serve.

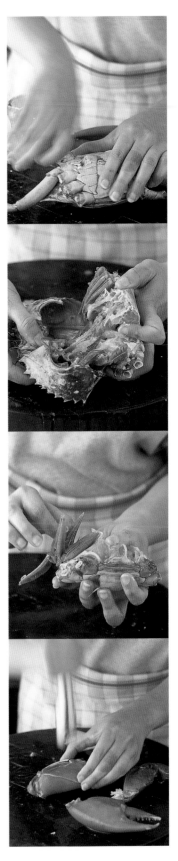

Pull the large front claws off the crab, pull the body open and remove the gills. Crack the larger claws with the handle of a cleaver.

SNAPPER WITH GREEN BANANA AND MANGO

GREEN BANANA IS VERY STARCHY, MUCH MORE LIKE A VEGETABLE THAN A FRUIT. HERE IT USED IN A YELLOW CURRY ALONGSIDE ANOTHER FRUIT, GREEN MANGO, WHICH ACTS AS A SOURING AGENT. RAW VEGETABLES ARE OFTEN SERVED AS AN ACCOMPANIMENT TO COUNTERACT THE CHILLI HEAT.

1 teaspoon salt
1 teaspoon ground turmeric
1 small green banana or plantain,
   thinly sliced
60 ml (¼ cup) coconut cream
   (page 551)
2 tablespoons yellow curry paste
   (page 559) or bought paste
1 tablespoon fish sauce
1 teaspoon palm sugar
400 g (14 oz) snapper or other
   white fish fillets, cut into
   large cubes
315 ml (1¼ cups) coconut milk
   (page 279)
1 small green mango, cut into
   thin slices
1 large green chilli, finely sliced
12 Thai sweet basil leaves

SERVES 4

BRING a small saucepan of water to the boil. Add the salt, turmeric and banana slices and simmer for 10 minutes, then drain.

PUT the coconut cream in a wok or saucepan and simmer over a medium heat for about 5 minutes, or until the cream separates and a layer of oil forms on the surface. Stir the cream if it starts to brown around the edges. Add the curry paste, stir well to combine and cook until fragrant. Add the fish sauce and sugar and cook for another 2 minutes or until the mixture begins to darken.

ADD the fish pieces and stir well to coat the fish in the curry mixture. Slowly add the coconut milk until it has all been incorporated.

ADD the banana, mango, green chilli and most of the basil leaves to the pan and gently stir to combine all the ingredients, cooking for a minute or two. Garnish with the remaining basil.

The fruit is added towards the end of cooking.

Green mangoes.

SALMON EN PAPILLOTE WITH HERB SAUCE

4 x 200 g (7 oz) salmon fillets, skinned
10 g (⅓ oz) butter, melted
8 thin slices of lemon, halved

HERB SAUCE
300 ml (1¼ cup) fish stock
100 ml (⅓ cup) dry white wine
2 shallots, finely chopped
250 ml (1 cup) double cream
4 tablespoons finely chopped herbs such as chervil, chives, parsley, tarragon or sorrel

SERVES 4

PREHEAT the oven to 200°C (400°F/Gas 6).

REMOVE any bones from the salmon fillets: you may need to use tweezers to do this. Cut out four 30 cm (12 inch) greaseproof paper circles. Fold each circle in half, then open out again and brush with melted butter. Place a salmon fillet on one half of each paper circle, lay four half slices of lemon on top, season, then fold the other half of the paper over the fish to enclose it. Seal the parcels by folding the two edges of greaseproof paper tightly together. Put on a baking tray and bake for 10–15 minutes (depending on the thickness of the salmon), or until the fish is firm to the touch.

TO MAKE the herb sauce, put the stock, wine and shallots in a pan and simmer until the mixture has reduced to a syrup (you should have about 5 tablespoons of liquid left). Add the cream and bubble for a few minutes to thicken slightly. Season and gently stir in the herbs. Serve each diner a parcel to unwrap at the table with the herb sauce in a separate bowl.

Wrap the pieces of salmon in large circles of greaseproof paper to seal in the flavours while they bake.

SKATE WITH BLACK BUTTER

COURT BOUILLON
250 ml (1 cup) white wine
1 onion, sliced
1 carrot, sliced
1 bay leaf
4 black peppercorns

4 x 250 g (9 oz) skate wings, skinned
100 g (3 oz) unsalted butter
1 tablespoon chopped parsley
1 tablespoon capers, rinsed, squeezed dry and chopped

SERVES 4

TO MAKE the court bouillon, put the wine, onion, carrot, bay leaf, peppercorns and 1 litre (4 cups) water into a large deep frying pan, bring to the boil and simmer for 20 minutes. Strain the court bouillon and return to the cleaned frying pan.

ADD the skate and simmer for 10 minutes, or until it flakes when tested with the point of a knife. Lift out the fish, drain, cover and keep warm.

HEAT the butter in a frying pan and cook over moderate heat for 2 minutes until it turns brown to make a *beurre noisette*. Remove from the heat and stir in the parsley, capers, salt and pepper.

POUR the sauce over the top of the fish and serve immediately. You can lift the fillet off each side of the fish first, if you prefer.

SKATE WITH BLACK BUTTER

STEAMED MUSSELS WITH BLACK BEAN SAUCE

MUSSELS ARE NOT EATEN AS MUCH IN CHINA AS CLAMS, HOWEVER, THEY ARE ENJOYED IN SEASIDE AREAS. THIS RECIPE WORKS EQUALLY WELL WITH CLAMS IF YOU PREFER.

Scrub off any barnacles from the mussels, then remove the beards (byssus) by tugging on them firmly.

1 kg (2 lb 3 oz) mussels
1 tablespoon oil
1 garlic clove, finely chopped
1/2 teaspoon finely chopped ginger
2 spring onions (scallions), finely chopped
1 red chilli, chopped
1 tablespoon light soy sauce
1 tablespoon Shaoxing rice wine
1 tablespoon salted, fermented black beans, rinsed and mashed
2 tablespoons chicken and meat stock (page 565)
few drops of roasted sesame oil

SERVES 4

SCRUB the mussels, remove any beards, and throw away any that do not close when tapped on the work surface.

PLACE the mussels in a large dish in a steamer. Steam over simmering water in a covered wok for 4 minutes, discarding any that do not open after this time.

MEANWHILE, HEAT the oil in a small saucepan. Add the garlic, ginger, spring onion and chilli and cook, stirring, for 30 seconds. Add the remaining ingredients, and blend well. Bring to the boil, then reduce the heat and simmer for 1 minute.

TO SERVE, remove and discard the top shell of each mussel, pour 2 teaspoons of the sauce into each mussel and serve on the shell.

CLAMS IN YELLOW BEAN SAUCE

CLAMS ARE IMMENSELY POPULAR IN CHINA AND ARE SEEN AS A SYMBOL OF GOOD FORTUNE AS THEIR SHELLS ARE SAID TO LOOK LIKE COINS. THIS IS A VERY SIMPLE RECIPE FOR THEM.

CLAMS IN YELLOW BEAN SAUCE

1.5 kg (3 lb 5 oz) hard-shelled clams
1 tablespoon oil
2 garlic cloves, crushed
1 tablespoon grated ginger
2 tablespoons yellow bean sauce
125 ml (1/2 cup) chicken stock (page 565)
1 spring onion (scallion), sliced

SERVES 4

WASH the clams in several changes of cold water, leaving them for a few minutes each time to remove any grit. Scrub the clams well, discarding any that remain open. Drain well.

HEAT a wok over high heat, add the oil and heat until very hot. Stir-fry the garlic and ginger for 30 seconds, then add the bean sauce and clams and toss together. Add the stock and stir for 3 minutes until the clams have opened, discarding any that do not open after this time. Season with salt and white pepper. Transfer the clams to a plate and sprinkle with spring onion.

POULTRY

COQ AU VIN

A DISH ALLEGEDLY PREPARED BY CAESAR WHEN BATTLING THE GAULS, WHO SENT HIM A SCRAWNY CHICKEN AS A MESSAGE OF DEFIANCE. CAESAR COOKED IT IN WINE AND HERBS AND INVITED THEM TO EAT, THUS DEMONSTRATING THE OVERWHELMING SOPHISTICATION OF THE ROMANS.

2 x 1.6 kg (3½ lb) chickens
1 bottle red wine
2 bay leaves
2 thyme sprigs
250 g (9 oz) bacon, diced
60 g (2 oz) butter
20 pickling or pearl onions
250 g (9 oz) button mushrooms
1 teaspoon oil
30 g (1 oz) plain flour
1 litre (4 cups) chicken stock
125 ml (½ cups) brandy
2 teaspoons tomato purée
1½ tablespoons softened butter
1 tablespoon plain flour
2 tablespoons chopped parsley

SERVES 8

JOINT each chicken into eight pieces by removing both legs and cutting between the joint of the drumstick and the thigh. Cut down either side of the backbone and lift it out. Turn the chicken over and cut through the cartilage down the centre of the breastbone. Cut each breast in half, leaving the wing attached to the top half.

PUT the wine, bay leaves, thyme and some salt and pepper in a bowl and add the chicken. Cover and leave to marinate, preferably overnight.

BLANCH the bacon in boiling water, then drain, pat dry and sauté in a frying pan until golden. Lift out onto a plate. Melt a quarter of the butter in the pan, add the onions and sauté until browned. Lift out and set aside.

MELT another quarter of the butter, add the mushrooms, season with salt and pepper and sauté for 5 minutes. Remove and set aside.

DRAIN the chicken, reserving the marinade, and pat the chicken dry. Season. Add the remaining butter and the oil to the frying pan, add the chicken and sauté until golden. Stir in the flour.

TRANSFER the chicken to a large saucepan or casserole and add the stock. Pour the brandy into the frying pan and boil, stirring, for 30 seconds to deglaze the pan. Pour over the chicken. Add the marinade, onions, mushrooms, bacon and tomato purée. Cook over moderate heat for 45 minutes, or until the chicken is cooked through.

IF the sauce needs thickening, lift out the chicken and vegetables and bring the sauce to the boil. Mix together the butter and flour to make a *beurre manié* and whisk into the sauce. Boil, stirring, for 2 minutes until thickened. Add the parsley and return the chicken and vegetables to the sauce.

Cooking the chicken with the skin on keeps the flesh moist.

Butchers shops in Kerala advertise their wares through pictures. Lamb or goat and chicken are the most popular.

CARDAMOM CHICKEN

THIS DISH HAS A HIGHLY AROMATIC SAUCE FLAVOURED WITH CARDAMOM. THE YOGHURT MAKES THE SAUCE DELICIOUSLY CREAMY. IF YOU DON'T MAKE YOUR OWN YOGHURT, DRAIN COMMERCIAL YOGHURT OVERNIGHT. THIS MAKES THE SAUCE MUCH RICHER BY GETTING RID OF ANY EXCESS LIQUID.

1.5 kg (3 lb 5 oz) chicken or chicken pieces
25 cardamom pods
4 garlic cloves, crushed
3 cm (1¼ inch) piece of ginger, grated
300 ml (1¼ cups) thick natural yoghurt (page 554)
1½ teaspoons ground black pepper
grated rind of 1 lemon
2 tablespoons ghee or oil
400 ml (1½ cups) coconut milk (page 551)
6 green chillies, pricked all over
2 tablespoons chopped coriander (cilantro) leaves
3 tablespoons lemon juice

SERVES 4

IF USING a whole chicken, cut it into eight pieces by removing both legs and cutting between the joint of the drumstick and thigh. Cut down either side of the backbone and remove the backbone. Turn the chicken over and cut through the cartilage down the centre of the breastbone. Cut each breast in half, leaving the wing attached to the top half. Trim off the wing tips. Remove the skin if you prefer.

REMOVE the seeds from the cardamom pods and crush them in a spice grinder or pestle and mortar. In a blender, mix the garlic and ginger with enough of the yoghurt (about 50 ml (¼ cup)) to make a paste, or, if you prefer, mix them with a spoon. Add the cardamom, pepper and grated lemon rind. Spread this over the chicken pieces, cover,
and leave in the fridge overnight.

HEAT the ghee or oil in a karhai or heavy-based frying pan over low heat and brown the chicken pieces all over. Add the remaining yoghurt and coconut milk to the pan, bring to the boil, then add the whole chillies and the coriander leaves. Simmer for 20–30 minutes or until the chicken is cooked through. Season with salt, to taste, and stir in the lemon juice.

Pistachios ripen on a tree in Sicily.

Marsala is a fortified wine that takes its name from the town in Sicily where the grapes are grown. It was created by an English wine shipper in 1773, who added grape spirit to wine to prevent it spoiling at sea.

ROAST TURKEY WITH PISTACHIO STUFFING

ITALIAN ROAST TURKEY IS TRADITIONALLY SERVED WITH *MOSTARDA DI CREMONA*, A TYPE OF ITALIAN CHUTNEY, MADE FROM CANDIED FRUIT SUCH AS PEAR, APRICOT, MELON AND ORANGE PRESERVED WITH MUSTARD, HONEY, WINE AND SPICES. YOU CAN ALSO USE THIS RECIPE TO ROAST GUINEA FOWL.

STUFFING
45 g (1½ oz) shelled pistachio nuts
100 g (3 oz) prosciutto, finely
   chopped
220 g (8 oz) minced pork
220 g (8 oz) minced chicken
1 egg
90 ml (⅓ cup) double cream
150 g (5 oz) chestnut purée
½ teaspoon finely chopped sage
   or ¼ teaspoon dried sage
pinch of cayenne pepper

1 x 3 kg (6½ lb) turkey
300 g (10 oz) butter, softened
1 onion, roughly chopped
4 sage leaves
1 rosemary sprig
½ celery stalk, cut into 2–3 pieces
1 carrot, cut into 3–4 pieces
250 ml (1 cup) dry white wine
125 ml (½ cup) dry Marsala
250 ml (1 cup) chicken stock

SERVES 8

TO MAKE the stuffing, preheat the oven to 170°C (325°F/Gas 3). Spread the pistachio nuts on a baking tray and toast for 6–8 minutes. Place in a bowl with the other stuffing ingredients, season well and mix together thoroughly.

FILL the turkey cavity with the stuffing and sew up the opening with kitchen string. Cross the legs and tie them together, and tuck the wings behind the body. Rub the skin with 100 g (3 oz) of the butter. Put the onion in the centre of a roasting tin and place the turkey on top, breast up. Add another 100 g (3 oz) of butter to the tin with the sage, rosemary, celery and carrot. Pour the white wine and Marsala over the top. Roast for 2½–3 hours, basting several times. Cover with buttered greaseproof paper when the skin becomes golden brown.

TRANSFER the turkey to a carving plate and leave to rest in a warm spot. Put the vegetables from the pan into a food processor and blend, or push them through a sieve. Add the pan juices and scrapings from the bottom of the tin and blend until smooth. Transfer the mixture to a saucepan, add the remaining 100 g (3 oz) of butter and the chicken stock and bring to the boil. Season and cook until thickened to a good gravy consistency. Transfer to a gravy boat.

CARVE the turkey and serve with stuffing and gravy, and preferably *mostarda di Cremona*.

SPICY GROUND DUCK

THIS RECIPE IS A SPECIALITY FROM AROUND UBON RACHATHANI, THAILAND. YOU CAN USE MINCED CHICKEN INSTEAD OF DUCK. SERVE WITH RAW VEGETABLES SUCH AS SNAKE BEANS, CABBAGE AND FIRM, CRISP LETTUCE.

Pound the dry-fried rice in a pestle and mortar until it forms a powder. Alternatively, you can use a small blender.

1 tablespoon jasmine rice
280 g (10 oz) minced (ground) duck
3 tablespoons lime juice
1 tablespoon fish sauce
2 lemon grass stalks, white part
    only, finely sliced
50 g (2 oz) Asian shallots,
    finely sliced
5 makrut (kaffir) lime leaves,
    finely sliced
5 spring onions (scallions),
    finely chopped
¼–½ teaspoon roasted chilli powder,
    according to taste
a few lettuce leaves
a few mint leaves, for garnish
raw vegetables such as snake
    beans, cut into lengths, cucumber
    slices, thin wedges of cabbage,
    halved baby tomatoes, to serve

SERVES 4

DRY-FRY the rice in a small pan over a medium heat. Shake the pan to move the rice around, for 6–8 minutes, or until the rice is brown. Using a pestle and mortar or a small blender, pound or blend the rice until it almost forms a powder.

IN a saucepan or wok, cook the duck with the lime juice and fish sauce over a high heat. Crumble and break the duck until the meat has separated into small pieces. Cook until light brown. Dry, then remove from the heat.

ADD the rice powder, lemon grass, shallots, makrut lime leaves, spring onions and chilli powder to the duck and stir together. Taste, then adjust the seasoning if necessary.

LINE a serving plate with lettuce leaves. Spoon the duck over the leaves, then garnish with mint leaves. Arrange the vegetables on a separate plate.

QUAIL MASALA

QUAIL IS AN EXOTIC DISH, EVEN IN INDIA. MANY OF THE ROYAL HOUSEHOLDS TRADITIONALLY USED QUAIL IN MANY DIFFERENT WAYS. HERE IT IS INCORPORATED INTO A DRY-STYLE, STEAMED RECIPE. TENDER YOUNG CHICKEN OR POUSSIN CAN BE SUCCESSFULLY USED INSTEAD.

6 x 150 g (5 oz) quails

MARINADE
100 g (3 oz) blanched almonds
3 garlic cloves, crushed
3 cm (1¼ inch) piece of ginger,
    grated
½ onion, finely chopped
½ teaspoon chilli powder
½ teaspoon ground cloves
½ teaspoon ground cinnamon
1 teaspoon ground cumin
1 teaspoon garam masala
    (page 556)
2 tablespoons mint leaves,
    finely chopped
200 ml thick natural yoghurt
    (page 554)
1 teaspoon jaggery or
    soft brown sugar

RICE STUFFING
60 g (2 oz) rice
1 teaspoon amchoor powder
50 g (2 oz) chopped pine nuts
1½ tablespoons lemon juice

2 young banana leaves
3 tablespoons lemon juice
cucumber slices
mango or green mango slices
mint leaves

SERVES 6

CLEAN the quails by rinsing them well and wiping them dry. Prick the flesh all over so that the marinade will penetrate the meat.

TO MAKE the marinade, grind the almonds in a food processor or finely chop them with a knife, then mix them with the remaining marinade ingredients. Coat the quails evenly with the marinade, then cover and marinate for 4 hours, or overnight, in the fridge.

TO MAKE the rice stuffing, preheat the oven to 200°C (400°F/Gas 6). Cook the rice in boiling water for 15 minutes or until just tender. Drain well and allow to cool. Combine the rice, amchoor powder, pine nuts and lemon juice and season with salt. Just before cooking, fill the quails with the rice stuffing and brush some marinade on the quails. If you are making the stuffing in advance, make sure you refrigerate it until you are ready to use it.

CUT the banana leaves into neat pieces big enough to wrap a quail. Soften the leaves by dipping them into a pan of very hot water. Wipe them dry as they become pliant. If you can't get banana leaves, use foil. Brush with oil.

WRAP each quail individually in a piece of banana leaf, drizzling with any excess marinade. Tie firmly with a piece of kitchen string. Place the parcels, with the seam side up, on a rack above a baking tray and bake for 25–30 minutes. Check to see if the quails are cooked by opening one—the flesh should be slightly pink but the juices should run clear when the flesh is pierced. If necessary, cook the quails for another 5 minutes. Open the packets completely for 3 minutes at the end of cooking, to brown the quail slightly. Sprinkle a dash of lemon juice over each quail. Serve in the packets with some sliced cucumber, sliced mango and mint leaves.

To make sure none of the flavour or juices escape while the quails cook, wrap them in banana leaves as if they are little parcels.

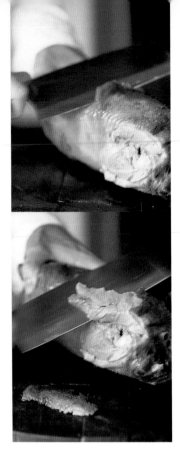

Carve the duck so that each slice has some crispy skin and tender meat. The skin can also be eaten separately, wrapped in the pancakes, while the meat is used in a stir-fry.

Commercially made pancakes are available in Asian shops, fresh or frozen, or from restaurants that sell take-away ducks and barbecued meat.

PEKING DUCK

THIS DISH OWES ITS REPUTATION NOT SO MUCH TO THE WAY IT IS COOKED, BUT TO THE WAY IT IS THEATRICALLY CARVED AND EATEN ROLLED INTO PANCAKES. IN RESTAURANTS, THE DUCK IS COOKED IN A SPECIAL OVEN, BUT THIS RECIPE HAS BEEN MODIFIED FOR THE HOME KITCHEN.

2.5 kg (5½ lb) duck
2 tablespoons maltose or honey, dissolved in 2 tablespoons water
125 ml (½ cup) hoisin sauce or plum sauce
24 Mandarin pancakes (page 571)
6–8 spring onions (scallions), shredded
½ cucumber, shredded

SERVES 6

CUT the wing tips off the duck with a pair of poultry shears. Rinse the duck, drain, and remove any fat from the cavity opening and around the neck. Cut off and discard the parson's nose. Plunge the duck into a pot of boiling water for 2–3 minutes to tighten the skin. Remove and drain, then dry thoroughly.

WHILE the skin is still warm, brush the duck all over with the maltose or honey and water solution, then hang it up to dry in a cool and airy place for at least 6 hours, or overnight, or leave it uncovered in the fridge.

PREHEAT the oven to 200°C (400°F/Gas 6). Place the duck, breast side up, on a rack in a roasting tin, and cook without basting or turning for 1½ hours. Check to make sure the duck is not getting too dark and, if it is, cover it loosely with foil.

TO SERVE, remove the crispy duck skin in small slices by using a sharp carving knife, then carve the meat, or carve both together. Arrange on a serving plate.

TO EAT, spread about 1 teaspoon of the hoisin sauce or plum sauce in the centre of a pancake, add a few strips of spring onion, cucumber, duck skin and meat, roll up the pancake and turn up the bottom edge to prevent the contents from falling out.

GREEN CURRY WITH CHICKEN

THIS FAMILIAR CLASSIC, WHICH SHOULD NEVER BE EXTREMELY HOT, HAS AS ITS BASE A PASTE OF CHILLIES, GALANGAL AND LEMON GRASS. BITTER VEGETABLES SUCH AS THAI EGGPLANT OFFSET THE SWEETNESS OF THE COCONUT CREAM. TENDER STEAK CAN BE USED INSTEAD OF CHICKEN.

60 ml (¼ cup) coconut cream
(page 551)
2 tablespoons green curry paste
(page 559) or bought paste
350 g (12 oz) skinless chicken thigh
fillets, sliced
440 ml (1¾ cups) coconut milk
(page 551)
2½ tablespoons fish sauce
1 tablespoon palm sugar
350 g (12 oz) mixed Thai eggplants
(aubergines), cut into quarters,
and pea eggplants (aubergines)
50 g (2 oz) galangal, julienned
7 makrut (kaffir) lime leaves,
torn in half
a handful of Thai sweet basil leaves,
for garnish
1 long red chilli, seeded and finely
sliced, for garnish

SERVES 4

PUT the coconut cream in a wok or saucepan and simmer over a medium heat for about 5 minutes, or until the cream separates and a layer of oil forms on the surface. Stir the cream if it starts to brown around the edges. Add the curry paste, stir well to combine and cook until fragrant.

ADD the chicken and stir for a few minutes. Add nearly all of the coconut milk, the fish sauce and palm sugar and simmer over a medium heat for another 5 minutes.

ADD the eggplants and cook, stirring occasionally, for about 5 minutes or until the eggplants are cooked. Add the galangal and makrut lime leaves. Taste, then adjust the seasoning if necessary. Spoon into a serving bowl and sprinkle with the last bit of coconut milk, as well as the basil leaves and chilli slices.

Various types of eggplant are used in Thailand and the bitter taste is very popular. They don't take long to cook.

DUCK A L'ORANGE

DUCK CAN BE FATTY, WHICH IS WHY IT SHOULD BE PRICKED ALL OVER AND COOKED ON A RACK TO LET THE FAT DRAIN AWAY. THE REASON THAT DUCK A L'ORANGE WORKS SO PERFECTLY AS A DISH, IS THAT THE SWEET ACIDITY OF THE CITRUS FRUIT CUTS THROUGH THE RICH DUCK FAT.

5 oranges
1 x 2 kg (4½ lb) duck
2 cinnamon sticks
15 g (½ oz) mint leaves
95 g (3 oz) light brown sugar
125 ml (½ cup) cider vinegar
80 ml (⅓ cup) Grand Marnier
30 g (1 oz) butter

SERVES 4

PREHEAT the oven to 150°C (300°F/Gas 2). Halve two of the oranges and rub them all over the duck. Place them inside the duck cavity with the cinnamon sticks and mint. Tie the legs together and tie the wings together. Prick all over with a fork so that the fat can drain out as the duck cooks.

PUT the duck on a rack, breast side down, and put the rack in a shallow roasting tin. Roast for 45 minutes, turning the duck halfway through.

MEANWHILE, zest and juice the remaining oranges (if you don't have a zester, cut the orange peel into thin strips with a sharp knife). Heat the sugar in a saucepan over low heat until it melts and then caramelizes: swirl the pan gently to make sure it caramelizes evenly. When the sugar is a rich brown, add the vinegar (be careful as it will splutter) and boil for 3 minutes. Add the orange juice and Grand Marnier and simmer for 2 minutes.

Adding the orange juice to the caramel sauce.

BLANCH the orange zest in boiling water for 1 minute three times, changing the water each time. Refresh under cold water, drain and reserve.

REMOVE the excess fat from the tin. Increase the oven temperature to 180°C (350°F/Gas 4). Spoon some of the orange sauce over the duck and roast for 45 minutes, spooning the remaining sauce over the duck every 5–10 minutes and turning the duck to baste all sides.

REMOVE the duck from the oven, cover with foil and strain the juices back into a saucepan. Skim off any excess fat and add the orange zest and butter to the saucepan. Stir to melt the butter. Reheat the sauce and serve over the duck.

A butcher's shop in Paris.

STIR-FRIED SQUAB IN LETTUCE LEAVES

THIS DISH IS A CANTONESE CLASSIC, SOMETIMES CALLED SAN CHOY BAU, AND THE LITTLE PARCELS, WITH THE CONTRAST BETWEEN THEIR WARM FILLING AND THE COLD LETTUCE, ARE WONDERFUL. IF SQUAB IS UNAVAILABLE, CHICKEN MAY BE USED INSTEAD.

In China, all poultry is sold live in the markets so there is no doubting its freshness.

12 soft lettuce leaves, such as butter lettuce
250 g (9 oz) squab or pigeon breast meat
450 g (1 lb) centre-cut pork loin, trimmed
90 ml (⅓ cup) light soy sauce
3½ tablespoons Shaoxing rice wine
2½ teaspoons roasted sesame oil
8 dried Chinese mushrooms
240 g (8 oz) peeled water chestnuts
120 ml (½ cup) oil
2 spring onions (scallions), finely chopped
2 tablespoons finely chopped ginger
1 teaspoon salt
1 teaspoon sugar
1 teaspoon cornflour

SERVES 6

RINSE the lettuce and separate the leaves. Drain thoroughly, then lightly pound each leaf with the flat side of a cleaver. Arrange the flattened leaves in a basket or on a platter and set aside.

MINCE the squab meat in a food processor or chop very finely with a sharp knife. Mince the pork to the same size as the squab. Place the squab and pork in a bowl with 2 tablespoons of the soy sauce, 1½ tablespoons of the rice wine and 1 teaspoon of the sesame oil, and toss lightly. Marinate in the fridge for 20 minutes.

SOAK the dried mushrooms in boiling water for 30 minutes, then drain and squeeze out any excess water. Remove and discard the stems and chop the caps. Blanch the water chestnuts in a pan of boiling water for 1 minute, then refresh in cold water. Drain, pat dry and roughly chop them.

HEAT a wok over high heat, add 3 tablespoons of the oil and heat until very hot. Stir-fry the meat mixture, mashing and separating the pieces, until browned. Remove and drain. Reheat the wok, add 3 tablespoons more of the oil and heat until very hot. Stir-fry the spring onion and ginger, turning constantly, for 10 seconds, or until fragrant. Add the mushrooms and stir-fry for 5 seconds, turning constantly. Add the water chestnuts and stir-fry for 15 seconds, or until heated through. Add the remaining soy sauce, rice wine and sesame oil with the salt, sugar, cornflour and 125 ml (½ cup) water. Stir-fry, stirring constantly, until thickened. Add the cooked meat mixture and toss lightly.

TO SERVE, place some of the stir-fried meat in a lettuce leaf, roll up and eat.

A restaurant in Beijing.

CHICKEN CACCIATORA

JUST LIKE THE FRENCH *CHASSEUR*, CACCIATORA MEANS 'HUNTER'S STYLE'. THE DISH IS ORIGINALLY FROM CENTRAL ITALY, BUT LIKE SO MUCH ITALIAN FARE, EVERY REGION HAS PUT ITS OWN TWIST ON THE RECIPE. THIS ONE, WITH TOMATOES, IS PROBABLY THE MOST WIDELY TRAVELLED.

3 tablespoons olive oil
1 large onion, finely chopped
3 garlic cloves, crushed
1 stalk celery, finely chopped
150 g (5 oz) pancetta, finely
    chopped
125 g (4 oz) button mushrooms,
    thickly sliced
4 chicken drumsticks
4 chicken thighs
90 ml (⅓ cup) dry vermouth or dry
    white wine
2 x 400 g (14 oz) tins chopped
    tomatoes
¼ teaspoon brown sugar
1 oregano sprig, plus 4–5 sprigs
    to garnish
1 rosemary sprig
1 bay leaf

SERVES 4

HEAT half the oil in a large casserole. Add the onion, garlic and celery and cook, stirring from time to time, over moderately low heat for 6–8 minutes until the onion is golden.

ADD the pancetta and mushrooms, increase the heat and cook, stirring occasionally, for 4–5 minutes. Spoon out onto a plate and set aside.

ADD the remaining olive oil to the casserole and lightly brown the chicken pieces, a few at a time. Season them as they brown. Spoon off any excess fat and return all the pieces to the casserole. Add the vermouth, increase the heat and cook until the liquid has almost evaporated.

ADD the tomatoes, sugar, oregano, rosemary, bay leaf and 75 ml (¼ cup) cold water. Bring to the boil then stir in the reserved pancetta mixture. Cover and leave to simmer for 20 minutes, or until the chicken is tender but not falling off the bone.

IF the liquid is too thin, remove the chicken from the casserole, increase the heat and boil until thickened. Discard the sprigs of herbs and taste for salt and pepper. Toss in the additional oregano sprigs and the dish is ready to serve.

Early morning shopping in Bologna.

This curry, with its combination of coconut milk, duck and fruit, is very rich. Cook the lychees for only a few minutes.

RED CURRY WITH ROASTED DUCK AND LYCHEES

IN THAILAND, THIS SPECIALITY DISH IS OFTEN SERVED DURING THE TRADITIONAL FAMILY FEASTING THAT ACCOMPANIES CELEBRATIONS INCLUDING THE ORDINATION OF BUDDHIST MONKS, WEDDINGS AND NEW YEAR. THIS IS VERY RICH, SO SERVE IT ALONGSIDE A SALAD TO CUT THROUGH THE SAUCE.

60 ml (¼ cup) coconut cream (page 551)

2 tablespoons red curry paste (page 558) or bought paste

½ roasted duck, boned and chopped

440 ml (1¾ cups) coconut milk (page 551)

2 tablespoons fish sauce

1 tablespoon palm sugar

225 g (8 oz) tin lychees, drained

110 g (4 oz) baby tomatoes

7 makrut (kaffir) lime leaves, torn in half

a handful of Thai sweet basil leaves, for garnish

1 long red chilli, seeded and finely sliced, for garnish

SERVES 4

PUT the coconut cream in a wok or saucepan and simmer over a medium heat for about 5 minutes, or until the cream separates and a layer of oil forms on the surface. Stir the cream if it starts to brown around the edges. Add the curry paste, stir well to combine and cook until fragrant.

ADD the roasted duck and stir for 5 minutes. Add the coconut milk, fish sauce and palm sugar and simmer over a medium heat for another 5 minutes. Add the lychees and baby tomatoes and cook for 1–2 minutes. Add the makrut lime leaves. Taste, then adjust the seasoning if necessary. Spoon into a serving bowl and sprinkle with the basil leaves and sliced chilli.

TANDOORI CHICKEN

TRADITIONALLY COOKED IN A TANDOOR (CLAY OVEN), THIS IS PERHAPS THE MOST POPULAR CHICKEN DISH FROM NORTHERN INDIA, WHERE IT IS SERVED WITH NAAN AND LACCHA. YOU CAN NEVER GET EXACTLY THE SAME RESULTS AT HOME BUT THIS IS A VERY GOOD APPROXIMATION.

1.5 kg (3 lb 5 oz) chicken or skinless chicken thighs and drumsticks

MARINADE
2 teaspoons coriander (cilantro) seeds
1 teaspoon cumin seeds
1 onion, roughly chopped
3 garlic cloves, roughly chopped
5 cm (2 inch) piece of ginger, roughly chopped
250 ml (1 cup) thick natural yoghurt (page 554)
grated rind of 1 lemon
3 tablespoons lemon juice
2 tablespoons clear vinegar
1 teaspoon paprika
2 teaspoons garam masala (page 556)
1/2 teaspoon tandoori food colouring (optional)

2 tablespoons ghee
onion rings
lemon wedges

SERVES 4

REMOVE the skin from the chicken and cut the chicken in half. Using a sharp knife, make 2.5 cm (1/8 inch) long diagonal incisions on each limb and breast, taking care not to cut through to the bone. If using thighs and drumsticks, trim away any excess fat and make an incision in each piece.

TO MAKE the marinade, place a frying pan over low heat and dry-roast the coriander seeds until aromatic. Remove and dry-roast the cumin seeds. Grind the roasted seeds to a fine powder using a spice grinder or pestle and mortar. In a food processor, blend all the marinade ingredients to form a smooth paste. Season with salt, to taste. If you don't have a food processor, chop the onion, garlic and ginger more finely and mix with the rest of the ingredients in a bowl.

MARINATE the chicken in the spicy yoghurt marinade for at least 8 hours, or overnight. Turn the chicken occasionally in the marinade to ensure that all sides are soaked.

HEAT the oven to 200°C (400°F/Gas 6). Place the chicken on a wire rack on a baking tray. Cover with foil and roast on the top shelf for about 45–50 minutes or until cooked through (test by inserting a skewer into a thigh—the juices should run clear). Baste the chicken with the marinade once during cooking. Remove the foil 15 minutes before the end of cooking, to brown the tandoori mixture. Preheat the grill (broiler) to its highest setting.

PRIOR to serving, while the chicken is still on the rack, heat the ghee, pour it over the chicken halves and cook under the grill for 5 minutes to blacken the edges of the chicken like a tandoor. Serve the chicken garnished with onion rings and lemon wedges.

Newly made yoghurt is left to set in porous earthenware bowls, which help to drain and thicken it.

Dried jujubes, or Chinese dates.

Chopping ginger outside a shop in Chengdu.

YUNNAN POT CHICKEN

A YUNNAN POT IS AN EARTHENWARE SOUP POT WITH A CHIMNEY. THE POT COOKS FOOD BY 'CLOSED STEAMING', WHICH GIVES A CLEARER, MORE INTENSELY FLAVOURED STOCK THAN ORDINARY STEAMING. INSTEAD OF A YUNNAN POT, YOU CAN USE A CLAY POT OR CASSEROLE INSIDE A STEAMER.

25 jujubes (dried Chinese dates)
1.5 kg (3 lb 5 oz) chicken
6 wafer-thin slices dang gui (dried angelica)
6 slices ginger, smashed with the flat side of a cleaver
6 spring onions (scallions), ends trimmed, smashed with the flat side of a cleaver
60 ml (¼ cup) Shaoxing rice wine
½ teaspoon salt

SERVES 6

SOAK the jujubes in hot water for 20 minutes, then drain and remove the stones.

RINSE the chicken, drain, and remove any fat from the cavity opening and around the neck. Cut off and discard the parson's nose. Using a cleaver, cut the chicken through the bones into square 4 cm (1½ inch) pieces. Blanch the chicken pieces in a pan of boiling water for 1 minute, then refresh in cold water and drain thoroughly.

ARRANGE the chicken pieces, jujubes, dang gui, ginger and spring onions in a clay pot or casserole about 24 cm (10 inches) in diameter. Pour the rice wine and 1 litre (4 cups) boiling water over the top and add the salt. Cover the clay pot or casserole tightly, adding a layer of wet muslin between the pot and lid to form a good seal if necessary, and place it in a steamer.

STEAM over simmering water in a covered wok for about 2 hours, replenishing with boiling water during cooking.

REMOVE the pot from the steamer and skim any fat from the surface of the liquid. Discard the dang gui, ginger and spring onions. Taste and season if necessary. Serve directly from the pot.

TARRAGON CHICKEN

TARRAGON HAS A DELICATE, BUT DISTINCTIVE, LIQUORICE FLAVOUR AND IS ONE OF THE HERBS THAT GOES INTO THE FRENCH *FINES HERBES* MIXTURE. IT IS KNOWN AS A PARTICULARLY GOOD PARTNER FOR CHICKEN, WITH A TARRAGON CREAM SAUCE MAKING A CLASSIC COMBINATION.

1½ tablespoons chopped tarragon
1 small garlic clove, crushed
50 g (2 oz) butter, softened
1 x 1.6 kg (3½ lb) chicken
2 teaspoons oil
150 ml (⅔ cup) chicken stock
2 tablespoons white wine
1 tablespoon plain flour
1 tablespoon tarragon leaves
150 ml (⅔ cup) double cream

SERVES 4

PREHEAT the oven to 200°C (400°F/Gas 6). Mix together the chopped tarragon, garlic and half the butter. Season with salt and pepper and place inside the cavity of the chicken. Tie the legs together and tuck the wing tips under.

HEAT the remaining butter with the oil in a large casserole dish over low heat and brown the chicken on all sides. Add the chicken stock and wine. Cover the casserole and bake in the oven for 1 hour 20 minutes, or until the chicken is tender and the juices run clear when the thigh is pierced with a skewer. Remove the chicken, draining all the juices back into the casserole. Cover with foil and a tea towel and leave the chicken to rest.

SKIM a tablespoon of the surface fat from the cooking liquid and put it in a small bowl. Skim the remainder of the fat from the surface and throw this away. Add the flour to the reserved fat and mix until smooth. Whisk quickly into the cooking liquid and stir over moderate heat until the sauce boils and thickens.

STRAIN the sauce into a clean saucepan and add the tarragon leaves. Simmer for 2 minutes, then stir in the cream and reheat without boiling. Season with salt and pepper. Carve the chicken and spoon the sauce over the top to serve.

Brown the chicken to seal before adding the stock and wine.

Buying cooked chickens and meat from a market rotisserie.

BANG BANG CHICKEN

THIS CLASSIC SICHUANESE COLD PLATTER IS MADE FROM CHICKEN, CUCUMBER AND BEAN THREAD NOODLES, MIXED IN A SESAME OR PEANUT SAUCE. THE SESAME DRESSING IS THE AUTHENTIC ONE BUT THE PEANUT VERSION IS ALSO VERY GOOD.

1¹/₂ cucumbers
1 teaspoon salt
30 g (1 oz) bean thread noodles
1 teaspoon roasted sesame oil
250 g (9 oz) cooked chicken, cut into shreds
2 spring onions (scallions), green part only, finely sliced

SESAME DRESSING
¹/₄ teaspoon Sichuan peppercorns
3 garlic cloves
2 cm (³/₄ inch) piece ginger
¹/₂ teaspoon chilli sauce
3 tablespoons toasted sesame paste
2 tablespoons roasted sesame oil
2¹/₂ tablespoons light soy sauce
1 tablespoon Shaoxing rice wine
1 tablespoon Chinese black rice vinegar
1 tablespoon sugar
3 tablespoons chicken stock (page 565)

OR

PEANUT DRESSING
60 g (2 oz) smooth peanut butter
1 teaspoon light soy sauce
1¹/₂ tablespoons sugar
2 teaspoons Chinese black rice vinegar
1 tablespoon Shaoxing rice wine
1 tablespoon roasted sesame oil
1 spring onion (scallion), finely chopped
1 tablespoon finely chopped ginger
1 teaspoon chilli sauce
2¹/₂ tablespoons chicken stock (page 565)

SERVES 6

SLICE the cucumbers lengthways and remove most of the seeds. Cut each half crossways into thirds, then cut each piece lengthways into thin slices that are 5 cm (2 inches) long and 1 cm (¹/₂ inch) wide. Place the slices in a bowl, add the salt, toss lightly, and set aside for 20 minutes. Pour off the water that has accumulated.

TO MAKE the sesame dressing, put the Sichuan peppercorns in a frying pan and cook over medium heat, stirring occasionally, for 7–8 minutes, or until golden brown and very fragrant. Cool slightly, then crush into a powder. Combine the garlic, ginger, chilli sauce, sesame paste, sesame oil, soy sauce, rice wine, vinegar, sugar and stock in a blender, food processor or mortar and pestle. Blend to a smooth sauce the consistency of double cream. Stir in the Sichuan peppercorn powder. Pour into a bowl and set aside.

TO MAKE the peanut dressing, combine the peanut butter, soy sauce, sugar, vinegar, rice wine, sesame oil, spring onion, ginger, chilli sauce and stock in a blender, food processor or mortar and pestle. Blend until the mixture is the consistency of double cream, adding a little water if necessary. Pour into a bowl and set aside.

SOAK the bean thread noodles in hot water for 10 minutes, then drain and cut into 8 cm (3¹/₄ inch) lengths. Blanch the noodles in a pan of boiling water for 3 minutes, then refresh in cold water and drain again. Toss the noodles in the sesame oil and arrange them on a large platter. Arrange the cucumber slices on top. Place the chicken shreds on top of the cucumber. Just before serving, pour the sesame or peanut dressing over the chicken. Sprinkle with the spring onion and serve.

CHICKEN WITH CHILLI JAM

CHILLI JAM, OR ROASTED CHILLI PASTE, IS USED AS A RELISH, CONDIMENT AND INGREDIENT IN VARIOUS THAI DISHES. HERE IT ADDS A MORE COMPLEX SWEET, CHILLI FLAVOUR THAN JUST USING CHILLIES. ADD THE SMALLER AMOUNT BEFORE TASTING, THEN ADD A LITTLE MORE IF YOU NEED TO.

2 teaspoons fish sauce
2 tablespoons oyster sauce
60 ml (¼ cup) coconut milk
    (page 551)
½ teaspoon sugar
2½ tablespoons vegetable oil
6 garlic cloves, finely chopped
1–1½ tablespoons chilli jam
    (page 561), to taste
500 g (1 lb 2 oz) skinless chicken
    breast fillets, finely sliced
a handful of holy basil leaves
1 long red or green chilli,
    seeded and finely sliced,
    for garnish

SERVES 4

MIX the fish sauce, oyster sauce, coconut milk and sugar in a small bowl.

HEAT the oil in a wok or frying pan and stir-fry half the garlic over a medium heat until light brown. Add half the chilli jam and stir-fry for another 2 minutes or until fragrant. Add half of the chicken and stir-fry over a high heat for 2–3 minutes. Remove from the wok. Repeat with the remaining garlic, chilli jam and chicken. Return all the chicken to the wok.

ADD the fish sauce mixture to the wok and stir-fry for a few more seconds or until the chicken is cooked. Taste, then adjust the seasoning if necessary. Stir in the basil leaves. Garnish with chilli slices.

Mixing the sauce ingredients together before you start cooking means you can just pour it in when you need to.

Salt harvested from the Gulf of Thailand.

POLLO ALLA DIAVOLA

DEVIL'S CHICKEN ORIGINATED IN THE TUSCAN KITCHEN. THE CHICKEN IS BUTTERFLIED, THEN MARINATED IN OLIVE OIL AND CHILLI. TRADITIONALLY THE BIRD WOULD BE COOKED ON A GRILL OVER AN OPEN FIRE—THE FLAMES LICKING UP FROM BELOW LIKE THE FIRES OF THE DEVIL.

2 x 900 g (2 lb) chickens
150 ml (⅔ cup) olive oil
juice of 1 large lemon
2 sage leaves
3–4 very small red chillies, finely minced, or ½ teaspoon dried chilli flakes
2 shallots
2 garlic cloves
4 tablespoons chopped parsley
2½ tablespoons softened butter
lemon slices

SERVES 4

SPLIT each chicken through the breastbone and press open to form a butterfly, joined down the back. Flatten with your hand to give a uniform surface for cooking. Place in a shallow dish large enough to take both chickens side by side.

MIX together the olive oil, lemon juice, sage and chilli in a bowl and season well with salt and pepper. Pour over the chicken and leave to marinate in the fridge for 30 minutes. Turn the chickens and leave for a further 30 minutes.

MEANWHILE, chop the shallots, garlic, parsley and butter in a blender or food processor until fine and paste-like. (If you want to do this by hand, chop the vegetables and then mix them into the softened butter.) Season with salt and pepper. Preheat the grill (broiler).

PLACE the chickens, skin side down, on a grill tray. Position about 10 cm (4 inches) below the heat and grill for 10 minutes, basting with the marinade once or twice. Turn the chickens and grill, basting occasionally, for another 10–12 minutes, or until the juices run clear when a thigh is pierced deeply with a skewer.

SPREAD the butter paste over the skin of the chickens with a knife. Reduce the heat and grill for about 3 minutes until the coating is lightly browned. Serve hot or cold, with lemon wedges.

Wild chillies have been eaten in Mexico since 7000 BC. It is likely that the plants were brought to Europe by Columbus—the chilli reached southern Italy in 1526 and, as in many other countries, was absorbed into local dishes.

PARSI CHICKEN WITH APRICOTS

IN THIS DELICIOUS PARSI DISH FROM MUMBAI (BOMBAY), THE USE OF DRIED APRICOTS, JAGGERY AND VINEGAR GIVE A SWEET SOUR FLAVOUR. THE POTATO STRAWS MAKE AN UNUSUAL GARNISH AND ADD A CONTRASTING CRUNCHY TEXTURE TO ENHANCE THE RECIPE.

1.5 kg (3 lb 5 oz) chicken or
 chicken pieces
3 tablespoons oil
2 large onions, finely sliced
1 clove garlic, finely chopped
4 cm (1½ inch) piece of ginger,
 finely chopped
3 dried chillies
1½ teaspoons garam masala
 (page 556)
2 tablespoons tomato purée
1 teaspoon salt
2 tablespoons clear vinegar
1½ tablespoons jaggery
 or soft brown sugar
12 dried apricots

POTATO STRAWS
1 large waxy potato
1 tablespoon salt
oil for deep-frying

SERVES 4

IF USING a whole chicken, cut it into eight pieces by removing both legs and cutting between the joint of the drumstick and thigh. Cut down either side of the backbone and remove the backbone. Turn the chicken over and cut through the cartilage down the centre of the breastbone. Cut each breast in half, leaving the wing attached to the top half. Trim off the wing tips.

HEAT the oil in a karhai or casserole. Add the onion and stir over medium heat until softened and starting to brown. Stir in the garlic, ginger, dried chillies and garam masala, then add all the chicken pieces. Stir and brown the chicken for 5 minutes, taking care not to burn the onion. Add the tomato purée, salt and 250 ml (1 cup) water. Bring to the boil, then reduce the heat, cover and simmer gently for 20 minutes.

ADD the vinegar, jaggery and dried apricots to the pan, cover and simmer for another 15 minutes.

TO MAKE the potato straws, grate the potato on the largest holes of a grater, then put in a large bowl with about 1.5 litres (6 cups) water and the salt. Stir and remove some potato a handful at a time, squeezing and patting it dry on a tea towel. Fill a karhai or deep, heavy-based saucepan one-third full with oil. Heat the oil slowly to 160°C/315°F (a cube of bread will brown in 30 seconds), then add a small handful of potato. Be careful not to add too much as it will make the oil bubble and rise up the pan at first. When the potato is golden and crisp, remove it and drain on paper towels. Cook all the potato in the same way.

SERVE the chicken pieces garnished with the potato straws.

Street decorations on a busy street in Mumbai (Bombay) during the festival of Divali.

DRUNKEN CHICKEN

THERE ARE SEVERAL VERSIONS OF THIS POPULAR DISH, BUT IN THIS SIMPLE RECIPE, THE CHICKEN IS STEAMED IN THE 'DRUNKEN' SAUCE, WHICH IS THEN POURED OVER TO SERVE.

1.5 kg (3 lb 5 oz) chicken
150 ml (⅔ cup) Shaoxing rice wine
3 tablespoons Chinese spirit (Mou Tai) or brandy
3 slices ginger
3 spring onions (scallions), cut into short lengths
2 teaspoons salt
¼ teaspoon freshly ground black pepper
coriander (cilantro) leaves

SERVES 4

RINSE the chicken, drain, and remove any fat from the cavity opening and around the neck. Cut off and discard the parson's nose. Blanch the chicken in a pan of boiling water for 2–3 minutes, then refresh in cold water.

PLACE the chicken, breast side down, in a bowl. Add the rice wine, Chinese spirit, ginger, spring onion and half the salt. Place the bowl in a steamer. Cover and steam over simmering water in a wok for 1½ hours, replenishing with boiling water during cooking. Transfer the chicken to a dish, breast side up, reserving the cooking liquid.

POUR half the liquid into a wok or saucepan and add the remaining salt and the pepper. Bring to the boil, then pour the sauce over the chicken. Using a cleaver, cut the chicken through the bones into bite-size pieces. Garnish with the coriander.

DRUNKEN CHICKEN

THREE-CUP CHICKEN

THREE-CUP CHICKEN IS SO CALLED BECAUSE THE ORIGINAL RECIPE USES ONE CUP EACH OF RICE WINE, SOY SAUCE AND LARD. CHRISTINE YAN OF YMING RESTAURANT IN LONDON MODIFIED IT HERE BY SUBSTITUTING THE LARD WITH STOCK, AND THE RESULT IS A MUCH HEALTHIER DISH.

450 g (1 lb) skinless chicken thigh fillet
1 tablespoon cornflour
1 tablespoon oil
2 spring onions (scallions), cut to short lengths
4 small pieces ginger
3 tablespoons Shaoxing rice wine
3 tablespoons light soy sauce
100 ml (⅓ cup) chicken and meat stock (page 565)
½ teaspoon roasted sesame oil

SERVES 4

CUT the chicken into 2 cm (¾ inch) cubes. Combine the cornflour with enough water to make a paste and toss the chicken cubes in the paste to coat.

HEAT the oil in a small clay pot or casserole, lightly brown the chicken with the spring onion and ginger, then add the rice wine, soy and stock. Bring to the boil, then reduce the heat and simmer, covered, for 20–25 minutes. There should be a little liquid left—if there is too much, boil it off. Add the sesame oil and serve the chicken hot from the pot.

A sign proclaims 'Thai-style chicken feet' for sale at an outside stall in Chengdu.

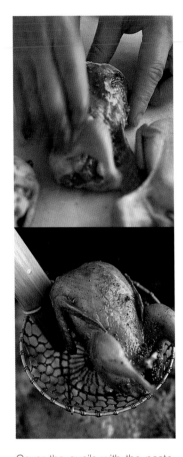

DEEP-FRIED QUAIL

QUAIL WORKS WELL FOR DISHES THAT WOULD PROBABLY TRADITIONALLY HAVE USED PIGEON OR TURTLE DOVE. CHICKEN PIECES CAN ALSO BE USED BUT THE QUAILS LOOK MORE ATTRACTIVE ON THE PLATE. SERVE ALONGSIDE VEGETABLE DISHES OR USE AS A STARTER.

5 white peppercorns
5 coriander (cilantro) seeds
¼ teaspoon cumin seeds
1 star anise
2 garlic cloves
2 tablespoons soy sauce
½ teaspoon palm sugar
4 quails
oil, for deep-frying
roasted chilli sauce (page 561) or
    sweet chilli sauce (page 562),
    to serve

SERVES 4

USING a pestle and mortar, pound together the peppercorns, coriander seeds, cumin seeds, star anise and a pinch of salt. Add the garlic, soy sauce and palm sugar and pound to a paste.

RUB the paste all over the quails, cover and marinate in the refrigerator for at least 3 hours.

HEAT the oil in a wok until a piece of bread dropped into it sizzles and turns brown. Pat the quails dry with paper towels. Add the quails and fry them for about 10 minutes, turning them so that they cook on all sides. Make sure the oil gets inside the quails as well.

DRAIN well and sprinkle with a little more salt. Cut into quarters and serve with roasted chilli sauce or sweet chilli sauce.

Cover the quails with the paste, then marinate them. Remove the cooked quail from the oil with a slotted spoon.

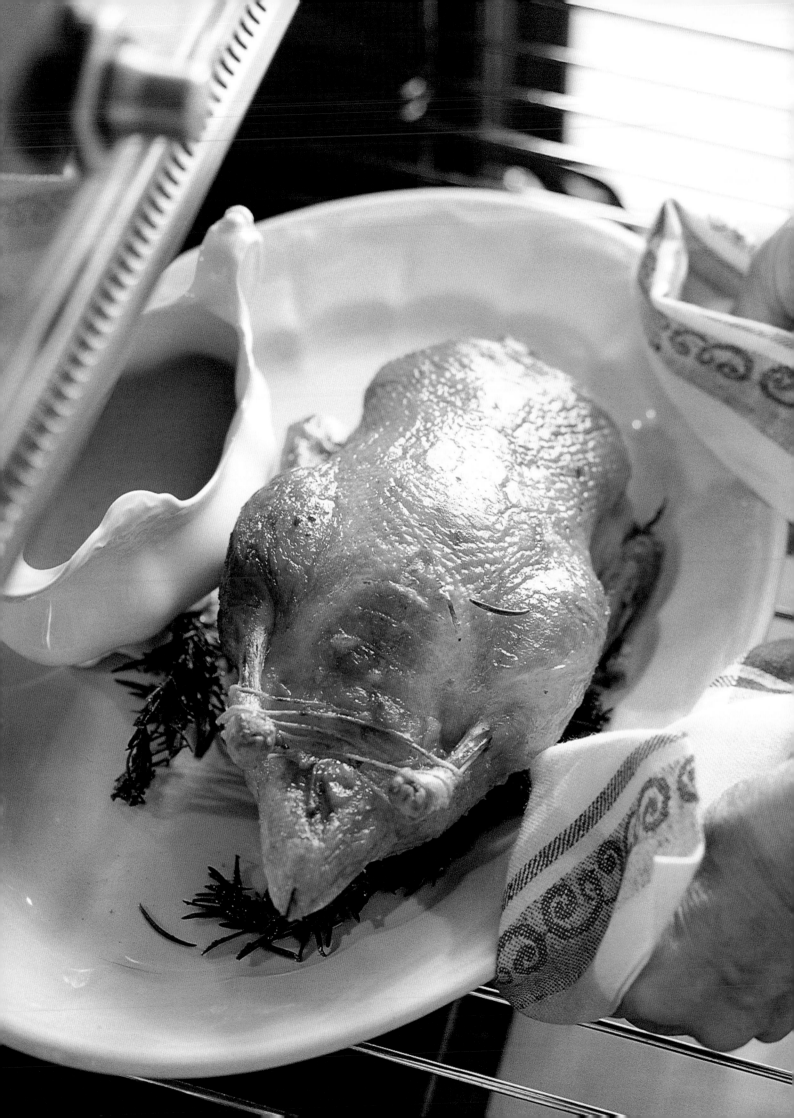

ROAST DUCK WITH PARMA HAM

PARMA HAM WAS SUPPOSEDLY SERVED TO HANNIBAL AT A BANQUET IN THE CITY IN 217 BC. TODAY ITS PRODUCTION IS A LICENSED INDUSTRY, WITH ONLY HAM FROM THE EMILIA-ROMAGNA REGION TAKING THE NAME. THESE HAMS HAVE THE DUCAL CROWN OF PARMA BRANDED ON THEIR SKIN.

2 thick slices 'country-style' bread,
  such as ciabatta, crusts removed
125 ml (½ cup) milk
1 x 2 kg (4½ lb) duck
6 thick slices Parma ham
3 garlic cloves, crushed
120 g (4 oz) minced pork
120 g (4 oz) minced veal
2 shallots, finely chopped
2 tablespoons grated Parmesan
1 tablespoon finely chopped parsley
1 egg
75 ml (¼ cup) olive oil
60 g (2 oz) lard or butter
2 rosemary sprigs
4 tablespoons grappa or brandy
250 ml (1 cup) chicken stock
3 tablespoons double cream

SERVES 4

PREHEAT the oven to 220°C (425°F/Gas 7). Soak the bread in the milk. Remove any excess skin and fat from the duck, leaving just enough skin to sew the cavity closed later.

BRING a large saucepan of water to the boil. Prick the skin of the duck all over and put it into the boiling water with a teaspoon of salt. Boil for 12 minutes. Remove and place, cavity side down, in a colander to drain for 10 minutes. Dry well all over, inside and out, with paper towels.

FINELY CHOP 2 slices of Parma ham and mix with the garlic, minced pork and veal, shallots, Parmesan and parsley. Squeeze the bread dry and add to the mixture. Add the egg, season and mix well. Fill the duck cavity with the stuffing then stitch closed with kitchen string. Tie the wings and legs together with string.

PUT the olive oil, lard and rosemary in a roasting tin and heat in the oven for 5 minutes. Put the duck in the middle, breast up, and roast for 10 minutes. Baste with the pan juices and lay the remaining slices of Parma ham over the breast, covering the legs as well. Reduce the temperature to 190°C (375°F/Gas 5) and roast for a further hour, basting several times. Remove the Parma ham, increase the heat to 210°C (415°F/Gas 6–7) and return to the oven for 10 minutes.

TRANSFER the duck to a carving plate and leave to rest for 10 minutes. Spoon all the fat out of the roasting tin, leaving just the duck juices, and place the tin over high heat on the stove. Add the grappa and cook until it is syrupy and almost evaporated, then add the chicken stock. Continue boiling until slightly thickened, then add the cream. Season well and strain into a sauceboat. Remove the string, carve the duck and stir any juices into the sauce before serving.

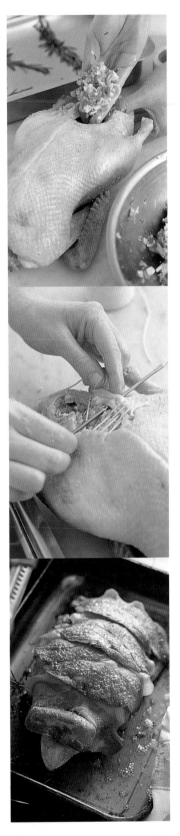

Stuff the duck, then stitch up the opening with kitchen string—you can buy special large needles from kitchen shops. The slices of ham prevent the duck drying out.

A shopping street in central Shanghai.

Ducks hanging up to dry after they have been plucked.

SHANGHAI SOY DUCK

THIS DUCK, SIMILAR TO CANTONESE SOY CHICKEN, IS TRADITIONALLY SERVED AT ROOM TEMPERATURE AS A FIRST COURSE, THOUGH THERE IS NO REASON WHY IT CAN'T BE SERVED AS A MAIN COURSE, HOT OR COLD. YOU CAN ALSO USE JOINTED PIECES OR DUCK BREASTS, JUST REDUCE THE COOKING TIME.

2.25 kg (5 lb) duck
2 teaspoons salt
4 spring onions (scallions), each
    tied in a knot
4 x 1 cm (½ inch) slices ginger,
    smashed with the flat side of a
    cleaver
6 star anise
3 cinnamon or cassia sticks
1 tablespoon Sichuan peppercorns
100 ml (⅓ cup) Shaoxing rice wine
200 ml (¾ cup) light soy sauce
100 ml (⅓ cup) dark soy sauce
100 g (3 oz) rock sugar

SERVES 4

RINSE the duck, drain, and remove any fat from the cavity opening and around the neck. Cut off and discard the parson's nose. Blanch the duck in a pan of boiling water for 2–3 minutes, then refresh in cold water, pat dry and rub the salt inside the cavity.

PLACE the duck, breast side up, in a clay pot or casserole, and add the spring onion, ginger, star anise, cinnamon, peppercorns, rice wine, soy sauces, rock sugar and enough water to cover. Bring to the boil, then reduce the heat and simmer, covered, for 40–45 minutes. Turn off the heat and leave the duck to cool in the liquid for 2–3 hours, transferring the clay pot to the fridge once it is cool enough. Leave in the fridge until completely cold (you can keep the duck in the liquid overnight and serve it the next day).

TO SERVE, remove the duck from the liquid and drain well. Using a cleaver, cut the duck through the bones into bite-size pieces.

TRADITIONALLY this dish is served at room temperature, but if you would like to serve it hot, put the clay pot with the duck and the liquid back on the stove and bring it to the boil. Simmer for 10 minutes, or until the duck is completely heated through.

MEAT AND GAME

RABBIT FRICASSÉE

THE NAME OF THE DISH COMES FROM AN OLD FRENCH WORD, *FRICASSER*, TO FRY. A FRICASSÉE IS A DISH OF WHITE MEAT, USUALLY CHICKEN, VEAL OR RABBIT, IN A VELOUTÉ SAUCE WITH EGG YOLKS AND CREAM. WILD RABBIT, IF YOU CAN GET IT, HAS A BETTER FLAVOUR THAN FARMED.

60 g (2 oz) clarified butter
1 x 1.5 kg (3 lb 5 oz) rabbit, cut into
   8 pieces
200 g (7 oz) button mushrooms
100 ml (⅓ cup) white wine
150 ml (⅔ cup) chicken stock
bouquet garni
100 ml (⅓ cup) oil
small bunch of sage
150 ml (⅔ cup) double cream
2 egg yolks

SERVES 4

HEAT half the clarified butter in a large saucepan, season the rabbit and brown in batches, turning once. Remove from the saucepan and set aside. Add the remaining butter to the saucepan and brown the mushrooms.

PUT the rabbit back into the saucepan with the mushrooms. Add the wine and boil for a couple of minutes before adding the stock and bouquet garni. Cover the pan tightly and simmer gently over very low heat for 40 minutes.

MEANWHILE, heat the oil in a small saucepan. Remove the leaves from the bunch of sage and drop them, a few at a time, into the hot oil. The leaves will immediately start to bubble around the edges. Cook them for 30 seconds, or until bright green and crispy. Make sure you don't overheat the oil or cook the leaves for too long or they will turn black and taste burnt. Drain the leaves on paper towels and sprinkle with salt.

LIFT the cooked rabbit and mushrooms out of the saucepan and keep warm. Discard the bouquet garni. Remove the pan from the heat, mix together the cream and egg yolks and stir quickly into the stock. Return to very low heat and cook, stirring, for about 5 minutes to thicken slightly (don't let the sauce boil or the eggs will scramble). Season with salt and pepper.

TO SERVE, pour the sauce over the rabbit and mushrooms and garnish with crispy sage leaves.

While the rabbit is simmering, deep-fry the sage until crispy.

245

CARAMEL PORK

CARAMEL PORK HAS A RELATIVELY SWEET FLAVOUR AND IS BEST SERVED WITH STEAMED JASMINE RICE OR STICKY RICE AND A SHARP-FLAVOURED DISH LIKE GREEN PAPAYA SALAD OR POMELO SALAD. CARAMEL PORK WILL KEEP FOR A FEW DAYS IN THE REFRIGERATOR AND CAN BE MADE IN ADVANCE.

vegetable oil, for deep-frying
75 g (3 oz) Asian shallots, finely
    sliced
6 garlic cloves, finely chopped
500 g (1 lb 2 oz) shoulder or leg
    of pork, cut into thin slices
1 tablespoon oyster sauce
1 tablespoon light soy sauce
1 tablespoon fish sauce
4 tablespoons palm sugar
¼ teaspoon ground white pepper

SERVES 4

HEAT 5 cm (2 inches) oil in a deep saucepan or wok over a medium heat and deep-fry the shallots until they are golden brown. Be careful not to burn them. Remove them from the wok with a slotted spoon and drain on paper towels.

DRAIN the oil from the saucepan or wok, leaving 2 tablespoons in the pan. Stir-fry the garlic in the oil until light brown, then add the pork and stir-fry for a few minutes. Add the oyster sauce, light soy sauce, fish sauce, sugar and ground pepper and continue cooking for about 5 minutes, or until all the liquid has evaporated and the mixture forms a thick sticky sauce.

SPOON onto a serving plate and sprinkle with the crispy shallots. Serve as required.

Palm sugar on sale.

BRAISED PORK

1 large pork hock or 2 small ones
oil, for deep-frying
2 coriander (cilantro) roots, chopped
4 garlic cloves, crushed
2 teaspoons ground white pepper
4 slices of ginger
2 star anise
1 cinnamon stick
2 tablespoons palm sugar
2 tablespoons fish sauce
2 tablespoons ketchap manis
1.5 litres (6 cups) chicken stock
4 hard-boiled eggs, shells removed

SERVES 4

PUT the pork hock in a saucepan of salted water and bring to the boil. Drain and repeat, then pat dry with paper towels. Heat a wok one-quarter filled with oil until the oil is very hot. Carefully add the dried pork hock to the wok and fry on all sides until brown. Loosely cover the wok with a lid if the oil spits too much. Remove the hock and drain away all but a tablespoon of the oil.

FRY the coriander roots, garlic and pepper briefly, then add the ginger, star anise and cinnamon stick and fry for a minute. Add the palm sugar, fish sauce, ketchap manis and stock and bring to a boil. Add the hock and cook for 2 hours or until the hock meat starts to fall off the bone. Add the eggs and cook for 10 minutes. Season with salt and serve with jasmine rice.

BRAISED PORK

BOLLITO MISTO

THIS MEAL REQUIRES A TRIP TO A REALLY GOOD BUTCHER. IF YOU ARE LUCKY ENOUGH TO FIND A ZAMPONE (PORK SAUSAGE STUFFED INTO A PIG'S TROTTER), USE IT INSTEAD OF THE COTECHINO. YOU WILL ONLY NEED A LITTLE OF THE COOKING LIQUID FOR SERVING—KEEP THE REST FOR MAKING SOUP.

1 x 800 g (1 lb 12 oz) cotechino
  sausage
1 x 1.25 kg (2 lb 12 oz) small beef
  tongue
3 parsley sprigs
4 baby carrots
1 celery stalk, sliced
2 onions, roughly chopped
10 peppercorns
2 bay leaves
1 x 1.25 kg (1 lb 12 oz) beef brisket
1 tablespoon tomato purée
1 x 900 g (2 lb) chicken
12 whole baby turnips
18 small onions, such as pickling
  or pearl onions

SERVES 8

BRING a saucepan of water to the boil. Prick the casing of the cotechino sausage and add to the pan. Reduce the heat, cover the saucepan and simmer for about 1¹/₂ hours, or until tender. Leave in the cooking liquid until ready to use.

MEANWHILE, bring a stockpot or very large saucepan of water to the boil. Add the tongue, parsley, carrots, celery, chopped onion, peppercorns, bay leaves and 1 teaspoon salt. Bring back to the boil, skim the surface and add the beef brisket and tomato purée. Cover the pan, reduce the heat and simmer for 2 hours, skimming the surface from time to time.

ADD the chicken, turnips and onions to the stockpot and simmer for a further hour. Top up with boiling water if necessary to keep the meat always covered. Add the cotechino for the last 20 minutes of cooking.

TURN OFF the heat and remove the tongue. Peel, trim and slice it, then arrange the slices on a warm platter. Slice the cotechino and beef and quarter the chicken. Arrange all the meats on the platter and surround them with the carrots, turnips and onions. Moisten with a little of the cooking liquid then take to the table. Serve with salsa verde (page 569) and *mostarda di Cremona*.

'Boiled meats' is a tradition in prosperous northern Italy, where cows and pigs are plentiful, with Piemonte generally accepted as the home of the best bollito misto. There, grand restaurants serve seven different meats with three sauces from a special trolley. Elsewhere, and when cooked at home for large family gatherings, the dish is a little less flamboyant, containing only two or three different meats.

Removing the seeds from the chillies will make the dish slightly milder. Gently stir the spices to evenly roast them.

The Indian version of the pestle and mortar. The base is the *sil* and the crushing stone the *nora*.

MANGALOREAN PORK BAFATH

MANGALOREAN FOOD IS SOUTH INDIAN WITH MANY OTHER INFLUENCES, INCLUDING PORTUGUESE. THIS RECIPE IS MILDLY SWEET BECAUSE OF THE KASHMIRI CHILLIES. THE PORK HAS OILS THAT ALMOST ROAST THE SPICES WITHIN THE MEAT WITH A BEAUTIFUL, AROMATIC RESULT.

20 red Kashmiri chillies, seeded
2 teaspoons coriander (cilantro) seeds
1 teaspoon cumin seeds
1/2 teaspoon ground turmeric
10 black peppercorns
2 tablespoons tamarind purée (page 554)
1.5 kg boneless pork leg or shoulder, cut into 3 cm (1 1/4 inch) cubes
1 tablespoon oil
2 onions, cut into 3 cm (1 1/4 inch) pieces
2 cm (3/4 inch) piece of ginger, finely chopped
6 green chillies, slit lengthwise into halves
8 cloves
2 cm (3/4 inch) piece of cinnamon stick, pounded roughly
1 tablespoon dark vinegar
3 garlic cloves, finely chopped
1 green chilli, extra, seeded, finely sliced lengthwise

SERVES 6

PLACE a small frying pan over low heat and dry-roast the chillies, coriander seeds, cumin seeds, ground turmeric and peppercorns until aromatic. Grind the roasted mixture to a fine powder using a spice grinder or pestle and mortar.

MIX all the roasted, ground ingredients with the tamarind and meat. Cover and marinate in the fridge for 2 hours.

HEAT the oil in a karhai or casserole over high heat, add the meat mixture in batches and brown all over. Return all the meat to the pan, then add the onion, ginger, chilli, cloves and cinnamon. Stir thoroughly to mix with the pork. Reduce the heat to low and cook for about 20 minutes, until the meat juices appear and mix with the spice, creating a thick sauce.

ADD the vinegar, garlic and 200 ml (3/4 cup) water and cook for 1–1 1/4 hours, until the pork is very tender. Season with salt, to taste. Cook until the oil separates from the spice mixture, which indicates the meat is ready. You can skim off the oil or blot it from the surface with paper towels if you prefer. Garnish with the chilli before serving.

Use the same frying pan for browning all the ingredients separately. Once you have made the sauce, return the kidneys and chipolatas to the pan.

KIDNEYS TURBIGO

THIS STEW OF KIDNEYS, SAUSAGES AND ONIONS IS NAMED AFTER THE TOWN OF TURBIGO IN LOMBARDY, THE SITE OF TWO FAMOUS FRENCH MILITARY VICTORIES OVER THE AUSTRIAN ARMY IN THE NINETEENTH CENTURY.

8 lamb kidneys
60 g (2 oz) butter
8 chipolata sausages
12 small pickling or pearl onions or shallots
125 g (4 oz) button mushrooms, sliced
1 tablespoon plain flour
2 tablespoons dry sherry
2 teaspoons tomato purée
250 ml (1 cup) beef stock
2 tablespoons finely chopped parsley

CROUTES
oil, for brushing
2 garlic cloves, crushed
12 slices baguette, cut on an angle

SERVES 4

TRIM, halve and cut the white membrane from the kidneys with scissors. Heat half the butter in a large frying pan and cook the kidneys for 2 minutes to brown all over. Remove to a plate. Add the chipolatas to the frying pan and cook for 2 minutes until browned all over. Remove to a plate. Cut in half on the diagonal.

LOWER the heat and add the remaining butter to the frying pan. Cook the onions and mushrooms, stirring, for 5 minutes until soft and golden brown.

MIX TOGETHER the flour and sherry to make a smooth paste. Add the tomato purée and stock and mix until smooth.

REMOVE the frying pan from the heat and stir in the stock mixture. Return to the heat and stir until boiling and slightly thickened. Season well with salt and pepper. Return the kidneys and chipolatas to the sauce. Lower the heat, cover the pan and simmer for 25 minutes, or until the kidneys are cooked. Stir occasionally.

MEANWHILE, to make the croutes, preheat the oven to 180°C (350°F/Gas 4). Mix together the oil and garlic and brush over the bread slices. Place on a baking tray and bake for 3–4 minutes. Turn over and bake for a further 3 minutes until golden brown. Sprinkle the kidneys with parsley and serve with the croutes on one side.

RED-COOKED BEEF

THIS IS BASICALLY A STEW, SLOW-COOKED IN AN EQUAL MIXTURE OF SOY SAUCE, RICE WINE AND GINGER. THIS DISH IS A VERY HOME-STYLE ONE, MORE LIKELY FOUND IN SOMEONE'S KITCHEN THAN ON A RESTAURANT MENU.

500 g (1 lb 2 oz) shin of beef or
   stewing or braising beef, trimmed
3 tablespoons Shaoxing rice wine
3 slices ginger
3 tablespoons dark soy sauce
50 g (2 oz) rock sugar
300 g (10 oz) carrots
1 teaspoon salt

SERVES 4

CUT the beef into 1.5 cm (½ inch) cubes and put in a clay pot or casserole with enough water to cover. Add the rice wine and ginger, bring to the boil, skim off any scum, then simmer, covered, for 35–40 minutes. Add the soy and sugar and simmer for 10–15 minutes.

CUT the carrots into pieces roughly the same size as the beef, add to the saucepan with the salt and cook for 20–25 minutes.

RED-COOKED BEEF

FIVE-SPICE BEEF

THIS IS A DELICIOUS BEEF RECIPE THAT IS VERY SIMPLE TO PREPARE. THE LIQUID IN WHICH THE BEEF HAS BEEN COOKED CAN BE REUSED FOR COOKING OTHER TYPES OF MEAT OR POULTRY, AND IS KNOWN AS LUSHUI ZHI—A 'MASTER SAUCE'.

750 g (1 lb 10 oz) shin of beef or
   stewing or braising beef, trimmed
2 spring onions (scallions), each tied
   in a knot
3 slices ginger, smashed with the
   flat side of a cleaver
4 tablespoons Chinese spirit
   (Mou Tai) or brandy
1.5 litres (6 cups) chicken and meat
   stock (page 565)
1 teaspoon salt
4 tablespoons light soy sauce
3 tablespoons dark soy sauce
1 tablespoon five-spice powder
150 g (5 oz) rock sugar
1 spring onion (scallion), finely
   sliced
1 teaspoon roasted sesame oil

SERVES 8

CUT the beef into two to three long strips and place in a clay pot or casserole with the spring onions, ginger, Chinese spirit and stock. Bring to the boil and skim off any scum. Simmer, covered, for 15–20 minutes.

ADD the salt, soy sauces, five-spice powder and sugar to the beef, return to the boil, then simmer, covered, for 25–30 minutes.

LEAVE the beef in the liquid to cool for 1 hour, then remove, drain, and cool for 3–4 hours. Just before serving, slice thinly across the grain and sprinkle with the spring onion and sesame oil.

Tying the spring onions into knots bruises the flesh and allows more flavour to come out.

Cassoulet can be time-consuming to prepare as the different ingredients are cooked separately and then layered in a deep casserole. Liquid is added up to the top of the beans.

CASSOULET

CASSOULET TAKES ITS NAME FROM THE TRADITIONAL CASSEROLE DISH USED FOR COOKING THIS STEW. IT VARIES REGIONALLY IN THE SOUTH OF FRANCE, WITH THE BEST-KNOWN VERSIONS HAILING FROM CARCASSONNE, TOULOUSE AND CASTELNAUDARY.

400 g (14 oz) dried haricot beans
bouquet garni
1/2 large onion, cut into quarters
2 garlic cloves, crushed
225 g (8 oz) salt pork or unsmoked
  bacon, cut into cubes
15 g (1/2 oz) clarified butter
400 g (14 oz) lamb shoulder
350 g (12 oz) boiling sausages
  (*saucisses à cuire*)
1 celery stalk, sliced
4 pieces duck confit or 4 pieces
  roasted duck
6 large tomatoes
180 g (6 oz) Toulouse sausage
4 slices baguette, made into
  crumbs

SERVES 6

PUT the beans in a bowl and cover with cold water. Soak overnight, then drain and rinse.

PUT the beans in a large saucepan with the bouquet garni, onion, garlic and salt pork. Add 2–3 litres of cold water, bring to the boil and then simmer for 1 hour.

HEAT the clarified butter in a frying pan. Cut the lamb into eight pieces and brown in the butter. Add the lamb, boiling sausage, celery and duck confit to the top of the beans and push into the liquid. Score a cross in the top of each tomato, plunge into boiling water for 20 seconds, then peel the skin away from the cross. Chop the tomatoes finely, discarding the cores, and add to the top of the cassoulet. Push into the liquid and cook for a further hour.

BROWN the Toulouse sausage in the frying pan and add to the top of the cassoulet. Push into the liquid and cook for 30 minutes more. Preheat the oven to 160°C (315°F/Gas 2–3).

DISCARD the bouquet garni. Strain the liquid into a saucepan and boil over moderate heat until reduced by two-thirds. Remove all the meat from the saucepan and slice the sausages and pull the duck meat from the bones. Layer the meat and beans, alternately, in a deep casserole. Pour in the liquid, to come no higher than the top of the beans.

SPRINKLE the cassoulet with the breadcrumbs and bake for 40 minutes. Every 10 minutes, break the breadcrumb crust with the back of a spoon to let a little liquid come through. If the beans look a bit dry, add a little stock or water to the edge of the dish. Serve straight from the casserole.

MOGHUL-STYLE LAMB

FOR THIS DISH, THE LAMB IS MARINATED, PREFERABLY OVERNIGHT, BEFORE IT IS COOKED. THIS ENSURES THAT THE MEAT IS TENDER AND FULL OF FLAVOUR. THE CREAM IS ADDED TO TEMPER THE STRONG COMBINATION OF SPICES.

6 garlic cloves, roughly chopped
4 cm (1½ inch) piece of ginger, roughly chopped
50 g (2 oz) blanched almonds
2 onions, thinly sliced
750 g (1 lb 10 oz) boneless leg or shoulder of lamb, cut into 2.5 cm (1 inch) cubes
2 teaspoons coriander (cilantro) seeds
40 g (1 oz) ghee
7 cardamom pods
5 cloves
1 cinnamon stick
1 teaspoon salt
300 ml (1¼ cups) single cream
½ teaspoon cayenne pepper
½ teaspoon garam masala (page 556)
flaked toasted almonds

SERVES 4

BLEND the garlic, ginger, almonds and 50 g (2 oz) of the onion in a blender or food processor. If you don't have a blender, finely chop them with a knife or grind together in a pestle and mortar. Add a little water if necessary to make a smooth paste, then put in a bowl with the lamb and mix thoroughly to coat the meat. Cover and marinate in the fridge for 2 hours, or overnight.

PLACE a small frying pan over low heat, dry-roast the coriander seeds until aromatic, then grind to a fine powder using a spice grinder or pestle and mortar.

HEAT the ghee in a karhai or casserole. Add the cardamom pods, cloves and cinnamon stick and, after a few seconds, add the remaining onion and fry until it is soft and starting to brown. Transfer the onion to a plate.

FRY the meat and marinade in the pan until the mixture is quite dry and has started to brown a little. Add 150 ml (⅔ cup) hot water to the pan, cover tightly and cook over low heat for 30 minutes, stirring occasionally.

ADD the ground coriander, salt, cream, cayenne pepper and cooked onion to the pan, cover and simmer for another 30 minutes, or until the lamb is tender. Stir occasionally to prevent the lamb from sticking to the pan. Remove the cardamom pods, cloves and cinnamon stick, then stir in the garam masala. Sprinkle with flaked almonds.

The remains of an ancient college built in 1354 in Haus Khas village, Delhi.

VEAL INVOLTINI

INVOLTINI MEANS 'LITTLE BUNDLES' AND IF YOU TRAVEL AROUND ITALY YOU'LL FIND THIS RECIPE IN MANY GUISES. TRADITIONALLY INVOLTINI WERE MADE WITH MEAT OR FISH, STUFFED WITH BREADCRUMBS, PINENUTS AND CURRANTS. YOU COULD ALSO USE TURKEY OR CHICKEN BREAST.

Escalopes of veal are usually pounded with a meat mallet before use, giving a thin tender meat that can be wrapped around fillings and fried quickly. Tie the involtini with kitchen string to prevent them unravelling while you're frying.

8 asparagus spears
4 veal escalopes
4 thin slices mortadella (preferably with pistachio nuts)
4 thin slices Bel Paese
plain flour, seasoned with salt and pepper
3 tablespoons butter
1 tablespoon olive oil
3 tablespoons dry Marsala

SERVES 4

WASH the asparagus and remove the woody ends (hold each spear at both ends and bend it gently—it will snap at its natural breaking point). Blanch the asparagus in boiling salted water for 3 minutes. Drain, reserving 3 tablespoons of the liquid.

PLACE each veal escalope between two sheets of clingfilm and pound with a meat mallet to make a 12 x 18 cm (5 x 7 inch) rectangle. Season lightly with salt and pepper. Trim both the mortadella and cheese slices to just a little smaller than the veal.

COVER each piece of veal with a slice of mortadella, then a slice of cheese. Place an asparagus spear in the centre, running across the shortest width, with the tip slightly overhanging the veal at one end. Place another asparagus spear alongside, but with its tip overhanging the other end. Roll each veal slice up tightly and tie in place at each end with kitchen string. Roll in the seasoned flour to coat.

HEAT 2 tablespoons of the butter with the olive oil in a frying pan. Fry the rolls over low heat for about 10 minutes, turning frequently, until golden and tender. Transfer to a hot serving dish and keep warm.

ADD the Marsala, the reserved asparagus liquid and the remaining butter to the pan and bring quickly to the boil. Simmer for 3–4 minutes, scraping up the bits from the base of the pan. The juices will reduce and darken. Taste for seasoning, then spoon over the veal rolls and serve immediately.

CHAR SIU

CHAR SIU, OR BARBECUE PORK, IS A CANTONESE SPECIALITY THAT CAN BE SEEN HANGING IN CHINESE RESTAURANTS. CHAR SIU MEANS 'SUSPENDED OVER FIRE' AND IS TRADITIONALLY DYED A RED COLOUR.

MARINADE
1 tablespoon rock sugar
1 tablespoon yellow bean sauce
1 tablespoon hoisin sauce
1 tablespoon oyster sauce
1 tablespoon red fermented bean curd
1 tablespoon Chinese spirit (Mou Tai) or brandy
1/2 teaspoon roasted sesame oil

750 g (1 lb 10 oz) centre-cut pork loin, trimmed
2 tablespoons maltose or honey, dissolved with a little water

SERVES 4

TO MAKE the marinade, combine the ingredients. Cut the pork into 4 x 20 cm (1½ x 8 inch) strips, add to the marinade and leave in the fridge for at least 6 hours.

PREHEAT the oven to 220°C (425°F/Gas 7). Put a baking dish filled with 600 ml (2½ cups) boiling water in the bottom of the oven. Drain the pork, reserving the marinade. Put an S-shaped meat hook through one end of each strip and hang from the top rack. Cook for 10–15 minutes, then baste with the marinade. Reduce the heat to 180°C (350°F/Gas 4) and cook for 8–10 minutes. Cool for 2–3 minutes, then brush with the maltose and grill (broil) for 4–5 minutes, turning to give a charred look around the edges.

CUT the meat into slices. Pour 200 ml (¾ cup) liquid from the dish into the marinade. Bring to the boil and cook for 2 minutes. Strain and pour over the pork.

Hanging the char siu to roast above a tray of water creates a steamy atmosphere which helps keep the meat moist. Generally in China, char siu is bought from take-aways as most homes do not have an oven.

SPICY CRISPY PORK

750 g (1 lb 10 oz) belly pork, rind on
1 teaspoon salt
1 teaspoon five-spice powder

DIPPING SAUCE
2 tablespoons light soy sauce
1 tablespoon dark soy sauce
1 tablespoon chilli sauce (optional)

SERVES 6

SCRAPE the pork rind to make sure it is free of any bristles. Dry, then rub with the salt and five-spice powder. Leave uncovered in the fridge for at least 2 hours.

TO MAKE the dipping sauce, combine all of the ingredients.

PREHEAT the oven to 240°C (475°F/Gas 9). Place the pork, skin side up, on a rack in a roasting tin. Roast for 20 minutes, reduce the heat to 200°C (400°F/Gas 6) and cook for 40–45 minutes until crispy. Cut into pieces and serve with the sauce.

SPICY CRISPY PORK

262

VENISON WITH BLACKBERRY SAUCE

60 g (2 oz) clarified butter
12 pickling or pearl onions
150 g (5 oz) blackberries or
blackcurrants
3 tablespoons redcurrant jelly
16 x 50 g (2 oz) venison medallions
60 ml (¼ cup) red wine
410 ml (1⅔ cups) brown stock
½ tablespoon softened butter
½ tablespoon plain flour

SERVES 4

HEAT half the clarified butter in a saucepan. Add the onions, cover with crumpled wet greaseproof paper and a lid. Cook gently for 20–25 minutes, stirring occasionally, until brown and cooked. Put the berries in a saucepan with the redcurrant jelly and 3 tablespoons water. Boil for 5 minutes until the fruit is softened and the liquid syrupy.

SEASON the venison, heat the remaining clarified butter in a frying pan and cook in batches over high heat for 1–2 minutes. Remove the venison and keep warm. Add the wine to the pan and boil for 30 seconds. Add the stock and boil until reduced by half.

MIX together the butter and flour to make a *beurre manié* and whisk into the stock. Boil, stirring, for 2 minutes, then drain the syrup from the fruit into the stock to make a sauce. Stir well, season and serve with the venison and onions. Use the drained fruit as a garnish if you like.

Brown the venison in batches so that it fries without stewing. Drain the syrup from the fruit to add flavour to the sauce.

ROASTED PHEASANT WITH GARLIC AND SHALLOTS

1 x 1 kg (2 lb 3 oz) pheasant
½ teaspoon juniper or allspice
berries, lightly crushed
a few parsley sprigs
30 g (1 oz) butter
6 rashers streaky bacon
6 shallots, unpeeled
6 garlic cloves, unpeeled
1 teaspoon plain flour
100 ml (½ cup) chicken stock

SERVES 2

PREHEAT the oven to 200°C (400°F/Gas 6). Rub the pheasant with salt, pepper and the juniper berries. Fill the cavity with the parsley and butter, tie the legs together and tuck the wing tips under. Place in a small roasting tin and lay the bacon over the pheasant to prevent it drying out. Scatter with the unpeeled shallots and garlic and roast for 20 minutes. Remove the bacon and roast for a further 10 minutes.

REMOVE the shallots, garlic and pheasant from the tin and cut off the pheasant legs. Put the legs back in the tin and cook for another 5 minutes, then remove and keep all the pheasant warm.

TO MAKE the gravy, transfer the roasting tin to the stovetop. Stir in the flour and cook, stirring, for 2 minutes. Add the stock and bring to the boil, whisking constantly. Boil for 2 minutes to thicken slightly, then strain the gravy. Serve the pheasant, shallots and garlic with a little gravy poured over.

ROASTED PHEASANT WITH GARLIC AND SHALLOTS

As with many Thai curries, this one cooks relatively quickly. Keep the meat moving around the wok until you add the liquid.

PANAENG BEEF CURRY

PANAENG CURRY IS A DRY, RICH, THICK CURRY MADE WITH SMALL AMOUNTS OF COCONUT MILK AND A DRY (PANAENG) CURRY PASTE, WHICH HAS RED CHILLIES, LEMON GRASS, GALANGAL AND PEANUTS. IT IS NOT TOO HOT AND HAS A SWEET AND SOUR TASTE. YOU CAN USE ANY TENDER CUT OF BEEF.

2 tablespoons vegetable oil
2 tablespoons dry curry paste
  (page 560) or bought paste
700 g (1 lb 9 oz) beef flank steak,
  sliced into strips
185 ml (¾ cup) coconut milk
  (page 551)
1 tablespoon fish sauce
1 tablespoon palm sugar
3 tablespoons tamarind purée
  (page 554)
2 makrut (kaffir) lime leaves, finely
  sliced, for garnish
½ long red chilli, seeded and finely
  sliced, for garnish
cucumber relish (page 563),
  to serve

SERVES 4

HEAT the oil in a saucepan or wok and stir-fry the curry paste over a medium heat for 2 minutes or until fragrant.

ADD the beef and stir for 5 minutes. Add nearly all of the coconut milk, the fish sauce, palm sugar and tamarind purée and reduce to a low heat. Simmer, uncovered, for 5–7 minutes. Although this is meant to be a dry curry, you can add a little more water during cooking if you feel it is drying out too much. Taste, then adjust the seasoning if necessary.

SPOON the curry into a serving bowl, spoon the last bit of coconut milk over the top and sprinkle with makrut lime leaves and chilli slices. Serve with cucumber relish.

Busy bustling Bangkok.

VITELLO TONNATO

THERE ARE TWO VERSIONS OF THIS NORTH ITALIAN DISH, BOTH FEATURING A SAUCE OF MASHED TUNA AND ANCHOVIES. IN THE OLDER, MILANESE, VERSION THE SAUCE IS THINNED WITH CREAM; THIS RECIPE IS FOR THE PIEMONTESE DISH, WHICH USES MAYONNAISE RATHER THAN CREAM.

1 x 1.25 kg (2 lb 12 oz) boneless
   rolled veal roast
500 ml (2 cups) dry white wine
500 ml (2 cups) chicken stock
2 garlic cloves
1 onion, quartered
1 carrot, roughly chopped
1 celery stalk, roughly chopped
2 bay leaves
3 cloves
10 peppercorns

SAUCE
95 g (3 oz) tin tuna in olive oil
15 g (½ oz) anchovy fillets
2 egg yolks
2 tablespoons lemon juice
125 ml (½ cup) olive oil

parsley sprigs
capers
thin lemon slices

SERVES 4

PUT the veal, wine, stock, garlic, onion, carrot, celery, bay leaves, cloves and peppercorns in a stockpot or very large saucepan. Add enough water to come two-thirds of the way up the veal and bring to the boil. Reduce the heat, cover the saucepan and simmer for 1¼ hours, or until tender. Leave to cool for 30 minutes, then remove the veal from the pan and strain the stock. Pour the stock into a saucepan and boil rapidly until reduced to about 250 ml (1 cup).

TO MAKE the sauce, purée the tuna and its oil with the anchovy fillets in a blender or small food processor. Add the egg yolks and 1 tablespoon of the lemon juice and process until smooth. With the motor running, slowly pour in the oil. Gradually add the reduced stock until the sauce has the consistency of a thin mayonnaise. (If you are doing this by hand, chop the tuna and anchovy finely, mix in the egg yolks and lemon juice and then whisk in the oil and stock.) Blend in the remaining lemon juice and season well.

TO SERVE, thinly slice the cold veal and arrange in overlapping slices down the centre of a serving platter. Spoon the sauce over the top and garnish with the parsley, capers and lemon slices.

Capers are usually available preserved in vinegar (these are best rinsed before use) but you will find that those preserved in salt are of a superior quality. Rinse well and pat dry before using.

The veal can be cooling in the stock while you make the sauce.

Harvesting bok choy in Liugan.

LION'S HEAD MEATBALLS

THIS DISH IS SO NAMED BECAUSE THE LARGE MEATBALLS ARE SAID TO LOOK LIKE LION'S HEADS SURROUNDED BY A MANE OF BOK CHOY. ORIGINALLY THE MEATBALLS TENDED TO BE MADE FROM PORK AND PORK FAT AND WERE COARSER IN TEXTURE.

450 g (1 lb) minced pork
1 egg white
4 spring onions (scallions), finely
    chopped
1 tablespoon Shaoxing rice wine
1 teaspoon grated ginger
1 tablespoon light soy sauce
2 teaspoons sugar
1 teaspoon roasted sesame oil
300 g (10 oz) bok choy
1 tablespoon cornflour
oil for frying
500 ml (2 cups) chicken and meat
    stock (page 565)

SERVES 4

PUT the pork and egg white in a food processor and process briefly until you have a fluffy mixture, or mash the pork mince in a large bowl and gradually stir in the egg white, beating the mixture well until it is fluffy. Add the spring onion, rice wine, ginger, soy sauce, sugar and sesame oil, season with salt and white pepper, and process or beat again briefly. Fry a small portion of the mixture and taste it, reseasoning if necessary. Divide the mixture into walnut-size balls.

SEPARATE the boy choy leaves and place in the bottom of a clay pot or casserole.

DUST the meatballs with cornflour. Heat a wok over high heat, add 1 cm (½ inch) oil and heat until very hot. Cook the meatballs in batches until they are browned all over. Drain well and add to the clay pot in an even layer. Pour off the oil and wipe out the wok.

REHEAT the wok over high heat until very hot, add the chicken stock and heat until it is boiling. Pour over the meatballs. Cover and bring very slowly to the boil. Simmer gently with the lid slightly open for 1½ hours, or until the meatballs are very tender. Serve the meatballs in the dish they were cooked in.

Roll the mixture into balls using the palms of your hands, then dust with cornflour to prevent them from sticking when you cook them.

271

ROAST VEAL STUFFED WITH HAM AND SPINACH

250 g (9 oz) spinach leaves
2 garlic cloves, crushed
2 tablespoons finely chopped
  parsley
2 teaspoons Dijon mustard
100 g (3 oz) ham on the bone,
  diced
finely grated zest of 1 lemon
1 x 600 g (1 lb 5 oz) piece
  boneless veal loin or fillet, beaten
  with a meat mallet to measure
  30 x 15 cm (12 x 6 inch)
  (ask your butcher to do this)
4 rashers streaky bacon
2 tablespoons olive oil
50 g (2 oz) butter
16 baby carrots
8 small potatoes, unpeeled
8 shallots
200 ml (¾ cup) dry (*Sercial*)
  Madeira

SERVES 4

PREHEAT the oven to 170°C (325°F/Gas 3). Wash the spinach and put in a large saucepan with just the water clinging to the leaves. Cover the pan and steam the spinach for 2 minutes or until just wilted. Drain, cool and squeeze dry with your hands. Chop and mix with the garlic, parsley, mustard, ham and lemon zest. Season well.

SPREAD the spinach filling over the centre of the piece of veal. Starting from one of the shorter sides, roll up like a swiss roll. Wrap the rashers of streaky bacon over the meat and season well. Tie with string several times along the roll to secure the bacon and make sure the roll doesn't unravel.

HEAT the olive oil and half the butter in a large frying pan and add the carrots, potatoes and shallots. Briefly brown the vegetables and then tip into a roasting tin. Brown the veal parcel on all sides, then place on top of the vegetables. Add 4 tablespoons of the Madeira to the frying pan and boil, stirring, for 30 seconds to deglaze the pan. Pour over the veal.

ROAST the meat for 30 minutes, then cover the top with foil to prevent overbrowning. Roast for another 45–60 minutes or until the juices run clear when you pierce the thickest part of the meat with a skewer. Wrap the meat in foil and leave to rest. Test the vegetables and return to the oven for a while if they're not yet tender. Remove them from the tin.

PLACE the roasting tin over moderate heat and add the rest of the Madeira. Allow it to bubble, then add the rest of the butter and season the sauce to taste. Slice the veal thickly and arrange the slices of meat on top of the vegetables. Pour over some of the Madeira sauce and serve the rest separately in a jug.

Spread the spinach filling over the piece of veal and then roll up like a swiss roll. Tie with string to keep the bacon rashers in place and prevent the veal unrolling.

BARBECUED PORK SPARE RIBS

2–3 garlic cloves, chopped

1 tablespoon chopped coriander (cilantro) roots or ground coriander

6 tablespoons palm sugar

7 tablespoons plum sauce or tomato ketchup

2 tablespoons light soy sauce

2 tablespoons oyster sauce

1 teaspoon ground pepper

½ teaspoon ground star anise (optional)

900 g (2 lb) pork spare ribs, chopped into 13–15 cm (5–6 inch) long pieces (baby back, if possible—ask your butcher to prepare it)

SERVES 4

USING a pestle and mortar or a small blender, pound or blend the garlic and coriander roots into a paste. In a large bowl, combine all the ingredients and rub the marinade all over the ribs with your fingers. Cover with plastic wrap and marinate in the refrigerator for at least 3 hours, or overnight.

PREHEAT the oven to 180°C/350°F/Gas 4 or heat a barbecue or grill (broiler). If cooking in the oven, place the ribs with all the marinade in a baking dish. Bake for 45–60 minutes, basting several times during cooking. If barbecuing, put the ribs on the grill, cover and cook for 45 minutes, turning and basting a couple of times. If the ribs do not go sufficiently brown, grill (broil) them for 5 minutes on each side until well browned and slightly charred. If using a grill, line the grill tray with foil. Cook the pork, turning several times and brushing frequently with the remaining sauce, until the meat is cooked through and slightly charred.

DEEP-FRIED PORK SPARE RIBS

5 coriander (cilantro) roots, chopped

3 garlic cloves, finely chopped

1 tablespoon fish sauce

1½ tablespoons oyster sauce

½ teaspoon ground white pepper

900 g (2 lb) pork spare ribs, chopped into 4–5 cm (1½–2 inch) long pieces (baby back, if possible—ask your butcher to prepare it)

vegetable oil, for deep-frying

sweet chilli sauce (page 562), to serve

SERVES 4

USING a pestle and mortar or a small blender, pound or blend the coriander roots and garlic into a paste. In a large bowl, combine the coriander paste, fish sauce, oyster sauce and ground pepper. Rub the marinade into the pork ribs using your fingertips, then cover and marinate in the refrigerator for at least 3 hours, or overnight.

HEAT 6 cm (2½ inches) oil in a wok or deep frying pan over a medium heat. When the oil seems hot, drop a small piece of garlic into it. If it sizzles immediately, the oil is ready. It is important not to have the oil too hot or the spare ribs will burn. Deep-fry half the spare ribs at a time for 15–20 minutes or until golden brown and cooked. Drain on paper towels. Serve with sweet chilli sauce.

DEEP-FRIED PORK SPARE RIBS

BARBECUED PORK SPARE RIBS

If you have time, leave the beef to marinate overnight to deepen the flavours of this dish.

BOEUF BOURGUIGNON

ALMOST EVERY REGION OF FRANCE HAS ITS OWN STYLE OF BEEF STEW, BUT BURGUNDY'S VERSION IS THE MOST WELL KNOWN. IF YOU CAN, MAKE IT A DAY IN ADVANCE TO LET THE FLAVOURS DEVELOP. SERVE WITH A SALAD OF ENDIVE, CHICORY AND WATERCRESS AND BREAD OR NEW POTATOES.

1.5 kg (3 lb 5 oz) beef blade or
   chuck steak
750 ml (3 cups) red wine (preferably
   Burgundy)
3 garlic cloves, crushed
bouquet garni
70 g (2½ oz) butter
1 onion, chopped
1 carrot, chopped
2 tablespoons plain flour
200 g (7 oz) bacon, cut into short
   strips
300 g (10 oz) shallots, peeled but
   left whole
200 g (7 oz) small button
   mushrooms

SERVES 6

CUT the meat into 4 cm (1½ inch) cubes and trim away any excess fat. Put the meat, wine, garlic and bouquet garni in a large bowl, cover with clingfilm and leave in the fridge for at least 3 hours and preferably overnight.

PREHEAT the oven to 160°C (315°F/Gas 2–3). Drain the meat, reserving the marinade and bouquet garni. Dry the meat on paper towels. Heat 30 g (1 oz) of the butter in a large casserole dish. Add the onion, carrot and bouquet garni and cook over low heat, stirring occasionally, for 10 minutes. Remove from the heat.

HEAT 20 g (⅔ oz) of the butter in a large frying pan over high heat. Fry the meat in batches for about 5 minutes or until well browned. Add to the casserole dish.

POUR the reserved marinade into the frying pan and boil, stirring, for 30 seconds to deglaze the pan. Remove from the heat. Return the casserole to high heat and sprinkle the meat and vegetables with the flour. Cook, stirring constantly, until the meat is well coated with the flour. Pour in the marinade and stir well. Bring to the boil, stirring constantly, then cover and cook in the oven for 2 hours.

HEAT the remaining butter in the clean frying pan and cook the bacon and shallots, stirring, for 8–10 minutes or until the shallots are softened but not browned. Add the mushrooms and cook, stirring occasionally, for 2–3 minutes or until browned. Drain on paper towels. Add the shallots, bacon and mushrooms to the casserole.

COVER the casserole and return to the oven for 30 minutes, or until the meat is soft and tender. Discard the bouquet garni. Season and skim any fat from the surface before serving.

BEEF WITH THAI SWEET BASIL LEAVES

THAI SWEET BASIL IS ONE OF THE TROPICAL HERBS WITH A DISTINCTIVE FLAVOUR AND PERFUME THAT INSTANTLY EVOKES THAI CUISINE. NO OTHER HERB WILL DO AS A SUBSTITUTE FOR THIS RECIPE. YOUR WOK SHOULD BE VERY HOT AND THE DISH SHOULD TAKE NO MORE THAN 7 OR 8 MINUTES TO COOK.

1 tablespoon fish sauce
3 tablespoons oyster sauce
4 tablespoons vegetable or
   chicken stock, or water
½ teaspoon sugar
2 tablespoons vegetable oil
4 garlic cloves, finely chopped
3 bird's eye chillies, lightly crushed
   with the side of a cleaver
500 g (1 lb 2 oz) tender rump or
   fillet steak, finely sliced
1 medium onion, cut into thin
   wedges
2 handfuls of Thai sweet basil
   leaves

SERVES 4

MIX the fish sauce, oyster sauce, stock and sugar in a small bowl.

HEAT the oil in the wok or frying pan and stir-fry half the garlic over a medium heat until light brown. Add half the crushed chillies and half the meat and stir-fry over a high heat for 2–3 minutes or until the meat is cooked. Remove from the wok and repeat with the remaining garlic, chillies and meat. Return all the meat to the wok.

ADD the onion and the fish sauce mixture and stir-fry for another minute.

ADD the basil leaves and stir-fry until the basil begins to wilt. Taste, then adjust the seasoning if necessary. Spoon onto a serving plate.

Warorot market.

VEAL SALTIMBOCCA

8 small veal escalopes
8 slices prosciutto
8 sage leaves
2 tablespoons olive oil
60 g (2 oz) butter
185 ml (⅔ cup) dry white wine or
    dry Marsala

SERVES 4

PLACE the veal between two sheets of clingfilm and pound with a meat mallet until an even thickness. Season lightly. Cut the prosciutto slices to the same size as the veal. Cover each piece of veal with a slice of prosciutto and place a sage leaf on top. Secure in place with a cocktail stick.

HEAT the oil and half the butter in a large frying pan. Add the veal in batches and fry, prosciutto up, over moderately high heat for 3–4 minutes, or until the veal is just cooked through. Transfer each batch to a hot plate as it is done.

POUR off the oil from the pan and add the wine. Cook over high heat until reduced by half, scraping up the bits from the bottom of the pan. Add the remaining butter and, when it has melted, season. Spoon over the veal to serve.

The cocktail stick will hold together the sage, prosciutto and veal. Take it out just before serving.

VEAL ALLA MILANESE

8 veal chops
2 eggs
60 g (2 oz) fine dried breadcrumbs
3 tablespoons grated Parmesan
3 tablespoons butter
1 tablespoon oil
4 lemon wedges dipped in finely
    chopped parsley

SERVES 4

CUT all the fat from the veal chops and trim the lower rib bone until it is clean of all fat and flesh. Place each chop between two sheets of clingfilm and pound the flesh with a meat mallet until it is half its original thickness.

LIGHTLY BEAT the eggs with salt and pepper and pour into a dish. Combine the breadcrumbs and Parmesan and place in another dish. Dip each chop into the egg, coating it on both sides. Shake off the excess egg, then coat the chop with the breadcrumb mix, pressing each side firmly into the crumbs. Place all the chops on a plate and chill for 30 minutes.

HEAT the butter and oil in a large frying pan. As soon as the butter stops foaming, add the chops and fry gently for 4 minutes on each side, until the breadcrumbs are deep golden. Serve immediately with the lemon wedges.

VEAL ALLA MILANESE

PORK CHOPS WITH BRAISED RED CABBAGE

Braise the red cabbage slowly to bring out the sweetness.

BRAISED RED CABBAGE
30 g (1 oz) clarified butter
1 onion, finely chopped
1 garlic clove, crushed
1 small red cabbage, shredded
1 dessert apple, peeled, cored and
    finely sliced
75 ml (¼ cup) red wine
1 tablespoon red wine vinegar
¼ teaspoon ground cloves
1 tablespoon finely chopped sage

15 g (½ oz) clarified butter
4 x 200 g (7 oz) pork chops,
    trimmed
75 ml (¼ cup) white wine
400 ml (1½ cups) chicken stock
3 tablespoons double cream
1½ tablespoons Dijon mustard
4 sage leaves

SERVES 4

TO BRAISE the cabbage, put the clarified butter in a large saucepan, add the onion and garlic and cook until softened but not browned. Add the cabbage, apple, wine, vinegar, cloves and sage and season with salt and pepper. Cover the pan and cook for 30 minutes over very low heat. Uncover the pan and cook, stirring, for a further 5 minutes to evaporate any liquid.

MEANWHILE, heat the clarified butter in a frying pan, season the chops and brown well on both sides. Add the wine and stock, cover and simmer for 20 minutes, or until the pork is tender.

REMOVE the chops from the frying pan and strain the liquid. Return the liquid to the pan, bring to the boil and cook until reduced by two-thirds. Add the cream and mustard and stir over very low heat without allowing to boil, until the sauce has thickened slightly. Pour over the pork chops and garnish with sage. Serve with the red cabbage.

PORK CHOPS WITH CALVADOS

60 g (2 oz) butter
2 dessert apples, cored, each cut
    into 8 wedges
½ teaspoon sugar
1½ tablespoons oil
4 x 200 g (7 oz) pork chops,
    trimmed
2 tablespoons Calvados
2 shallots, finely chopped
250 ml (1 cup) dry cider
125 ml (½ cup) chicken stock
150 ml (⅔ cup) double cream

SERVES 4

MELT half the butter in a frying pan, add the apple and sprinkle with the sugar. Cook over low heat, turning occasionally, until tender and glazed.

HEAT the oil in a frying pan and sauté the pork chops until cooked, turning once. Pour the excess fat from the pan, add the Calvados and flambé by lighting the pan with your gas flame or a match (stand well back when you do this and keep a pan lid handy for emergencies). Transfer the pork to a plate and keep warm.

ADD the remaining butter to the pan and cook the shallots until soft but not brown. Add the cider, stock and cream and bring to the boil. Reduce the heat and simmer for 15 minutes, or until reduced enough to coat the back of a spoon.

SEASON the sauce, add the pork and simmer for 3 minutes to heat through. Serve with the apple.

PORK CHOPS WITH
CALVADOS

KOFTA IN TOMATO AND YOGHURT SAUCE

EVERY NATION SEEMS TO HAVE A VERSION OF KOFTA, RANGING FROM MEATBALLS AND CROQUETTES TO RISSOLES AND DUMPLINGS. THIS RECIPE IS THE NORTH INDIAN WAY OF PREPARING THEM. THE RICH TOMATO AND YOGHURT SAUCE IS PERFECT WHEN SERVED WITH NAAN BREAD.

Cardamom pods are harvested by hand. They grow on small stalks at the base of the plant.

KOFTA

1 onion

500 g (1 lb 2 oz) minced lamb

2 cm (¾ inch) piece of ginger, grated

3 garlic cloves, finely chopped

2 green chillies, seeded and finely chopped

½ teaspoon salt

1 egg

TOMATO AND YOGHURT SAUCE

2 teaspoons coriander (cilantro) seeds

2 teaspoons cumin seeds

3 tablespoons oil

10 cm (4 inch) piece of cinnamon stick

6 cloves

6 cardamom pods

1 onion, finely chopped

½ teaspoon ground turmeric

1 teaspoon paprika

1 teaspoon garam masala (page 556)

½ teaspoon salt

200 g (7 oz) tin chopped tomatoes

150 ml (⅔ cup) thick natural yoghurt (page 554)

coriander (cilantro) leaves

SERVES 4

TO MAKE the kofta, grate the onion, put it in a sieve and use a spoon to press out as much of the liquid as possible. Put it in a bowl and combine with the lamb, ginger, garlic, green chilli, salt and the egg. Mix thoroughly, then divide into 20 equal portions and shape each into a ball. Cover with clingfilm and refrigerate for about 2 hours. Alternatively, the meatballs can be put in the freezer while the sauce is being prepared, then they will be sufficiently firm enough to stay in shape when they are added to the sauce.

TO MAKE the sauce, place a small frying pan over low heat and dry-roast the coriander seeds until aromatic. Remove, then dry-roast the cumin seeds. Grind the roasted mixture to a fine powder using a spice grinder or pestle and mortar.

HEAT the oil in a karhai or heavy-based frying pan over low heat. Add the cinnamon stick, cloves, cardamom pods and onion and fry until the onion is golden. Add all the ground spices and the salt and fry for about 30 seconds. Stir in the tomato, then remove from the heat and slowly stir in the yoghurt. Return the pan to the heat, slide in the chilled meatballs and bring to the boil. Simmer, uncovered, for 1 hour, over very low heat. It may be necessary to shake the pan from time to time to prevent the meatballs from sticking. If during cooking the sauce dries out, add 125 ml (½ cup) water as required and continue to cook for the full hour. Remove any whole spices before serving and serve garnished with coriander leaves.

LAMB STUFFED WITH COUSCOUS AND ALMONDS

THE ALMONDS GIVE THIS STUFFING A LOVELY CRUNCHY TEXTURE. WHEN YOU BUY THE MEAT, BE SURE TO TELL THE BUTCHER YOU ARE INTENDING TO STUFF THE LAMB AND YOU WILL NEED THE HOLE IN THE MEAT TO BE FAIRLY LARGE. SERVE WITH BOULANGÈRE POTATOES.

80 ml (⅓ cup) olive oil
1 small red capsicum (pepper)
1 small yellow capsicum (pepper)
35 g (1 oz) whole blanched
  almonds
1 small onion, chopped
4 garlic cloves
100 g (3 oz) eggplant, diced
400 g (14 oz) tin chopped tomatoes
pinch of sugar
1 tablespoon thyme leaves
2 teaspoons capers, rinsed and
  squeezed dry
8 black olives, pitted and finely
  chopped
50 g (2 oz) couscous
1 x 1.5 kg (3 lb 5 oz) tunnel-boned
  leg of lamb
½ small onion

GRAVY
1 tablespoon plain flour
1 teaspoon tomato purée
275 ml (1 cup) brown stock
100 ml (⅓ cup) red wine

SERVES 6

PREHEAT the oven to 200°C (400°F/Gas 6). Rub 1 tablespoon of oil over the capsicums and roast for 40–45 minutes, or until blackened. Cool, then peel and cut into long thin strips.

LIGHTLY TOAST the almonds in a dry frying pan, then chop. Heat 1 tablespoon of oil in the pan and cook the onion until softened. Crush 2 garlic cloves, add to the onion and cook for 5 minutes. Add 2 tablespoons of oil and the eggplant and cook for 10 minutes. Add the tomato and sugar and simmer until fairly dry. Remove from the heat and mix in the thyme, capers and olives. Cool.

POUR 100 ml (⅓ cup) boiling water onto the couscous. Leave for 5 minutes, then fluff the grains with a fork. Add the couscous, capsicums and almonds to the eggplant mixture and season well.

INCREASE the oven to 230°C (450°F/Gas 8). Push as much stuffing as you can into the cavity of the lamb. (Put any leftover stuffing in an ovenproof dish.) Fold the meat over the stuffing at each end and secure with skewers. Put the remaining cloves of garlic and the half onion in a roasting tin and place the lamb on top. Roast for 30 minutes, then reduce the oven to 180°C (350°F/Gas 4) and cook for 1½ hours (cover with foil if overbrowning). Bake any extra stuffing for the last 20 minutes.

TO MAKE the gravy, remove the meat from the tin, cover and leave to rest. Strain off all but 2 tablespoons of the fat from the tin, then place over moderate heat. Stir in the flour and tomato purée and gradually add the stock, stirring. Add the wine slowly, stirring until the gravy reaches the consistency you like. Season well. Slice the meat and serve with the gravy and any extra stuffing.

The couscous and almond filling should be fairly dry. Pack as much as you can into the lamb and cook the rest separately.

PORK BRAISED IN MILK

ASK YOUR BUTCHER TO CHINE AND SKIN THE PORK LOIN (CHINING MEANS REMOVING THE BACKBONE FROM THE RACK OF RIBS SO THAT YOU CAN CARVE BETWEEN THE RIBS). THE MILK AND LEMON SAUCE WILL APPEAR LUMPY AND CURDLED, BUT TASTES DELICIOUS—YOU CAN STRAIN IT IF YOU LIKE.

1 x 2.25 kg (5 lb) pork loin, chined and skinned
50 ml (¼ cup) olive oil
4 garlic cloves, cut in half lengthways
15 g (½ oz) sage or rosemary leaves
1 litre (4 cups) milk
grated zest of 2 lemons
juice of 1 lemon

SERVES 6

PREHEAT the oven to 200°C (400°F/Gas 6). Prepare the pork by trimming the fat to leave just a thin layer. The bone and fat keeps the pork moist.

HEAT the olive oil in a large roasting tin. Add the pork and brown the meat on all sides. Remove the pork and pour away the fat from the roasting tin. Add the garlic and sage to the tin and place the pork on top of them. Season with salt and pepper and pour the milk over the pork. Return to the heat and bring just to the boil. Remove the tin from the heat again, add the lemon zest and drizzle with the lemon juice.

TRANSFER to the oven and roast for about 20 minutes. Reduce the temperature to 150°C (300°F/Gas 2) and cook for a further 1–1¼ hours, depending on the thickness of the meat. If necessary, add a little more milk every so often, to keep the meat roasting in liquid. Baste the meat with the juices every 30 minutes. Do not cover, so that the juices reduce and the fat on the pork becomes crisp.

TO TEST if the pork is cooked, poke a skewer into the middle of the meat, count to ten and pull it out. Touch it on the inside of your wrist and, if it feels hot, the meat is cooked through. Leave the meat to rest for 10 minutes before carving.

STRAIN the sauce if you like (you don't need to, but it may look curdled) and serve with the meat. Delicious with braised fennel, cavolo nero or roasted vegetables.

Putting the garlic and sage in the tin and laying the pork on top makes a rack for the meat to prevent it boiling in its own juices instead of roasting. Pour the milk over the pork and roast uncovered so the skin crisps.

VENISON CASSEROLE

THIS FRENCH WINTER CASSEROLE IS SERVED UP DURING THE HUNTING SEASON IN POPULAR GAME AREAS SUCH AS THE ARDENNES, AUVERGNE AND ALSACE. VENISON BENEFITS FROM BEING MARINATED BEFORE COOKING, OTHERWISE IT CAN BE A LITTLE TOUGH.

The easiest way to mix the venison with the marinade is to toss together with your hands.

MARINADE
1/2 onion
4 cloves
8 juniper berries, crushed
8 black peppercorns, crushed
250 ml (1 cup) red wine
1 carrot, roughly chopped
1/2 celery stalk
2 bay leaves
2 garlic cloves
2 pieces lemon zest
5 rosemary sprigs

1 kg (2 lb 3 oz) venison, cubed
30 g (1 oz) plain flour
1 tablespoon vegetable oil
15 g (1/2 oz) clarified butter
8 shallots
500 ml (2 cups) brown stock
2 tablespoons redcurrant jelly
rosemary sprigs

SERVES 4

TO MAKE the marinade, cut the half onion into four pieces and stud each one with a clove. Mix together in a large bowl with the rest of the marinade ingredients. Add the venison, toss well and leave overnight in the fridge to marinate.

LIFT the venison out of the marinade (reserving the marinade), drain and pat dry with paper towels. Season the flour and use to coat the venison (the cleanest way to do this is to put the flour and venison in a plastic bag and toss well).

PREHEAT the oven to 160°C (315°F/Gas 2–3). Heat the oil and clarified butter in a large casserole dish, brown the shallots and then remove from the dish. Brown the venison in the oil and butter, then remove from the casserole.

STRAIN the marinade liquid through a sieve into the casserole and boil, stirring, for 30 seconds to deglaze. Pour in the stock and bring to the boil.

TIP the remaining marinade ingredients out of the sieve onto a piece of muslin and tie up in a parcel to make a bouquet garni. Add to the casserole with the venison. Bring the liquid to simmering point, then put the casserole in the oven. Cook for 45 minutes and then add the shallots. Cook for a further 1 hour.

DISCARD the bouquet garni, remove the venison and shallots from the cooking liquid and keep warm. Add the redcurrant jelly to the liquid and boil on the stovetop for 4–5 minutes to reduce by half. Strain the sauce and pour over the venison. Serve garnished with sprigs of rosemary.

MONGOLIAN HOTPOT

THE HOTPOT WAS INTRODUCED TO NORTHERN CHINA BY THE MONGOLIANS, BUT IT SOON BECAME SO POPULAR THAT REGIONAL VARIATIONS EVOLVED. TRADITIONALLY LAMB OR BEEF IS USED, AS IN THIS SLIGHTLY ADAPTED VERSION OF THE NORTHERN CLASSIC.

The Great Wall of China.

A hotpot restaurant in Yunnan.

350 g (12 oz) rump or sirloin steak, trimmed
1 tablespoon light soy sauce
80 ml (1/3 cup) Shaoxing rice wine
1/2 teaspoon roasted sesame oil
250 g (9 oz) Chinese cabbage, stems removed and leaves cut into 5 cm (2 inch) squares
1 tablespoon oil
2 garlic cloves, smashed with the flat side of a cleaver
750 ml (3 cups) chicken stock (page 565)
1/2 teaspoon salt
30 g (1 oz) bean thread noodles
225 g (8 oz) Chinese mushrooms (shiitake) or button mushrooms
180 g (6 oz) baby spinach

DIPPING SAUCE
2 tablespoons light soy sauce
1 tablespoon Shaoxing rice wine
1 teaspoon Chinese black rice vinegar
1 teaspoon sugar
1/2 teaspoon chilli sauce or dried chilli flakes (optional)
1/2 spring onion (scallion), finely chopped
1 teaspoon finely chopped ginger
1 garlic clove, finely chopped

SERVES 6

CUT the beef across the grain into paper-thin slices. Place in a bowl and add the soy sauce, 1 tablespoon of the rice wine and the sesame oil, toss lightly, and arrange the slices on a platter.

SEPARATE the hard cabbage pieces from the leafy ones. Heat a wok over high heat, add the oil and heat until very hot. Stir-fry the hard cabbage pieces and garlic for several minutes, adding 1 tablespoon of water. Add the leafy cabbage pieces and stir-fry for several minutes. Add the remaining rice wine, chicken stock and salt, and bring to the boil. Reduce the heat and simmer for 20 minutes.

SOAK the bean thread noodles in hot water for 10 minutes, then drain and cut into 15 cm (6 inch) lengths. Arrange the mushrooms, spinach and noodles on several platters and place on a table where a heated Mongolian hotpot has been set up. (If you do not have a Mongolian hotpot, use a pot and a hot plate, or an electric frying pan or an electric wok.)

COMBINE the dipping sauce ingredients and divide among six bowls. Put a bowl of dipping sauce at each diner's place.

POUR the cabbage soup mixture into the hotpot and bring to the boil. To eat, each diner takes a slice of meat, dips it into the hot stock until the meat is cooked, then dips the meat into the dipping sauce, and eats. The mushrooms, noodles and spinach are cooked in the same way and dipped in the sauce before eating. Supply small wire strainers to cook the noodles so they stay together. The mushrooms and noodles should cook for 5–6 minutes, but the spinach should only take about 1 minute. Once all the ingredients have been eaten, the soup is eaten.

OSSO BUCO ALLA MILANESE

OSSO BUCO IS A MILANESE DISH AND TRADITIONALLY TOMATOES ARE NOT USED IN THE COOKING OF NORTHERN ITALY. THE ABSENCE OF TOMATO THE MORE DELICATE FLAVOUR OF THE GREMOLATA TO FEATURE IN THIS CLASSIC OSSO BUCO. SERVE WITH *RISOTTO ALLA MILANESE* (PAGE 386).

12 pieces veal shank, about 4 cm
(1½ inches) thick
plain flour, seasoned with salt and
pepper
60 ml (¼ cup) olive oil
60 g (2 oz) butter
1 garlic clove
250 ml (1 cup) dry white wine
1 bay leaf or lemon leaf
pinch of allspice
pinch of ground cinnamon

GREMOLATA
2 teaspoons grated lemon rind
6 tablespoons finely chopped
parsley
1 garlic clove, finely chopped

thin lemon wedges

SERVES 4

TIE each piece of veal shank around its girth to secure the flesh, then dust with the seasoned flour. Heat the oil, butter and garlic in a large heavy saucepan big enough to hold the shanks in a single layer. Put the shanks in the pan and cook for 12–15 minutes until well browned. Arrange the shanks, standing them up in a single layer, pour in the wine and add the bay leaf, allspice and cinnamon. Cover the saucepan.

COOK at a low simmer for 15 minutes, then add 125 ml (½ cup) warm water. Continue cooking, covered, for about 45 minutes to 1 hour (the timing will depend on the age of the veal) until the meat is tender and you can cut it with a fork. Check the volume of liquid once or twice and add more warm water as needed. Transfer the veal to a plate and keep warm. Discard the garlic clove and bay leaf.

TO MAKE the gremolata, mix together the lemon rind, parsley and garlic. Increase the heat under the saucepan and stir for 1–2 minutes until the sauce is thick, scraping up any bits off the bottom of the saucepan as you stir. Stir in the gremolata. Season with salt and pepper if necessary and return the veal to the sauce. Heat through, then serve with the lemon wedges.

The pan for osso buco must be large enough to fit the shank pieces in a single layer so that they cook through evenly.

A greengrocer at Saint-Rèmy.

NAVARIN A LA PRINTANIÈRE

NAVARIN A LA PRINTANIÈRE IS TRADITIONALLY MADE TO WELCOME SPRING AND THE NEW CROP OF YOUNG VEGETABLES. NAVARINS, OR STEWS, CAN ALSO BE MADE ALL YEAR ROUND, USING OLDER WINTER ROOT VEGETABLES SUCH AS POTATOES, CARROTS AND TURNIPS.

1 kg (2 lb 3 oz) lean lamb shoulder
30 g (1 oz) butter
1 onion, chopped
1 garlic clove, crushed
1 tablespoon plain flour
500 ml (2 cups) brown stock
bouquet garni
18 baby carrots
8 large-bulb spring onions
   (scallions)
200 g (7 oz) baby turnips
175 g (6 oz) small potatoes
150 g (5 oz) peas, fresh or frozen

SERVES 6

TRIM the lamb of any fat and sinew and then cut it into bite-sized pieces. Heat the butter over high heat in a large casserole. Brown the lamb in two or three batches, then remove from the casserole.

ADD the onion to the casserole and cook, stirring occasionally, over moderate heat for 3 minutes or until softened but not browned. Add the garlic and cook for a further minute or until aromatic.

RETURN the meat and any juices to the casserole and sprinkle with the flour. Stir over high heat until the meat is well coated and the liquid is bubbling, then gradually stir in the stock. Add the bouquet garni and bring to the boil. Reduce the heat to low, cover the casserole and cook for 1¼ hours.

TRIM the carrots, leaving a little bit of green stalk, and do the same with the spring onions and baby turnips. Cut the potatoes in half if they are large.

ADD the vegetables to the casserole dish, bring to the boil and simmer, covered, for 15 minutes or until the vegetables are tender. (If you are using frozen peas, add them right at the end so they just heat through.) Season with plenty of salt and pepper before serving.

Brown the lamb in a couple of batches so that you don't lower the temperature by overcrowding. Once all the meat is browned and coated with flour, slowly stir in the stock.

A meat stall in an outdoor market in Sichuan.

Chinese spirits are sold in fancy packaging. The Wuliangye shown here is made from five grains: sorghum, corn, wheat and two kinds of rice.

SPARERIBS WITH SWEET-AND-SOUR SAUCE

THIS DELICIOUS DISH IS CANTONESE IN ORIGIN. THE SAUCE SHOULD BE BRIGHT AND TRANSLUCENT, THE MEAT TENDER AND SUCCULENT, AND THE FLAVOUR NEITHER TOO SWEET NOR TOO SOUR. IF YOU PREFER YOU CAN USE A BONELESS CUT OF PORK SUCH AS LOIN.

500 g (1 lb 2 oz) Chinese-style pork spareribs
1/4 teaspoon salt
1/4 teaspoon freshly ground black pepper
1 teaspoon sugar
1 tablespoon Chinese spirit (Mou Tai) or brandy
1 egg yolk, beaten
1 tablespoon cornflour
oil for deep-frying

SAUCE
1 tablespoon oil
1 small green capsicum (pepper), shredded
3 tablespoons sugar
2 tablespoons clear rice vinegar
1 tablespoon light soy sauce
1 tablespoon tomato purée
1/4 teaspoon roasted sesame oil
50 ml (1/4 cup) chicken and meat stock (page 565)
2 teaspoons cornflour

SERVES 4

ASK the butcher to cut the slab of spareribs crosswise into thirds that measure 4–5 cm (1½–2 inches) in length, or use a cleaver to do so yourself. Cut the ribs between the bones to separate them. Put the pieces in a bowl with the salt, pepper, sugar and Chinese spirit. Marinate in the fridge for at least 35 minutes, turning occasionally.

MEANWHILE, blend the egg yolk with the cornflour and enough water to make a thin batter. Remove the spareribs from the marinade and coat them with the batter.

FILL a wok one quarter full of oil. Heat the oil to 180°C (350°F), or until a piece of bread fries golden brown in 15 seconds when dropped in the oil. Fry the spareribs in batches for 5 minutes until they are crisp and golden, stirring to separate them, then remove and drain. Reheat the oil and fry the spareribs again for 1 minute to darken their colour. Remove and drain well on crumpled paper towels. Keep warm in a low oven.

TO MAKE the sauce, heat a wok over high heat, add the oil and heat until very hot. Stir-fry the green capsicum for a few seconds, then add the sugar, rice vinegar, soy sauce, tomato purée, sesame oil and stock, and bring to the boil. Combine the cornflour with enough water to make a paste, add to the sauce and simmer until thickened. Add the spareribs and toss to coat them with the sauce. Serve hot.

A tea-seller in Guangzhou.

VEGETABLES

A vegetable stall in Lyon market.

Crème fraîche is regularly used in place of cream in French kitchens.

PURÉE OF SPINACH

PURÉE OF SWEDES

IT IS EASIEST TO MAKE VEGETABLE PURÉES IN A FOOD PROCESSOR OR BLENDER BUT, IF YOU DON'T HAVE ONE, MASH THEM WITH A POTATO MASHER OR USE A FOODMILL. NEVER PURÉE POTATOES IN A PROCESSOR OR BLENDER—THEY BECOME GLUEY.

1 kg (1 lb 3 oz) swedes, peeled
  and chopped
50 g (2 oz) butter
1 tablespoon crème fraîche

SERVES 4

PUT the swede in a saucepan, half-cover with water and add 1 teaspoon salt and 20 g (⅔ oz) of the butter. Bring to the boil and then reduce the heat, cover, and simmer for 30 minutes or until tender. Drain, reserving the cooking liquid.

PROCESS the swede in a food processor or blender with enough of the cooking liquid to make a purée. Spoon into a saucepan and stir in the remaining butter and the crème fraîche. Reheat gently for a couple of minutes, stirring all the time.

PURÉE OF JERUSALEM ARTICHOKES

750 g (1 lb 10 oz) Jerusalem
  artichokes, peeled
250 g (9 oz) potatoes, halved
20 g (⅔ oz) butter
2 tablespoons crème fraîche

SERVES 4

COOK the artichokes in boiling salted water for 20 minutes or until tender. Drain and then mix in a food processor or blender to purée.

COOK the potatoes in boiling salted water for 20 minutes, then drain and mash. Add to the artichoke with the butter and crème fraîche. Season, beat well and serve at once.

PURÉE OF SPINACH

1 kg (2 lb 3 oz) spinach leaves
50 g (2 oz) butter, cubed
4 tablespoons crème fraîche
1/2 teaspoon nutmeg

SERVES 4

WASH the spinach and put in a large saucepan with just the water clinging to the leaves. Cover the pan and steam the spinach for 2 minutes, or until just wilted. Drain, cool and squeeze dry with your hands. Finely chop.

PUT the spinach in a small saucepan and gently heat through. Increase the heat and gradually add the butter, stirring all the time. Add the crème fraîche and stir into the spinach until it is glossy. Season well and stir in the nutmeg.

SHEBU BHAJI

DILL IS A HERB THAT CAN BE USED IN ABUNDANCE, AS IT IS IN THIS DISH, WITHOUT BEING OVERPOWERING. IT HAS A MILD BUT VERY DISTINCTIVE FLAVOUR.

200 g (7 oz) potatoes
200 g (7 oz) dill
2 tablespoons oil
2 garlic cloves, chopped
1/4 teaspoon ground turmeric
1 teaspoon black mustard seeds
pinch of asafoetida
1 dried chilli

SERVES 2

CUT the potatoes into 2.5 cm (1 inch) cubes and cook in a saucepan of simmering water for 15 minutes or until just tender. Drain well.

WASH the dill in several changes of water and trim off the tough stalks. Roughly chop the dill.

HEAT the oil in a heavy-based saucepan, add the garlic and fry for 30 seconds over low heat. Add the turmeric, mustard seeds, asafoetida and the whole chilli, cover and briefly allow the seeds to pop. Stir in the potato until well mixed. Add the dill, cover and cook over low heat for 5 minutes. The dill contains sufficient moisture to cook without the addition of any water. Season with salt, to taste.

MOOLI BHAJI

THE ASIAN RADISH, OR MOOLI AS IT IS ALSO KNOWN, IS MUCH MILDER IN FLAVOUR THAN ITS WESTERN COUNTERPART. IT LOOKS LIKE A HUGE, WHITE CARROT AND HAS A CRISP, JUICY FLESH. BHAJI IS THE NAME GIVEN TO MANY VEGETABLE DISHES AND LOOSELY IT MEANS FRIED VEGETABLES.

500 g (1 lb 2 oz) mooli
25 g grated coconut (page 555)
2 tablespoons oil
1/4 teaspoon black mustard seeds
1 onion, chopped
1/4 teaspoon ground turmeric
pinch of asafoetida
1 green chilli, finely chopped

SERVES 4

CUT the mooli into batons. Heat a frying pan over low heat and dry-roast the coconut, stirring constantly until it browns lightly.

HEAT the oil in a karhai or heavy-based saucepan over low heat. Add the mustard seeds, cover and allow to pop briefly. Add the onion and cook until lightly browned. Stir in the turmeric, asafoetida, chilli and the mooli until well mixed. Add 125 ml (1/2 cup) water and simmer for 5–7 minutes, until the mooli is cooked through and tender. Season with salt, to taste. Garnish with the coconut.

MOOLI BHAJI

Frying the eggplant slices first adds flavour to the finished dish.

EGGPLANT PARMIGIANA

PARMIGIANA IS A DECEPTIVE NAME FOR THIS DISH, AS THE RECIPE DOES NOT, IN FACT, HAIL FROM THAT CITY. INSTEAD ITS CREATION IS CLAIMED BY ALMOST EVERY REGION OF ITALY, BUT THE USE OF MOZZARELLA AND TOMATOES INDICATES A DISH FROM THE SOUTH.

1.5 kg (3 lb 5 oz) eggplant
　(aubergines)
plain flour
350 ml (1½ cups) olive oil
500 ml (2 cups) tomato passata
2 tablespoons roughly torn basil
　leaves
250 g (9 oz) mozzarella, grated
90 g (3 oz) Parmesan, grated

SERVES 8

THINLY SLICE the eggplants lengthways. Layer the slices in a large colander, sprinkling salt between each layer. Leave for 1 hour to extract the bitter juices. Rinse and pat the slices dry on both sides with paper towels. Coat the eggplant slices lightly with flour.

PREHEAT the oven to 180°C (350°F/Gas 4) and grease a 32 x 20 cm (13 x 8 inch) shallow casserole or baking tray.

HEAT 125 ml (½ cup) of the olive oil in a large frying pan. Quickly fry the eggplant in batches over moderately high heat until crisp and golden on both sides. Add more olive oil as needed, and drain well on paper towels as you remove each batch from the pan.

MAKE a slightly overlapping layer of eggplant slices over the base of the dish. Season with pepper. Spoon 4 tablespoons of passata over the eggplant and scatter a few pieces of basil on top. Sprinkle with some mozzarella, followed by some Parmesan. Continue with this layering until you have used up all the ingredients.

BAKE for 30 minutes. Remove from the oven and allow to cool for 30 minutes before serving.

WING BEAN SALAD

THIS IS A FRESH, CRUNCHY SALAD THAT LOOKS GOOD ON THE TABLE. WING BEANS HAVE FOUR
FRILLY EDGES TO THEM AND AN INTERESTING CROSS SECTION WHEN CUT.

oil, for frying
75 g (3 oz) Asian shallots,
    finely sliced
175 g (6 oz) wing beans
55 g (2 oz) cooked chicken, shredded
1 lemon grass stalk, white part only,
    finely sliced
2 tablespoons dried shrimp, ground
1½ tablespoons fish sauce
3–4 tablespoons lime juice
½ long red chilli or 1 small red chilli,
    finely chopped
55 g (2 oz) whole salted roasted
    peanuts
125 ml (½ cup) coconut milk
    (page 551), for garnish

SERVES 4

HEAT 2.5 cm (1 inch) oil in a wok or deep frying
pan over a medium heat. Deep-fry the shallots for
3–4 minutes until they are light brown (without
burning them). Lift out with a slotted spoon and
drain on paper towels.

SLICE the wing beans diagonally into thin pieces.
Blanch the wing beans in boiling water for
30 seconds, then drain and put them in cold
water for 1–2 minutes. Drain and transfer to a
bowl. Add the cooked chicken, lemon grass,
dried shrimp, fish sauce, lime juice, chilli and
half the peanuts. Mix with a spoon. Taste, then
adjust the seasoning if necessary.

PUT the wing bean salad in a serving bowl, drizzle
with coconut milk and sprinkle with the crispy
shallots and the rest of the peanuts.

STIR-FRIED WATER SPINACH

THE VEGETABLE THAT THE CHINESE CALL 'ONG CHOY' IS POPULAR IN THAILAND WHERE IT'S CALLED
'PHAK BUNG'. IT HAS LONG THIN STALKS AND LEAFY TOPS, ALL OF WHICH ARE GOOD TO EAT. BUY IT
FROM ASIAN SUPERMARKETS WHERE IT IS SOMETIMES CALLED MORNING GLORY.

1½ tablespoons oyster sauce
1 teaspoon fish sauce
1 tablespoon yellow bean sauce
¼ teaspoon sugar
1½ tablespoons vegetable oil
2–3 garlic cloves, finely chopped
350 g (12 oz) water spinach, cut
    into 5 cm (2 inch) lengths
1 red bird's eye chilli, slightly
    crushed (optional)

SERVES 4

MIX the oyster sauce, fish sauce, yellow bean
sauce and sugar in a small bowl.

HEAT the oil in a wok or a frying pan and stir-fry
the garlic over a medium heat until light brown.
Increase the heat to very high, add the stalks
of the water spinach and stir-fry for 1–2 minutes.
Add the leaves of the water spinach, the sauce
mixture and the crushed chilli and stir-fry for
another minute.

STIR-FRIED WATER SPINACH

WING BEAN SALAD

BOULANGÈRE POTATOES

1 kg (2 lb 3 oz) potatoes
1 large onion
2 tablespoons finely chopped
    parsley
500 ml (2 cups) hot chicken or
    vegetable stock
25 g (1 oz) butter, cubed

SERVES 6

PREHEAT the oven to 180°C (350°F/Gas 4).

THINLY SLICE the potatoes and onion with a
mandolin or sharp knife. Build up alternate layers
of potato and onion in a 20 x 10 cm (8 x 4 inch)
deep dish, sprinkling parsley, salt and plenty of
black pepper between each layer. Finish with a
layer of potato. Pour the stock over the top and
dot with butter.

BAKE, covered with foil, on the middle shelf of the
oven for 30 minutes, then remove the foil and
lightly press down on the potatoes to keep them
submerged in the stock. Bake for another
30 minutes, or until the potatoes are tender and
the top golden brown. Serve piping hot.

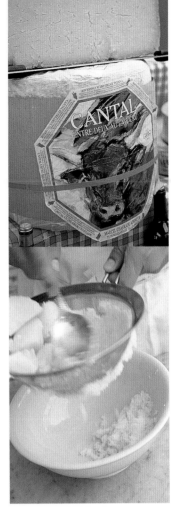

ALIGOT

THIS SPECIALITY OF THE AUVERGNE REGION IN FRANCE IS A POTATO PURÉE BEATEN TOGETHER WITH
CANTAL CHEESE TO MAKE A STRETCHY ELASTIC MIXTURE. CANTAL IS A SEMI-HARD SMOOTH CHEESE—
USE MILD CHEDDAR IF YOU CAN'T FIND IT.

Pushing the mashed potato
through a sieve will ensure that
the aligot is smooth.

800 g (1 lb 12 oz) floury potatoes,
    cut into even-sized pieces
75 g (2½ oz) butter
2 garlic cloves, crushed
3 tablespoons milk
300 g (10 oz) Cantal (or mild
    Cheddar), grated

SERVES 4

COOK the potatoes in boiling salted water for
20–30 minutes, or until tender. Meanwhile, melt
the butter in a small saucepan over low heat and
add the garlic. Mash the potatoes and then sieve
to give a really smooth purée (don't use a food
processor or they will become gluey).

RETURN the potato purée to the saucepan over
gentle heat and add the garlic butter and milk. Mix
together well and then add the cheese, handful by
handful. Beat in the cheese—once it has melted
the mixture will be stretchy. Season with salt and
pepper before serving.

ALIGOT

FLASH-COOKED PEA SHOOTS WITH GARLIC

PEA SHOOTS ARE THE DELICATE LEAVES AT THE TOP OF PEA PLANTS. THEY ARE PARTICULARLY GOOD WHEN STIR-FRIED SIMPLY WITH A LITTLE OIL AND GARLIC. IF UNAVAILABLE, SPINACH OR ANY OTHER LEAFY GREEN MAY BE SUBSTITUTED.

Selling pea shoots in Dali.

350 g (12 oz) pea shoots
1 teaspoon oil
2 garlic cloves, finely chopped
1¹/₂ tablespoons Shaoxing rice wine
¹/₄ teaspoon salt

SERVES 6

TRIM the tough stems and wilted leaves from the pea shoots. Wash well and dry thoroughly.

HEAT a wok over high heat, add the oil and heat until very hot. Add the pea shoots and garlic and toss lightly for 20 seconds, then add the rice wine and salt, and stir-fry for 1 minute, or until the shoots are slightly wilted, but still bright green. Transfer to a platter, leaving behind most of the liquid. Serve hot, at room temperature, or cold.

STIR-FRIED LOTUS ROOT

THE LOTUS IS A SYMBOL OF PURITY IN BUDDHIST CULTURE AS THE ROOTS, WHICH GROW IN MUD, ARE CLEAN AND PURE DESPITE THEIR MUDDY ORIGINS. LOTUS ROOT CAN BE EATEN RAW OR COOKED AND HAS A CRISP, CRUNCHY TEXTURE.

450 g (1 lb) fresh lotus root or 350 g (12 oz) ready-prepared lotus root
1 tablespoon oil
1 garlic clove, thinly sliced
10 very thin slices ginger
2 spring onions (scallions), finely chopped
50 g (2 oz) Chinese ham, rind removed, diced
1 tablespoon Shaoxing rice wine
1 tablespoon light soy sauce
1 teaspoon sugar

SERVES 4

IF USING fresh lotus root, peel, cut into slices, wash well and drain thoroughly. Ready-prepared lotus root just needs to be washed, sliced and drained thoroughly.

HEAT a wok over high heat, add the oil and heat until very hot. Stir-fry the garlic and ginger for 30 seconds. Add the spring onion, ham and lotus root and stir-fry for 1 minute, then add the rice wine, soy sauce and sugar and cook for 2–3 minutes, or until the lotus root is tender but still crisp.

STIR-FRIED LOTUS ROOT

SPICED BANANA FLOWER

ALL PARTS OF THE BANANA PLANT ARE USED IN DIFFERENT WAYS: THE LEAVES AS AN AROMATIC FOOD WRAPPER AND AS A 'PLATE' FOR INDIAN MEALS; AND THE FRUIT, FLOWER, AND TENDER INNER RINGS OF THE STEM ARE EATEN. WEAR PLASTIC GLOVES TO STOP THE SAP STAINING YOUR HANDS.

1 banana flower
1/2 lemon
200 g (7 oz) prawns
20 g (2/3 oz) grated coconut
(page 555)
1 tablespoon oil
120 ml (1/2 cup) lime juice
1 red chilli, finely chopped
2 tablespoons jaggery or
soft brown sugar
1 tablespoon grated lime rind,
or lime leaves
mint leaves

SERVES 4

PEEL off one leaf at a time from the banana flower. Remove the yellow, stick-like immature bananas and discard both them and the leaves until you reach the white inner core. Chop off the top end and discard it. Chop what is left into quarters and soak it in a bowl of water with 1 teaspoon salt for 1 hour. Drain the banana flower, transfer to a saucepan, cover with fresh water and add the juice from the half lemon. Bring to the boil and cook for 15–20 minutes, or until soft. The banana flower will darken in colour as it cooks. Drain and slice into julienne strips. Peel and devein the prawns and cut each in half.

PLACE a heavy-based frying pan over low heat and dry-roast the coconut, stirring constantly until the coconut is golden brown. Finely grind in a pestle and mortar or in a spice grinder.

HEAT the oil in the frying pan and fry the prawns until they are pink and cooked through. Mix the prawns with the lime juice, chilli, jaggery and lime rind. Season with salt, to taste, then leave to cool.

JUST before serving, add the banana hearts and coconut to the prawns and toss well. Serve cold, garnished with the mint leaves.

Peel off the leaves and immature bananas until you reach the core, then chop off the end. Soak the quarters of core in salted water.

315

VEGETABLE TORTE

150 g (5 oz) asparagus
4 tablespoons olive oil
1 onion, chopped
1 zucchini, halved lengthways and
   finely sliced
2 large garlic cloves, crushed
100 g (3 oz) spinach, stalks
   removed if necessary
1 tablespoon chopped basil
75 g (2½ oz) Parmesan, grated
250 g (9 oz) ricotta
250 g (9 oz) mascarpone
4 eggs

SERVES 4

WASH the asparagus and remove the woody ends (hold each spear at both ends and bend it gently—it will snap at its natural breaking point). Remove the spear tips of the asparagus and slice the remaining stems. Bring a small saucepan of salted water to the boil and cook the asparagus stems for about 2 minutes. Add the tips and cook for 1 minute. Drain the asparagus and set aside.

PREHEAT the oven to 180°C (375°F/Gas 4). Heat the olive oil in a saucepan and cook the onion until soft. Increase the heat and add the zucchini. Cook until the zucchini is soft and golden brown, stirring occasionally. Add the garlic and cook for 1 minute more. Finally, add the spinach and mix briefly until just wilted.

REMOVE the pan from the heat, add the asparagus and the basil, season with salt and pepper and set aside to cool.

GREASE a 20 cm (8 inch) springform tin with butter and dust with about 1 tablespoon of the Parmesan. Mix together the ricotta, mascarpone, eggs and 50 g (2 oz) Parmesan and add it to the cooled vegetables. Mix well and taste for seasoning.

SPOON the mixture into the tin and scatter with the remaining Parmesan. Place in the oven, on a tray to catch any drips, and cook for about 30 minutes. The top should be light golden brown and the mixture still wobble slightly in the centre. Leave to cool for 30 minutes, then chill in the fridge for about 3 hours, until the torte has set. Serve with a simple rocket or mixed leaf salad.

Lighting candles at a
Buddhist temple.

Tiger lily buds, or golden
needles, are dried unopened
lilies. When reconstituted they
resemble limp bean sprouts.

BUDDHA'S DELIGHT

THE ORIGINAL RECIPE FOR THIS WELL-KNOWN VEGETARIAN DISH USED NO LESS THAN EIGHTEEN DIFFERENT INGREDIENTS TO REPRESENT THE EIGHTEEN BUDDHAS. NOWADAYS, ANYTHING BETWEEN SIX TO EIGHT INGREDIENTS IS USUAL PRACTICE.

25 g (1 oz) tiger lily buds
6–8 dried Chinese mushrooms
10 g (1/3 oz) dried black fungus
   (wood ears)
150 g (5 oz) braised gluten, drained
50 g (2 oz) bean curd puffs
100 g (3 oz) bean sprouts
1 carrot
4 tablespoons oil
50 g (2 oz) snowpeas, ends
   trimmed
1 teaspoon salt
1/2 teaspoon sugar
4 tablespoons vegetable stock
   (page 565)
2 tablespoons light soy sauce
1/2 teaspoon roasted sesame oil

SERVES 4

SOAK the tiger lily buds in boiling water for 30 minutes. Rinse and drain the tiger lily buds, and trim off any roots if they are hard. Soak the dried mushrooms in boiling water for 30 minutes, then drain and squeeze out any excess water. Remove and discard the stems and cut the caps in half (or quarters if large). Soak the dried black fungus in cold water for 20 minutes, then drain and squeeze out any excess water. Cut any large pieces of fungus in half.

CUT the gluten and bean curd into small pieces. Wash the bean sprouts, discarding any husks and straggly end pieces, and dry thoroughly. Diagonally cut the carrot into thin slices.

HEAT a wok over high heat, add the oil and heat until very hot. Stir-fry the carrot for 30 seconds, then add the snowpeas and bean sprouts. Stir-fry for 1 minute, then add the gluten, bean curd, tiger lily buds, mushrooms, black fungus, salt, sugar, stock and soy sauce. Toss everything together, then cover and braise for 2 minutes at a gentle simmer.

ADD the sesame oil, toss it through the mixture and serve hot or cold.

SPICY EGGPLANT

THIS IS A WONDERFUL DISH IN WHICH EGGPLANT IS COOKED WITH PICKLING STYLE SPICES. THE EGGPLANT CAN BE SERVED AS PART OF AN INDIAN FEAST OR AS A SPICY ACCOMPANIMENT. IT IS ALSO GOOD AS A VEGETARIAN MAIN DISH WITH RICE AND SOME YOGHURT.

800 g (1 lb 12 oz) eggplant
(aubergine), cut into wedges
4–5 cm (1½–2 inches) long
400 g ripe tomatoes or 400 g
(14 oz) tin chopped tomatoes
2.5 cm (1 inch) piece of ginger,
grated
6 garlic cloves, crushed
300 ml (1¼ cups) oil
1 teaspoon fennel seeds
½ teaspoon kalonji (nigella seeds)
1 tablespoon ground coriander
(cilantro)
¼ teaspoon ground turmeric
½ teaspoon cayenne pepper
1 teaspoon salt

SERVES 6

PUT the eggplant pieces in a colander, sprinkle them with salt and leave them for 30 minutes to allow any bitter juices to run out. Rinse, squeeze out any excess water, then pat dry with paper towels. If using fresh tomatoes, score a cross in the top of each and plunge into boiling water for 20 seconds. Drain and peel away from the cross. Roughly chop the tomatoes, discarding the cores and seeds and reserving any juices.

PUREE the ginger and garlic with one-third of the tomato in a blender or food processor. If you don't have a blender, finely chop the tomatoes and mix with the ginger and garlic.

HEAT 125 ml (½ cup) of the oil in a large, deep, heavy-based frying pan and when hot, add as many eggplant pieces as you can fit in a single layer. Cook over medium heat until brown on both sides, then transfer to a sieve over a bowl so that the excess oil can drain off. Add the remaining oil to the pan as needed and cook the rest of the eggplant in batches.

REHEAT the oil that's left in the pan and add the fennel seeds and kalonji. Cover and allow to pop for a few seconds. Add the tomato and ginger mixture and the remaining ingredients, except the eggplant. Cook, stirring regularly for 5–6 minutes, until the mixture becomes thick and fairly smooth (be careful as it may spit at you). Carefully add the cooked eggplant so the pieces stay whole, cover the pan and cook gently for about 10 minutes.

STORE the eggplant in the sauce in the fridge. Pour off any excess oil before serving. The eggplant can either be served cold or gently warmed through.

Drain the fried eggplant to get rid of any excess oil.

FENNEL, TOMATO AND GARLIC GRATIN

1 kg (2 lb 3 oz) fennel bulbs
80 ml (⅓ cup) olive oil
1 large red onion, halved and thinly
    sliced
2 garlic cloves, crushed
500 g (1 lb 2 oz) tomatoes

GRATIN TOPPING
60 g (2 oz) white bread, broken into
    coarse crumbs
65 g (2 oz) Parmesan, grated
2 teaspoons grated lemon zest
1 garlic clove, crushed

SERVES 4

PREHEAT the oven to 200°C (400°F/Gas 6). Grease a 21 cm (8½ inch) square gratin dish with melted butter or oil. Cut the fennel in half lengthways, then slice thinly.

HEAT the oil in a large frying pan. Cook the onion for 3–4 minutes until softened but not browned. Add the garlic and cook for 2 minutes. Add the fennel and cook, stirring frequently, for 7 minutes until softened and lightly golden brown.

SCORE a cross in the top of each tomato, plunge into boiling water for 20 seconds and then peel the skin away from the cross. Chop roughly and add to the fennel. Cook, stirring frequently, for 5 minutes until the tomato is softened. Season well and pour into the dish.

TO MAKE the gratin topping, mix together all the ingredients, sprinkle over the vegetables and bake for 15 minutes, or until golden brown and crisp. Serve immediately.

To make the vegetable tian, arrange a layer of courgettes in the dish, then top with cheese, the tomato mixture and thyme.

VEGETABLE TIAN

60 ml (¼ cup) olive oil
500 g (1 lb 2 oz) zucchinis, thickly
    sliced on the diagonal
4 garlic cloves, crushed
pinch of nutmeg
650 g (1 lb 7 oz) tomatoes
2 red onions, chopped
60 ml (¼ cup) white wine
20 g (⅔ oz) chopped flat-leaf
    parsley
125 g (4 oz) Gruyère, grated
a few small thyme sprigs

SERVES 4

PREHEAT the oven to 180°C (350°F/Gas 4). Grease a 15 x 25 cm (6 x 10 inch) ovenproof dish with melted butter or oil. Heat half the oil in a large frying pan and add the zucchini and half the garlic. Cook, stirring, over low heat for 8 minutes, or until just beginning to soften. Season well with salt, pepper and nutmeg. Spread evenly into the dish.

SCORE a cross in the top of each tomato, plunge into boiling water for 20 seconds and then peel the skin away from the cross. Chop roughly. Cook the onion in the remaining oil over low heat for 5 minutes, stirring often. Add the remaining garlic, tomato, wine and parsley. Cook, stirring often, for 10 minutes until all the liquid has evaporated.

SPRINKLE the cheese over the zucchinis and spread the tomato mixture over the top. Scatter with thyme sprigs and bake for 20 minutes, or until heated through.

VEGETABLE TIAN

STUFFED OKRA

STUFFED OKRA IS SERVED AS A DELICACY IN NORTHERN INDIAN HOMES. ONE HAS TO PREPARE THIS DISH WITH A LITTLE LOVE AND A LOT OF PATIENCE BUT ALL EFFORTS ARE REWARDED WHEN THE FINAL DISH IS PRESENTED AT THE TABLE. IT IS DELICIOUS SERVED WITH INDIAN BREADS.

1 red onion, roughly chopped
4 garlic cloves, roughly chopped
10 cm (4 inch) piece of ginger, grated
5 teaspoons ground cumin
1 tablespoon ground coriander (cilantro)
2 teaspoons ground turmeric
1 teaspoon chilli powder
2 teaspoons garam masala (page 556)
1 teaspoon ground black pepper
1 tablespoon salt
550 g (1 lb 3 oz) okra
120 ml (½ cup) oil
pinch of asafoetida

SERVES 6

COMBINE the onion, garlic and ginger in a food processor and blend them to form a paste, or chop them all finely and pound them together in a pestle and mortar. Transfer to a bowl and add 4 teaspoons of the cumin, the coriander, 1¼ teaspoons of the turmeric, the chilli powder and garam masala and mix well. Stir in the pepper and 3 teaspoons of the salt.

CUT off the bottoms of the okra, then use a knife to make a slit lengthwise in each of them, stopping just short of the tail end. Using your hands or a small knife, put a little of the spice mixture into the insides of the okra. Some of it will ooze out but don't worry. This process will take a little time but the end result is delicious. Carefully cut all the okra into 1 cm pieces, or if you prefer, you can leave them whole.

HEAT the oil in a karhai or large, wide, heavy-based frying pan over low heat. Add the asafoetida and remaining turmeric to the pan and stir it around so that the oil absorbs the flavour. Add the okra and stir so it is coated in the flavoured oil. Add 2 tablespoons water. Cover and cook for 10 minutes, shaking the pan occasionally to prevent the okra sticking to the pan (add 2 more tablespoons of water if necessary).

ADD the remaining salt and remaining ground cumin to the pan. Shake the pan, then simmer the mixture for 5–10 minutes, until the okra is quite soft. The okra will retain a slight crunch on the outside because of its unique texture.

Stuffing the okra adds an extra dimension to the flavour. Use a small knife to help you slide the stuffing into each piece.

SPICY TOMATO DIPPING SAUCE

THIS FAMOUS DIPPING SAUCE FROM THAILAND SHOULD BE SERVED AS A MAIN COURSE WITH BLANCHED VEGETABLES SUCH AS WEDGES OF EGGPLANT OR CABBAGE, PIECES OF SNAKE BEAN OR PUMPKIN, AND ASPARAGUS SPEARS. PIECES OF DEEP-FRIED PORK SKIN ARE ALSO SUITABLE.

1 dried long red chilli
1 lemon grass stalk, white part only,
    finely sliced
4 Asian shallots, finely chopped
2–3 garlic cloves, roughly chopped
½ teaspoon shrimp paste
1½ tablespoons vegetable oil
175 g (6 oz) minced (ground) fatty
    pork
450 g (1 lb) tomatoes,
    finely chopped
2 tablespoons fish sauce
1 tablespoon sugar
3 tablespoons tamarind purée
mixed vegetables, such as wedges
    of eggplant (aubergine), pieces of
    snake bean, wedges of cabbage,
    asparagus spears, baby corn,
    pieces of pumpkin, to serve
a few coriander (cilantro) leaves,
    for garnish
pieces of pork skin, deep-fried,
    to serve

SERVES 4

SLIT the chilli lengthways with a sharp knife and discard all the seeds. Soak the chilli in hot water for 1–2 minutes or until soft, then drain and chop roughly. Using a pestle and mortar, pound the chilli, lemon grass, shallots and garlic into a paste. Add the shrimp paste and mix well. Alternatively, use a small processor or blender to grind or blend the chilli, lemon grass, shallots, garlic and shrimp paste into a smooth paste.

HEAT the oil in a saucepan or wok and stir-fry the paste over a medium heat for 2 minutes or until fragrant. Add the minced pork and stir for 2–3 minutes. Add the tomatoes, fish sauce, sugar and tamarind. Reduce the heat and gently simmer for 25–30 minutes or until the mixture is thick.

BLANCH briefly any tough vegetables such as eggplant, snake beans, asparagus and pumpkin. Drain well.

TASTE the sauce, then adjust with more tamarind, sugar or chilli if necessary. This dish should have three flavours: sweet, sour and lightly salted. Spoon into a serving bowl and garnish with coriander leaves. Serve with a mixture of blanched vegetables and deep-fried pork skin.

VEGETABLE TIMBALES

270 g (10 oz) carrots, chopped
270 g (10 oz) watercress, trimmed
270 g (10 oz) red capsicum
   (pepper)
180 ml (⅔ cup) double cream
7 egg yolks
pinch of nutmeg

SERVES 4

PREHEAT the oven to 160°C (315°F/Gas 2–3). Steam the carrot until soft. Wash the watercress and put in a saucepan with just the water clinging to the leaves. Cover the pan and steam the watercress for 2 minutes, or until just wilted. Drain, cool and squeeze dry with your hands.

PREHEAT the grill (broiler). Cut the capsicums in half, remove the seeds and membrane and place, skin side up, under the hot grill until the skin blackens and blisters. Leave to cool before peeling away the skin.

PURÉE each vegetable individually in a food processor, adding a third of the cream to the carrot to make a smooth purée. Pour the capsicum purée into a saucepan and stir over moderate heat until thickened. Put each purée in its own bowl to cool, then divide the remaining cream between the capsicum and watercress purées.

STIR 2 egg yolks into each purée. Divide the last yolk between the watercress and capsicum purées. Season with salt, pepper and nutmeg.

GREASE four timbale moulds and divide the carrot purée equally among them. Smooth the surface. Spoon the watercress purée on top and smooth the surface. Top with the capsicum purée. Put the moulds in a roasting tin and pour in hot water to come halfway up the sides of the timbales. Cook in this bain-marie for 1¼ hours.

TO SERVE, hold a plate on top of each timbale and then tip it upside down. Give the plate and timbale one sharp shake and the timbale will release itself. Serve with a salad and baguette.

Smooth each layer as you put it in the mould, so the timbale is neat and even when turned out.

BABY EGGPLANT AND CHERRY TOMATO STIR-FRY

ALTHOUGH A MIXTURE OF THAI EGGPLANTS OF DIFFERENT COLOURS WILL MAKE THIS DISH MORE VISUALLY APPEALING, JUST ONE TYPE WILL DO FINE. THE EGGPLANTS MAY DISCOLOUR WHEN YOU COOK THEM BUT DON'T WORRY AS THE FLAVOUR WON'T BE AFFECTED.

12 small round Thai eggplants
(aubergines), green, yellow
or purple
1 teaspoon fish sauce,
plus 1 tablespoon
1 tablespoon vegetable oil
1 small red chilli, chopped
1 tablespoon finely sliced ginger
2 Asian shallots, finely chopped
1 garlic clove, chopped
150 g (5 oz) cherry tomatoes
2 tablespoons black vinegar
2 tablespoons palm sugar
12–18 Thai sweet basil leaves

SERVES 4

CUT each eggplant in half and toss them in a bowl with 1 teaspoon fish sauce. Put about 8 cm (3 inches) of water in a wok and bring to the boil. Place the eggplants in a bamboo steamer, place the steamer over the boiling water and steam the eggplants for 15 minutes.

HEAT the oil in a wok, add the chilli, ginger, shallots and garlic and cook for 15 seconds. Add the eggplants and tomatoes and toss well. Add the black vinegar, sugar and remaining fish sauce and cook for 2–3 minutes, until the sauce thickens. Stir in the basil leaves and serve.

STIR-FRIED BROCCOLI WITH
OYSTER SAUCE

STIR-FRIED BROCCOLI WITH OYSTER SAUCE

350 g (12 oz) Chinese broccoli,
cut into pieces
1 tablespoon vegetable oil
2 garlic cloves, finely chopped
1 tablespoon oyster sauce
1 tablespoon light soy sauce

SERVES 4

BLANCH the Chinese broccoli in boiling salted water for 2–3 minutes, then drain thoroughly.

HEAT the oil in a wok or frying pan and stir-fry the garlic over a medium heat until light brown. Add the Chinese broccoli and half of the oyster sauce and the light soy sauce. Stir-fry over a high heat for 1–2 minutes until the stems are just tender. Drizzle with the remaining oyster sauce.

CHARGRILLED RADICCHIO

2 heads radicchio
60 ml (¼ cup) olive oil
1 teaspoon balsamic vinegar

SERVES 4

TRIM the radicchio, discarding the outer leaves. Slice into quarters lengthways and rinse well. Drain, then pat dry with paper towels.

PREHEAT a griddle to hot. Lightly sprinkle the radicchio with some of the olive oil and season. Cook for 2–3 minutes, until the under leaves soften and darken, then turn to cook the other side. Transfer to a dish and sprinkle with the remaining oil and vinegar. Serve hot with grilled meats, or cold as part of an antipasto platter.

There are several types of radicchio available in Italy, all from the North. This round variety, *rossa di Verona*, is from Chioggia. The longer-leaved type is from Treviso.

CARDOONS WITH PARMESAN

CARDOONS, LIKE ARTICHOKES, ARE A TYPE OF THISTLE, GROWN FOR THEIR STALKS. THEY BROWN WHEN CUT, SO USE A STAINLESS STEEL KNIFE AND KEEP THEM IN ACIDULATED WATER. THE SICILIANS ALSO CALL THE YOUNG STALKS OF ARTICHOKES CARDOONS AND COOK THEM IN THE SAME WAY.

juice of 1 lemon
750 g (1 lb 10 oz) cardoons
1 tablespoon plain flour
60 g (2 oz) butter
1 small onion, thinly sliced
4 tablespoons grated Parmesan

SERVES 4

PUT half the lemon juice in a large bowl of cold water. Discard the green leaves, outer stalks and tough parts of the cardoons, leaving the tender white stalks. Cut into 8 cm (3¼ inch) lengths and toss into the bowl of water.

BRING a large saucepan of water to the boil. Add the remaining lemon juice, the flour and a large pinch of salt. Add the cardoons. Simmer for about 50 minutes, or until tender. Drain and plunge into a bowl of cold water. Remove the strings with a knife, as you would with celery.

PREHEAT the oven to 180°C (350°F/Gas 4) and grease a shallow 25 x 15 cm (10 x 6 inch) casserole or baking tray. Melt the butter in a small frying pan and add the onion. Cook over low heat for 10 minutes until soft and golden.

LAYER half the cardoons over the base of the casserole and season with pepper. Spoon half the onion over the top and sprinkle with half the Parmesan. Repeat these layers and bake in the oven for 30 minutes.

CARDOONS WITH PARMESAN

Preserved mustard cabbage *(bottom, second from left)* for sale in Beijing.

DOUBLE-COOKED YARD-LONG BEANS

THIS SICHUANESE RECIPE IS SO NAMED BECAUSE THE BEANS, AFTER BEING FRIED UNTIL TENDER, ARE THEN COOKED AGAIN WITH SEASONINGS AND A SAUCE. TRADITIONALLY YARD-LONG, OR SNAKE, BEANS ARE USED. THESE ARE AVAILABLE IN CHINESE SHOPS, BUT FRENCH BEANS ARE ALSO DELICIOUS.

1 kg (2 lb 3 oz) yard-long (snake) beans or French beans, trimmed
150 g (5 oz) minced pork or beef
2 tablespoons light soy sauce
1¹/₂ tablespoons Shaoxing rice wine
¹/₂ teaspoon roasted sesame oil
oil for deep-frying
5 tablespoons finely chopped preserved mustard cabbage
3 spring onions (scallions), finely chopped
1¹/₂ teaspoons sugar

SERVES 6

DIAGONALLY cut the beans into 5 cm (2 inch) pieces. Lightly chop the minced meat with a cleaver until it goes slightly fluffy. Put the meat in a bowl, add 1 teaspoon of the soy sauce, 1 teaspoon of the rice wine and the sesame oil and stir vigorously to combine.

FILL a wok one quarter full of oil. Heat the oil to 180°C (350°F), or until a piece of bread fries golden brown in 15 seconds when dropped in the oil. Add a third of the beans, covering the wok with the lid as they are placed in the oil to prevent the oil from splashing. Cook for 3¹/₂–4 minutes, stirring constantly, until they are tender and golden brown at the edges. Remove with a wire sieve or slotted spoon and drain. Reheat the oil and repeat with the remaining beans. Pour the oil from the wok, leaving 1 tablespoon.

REHEAT the reserved oil over high heat until very hot, add the minced meat and stir-fry until the colour changes, mashing and chopping to separate the pieces of meat. Push the meat to the side and add the preserved mustard cabbage and spring onion. Stir-fry over high heat for 15 seconds, or until fragrant. Add the beans with the remaining soy sauce and rice wine, sugar and 1 tablespoon water, and return the meat to the centre of the pan. Toss lightly to coat the beans with the sauce.

Meat, such as this pork, is minced by hand using two cleavers at a market.

A vegetable shop in Kerala.

CAULIFLOWER WITH MUSTARD

THIS IS A LOVELY DISH USING CAULIFLOWER AND MANY SPICES. IN INDIA, THE VARIATIONS OF THIS DISH ALL PUT THE EMPHASIS ON QUITE DIFFERENT SPICE COMBINATIONS. THIS MUSTARDY ONE GOES WELL WITH RICE AND PIECES OF ROTI BUT IS ALSO A GOOD ACCOMPANIMENT TO MEAT DISHES.

2 teaspoons yellow mustard seeds
2 teaspoons black mustard seeds
1 teaspoon ground turmeric
1 teaspoon tamarind purée
   (page 554)
2–3 tablespoons mustard oil or oil
2 garlic cloves, finely chopped
1/2 onion, finely chopped
600 g (1 lb 5 oz) cauliflower, broken
   into small florets
3 mild green chillies, seeded
   and finely chopped
2 teaspoons kalonji (nigella seeds)

SERVES 4

GRIND the mustard seeds together to a fine powder in a spice grinder or pestle and mortar. Mix with the turmeric, tamarind purée and 100 ml (1/3 cup) water to form a smooth, quite liquid paste.

HEAT 2 tablespoons oil in a karhai or large, heavy-based saucepan over medium heat until almost smoking. Reduce the heat to low, add the garlic and onion and fry until golden. Cook the cauliflower in batches, adding more oil if necessary, and fry until lightly browned. Add the chilli and fry for 1 minute, or until tinged with brown around the edges.

RETURN all the cauliflower to the pan, sprinkle it with the mustard mixture and kalonji and stir well. Increase the heat to medium and bring to the boil, even though there's not much sauce. Reduce the heat to low, cover and cook until the cauliflower is nearly tender and the seasoning is dry. You may have to sprinkle a little more water on the cauliflower as it cooks to stop it sticking to the pan. If there is still excess liquid when the cauliflower is cooked, simmer with the lid off until it dries out. Season with salt, to taste, and remove from the heat.

RATATOUILLE

THE NAME RATATOUILLE COMES FROM THE FRENCH WORD FOR 'MIX' AND WAS PREVIOUSLY USED AS A FAMILIAR TERM FOR ANY STEW. THIS RECIPE FOLLOWS THE TRADITIONAL VERSION, WITH EACH INGREDIENT BEING FRIED SEPARATELY BEFORE THE FINAL SIMMERING.

4 tomatoes
2 tablespoons olive oil
1 large onion, diced
1 red capsicum (pepper), diced
1 yellow capsicum (pepper), diced
1 eggplant (aubergine), diced
2 zucchinis (courgettes), diced
1 teaspoon tomato purée
1/2 teaspoon sugar
1 bay leaf
3 thyme sprigs
2 basil sprigs
1 garlic clove, crushed
1 tablespoon chopped parsley

SERVES 4

SCORE a cross in the top of each tomato, plunge into boiling water for 20 seconds and then peel the skin away from the cross. Chop roughly.

HEAT the oil in a frying pan. Add the onion and cook over low heat for 5 minutes. Add the capsicums and cook, stirring, for 4 minutes. Remove from the pan and set aside.

FRY the eggplant until lightly browned all over and then remove from the pan. Fry the zucchini until browned and then return the onion, peppers and aubergine to the pan. Add the tomato purée, stir well and cook for 2 minutes. Add the tomato, sugar, bay leaf, thyme and basil, stir well, cover and cook for 15 minutes. Remove the bay leaf, thyme and basil.

MIX TOGETHER the garlic and parsley and add to the ratatouille at the last minute. Stir and serve.

You can braise white chicory or the purple-tipped variety. Both should be pale yellow, rather than green and bitter.

BRAISED CHICORY

8 chicory heads
1 tablespoon butter
1 teaspoon brown sugar
2 teaspoons tarragon vinegar
100 ml (1/3 cup) chicken stock
2 tablespoons double cream

SERVES 4

TRIM the ends from the chicory. Melt the butter in a deep frying pan and fry the chicory briefly on all sides. Add the sugar, vinegar and chicken stock and bring to the boil. Reduce the heat to a simmer and cover the pan.

SIMMER GENTLY for 30 minutes, or until tender, turning halfway through. Take the lid off the pan and simmer until nearly all the liquid has evaporated. Stir in the cream and serve.

BRAISED CHICORY

STIR-FRIED SNAKE BEANS

SNAKE BEANS ARE VERY LONG GREEN BEANS AND ARE USUALLY SOLD IN COILS. YOU CAN LEAVE OUT THE CHICKEN IF YOU PREFER, BUT REMEMBER THAT THIS STILL WON'T BE A VEGETARIAN DISH AS IT CONTAINS RED CURRY PASTE, WHICH HAS FISH SAUCE AND SHRIMP PASTE IN IT.

2 tablespoons vegetable oil
2 teaspoons red curry paste
    (page 558) or bought paste
350 g (12 oz) skinless chicken
    breast fillet, finely sliced
350 g (12 oz) snake beans,
    cut diagonally into 2.5 cm
    (1 inch) pieces
1 tablespoon fish sauce
25 g (1 oz) sugar
4 makrut (kaffir) lime leaves,
    very finely shredded

SERVES 4

HEAT the oil in a wok or frying pan and stir-fry the red curry paste over a medium heat for 2 minutes or until fragrant. Add the chicken and stir for 4–5 minutes or until the chicken is cooked. Add the beans, fish sauce and sugar. Stir-fry for another 4–5 minutes.

TRANSFER to a serving plate and sprinkle with the makrut lime leaves.

PUMPKIN WITH CHILLI AND BASIL

PUMPKIN WITH CHILLI AND BASIL

3 tablespoons dried shrimp
½ teaspoon shrimp paste
2 coriander (cilantro) roots
10–12 white peppercorns
2 garlic cloves, chopped
2 Asian shallots, chopped
125 ml (½ cup) coconut cream
    (page 551)
300 g (10 oz) butternut pumpkin
    (squash), cut into 4 cm (1½ inch)
    cubes
2 large red chillies, cut lengthways
125 ml (½ cup) coconut milk
    (page 551)
1 tablespoon fish sauce
1 tablespoon palm sugar
2 teaspoons lime juice
12 Thai sweet basil leaves

SERVES 4

SOAK 2 tablespoons of the dried shrimp in a small bowl of water for 20 minutes, then drain.

PUT the remaining dried shrimp, shrimp paste, coriander roots, peppercorns, garlic and shallots in a pestle and mortar or food processor and pound or blend to a paste.

BRING the coconut cream to a boil in a saucepan and simmer for 5 minutes. Add the paste and stir to combine. Cook for another 2–3 minutes, then add the pumpkin, chillies, rehydrated shrimp and coconut milk. Stir to combine all the ingredients and simmer for 10–15 minutes, until the pumpkin is just tender. Don't let the pumpkin turn to mush.

ADD the fish sauce, palm sugar and lime juice to the pan and cook for another 2–3 minutes. Stir in the basil leaves before serving.

SPINACH KOFTA IN YOGHURT SAUCE

THIS VEGITARIAN DISH IS QUITE SUBSTANTIAL. YOU CAN EAT THE YOGHURT SAUCE AND THE SPINACH KOFTA AS SEPARATE DISHES BUT THEY GO VERY WELL TOGETHER AS IN THIS RECIPE.

YOGHURT SAUCE

375 ml (1 1/2 cups) thick natural
    yoghurt (page 554)
4 tablespoons besan flour
1 tablespoon oil
2 teaspoons black mustard seeds
1 teaspoon fenugreek seeds
6 curry leaves
1 large onion, finely chopped
3 garlic cloves, crushed
1 teaspoon ground turmeric
1/2 teaspoon chilli powder

SPINACH KOFTAS

1 bunch spinach (about 450 g/1 lb),
    leaves picked off the stems, or
    500 g (1 lb 2 oz) frozen spinach,
    thawed and drained
170 g (6 oz) besan flour
1 red onion, finely chopped
1 ripe tomato, finely diced
2 garlic cloves, crushed
1 teaspoon ground cumin
2 tablespoons coriander (cilantro)
    leaves

oil for deep-frying
coriander leaves (optional)

SERVES 6

TO MAKE the yoghurt sauce, in a large bowl, whisk the yoghurt, besan flour and 750 ml (3 cups) water to a smooth paste. Heat the oil in a heavy-based saucepan or deep frying pan over low heat. Add the mustard and fenugreek seeds and the curry leaves, cover and allow the seeds to pop for 1 minute. Add the onion and cook for 5 minutes, or until soft and starting to brown. Add the garlic and stir for 1 minute, or until soft. Add the turmeric and chilli powder and stir for 30 seconds. Add the yoghurt mixture, bring to the boil and simmer over low heat for 10 minutes. Season with salt, to taste.

TO MAKE the spinach koftas, blanch the spinach in boiling water for 1 minute and refresh in cold water. Drain, squeeze out any extra water by putting the spinach between two plates and pushing them together. Finely chop the spinach. Combine with the remaining kofta ingredients and up to 60 ml (1/4 cup) of water, a little at a time, adding enough to make the mixture soft but not sloppy. If it becomes too sloppy, add more besan flour. Season with salt, to taste. (To test the seasoning, fry a small amount of the mixture and taste it.) Shape the mixture into balls by rolling it in dampened hands, using 1 tablespoon of mixture for each.

FILL a karhai or heavy-based saucepan one-third full with oil and heat to 180°C/350°F (a cube of bread will brown in 15 seconds). Lower the koftas into the oil in batches and fry until golden and crisp. Don't overcrowd the pan. Remove the koftas as they cook, shake off any excess oil and add them to the yoghurt sauce.

GENTLY reheat the yoghurt sauce and sprinkle with the coriander leaves if using.

CHINESE BROCCOLI WITH SOY SAUCE

CHINESE BROCCOLI (GAI LAN) IS A VERSATILE, HEALTHY VEGETABLE THAT IS QUICK TO PREPARE. THERE IS NO WASTE AS BOTH THE LEAVES AND STALKS ARE EATEN. IT CAN BE SERVED WITH MORE COMPLICATED SAUCES BUT GOES EQUALLY WELL WITH A LIGHT DRIZZLE OF SOY AND OYSTER SAUCE.

400–500 g (1 lb) Chinese broccoli
  (gai lan)
2 tablespoons oil
1 tablespoon oyster sauce
2 tablespoons light soy sauce

SERVES 4

WASH the broccoli well. Discard any tough-looking stems and cut the rest of the stems in half. Blanch the broccoli in a pan of boiling water for 2 minutes, or until the stems and leaves are just tender, then refresh in cold water and dry thoroughly. Arrange in a serving dish.

HEAT a wok over high heat, add the oil and heat until very hot. Carefully pour the hot oil over the Chinese broccoli (it will splatter). Gently toss the oil through the Chinese broccoli and drizzle with the oyster sauce and soy sauce. Serve hot.

Chinese broccoli (gai lan) comes in both the more common green and a dark purple variety.

STIR-FRIED BOK CHOY

BOK CHOY COMES IN SEVERAL VARIETIES AND SIZES. SOME TYPES HAVE LONG WHITE STEMS AND VERY GREEN LEAVES, WHEREAS OTHERS, SUCH AS SHANGHAI (BABY) BOK CHOY, HAVE SHORTER PALE-GREEN STEMS AND LEAVES. ALL TYPES ARE INTERCHANGEABLE IN RECIPES.

400 g (14 oz) bok choy
2 tablespoons oil
2 garlic cloves, smashed with the
  flat side of a cleaver
3 thin slices ginger, smashed with
  the flat side of a cleaver
3 tablespoons chicken stock
  (page 565)
1 teaspoon sugar
salt or light soy sauce, to taste
1 teaspoon roasted sesame oil

SERVES 4

CUT the bok choy into 5–8 cm (2–3¼ inch) lengths. Trim off any roots that may hold the pieces together, then wash well and dry thoroughly.

HEAT a wok over high heat, add the oil and heat until very hot. Stir-fry the garlic and ginger for 30 seconds. Add the bok choy and stir-fry until it begins to wilt, then add the stock and sugar and season with the salt or soy sauce. Simmer, covered, for 2 minutes, or until the stems and leaves are tender but still green. Add the sesame oil and serve hot.

CHINESE BROCCOLI WITH
SOY SAUCE

SIDE DISHES

PINEAPPLE CHUTNEY

THIS QUICK AND SIMPLE FRESH PINEAPPLE CHUTNEY CAN BE ENJOYED AS PART OF ANY MAIN MEAL INCLUDING MEAT AND POULTRY OR FISH AND SEAFOOD DISHES. THE ACIDITY OF THE PINEAPPLE WILL CUT THROUGH ANY RICH DISHES AND MAKE A REFRESHING CONTRAST.

2 small or 1 large pineapple,
  slightly green
1 teaspoon salt
1 red onion, thinly sliced into
  half rings
4 red chillies, seeded and finely
  chopped
4 garlic cloves, finely chopped
2 teaspoons ginger juice
  (page 554)
30 g (1 oz) icing sugar, or to taste
6 tablespoons lime juice, or to taste

SERVES 6

PEEL the pineapple by cutting down the outside in strips. Remove any remaining eyes, then slice the pineapple lengthwise and remove the tough central core.

RUB the pineapple with the salt and leave it to sit for a few minutes in a colander to draw out some of the juices. Rinse, then chop into small chunks and drain well on paper towels.

MIX all the ingredients together in a bowl, adding enough sugar, lime juice, pepper and salt to achieve a balanced flavour. Chill and serve.

PODI

PODI

PODI IS A COARSE POWDER USED AS A DIP OR AS A SEASONING. EAT IT WITH IDLI OR USE IT AS A SCATTER SEASONING FOR STEAMED VEGETABLES OR SALADS. THIS WILL MAKE ENOUGH TO LAST A LONG TIME SO STORE IT IN A JAR AND USE IT AS YOU NEED IT (YOU CAN MAKE HALF IF YOU WISH).

110 g (4 oz) urad dal
100 g (3½ oz) chana dal
10 g (⅓ oz) dried chillies
75 g (2½ oz) sesame seeds
½ teaspoon sugar
½ teaspoon salt
1 tablespoon ghee

MAKES 220 G (8 OZ)

PLACE a small frying pan over low heat and dry-roast the urad dal, stirring constantly until brown. Remove from the pan and repeat with the chana dal, dried chillies and sesame seeds. Grind the roasted mixture to a powder with the sugar and salt, using a spice grinder or pestle and mortar. Cool completely and store in a jar or an airtight container.

WHEN ready to serve, heat the ghee in a frying pan and add 2 teaspoons of podi per person. Toss together until well mixed.

SWEET TOMATO CHUTNEY

THIS IS AN EASY STORE-CUPBOARD CHUTNEY. IT IS AN ESPECIALLY HANDY RECIPE IF YOU HAVE AN ABUNDANCE OF VERY RIPE TOMATOES. IF YOU CAN'T FIND CLEAR VINEGAR USE WHITE VINEGAR.

8 garlic cloves, roughly chopped
5 cm (2 inch) piece of ginger, roughly chopped
2 x 400 g (14 oz) tins chopped tomatoes or 800g (1 lb 12 oz) peeled fresh tomatoes
300 ml clear vinegar
350 g jaggery or soft brown sugar
2 tablespoons sultanas
2 teaspoons salt
3/4 teaspoon cayenne pepper
chilli powder (optional)

MAKES 500 ML (2 CUPS)

COMBINE the garlic, ginger and half of the tomatoes in a blender or food processor and blend until smooth. If you don't have a blender, crush the garlic, grate the ginger and push the tomatoes through a sieve before mixing them all together.

PUT the rest of the tomatoes, the vinegar, sugar, sultanas and salt in a large, heavy-based saucepan. Bring to the boil and add the garlic and ginger mixture. Reduce the heat and simmer gently for 1 1/2–1 3/4 hours, stirring occasionally, until the mixture is thick enough to fall off a spoon in sheets. Make sure the mixture doesn't catch on the base.

ADD the cayenne pepper. For a hotter chutney, add a little chilli powder. Leave to cool, then pour into sterilized jars (wash two 250 ml/1 cup jars in boiling water and dry them in a warm oven). Store in a cool place, or in the fridge after opening.

Shelled tamarind husk and pulp.

TAMARIND AND RAISIN CHUTNEY

2 teaspoons fennel seeds
250 ml (1 cup) tamarind purée (page 554)
50 g (2 oz) pitted dates, chopped
30 g (1 oz) raisins
1 teaspoon chilli powder
180 g (6 oz) jaggery or soft brown sugar
1 tablespoon oil
1/2 teaspoon black mustard seeds
6 green chillies, slit in half and seeded but left whole

MAKES 250 ML (1 CUP)

PLACE a small frying pan over low heat and dry-roast the fennel seeds, stirring constantly until aromatic. Grind the seeds to a fine powder using a spice grinder or pestle and mortar. Mix the ground fennel with the tamarind, dates, raisins, chilli powder, jaggery and a pinch of salt.

HEAT the oil in a large, heavy-based saucepan over medium heat, add the mustard seeds, then cover and shake the pan until they start to pop. Add the date mixture and chillies, bring to the boil and cook for about 3 minutes, until the mixture starts to thicken. Reduce the heat and simmer for 40 minutes until the chutney is thick enough to fall off a spoon in sheets. Cool, then put in a sterilized jar (wash the jar in boiling water and dry in a warm oven). Store in a cool place. Refrigerate after opening.

TAMARIND AND RAISIN CHUTNEY

CHURRI

THIS IS A VERY REFRESHING SIDE DISH WHICH IS TRADITIONALLY USED AS AN ACCOMPANIMENT TO BIRYANI BUT IT IS VERSATILE AND CAN BE SERVED WITH MOST INDIAN DISHES. THE YOGHURT AND BUTTERMILK HAVE A COOLING EFFECT WHEN CHURRI IS EATEN WITH HOT OR SPICY DISHES.

1 teaspoon cumin seeds
10 g (⅓ oz) mint leaves, roughly chopped
15 g (½ oz) coriander (cilantro) leaves, roughly chopped
2 cm (¾ inch) piece of ginger, roughly chopped
2 green chillies, roughly chopped
300 ml (1¼ cups) thick natural yoghurt (page 554)
300 ml (1¼ cups) buttermilk
1 onion, thinly sliced

SERVES 4

PLACE a small frying pan over low heat and dry-roast the cumin seeds until aromatic. Grind the seeds to a fine powder in a spice grinder or pestle and mortar.

CHOP the mint, coriander, ginger and chilli to a fine paste in a blender, or chop together finely with a knife. Add the yoghurt and buttermilk and a pinch of salt to the mixture and blend until all the ingredients are well mixed. Check the seasoning, adjust if necessary, then mix in the sliced onion and the ground cumin, reserving a little cumin to sprinkle on top.

The Charminar, Hyderabad.

CARROT PACHADI

THIS DELIGHTFUL CARROT SIDE DISH IS SIMILAR TO RAITA, PACHADI BEING THE SOUTHERN INDIAN TERM FOR A YOGHURT-BASED ACCOMPANIMENT. THIS GOES PARTICULARLY WELL WITH BIRYANI AND PULAO BUT IS SUITABLE FOR SERVING WITH MANY OTHER DISHES AS THE YOGHURT IS SOOTHING.

1 tablespoon oil
1 teaspoon black mustard seeds
2–3 dried chillies
¼ teaspoon asafoetida
1 stalk of curry leaves
600 ml (2½ cups) thick natural yoghurt (page 554)
4 carrots, finely grated
coriander (cilantro) leaves

SERVES 4

HEAT the oil in a small saucepan over medium heat, add the mustard seeds and chillies, then cover and shake the pan until the seeds start to pop. Remove from the heat and immediately stir in the asafoetida and curry leaves.

WHISK the yoghurt to remove any lumps, then mix in the grated carrot. Mix in the mustard seeds, chillies, asafoetida, curry leaves along with the oil, then season with salt, to taste. Garnish with coriander leaves.

CARROT PACHADI

LEGUMES

CHANA MASALA

CHANA MASALA IS SERVED UP BY TRAVELLING VENDORS IN BAZAARS OR ON THE STREETS OF INDIA, AND EATEN WITH PURIS. IT IS ENJOYED BY EVERYBODY AT ALL TIMES OF THE DAY AS A SNACK OR A LIGHT MEAL AND MAKES A GOOD ACCOMPANIMENT TO ANY INDIAN MEAL.

Asafoetida is used as a pungent seasoning in many dishes. It is also used in dishes made with pulses because it helps dissipate the gasses they create. Powdered versions like this often contain rice flour and turmeric as well.

Pulses are on sale all over India, in their uncooked form and also fried as snacks.

250 g (9 oz) chickpeas
1 large onion, roughly chopped
2 garlic cloves, roughly chopped
5 cm (2 inch) piece of ginger, roughly chopped
1 green chilli, chopped
160 ml (2/3 cup) oil
1 tablespoon ground cumin
1 tablespoon ground coriander (cilantro)
1 teaspoon chilli powder
pinch of asafoetida
2 tablespoons thick natural yoghurt (page 554)
2 1/4 tablespoons garam masala (page 556)
2 teaspoons tamarind purée (page 554)
1/2 lemon
3 green chillies, extra
1/4 teaspoon ground black pepper
3 teaspoons salt
2 teaspoons chaat masala (page 556)
1/2 red onion, sliced into thin rings
2 cm (3/4 inch) piece of ginger, cut into thin strips
coriander (cilantro) leaves, roughly chopped (optional)

SERVES 6

SOAK the chickpeas overnight in 2 litres (8 cups) of water. Drain, then put the chickpeas in a large saucepan with another 2 litres (8 cups) water. Bring to the boil, spooning off any scum from the surface, then simmer over low heat for 1–1 1/2 hours, until soft. It is important the chickpeas are soft at this stage as they won't soften once the sauce has been added. Drain, reserving the cooking liquid.

BLEND the onion, garlic, ginger and chopped chilli to a paste in a food processor or very finely chop them together with a knife.

HEAT the oil in a heavy-based saucepan over medium heat and fry the onion mixture until golden brown. Add the cumin, coriander, chilli powder and asafoetida, then stir for 1 minute. Add the yoghurt and stir for another minute. Stir in 2 tablespoons of the garam masala and pour in 1.25 litres (5 cups) of the reserved cooking liquid, a little at a time, stirring after each addition. Bring to the boil, then reduce the heat to simmering point.

ADD the tamarind purée, lemon, whole chillies, chickpeas, pepper and the salt. Partially cover the pan, simmer for 30 minutes, then remove the lemon. Cook the sauce for another 30 minutes, or until all the liquid has reduced, leaving the softened chickpeas coated in a rich dark brown sauce.

ADD the chaat masala and remaining garam masala and stir in the raw onion rings, ginger and coriander leaves if using.

Selling snacks in Yunnan.

Fresh bean curd and chilli pastes are readily available at the markets in China.

MA PO TOFU

A QUINTESSENTIAL SICHUANESE DISH, SUPPOSEDLY NAMED AFTER AN OLD WOMAN WHO SERVED THIS IN HER RESTAURANT AND WHOSE POCKMARKED COMPLEXION LED TO THE DISH BEING CALLED MA PO TOFU, 'POCKMARKED GRANDMOTHER'S TOFU'. SOFT BEAN CURD IS TRADITIONALLY USED.

750 g (1 lb 10 oz) soft or firm bean curd, drained
250 g (9 oz) minced beef or pork
2 tablespoons dark soy sauce
1 1/2 tablespoons Shaoxing rice wine
1/2 teaspoon roasted sesame oil
2 teaspoons Sichuan peppercorns
1 tablespoon oil
2 spring onions (scallions), finely chopped
2 garlic cloves, finely chopped
2 teaspoons finely chopped ginger
1 tablespoon chilli bean paste (toban jiang), or to taste
250 ml (1 cup) chicken and meat stock (page 565)
1 1/2 teaspoons cornflour
1 spring onion (scallion), finely shredded

SERVES 6

CUT the bean curd into cubes. Place the meat in a bowl with 2 teaspoons of the soy sauce, 2 teaspoons of the rice wine and the sesame oil, and toss lightly. Dry-fry the Sichuan peppercorns in a wok or pan until brown and aromatic, then crush lightly.

HEAT a wok over high heat, add the oil and heat until very hot. Stir-fry the meat until browned, mashing and chopping to separate the pieces. Remove the meat with a wire sieve or slotted spoon and heat the oil until any liquid from the meat has evaporated. Add the spring onion, garlic and ginger and stir-fry for 10 seconds, or until fragrant. Add the chilli bean paste and stir-fry for 5 seconds.

COMBINE the stock with the remaining soy sauce and rice wine. Add to the wok, bring to the boil, then add the bean curd and meat. Return to the boil, reduce the heat to medium and cook for 5 minutes, or until the sauce has reduced by a quarter. If you are using soft bean curd, do not stir or it will break up.

COMBINE the cornflour with enough water to make a paste, add to the sauce and simmer until thickened. Season if necessary. Serve sprinkled with the spring onion and Sichuan peppercorns.

PASTA WITH BORLOTTI BEANS

200 g (7 oz) dried borlotti beans
2 tablespoons olive oil
100 g (3 oz) pancetta, diced
1 celery stalk, chopped
1 onion, finely chopped
1 carrot, diced
1 garlic clove, crushed
3 tablespoons chopped parsley
1 bay leaf
400 g (14 oz) tin chopped
   tomatoes, drained
1.5 litres (6 cups) vegetable stock
150 g (5 oz) ditalini or macaroni
drizzle of extra virgin olive oil
grated Parmesan

SERVES 4

PLACE the beans in a large saucepan, cover with cold water and soak overnight. Drain and rinse under cold water.

HEAT the olive oil in a large saucepan and add the pancetta, celery, onion, carrot and garlic and cook over moderately low heat for 5 minutes until golden. Season with black pepper. Add the parsley, bay leaf, tomatoes, stock and borlotti beans and bring slowly to the boil. Reduce the heat and simmer for 1–1$\frac{1}{2}$ hours, or until the beans are tender, adding a little boiling water every so often to maintain the level.

ADD the pasta and simmer for about 6 minutes, or until the pasta is just *al dente*. Remove from the heat and leave to rest for 10 minutes. Serve warm with a drizzle of extra virgin olive oil over each bowl. Serve the Parmesan separately.

Chickpeas are grown in the south of Italy but appear in the cuisines of all regions, either whole or ground into *farinata* (flour).

PASTA WITH CHICKPEAS

250 g (9 oz) dried chickpeas
3 tablespoons olive oil
1 large onion, finely chopped
1 celery stalk, finely chopped
1 carrot, finely chopped
2 garlic cloves, crushed
1 rosemary sprig
pinch of crushed dried chilli
2 tablespoons tomato purée
1.5 litres (6 cups) vegetable stock
125 g (4 oz) small pasta shells
drizzle of extra virgin olive oil
grated Parmesan

SERVES 4

PUT the chickpeas in a large saucepan, cover with cold water and soak overnight. Drain and rinse under cold water.

HEAT the olive oil in a large saucepan, add the chopped vegetables, garlic and rosemary and cook over moderately low heat for 8 minutes. Add the chilli and season. Stir in the tomato purée and stock, then add the chickpeas. Bring to the boil. Reduce the heat and simmer for 1–1$\frac{1}{2}$ hours, or until the chickpeas are tender, adding a little boiling water every so often to maintain the level.

ADD the pasta and continue cooking until it is *al dente*. Remove the rosemary sprig. Drizzle with extra virgin olive oil and sprinkle with Parmesan.

PASTA WITH CHICKPEAS

SALT PORK WITH LENTILS

THE DRY CLIMATE AND VOLCANIC SOIL AROUND THE FRENCH TOWN OF LE PUY-EN-VELAY IN THE AUVERGNE ARE THE LUCKY COMBINATION THAT PRODUCES THE REGION'S SUPERIOR GREEN LENTIL. THEY ARE MORE EXPENSIVE THAN OTHER VARIETIES, BUT HAVE A SUPERB FLAVOUR.

1 kg (2 lb 3 oz) salt pork belly, cut into thick strips
1 small salt pork knuckle
1 large carrot, cut into chunks
200 g (7 oz) swede or turnips, peeled and cut into chunks
100 g (3 oz) leek, white part only, thickly sliced
1 parsnip, cut into chunks
1 onion, studded with 4 cloves
1 garlic clove
bouquet garni
2 bay leaves
6 juniper berries, slightly crushed
350 g (12 oz) puy lentils
2 tablespoons chopped parsley

SERVES 6

DEPENDING ON the saltiness of the pork you are using, you may need to soak it in cold water for several hours or blanch it before using. Ask your butcher whether to do this.

PUT the pork in a large saucepan with all the ingredients except the lentils and parsley. Stir thoroughly, then add just enough water to cover the ingredients. Bring to the boil, then reduce the heat, cover the pan and leave to simmer gently for 1¹/₄ hours.

PUT the lentils in a sieve and rinse under cold running water. Add to the saucepan and stir, then replace the lid and simmer for a further 45–50 minutes, or until the pork and lentils are tender.

DRAIN the pan into a colander, discarding the liquid. Return the contents of the colander to the saucepan, except for the whole onion which can be thrown away. Season the pork and lentils with plenty of black pepper and taste to see if you need any salt. Stir in the parsley.

Use a pan large enough to fit all the ingredients comfortably. Unlike other varieties, puy lentils keep their shape when cooked.

MUSHROOMS WITH TOFU

TOFU AND MUSHROOMS ARE COMMONLY USED TOGETHER IN CHINESE DISHES, JUST AS THEY ARE HERE IN THIS THAI DISH. THE BLANDNESS OF THE TOFU IS A CONTRAST TO BOTH THE TEXTURE AND FLAVOUR OF THE MUSHROOMS. FOR THE BEST FLAVOUR, USE THE TYPE OF MUSHROOMS SUGGESTED.

The mushrooms and tofu are cut into similarly sized pieces so that they cook evenly in the wok.

350 g (12 oz) firm tofu (bean curd)
1 teaspoon sesame oil
2 teaspoons light soy sauce
¼ teaspoon ground black pepper, plus some to sprinkle
1 tablespoon finely shredded ginger
5 tablespoons vegetable stock or water
2 tablespoons light soy sauce
2 teaspoons cornflour (cornstarch)
½ teaspoon sugar
1½ tablespoons vegetable oil
2 garlic cloves, finely chopped
200 g (7 oz) oyster mushrooms, hard stalks removed, cut in half if large
200 g (7 oz) shiitake mushrooms, hard stalks removed
2 spring onions (scallions), sliced diagonally, for garnish
1 long red chilli, seeded and finely sliced, for garnish

SERVES 2

DRAIN each block of tofu and cut into 2.5 cm (1 inch) pieces. Put them in a shallow dish and sprinkle with the sesame oil, light soy sauce, ground pepper and ginger. Leave to marinate for 30 minutes.

MIX the stock with the light soy sauce, cornflour and sugar in a small bowl until smooth.

HEAT the oil in a wok or frying pan and stir-fry the garlic over a medium heat until light brown. Add all the mushrooms and stir-fry for 3–4 minutes or until the mushrooms are cooked. Add the cornflour liquid, then carefully add the pieces of tofu and gently mix for 1–2 minutes. Taste, then adjust the seasoning if necessary.

SPOON onto a serving plate and sprinkle with spring onions, chilli slices and ground pepper.

Ringing the bells at Wat Phra That Doi Tung.

PARIPPU

A DISH THAT INCLUDES LENTILS OF SOME SORT IS A MUST AS PART OF ANY INDIAN MEAL. THIS RECIPE IS FROM THE SOUTH AND IS FLAVOURED WITH COCONUT AS WELL AS A TARKA OF FRIED ONION, CUMIN SEEDS, MUSTARD SEEDS AND CURRY LEAVES WHICH IS MIXED IN TOWARDS THE END OF COOKING.

225 g (8 oz) masoor dal (red lentils)
1 onion, roughly chopped
1 ripe tomato, roughly chopped
50 g (2 oz) creamed coconut,
  mixed with 250 ml (1 cup) water,
  or 250 ml (1 cup) coconut milk
  (page 551)
2 green chillies, chopped
1/4 teaspoon ground turmeric
1/2 teaspoon ground cumin
1/2 teaspoon ground coriander
  (cilantro)
2 tablespoons oil
1 teaspoon cumin seeds
1/2 teaspoon black mustard seeds
1 onion, very finely chopped
10 curry leaves

SERVES 4

PUT the lentils in a heavy-based saucepan with 500 ml (2 cups) water. Add the roughly chopped onion, tomato, creamed coconut or coconut milk, green chilli, turmeric, ground cumin and coriander, and bring to the boil. Simmer and cook, stirring occasionally until the lentils are cooked to a soft mush (masoor dal does not hold its shape when it cooks). This will take about 25 minutes. If all the water has evaporated before the lentils are cooked, add 125 ml (1/2 cup) of boiling water.

FOR the final seasoning (tarka), heat the oil in a small saucepan over low heat. Add the cumin seeds and mustard seeds, cover and allow the seeds to pop. Add the finely chopped onion and curry leaves and fry over low heat until the onion is golden brown. Pour the seasoned onions into the simmering lentils. Season with salt, to taste, and cook for another 5 minutes.

A woman binds curry leaves into neat bundles in the market.

FAGIOLI ALL'UCCELLETTO

350 g (12 oz) dried cannellini beans
bouquet garni
125 ml (½ cup) olive oil
2 garlic cloves
1 sage sprig, or ½ teaspoon dried sage
4 ripe tomatoes, peeled and chopped
1 tablespoon balsamic vinegar

SERVES 6

SOAK the beans in cold water overnight, then drain. Place in a large saucepan of cold water with the bouquet garni and bring to the boil. Add 2 tablespoons of the olive oil, reduce the heat and simmer for 1 hour. Add 1 teaspoon of salt and 500 ml (2 cups) boiling water and cook for a further 30 minutes, or until tender. Drain.

CUT the garlic cloves in half and put in a large saucepan with the sage and the remaining oil. Gently heat to infuse the flavours, but do not fry. Add the tomato and simmer for 10 minutes, then discard the garlic and the sprig of sage.

ADD the beans, season well and simmer for 15 minutes. Add a little boiling water at first to keep the pan moist, but then let the liquid evaporate towards the end of cooking. Stir the vinegar through just before serving. Serve hot.

The popularity of the bean has spread from its home region of Tuscany (whose inhabitants are affectionately known as the 'bean-eaters') to embrace the whole country. Many varieties of bean are bought dried and need to be soaked overnight before use.

BRAISED BORLOTTI BEANS

THESE BEANS ARE BEST EATEN WARM OR COLD RATHER THAN PIPING HOT STRAIGHT FROM THE STOVE. THEY KEEP WELL IN THE FRIDGE FOR UP TO SIX DAYS, BUT, IF YOU ARE MAKING THEM IN ADVANCE, DON'T ADD THE PARSLEY UNTIL YOU ARE READY TO SERVE.

350 g (12 oz) dried borlotti beans
440 ml (1½ cups) dry red wine
1 small onion, finely chopped
3 cloves
125 ml (½ cup) olive oil
1 rosemary sprig
3 garlic cloves, crushed
pinch of chilli flakes
3 tablespoons chopped parsley

SERVES 6

SOAK the beans in cold water overnight, then drain. Place in a large saucepan and add the wine, onion, cloves, half the olive oil and 875 ml (3½ cups) water. Cover and bring to the boil. Reduce the heat, remove the lid and simmer for 1 hour.

HEAT the remaining oil in a small saucepan. Strip the leaves off the rosemary sprig and chop finely. Place in the oil with the garlic and chilli and cook for 1 minute. Add to the beans and simmer for 30 minutes to1 hour, until the beans are tender.

DRAIN the beans, reserving the cooking liquid. Return the cooking liquid to the pan and simmer until it thickens. Season. Return the beans to the pan and simmer for a further 5 minutes. Stir in the parsley and cool for 15 minutes before serving.

BRAISED BORLOTTI BEANS

Transporting bean curd in Hangzhou.

The Temple of Heaven in Beijing.

NORTHERN-STYLE BEAN CURD

THIS DISH WAS APPARENTLY A FAVOURITE OF DOWAGER EMPRESS TZU-HSI IN THE NINETEENTH CENTURY, AND IT'S STILL A POPULAR CLASSIC IN CHINA TODAY. THE BEAN CURD IS FIRST FRIED, THEN SIMMERED SO THAT IT MELTS IN YOUR MOUTH.

1 kg (2 lb 3 oz) firm bean curd, drained
oil for deep-frying
120 g (4 oz) cornflour
2 eggs, lightly beaten
1 tablespoon finely chopped ginger
350 ml (1½ cups) chicken stock (page 565)
2 tablespoons Shaoxing rice wine
1 teaspoon salt, or to taste
½ teaspoon sugar
1½ teaspoons roasted sesame oil
2 spring onions (scallions), green part only, finely chopped

SERVES 6

HOLDING a cleaver parallel to the cutting surface, slice each bean curd cake in half horizontally. Cut each piece into 3 cm (1¼ inch) squares.

FILL a wok one quarter full of oil. Heat the oil to 190°C (375°F), or until a piece of bread fries golden brown in 10 seconds when dropped in the oil. Coat each piece of bean curd in the cornflour, then dip in the beaten egg to coat. Cook the bean curd in batches for 3–4 minutes on each side, or until golden brown. Remove with a wire sieve or slotted spoon and drain in a colander. Pour the oil from the wok, leaving 1 teaspoon.

REHEAT the reserved oil over high heat until very hot and stir-fry the ginger for 5 seconds, or until fragrant. Add the stock, rice wine, salt and sugar, and bring to the boil. Add the fried bean curd and pierce the pieces with a fork so that they will absorb the cooking liquid. Cook over medium heat for 20 minutes, or until all the liquid is absorbed. Drizzle the sesame oil over the bean curd, toss carefully to coat, sprinkle with the spring onion and serve.

An outdoor haircut in Beijing.

371

KALI DAL

DAL, WHICH IS BOTH THE NAME OF THE LENTILS, AND IN THIS CASE THE DISH, IS PART OF THE STAPLE DIET IN INDIA. THIS IS A SUMPTUOUS VERSION OF A SIMPLE DISH SERVED WITH ROTIS IN SIKH GURUDWARAS (TEMPLES). KALI MEANS BLACK AND THE GRAM IN THIS DISH HAVE A BLACK SKIN.

250 g (9 oz) whole black gram (sabat urad)
1 onion, roughly chopped
2 garlic cloves, roughly chopped
5 cm (2 inch) piece of ginger, roughly chopped
1 green chilli, roughly chopped
120 ml (½ cup) oil
2 tablespoons ground cumin
1 tablespoon ground coriander (cilantro)
2 teaspoons salt
¼ teaspoon chilli powder
3 tablespoons garam masala (page 556)
140 ml (½ cup) single cream

SERVES 6

PUT the whole black gram in a large, heavy-based saucepan, add 2 litres (8 cups) water and bring to the boil. Reduce the heat and simmer for 1 hour, or until the dal feels soft when pressed between the thumb and index finger. Most of the dal will split to reveal the creamy insides. Drain, reserving the cooking liquid.

BLEND the onion, garlic, ginger and chilli together in a food processor to form a paste, or finely chop them together with a knife. Heat the oil in a frying pan and fry the onion mixture over high heat, stirring constantly, until golden brown. Add the cumin and coriander and fry for 2 minutes. Add the dal and stir in the salt, chilli powder and garam masala. Pour 300 ml (1¼ cups) of the reserved dal liquid into the pan, bring to the boil, then reduce the heat and simmer for 10 minutes. Just before serving, stir in the cream and simmer for another 2 minutes to heat through.

A huge range of pulses and legumes are sold in the markets of India. These are eaten on a daily basis, often made into dal.

MASALA RAJMA

225 g (8 oz) kidney beans
3 tablespoons oil
½ onion, finely chopped
2 Indian bay leaves (cassia leaves)
5 cm (2 inch) piece of cinnamon stick
2 garlic cloves, finely chopped
¼ teaspoon ground turmeric
½ teaspoon ground coriander (cilantro)
½ teaspoon ground cumin
½ teaspoon garam masala (page 556)
3 dried chillies
2 cm (¾ inch) piece of ginger, grated

SERVES 4

SOAK the kidney beans overnight in 1.25 litres (5 cups) water in a large saucepan. Drain, return the beans to the saucepan with another 1.25 litres (5 cups) water and bring to the boil. Boil for 15 minutes, then reduce the heat and simmer for 1 hour, or until the kidney beans are tender. Drain, reserving the liquid.

HEAT the oil in a heavy-based saucepan over low heat. Add the onion, bay leaves, cinnamon and garlic and cook until the onion is lightly browned. Add the turmeric, coriander, cumin, garam masala, chillies and ginger and stir well. Add the beans with enough of their liquid to make a sauce. Bring to the boil and cook for 5 minutes, stirring constantly. Season with salt, to taste. If you wish, remove the chillies before serving.

MASALA RAJMA

RICE, NOODLES AND GRAINS

Gabriele Ferron cooking risotto at his restaurant in Isola della Scala.

For freshness, grate the Parmesan from a block as you need it. Take care as you fold in the asparagus tips—they break easily.

ASPARAGUS RISOTTO

THIS RISOTTO IS PARTICULARLY FLAVOURSOME BECAUSE THE ASPARAGUS STEMS ARE PUREED WITH THE STOCK AND SO ADDED TO THE RISOTTO DURING THE COOKING. THE ADDITION OF CREAM AT THE END GIVES A RICH CONSISTENCY.

1 kg (2 lb 3 oz) asparagus
500 ml (2 cups) chicken stock
500 ml (2 cups) vegetable stock
4 tablespoons olive oil
1 small onion, finely chopped
350 g (12 oz) risotto rice (arborio, vialone nano or carnaroli)
75 g (2½ oz) Parmesan, grated
3 tablespoons double cream

SERVES 4

WASH the asparagus and remove the woody ends (hold each spear at both ends and bend it gently—it will snap at its natural breaking point). Separate the tender spear tips from the stems.

COOK the asparagus stems in boiling water for 8 minutes, or until very tender. Drain and place in a blender with the chicken and vegetable stocks. Blend for 1 minute, then put in a saucepan, bring to the boil and maintain at a low simmer.

COOK the asparagus tips in boiling water for 1 minute, drain and refresh in iced water.

HEAT the olive oil in a large wide heavy-based saucepan. Add the onion and cook until softened but not browned. Add the rice and reduce the heat to low. Season and stir briefly to thoroughly coat the rice. Stir in a ladleful of the simmering stock and cook over moderate heat, stirring continuously. When the stock has been absorbed, stir in another ladleful. Continue like this for about 20 minutes, until all the stock has been added and the rice is *al dente*. (You may not need to use all the stock, or you may need a little extra—every risotto will be slightly different.)

ADD the Parmesan and cream and gently stir in the asparagus tips. Season with salt and pepper and serve hot.

A woman sorts through her rice by tossing it in the air to get rid of any chaff. In India rice often has to be picked over before use.

PULAO

PULAO OR PILAF CAN BE PLAIN OR A FESTIVE, ELABORATE DISH WITH FRUIT, NUTS AND SPICES AS HERE. RICE DISHES THAT REFLECT THESE FLAVOURS CAN BE FOUND AS FAR AFIELD AS SOUTHERN RUSSIA, PERSIA AND MOROCCO, A LEGACY OF DISHES TRAVELLING WITH CONQUERORS AND TRADERS.

500 g (1 lb 2 oz) basmati rice
1 teaspoon cumin seeds
4 tablespoons ghee or oil
2 tablespoons chopped almonds
2 tablespoons raisins or sultanas
2 onions, finely sliced
2 cinnamon sticks
5 cardamom pods
1 teaspoon sugar
1 tablespoon ginger juice
   (page 554)
15 saffron threads, soaked in
   1 tablespoon warm milk
2 Indian bay leaves (cassia leaves)
250 ml (1 cup) coconut milk
   (page 551)
2 tablespoons fresh or frozen peas
rosewater (optional)

SERVES 6

WASH the rice in a sieve under cold, running water until the water from the rice runs clear. Drain the rice and put in a saucepan, cover with water and soak for 30 minutes. Drain.

PLACE a small frying pan over low heat and dry-roast the cumin seeds until aromatic.

HEAT the ghee or oil in a karhai or heavy-based frying pan and fry the almonds and raisins until browned. Remove from the pan, fry the onion in the same ghee until dark golden brown, then remove from the pan.

ADD the rice, roasted cumin seeds, cinnamon, cardamom, sugar, ginger juice, saffron and salt to the pan and fry for 2 minutes, or until aromatic.

ADD the bay leaves and coconut milk to the pan, then add enough water to come about 5 cm (2 inches) above the rice. Bring to the boil, cover and cook over medium heat for 8 minutes, or until most of the water has evaporated.

ADD the peas to the pan and stir well. Reduce the heat to very low and cook until the rice is cooked through. Stir in the fried almonds, raisins and onion, reserving some for garnishing. Drizzle with a few drops of rosewater if you would like a more perfumed dish.

PEARL BALLS

THIS FAMOUS DISH ORIGINATED IN HUNAN PROVINCE, ONE OF CHINA'S MAJOR RICE BASINS. ONCE STEAMED, THE STICKY RICE THAT FORMS THE COATING FOR THESE MEATBALLS TURNS INTO PEARL-LIKE GRAINS. TRADITIONALLY, GLUTINOUS OR SWEET RICE IS USED, BUT YOU COULD USE RISOTTO RICE.

330 g (11 oz) glutinous or sweet rice
8 dried Chinese mushrooms
150 g (5 oz) peeled water chestnuts
450 g (1 lb) minced pork
1 small carrot, grated
2 spring onions (scallions), finely chopped
1¹/₂ tablespoons finely chopped ginger
2 tablespoons light soy sauce
1 tablespoon Shaoxing rice wine
1¹/₂ teaspoons roasted sesame oil
2¹/₂ tablespoons cornflour
soy sauce

SERVES 6

PUT the rice in a bowl and, using your fingers as a rake, rinse under cold running water to remove any dust. Drain the rice in a colander, then place it in a bowl with enough cold water to cover. Set aside for 1 hour. Drain the rice and transfer it to a baking tray in an even layer.

SOAK the dried mushrooms in boiling water for 30 minutes, then drain and squeeze out any excess water. Remove and discard the stems and chop the caps.

BLANCH the water chestnuts in a pan of boiling water for 1 minute, then refresh in cold water. Drain, pat dry and finely chop them.

PLACE the pork in a bowl, add the mushrooms, water chestnuts, carrot, spring onion, ginger, soy sauce, rice wine, sesame oil and cornflour. Stir the mixture vigorously to combine.

ROLL the mixture into 2 cm (¾ inch) balls, then roll each meatball in the glutinous rice so that it is completely coated. Lightly press the rice to make it stick to the meatball. Place the pearl balls well apart in three steamers lined with greaseproof paper punched with holes or some damp cheesecloth or muslin. Cover and steam over simmering water in a wok, reversing the steamers halfway through, for 25 minutes. If the rice is still *al dente*, continue to cook for a little longer until it softens. Serve with the soy sauce.

Roll the meatballs so they are completely coated in the glutinous rice, then press the rice on firmly so it sticks.

Score the insides of the squid tubes in a crisscross pattern.

EGG NOODLES WITH SEAFOOD

BA-MII ARE WHEAT FLOUR NOODLES, USUALLY MADE WITH EGG. STALLS SPECIALIZING IN BA-MII CAN BE FOUND ALL OVER THAILAND — NOODLE DISHES LIKE THIS ARE USUALLY EATEN AS A SNACK. SERVE WITH SLICED CHILLIES IN FISH SAUCE, DRIED CHILLI AND WHITE SUGAR FOR SEASONING.

8 raw prawns (shrimp)
2 squid tubes
250 g (9 oz) egg noodles
1 tablespoon vegetable oil
4 Asian shallots, smashed with the
    side of a cleaver
4 spring onions (scallions), cut into
    lengths and smashed with the
    side of a cleaver
2 cm (¾ inch) piece of ginger,
    finely shredded
2 garlic cloves, finely sliced
1 tablespoon preserved cabbage,
    rinsed and chopped (optional)
4 scallops, cut in half horizontally
1 tablespoon oyster sauce
2 teaspoons soy sauce
2 teaspoons fish sauce
½ bunch (1 cup) holy basil leaves

SERVES 4

PEEL and devein the prawns and cut each prawn along the back so it opens like a butterfly (leave each prawn joined along the base and at the tail, leaving the tail attached).

OPEN out the squid tubes and score the insides in a criss-cross pattern. Cut the squid tubes into squares.

COOK the egg noodles in boiling water, then drain and rinse.

HEAT the oil in a wok and add the shallots, spring onions, ginger, garlic and cabbage and stir-fry for 2 minutes. Add the prawns, squid and scallops one after the other, tossing after each addition, and cook for 3 minutes.

ADD the oyster and soy sauces and noodles and toss together. Add the fish sauce and holy basil and serve.

Preparing fish in Phetchaburi.

In China for this recipe, cassia bark *(middle)* is used more often than cinnamon.

CINNAMON BEEF NOODLES

1 teaspoon oil
10 spring onions (scallions), cut into
    4 cm lengths, lightly smashed
    with the flat side of a cleaver
10 garlic cloves, thinly sliced
6 slices ginger, smashed with the
    flat side of a cleaver
1¹/₂ teaspoons chilli bean paste
    (toban jiang)
2 cassia or cinnamon sticks
2 star anise
125 ml (¹/₂ cup) light soy sauce
1 kg (2 lb 3 oz) chuck steak,
    trimmed and cut into 4 cm
    (1¹/₂ inch) cubes
250 g (9 oz) rice stick noodles
250 g (9 oz) baby spinach
3 tablespoons finely chopped
    spring onion (scallion)

SERVES 6

HEAT a wok over medium heat, add the oil and heat until hot. Stir-fry the spring onion, garlic, ginger, chilli paste, cassia and star anise for 10 seconds, or until fragrant. Transfer to a clay pot, casserole or saucepan. Add the soy sauce and 2.25 litres (9 cups) water. Bring to the boil, add the beef, then return to the boil. Reduce the heat and simmer, covered, for 1¹/₂ hours, or until the beef is very tender. Skim the surface occasionally to remove impurities and fat. Remove and discard the ginger and cassia.

SOAK the noodles in hot water for 10 minutes, then drain and divide among six bowls. Add the spinach to the beef and bring to the boil. Spoon the beef mixture over the noodles and sprinkle with the spring onion.

LONGEVITY NOODLES

NOODLES IN CHINA SYMBOLIZE A LONG LIFE BECAUSE OF THEIR LENGTH AND ARE THEREFORE SERVED AT SPECIAL OCCASIONS SUCH AS BIRTHDAYS AND FEAST DAYS. THE NOODLES FOR THIS DISH CAN BE BOUGHT LABELLED AS LONGEVITY NOODLES.

LONGEVITY NOODLES

250 g (9 oz) precooked longevity or
    dried egg noodles
100 g (3 oz) bean sprouts
100 g (3 oz) fresh or tinned
    bamboo shoots, rinsed and
    drained
1 tablespoon oil
1 tablespoon finely chopped ginger
4 spring onions (scallions), thinly
    sliced
1 tablespoon light soy sauce
1 teaspoon roasted sesame oil
75 ml (¹/₃ cup) chicken stock
    (page 565)

SERVES 4

IF USING longevity noodles, cook in a pan of salted boiling water for 1 minute, drain, then rinse in cold water. If using dried egg noodles, cook in a pan of salted boiling water for 10 minutes, then drain. Wash the bean sprouts and drain thoroughly. Shred the bamboo shoots.

HEAT a wok over high heat, add the oil and heat until very hot. Stir-fry the ginger for a few seconds, then add the bean sprouts, bamboo shoots and spring onion and stir-fry for 1 minute. Add the soy sauce, sesame oil and stock and bring to the boil. Add the longevity or dried egg noodles and toss together until the sauce is absorbed.

Risotto rice comes in different types, all varying in absorbency. For this reason cooking times cannot be entirely accurate—just keep stirring until it is done.

MILANESE RISOTTO

MILANESE RISOTTO, THE CLASSIC ACCOMPANIMENT TO OSSO BUCO, TAKES ITS BRILLIANT YELLOW COLOUR FROM SAFFRON AND ITS RICH FLAVOUR FROM BEEF MARROW. IF BEEF MARROW IS HARD TO FIND, YOU CAN USE A FATTY PIECE OF LARDO, PROSCIUTTO OR PANCETTA, FINELY CHOPPED.

200 ml (¾ cup) dry white vermouth
   or white wine
large pinch of saffron threads
1.5 litres (6 cups) chicken stock
100 g (3 oz) butter
75 g (2½ oz) beef marrow
1 large onion, finely chopped
1 garlic clove, crushed
350 g (12 oz) risotto rice (arborio,
   vialone nano or carnaroli)
50 g (2 oz) Parmesan, grated

SERVES 6 AS A SIDE DISH

PUT the vermouth in a bowl, add the saffron and leave to soak. Put the stock in a saucepan, bring to the boil and then maintain at a low simmer.

MELT the butter and beef marrow in a large wide heavy-based saucepan. Add the onion and garlic and cook until softened but not browned. Add the rice and reduce the heat to low. Season and stir briefly to thoroughly coat the rice.

ADD the vermouth and saffron to the rice. Increase the heat and cook, stirring, until all the liquid has been absorbed. Stir in a ladleful of the simmering stock and cook over moderate heat, stirring continuously. When the stock has been absorbed, stir in another ladleful. Continue like this for about 20 minutes, until all the stock has been added and the rice is *al dente*. (You may not need to use all the stock, or you may need a little extra—every risotto will be slightly different.)

STIR IN a handful of Parmesan and serve the rest on the side for people to help themselves.

At Antica Riseria Ferron in the Veneto, rice is husked by hand then polished to produce perfect white grains.

CRISPY RICE NOODLES

THIS IS MADE BY DEEP-FRYING THE THINNEST RICE NOODLES INTO LIGHT AND CRISPY TANGLES. THESE ARE THEN TOSSED WITH SWEET AND SOUR SAUCE. THIS DISH SHOULD BE SERVED AS SOON AS IT IS COOKED OR THE NOODLES WILL LOSE THEIR CRISPINESS.

75 g (3 oz) rice vermicelli noodles
   (sen mii)
vegetable oil, for deep-frying
200 g (7 oz) firm tofu (bean curd),
   cut into matchsticks
75 g (3 oz) small Asian shallots or
   small red onions, finely sliced
150 g (5 oz) raw prawns (shrimp),
   peeled and deveined, tails intact
2 tablespoons fish sauce
2 tablespoons water or pickled
   garlic juice
1 tablespoon lime juice
2 tablespoons plum sauce
   (page 562) or tomato ketchup
1 tablespoon sweet chilli sauce
   (page 562)
4 tablespoons sugar
3 tablespoons palm sugar
3 small whole pickled garlic,
   finely sliced
110 g (1¼ cups) bean sprouts,
   tails removed, for garnish
3–4 spring onions (scallions),
   slivered, for garnish
1 long red chilli, seeded and
   cut into slivers, for garnish

SERVES 4

SOAK the noodles in cold water for 20 minutes, drain and dry very thoroughly on paper towels. Cut them into smaller lengths with a pair of scissors.

PUT the oil in the wok to a depth of about 8–10 cm (3–4 inches) and heat over a medium heat. Drop a piece of noodle into the wok. If it sinks and then immediately floats and puffs, the oil is ready. Drop a small handful of the noodles into the oil. Turn them once (it only takes seconds) and remove them as soon as they have swelled and turned a dark ivory colour. Remove the crispy noodles with a slotted spoon, hold over the wok briefly to drain, then transfer to a baking tray lined with paper towels to drain. Fry the remaining noodles in the same way. Break into smaller bits.

IN the same oil, deep-fry the tofu for 7–10 minutes or until golden and crisp. Remove and drain with a slotted spoon.

DEEP-FRY the shallots until crispy and golden brown. Remove with a slotted spoon and drain on paper towels.

DEEP-FRY the prawns for 1–2 minutes until they turn pink. Remove with a slotted spoon and drain on paper towels.

CAREFULLY pour off all the oil in the wok. Add the fish sauce, water, lime juice, plum sauce, sweet chilli sauce, sugar and palm sugar to the wok. Stir for 4–5 minutes over a low heat until slightly thick.

ADD half of the rice noodles and toss gently, mixing them into the sauce. Add the remaining noodles and tofu, prawns, pickled garlic and the shallots, tossing for 1–2 minutes until coated. Spoon onto a platter and garnish with bean sprouts, spring onions and chilli slivers.

Thai pickled garlic can be bought from Thai and Asian shops. Remove the crispy noodles and tofu with a slotted spoon.

Rice terraces at Longsheng.

A game of mahjong in Chengdu.

RAINBOW CONGEE

TO THE CHINESE, CONGEE IS A VERSATILE DISH. IT IS A FAVOURITE COMFORT FOOD, A DISH PREPARED

FOR CONVALESCENTS BECAUSE IT IS SO SOOTHING TO EAT, AND A FILLING AND FLAVOURFUL SNACK.

200 g (7 oz) short-grain rice
2 dried Chinese mushrooms
80 g (3 oz) snowpeas, ends
   trimmed
2 Chinese sausages (lap cheong)
2 tablespoons oil
1/4 red onion, finely diced
1 carrot, cut into 1 cm (1/2 inch) dice
2–2.25 litres (8–9 cups) chicken
   stock (page 565) or water
1/4 teaspoon salt
3 teaspoons light soy sauce

SERVES 6

PUT the rice in a bowl and, using your fingers as a rake, rinse under cold running water to remove any dust. Drain the rice in a colander.

SOAK the dried mushrooms in boiling water for 30 minutes, then drain and squeeze out any excess water. Remove and discard the stems and chop the caps into 5 mm (1/4 inch) dice. Cut the mangetout into 1 cm (1/2 inch) pieces.

PLACE the sausages on a plate in a steamer. Cover and steam over simmering water in a wok for 10 minutes, then cut them into 1 cm (1/2 inch) pieces. Heat a wok over medium heat, add the oil and heat until hot. Stir-fry the sausage until it is brown and the fat has melted out of it. Remove with a wire sieve or slotted spoon and drain. Pour the oil from the wok, leaving 1 tablespoon.

REHEAT the reserved oil over high heat until very hot. Stir-fry the red onion until soft and transparent. Add the mushrooms and carrot and stir-fry for 1 minute, or until fragrant.

PUT the mushroom mixture in a clay pot, casserole or saucepan and stir in 2 litres (8 cups) of stock or water, the salt, soy and the rice. Bring to the boil, then reduce the heat and simmer very gently, stirring occasionally, for 1 3/4–2 hours, or until it has a porridge-like texture and the rice is breaking up. If it is too thick, add the remaining stock and return to the boil. Toss in the mangetout and sausage, cover and stand for 5 minutes before serving.

RISOTTO NERO

YOU CAN SOMETIMES BUY THE INK SAC OF THE SQUID FROM YOUR FISHMONGER, ALTHOUGH MOST ARE LOST OR BURST BY THE TIME THE SQUID REACHES THE SHOP. THE LITTLE SACHETS OF INK ARE MORE EASILY FOUND. SQUID INK QUALIFIES AS SEAFOOD, SO DON'T SERVE THIS RISOTTO WITH PARMESAN.

2 medium-sized squid
1 litre (4 cups) fish stock
100 g (3 oz) butter
1 red onion, finely chopped
2 garlic cloves, crushed
350 g (12 oz) risotto rice (arborio,
    vialone nano or carnaroli)
3 sachets of squid or cuttlefish ink,
    or the ink sac of a large cuttlefish
150 ml (⅔ cup) white wine
2 teaspoons olive oil

SERVES 6 AS A STARTER

PREPARE the squid by pulling the heads and tentacles out of the bodies along with any innards. Cut the heads off below the eyes, leaving just the tentacles. Discard the heads and set the tentacles aside. Rinse the bodies, pulling out the transparent quills. Finely chop the bodies.

PUT the stock in a saucepan, bring to the boil and then maintain at a low simmer.

HEAT the butter in a large wide heavy-based saucepan and cook the onion until softened but not browned. Increase the heat and add the chopped squid. Cook for 3–5 minutes, or until the squid turns opaque. Add the garlic and stir briefly. Add the rice and reduce the heat to low. Season and stir briefly to thoroughly coat the rice.

SQUEEZE OUT the ink from the sachets and add to the rice with the wine. Increase the heat and stir until all the liquid has been absorbed.

STIR IN a ladleful of the simmering stock and cook over moderate heat, stirring continuously. When the stock has been absorbed, stir in another ladleful. Continue like this for about 20 minutes, until all the stock has been added and the rice is *al dente*. (You may not need to use all the stock, or you may need a little extra—every risotto will be slightly different.)

HEAT the olive oil in a frying pan and fry the squid tentacles quickly. Garnish the risotto with the tentacles and serve immediately.

Adding the wine to the ink and rice helps the ink dissolve and spread evenly through the risotto.

392

FRIED RICE WITH CRAB

FRIED RICE IS BEST MADE WITH DAY-OLD RICE, IN OTHER WORDS LEFTOVERS. USE A WOK FOR THE BEST RESULTS. CRAB, PREFERABLY FRESH IF POSSIBLE, GOES PARTICULARLY WELL WITH THE RICE.

2 tablespoons vegetable oil

4 garlic cloves, finely chopped

2 eggs

450 g (2½ cups) cooked jasmine rice, refrigerated overnight

110 g (4 oz) crab meat (drained well if tinned)

½ small onion, sliced

175 g (6 oz) tin water chestnuts, drained and sliced

2 tablespoons finely julienned ginger (optional)

1 tablespoon light soy sauce

1 teaspoon sugar

4 cooked crab claws, for garnish

½ long red chilli, seeded and finely sliced, for garnish

2 spring onions (scallions), finely chopped, for garnish

SERVES 4

HEAT the oil in a wok or frying pan and stir-fry the garlic over a medium heat until light brown. Using a spatula, move the fried garlic to the outer edges of the wok. Add the eggs and stir to scramble for 1–2 minutes. Add the cooked rice, crab meat and onion, stirring for 1– 2 minutes.

ADD the water chestnuts, ginger, light soy sauce and sugar and stir together for 1 minute. Taste, then adjust the seasoning if necessary.

SPOON onto a serving plate and garnish with the crab claws. Sprinkle with sliced chilli and spring onions.

Fresh water chestnuts.

Chinese, or black, mushrooms are also known as shiitake mushrooms. They can be bought fresh when in season and dried all year round.

BLACK MUSHROOM NOODLES

THIS VEGETARIAN NOODLE DISH IS STRONGLY FLAVOURED WITH CHINESE BLACK MUSHROOMS, CARROTS, LEEKS, GARLIC AND GINGER. TRADITIONALLY THE NOODLE CAKES ARE PAN-FRIED, BUT THEY CAN ALSO BE GRILLED (BROILED) UNTIL CRISP, WHICH USES LESS OIL.

275 g (10 oz) fresh or 175 g (6 oz) dried egg noodles
1 1/2 teaspoons roasted sesame oil
5 dried Chinese mushrooms
2 leeks, white part only
2 carrots
1 tablespoon oil
2 garlic cloves, finely chopped
1 tablespoon finely chopped ginger
2 tablespoons Shaoxing rice wine
2 tablespoons light soy sauce
1 tablespoon oyster sauce
1/4 teaspoon freshly ground black pepper
1 1/2 tablespoons cornflour

SERVES 4

COOK the noodles in salted boiling water for 2–3 minutes if fresh and 10 minutes if dried, then drain and combine with 1/2 teaspoon of the sesame oil.

PREHEAT the grill (broiler), shape the noodles into four mounds on a lightly oiled tray and grill (broil) for 10 minutes on each side, turning once, until golden brown. Keep warm in a low oven.

SOAK the dried mushrooms in boiling water for 30 minutes, then drain, reserving the soaking liquid, and squeeze out any excess water. Remove and discard the stems and shred the caps. Cut the leeks and carrots into 5 cm (2 inch) lengths, then into 1 cm (1/2 inch) wide strips. Wash well and dry thoroughly.

HEAT a wok over high heat, add the oil and heat until very hot. Stir-fry the garlic and ginger until fragrant. Add the leek and carrot and stir-fry for 1 minute. Add the rice wine and mushrooms and cook for 1 minute. Add the soy and oyster sauces, pepper, remaining sesame oil and 80 ml (1/3 cup) of the reserved liquid. Combine the cornflour with enough water to make a paste, add to the sauce and simmer until thickened. Put the noodles on a plate and spoon the sauce over.

SEVIAN KHEEMA

1 teaspoon cumin seeds
3 tablespoons ghee or oil
1 red onion, finely chopped
3 garlic cloves, crushed
2 cm (¾ inch) piece of ginger, grated
225 g (8 oz) minced lamb or beef
1 teaspoon ground black pepper
225 g (8 oz) sevian, broken into small pieces
3 tablespoons lime or lemon juice

SERVES 4

Sevian or vermicelli made from wheat flour are available as skeins of noodles or as bunches of straight lengths. Sometimes they are sold toasted.

PLACE a small frying pan over low heat, dry-roast the cumin until aromatic, then grind to a fine powder using a spice grinder or pestle and mortar.

HEAT 1 tablespoon ghee in a karhai or heavy-based frying pan and fry the onion, garlic and ginger for 3–4 minutes. Add the cumin, cook for 1 minute, then add the meat and cook for 8 minutes, or until the meat is dry, breaking up any lumps with the back of a fork. Season with the black pepper and salt, to taste, and remove from the pan.

HEAT the remaining ghee in the pan and fry the sevian for 1–2 minutes. Add the meat and fry for 1 minute. Add 150 ml (⅔ cup) water and cook until the sevian are tender, adding more water if necessary, but don't add too much at once. When cooked, sprinkle with the juice.

IDIYAPPAM

IDIYAPPAM

225 g (8 oz) rice sticks or vermicelli
4 tablespoons oil
50 g (2 oz) cashew nuts
½ onion, chopped
3 eggs
150 g (5 oz) fresh or frozen peas
10 curry leaves
2 carrots, grated
2 leeks, finely shredded
1 red capsicum (pepper), diced
2 tablespoons tomato ketchup
1 tablespoon soy sauce
1 teaspoon salt

SERVES 4

SOAK the rice sticks in cold water for 30 minutes, then drain and put them in a saucepan of boiling water. Remove from the heat and leave in the pan for 3 minutes. Drain and refresh in cold water.

HEAT 1 tablespoon oil in a frying pan and fry the cashews until golden. Remove, add the onion to the pan, fry until dark golden, then drain on paper towels. Cook the eggs in boiling water for 10 minutes to hard-boil, then cool them immediately in cold water. When cold, peel them and cut into wedges. Cook the peas in boiling water until tender.

HEAT the remaining oil in a frying pan and briefly fry the curry leaves. Add the carrot, leek and red capsicum and stir for 1 minute. Add the ketchup, soy sauce, salt and rice sticks and mix, stirring constantly to prevent the rice sticks from sticking to the pan. Serve on a platter and garnish with the peas, cashews, fried onion and egg wedges.

MUSHROOM RISOTTO

20 g (⅔ oz) dried porcini
  mushrooms
1 litre (4 cups) vegetable or chicken
  stock
2 tablespoons olive oil
1 tablespoon butter
1 small onion, finely chopped
2 garlic cloves, crushed
375 g (13 oz) risotto rice (arborio,
  vialone nano or carnaroli)
250 g (9 oz) mushrooms, sliced
pinch of nutmeg
45 g (1½ oz) Parmesan, grated
3 tablespoons finely chopped
  parsley

SERVES 4

SOAK the porcini in 500 ml (2 cups) boiling water for 30 minutes. Drain, retaining the liquid. Chop the porcini mushrooms and pass the liquid through a fine sieve. Put the stock in a saucepan, bring to the boil and then maintain at a low simmer.

HEAT the olive oil and butter in a large wide heavy-based saucepan. Cook the onion and garlic until softened but not browned. Add the rice and reduce the heat to low. Season and stir briefly to thoroughly coat the rice. Toss in the fresh mushrooms and nutmeg. Season and cook, stirring, for 1–2 minutes. Add the porcini and their liquid, increase the heat and cook until the liquid has been absorbed.

STIR IN a ladleful of stock and cook over moderate heat, stirring continuously. When the stock has been absorbed, stir in another ladleful. Continue like this for about 20 minutes, until all the stock has been added and the rice is *al dente*. (You may not need to use all the stock, or you may need a little extra.) Remove from the heat and stir in the Parmesan and parsley. Season and serve.

Dried porcini give an earthiness to dishes. When used with fresh mushrooms they add an attractive depth of flavour.

RISI E BISI

THE CONSISTENCY OF RISI E BISI IS THICK, HALFWAY BETWEEN A RISOTTO AND A SOUP IN TEXTURE
AND APPEARANCE. YOU CAN COOK IT THIN ENOUGH TO EAT WITH A SPOON, OR THICK ENOUGH TO USE
A FORK. SOME VERSIONS ARE VERY SIMPLE AND DO NOT EVEN INCLUDE PANCETTA.

1.5 litres (6 cups) chicken or
  vegetable stock
2 teaspoons olive oil
40 g (1 oz) butter
1 small onion, finely chopped
80 g (3 oz) pancetta, cut into small
  cubes
2 tablespoons chopped parsley
375 g (13 oz) shelled young peas
200 g (7 oz) risotto rice (arborio,
  vialone nano or carnaroli)
50 g (2 oz) Parmesan, grated

SERVES 4

PUT the stock in a saucepan, bring to the boil and then maintain at a low simmer. Heat the oil and half the butter in a large wide heavy-based saucepan and cook the onion and pancetta over low heat for 5 minutes until softened. Stir in the parsley and peas and add 2 ladlefuls of the stock. Simmer for 6–8 minutes.

ADD the rice and the remaining stock. Simmer until the rice is *al dente* and most of the stock has been absorbed. Stir in the remaining butter and the Parmesan, season and serve.

RISI E BISI

MUSHROOM RISOTTO

STIR-FRIED EGG NOODLES WITH VEGETABLES

2 tablespoons oyster sauce
1 tablespoon light soy sauce
1 teaspoon sugar
2 tablespoons vegetable oil
4 garlic cloves, finely chopped
225 g (8 oz) mixed Chinese broccoli
   florets, baby sweet corn,
   snake beans cut into lengths,
   snow peas (mangetout) cut into
   bite-sized pieces
250 g (9 oz) fresh egg noodles
45 g (½ cup) bean sprouts
3 spring onions (scallions), finely
   chopped
½ long red or green chilli, seeded
   and finely sliced
a few coriander (cilantro) leaves,
   for garnish

SERVES 4

COMBINE the oyster sauce, light soy sauce and sugar in a small bowl.

HEAT the oil in a wok or frying pan and stir-fry the garlic over a medium heat until lightly brown. Add all the mixed vegetables and stir-fry over a high heat for 1–2 minutes.

ADD the egg noodles and oyster sauce mixture to the wok and stir-fry for 2–3 minutes. Add the bean sprouts and spring onions. Taste, then adjust the seasoning if necessary.

SPOON onto a serving plate and garnish with chilli and coriander leaves.

FRIED RICE WITH PRAWNS AND CHILLI JAM

225 g (8 oz) raw prawns (shrimp)
3 tablespoons vegetable oil
4 garlic cloves, finely chopped
1 small onion, sliced
3 teaspoons chilli jam (page 561)
450 g (1 lb) cooked jasmine rice,
   refrigerated overnight
1 tablespoon light soy sauce
½ teaspoon sugar
1 long red chilli, seeded and
   finely sliced
2 spring onions (scallions),
   finely sliced
ground white pepper, for sprinkling
a few coriander (cilantro) leaves,
   for garnish

SERVES 4

PEEL and devein the prawns and cut each prawn along the back so it opens like a butterfly (leave each prawn joined along the base and at the tail, leaving the tail attached).

HEAT the oil in a wok or frying pan and stir-fry the garlic and onion over a medium heat until light brown. Add the chilli jam and stir for a few seconds or until fragrant. Add the prawns and stir-fry over a high heat for 2 minutes or until the prawns open and turn pink.

ADD the cooked rice, light soy sauce and sugar and stir-fry for 3–4 minutes. Add the chilli and spring onions and mix well. Taste, then adjust the seasoning if necessary.

SPOON onto a serving place and sprinkle with the white pepper and coriander leaves.

FRIED RICE WITH PRAWNS
AND CHILLI JAM

Lunch in Chengdu.

Make sure you separate all the minced meat as it cooks, or it will form large lumps and not resemble ants at all.

ANTS CLIMBING TREES

THE UNUSUAL NAME OF THIS SPICY SICHUANESE DISH IS SUPPOSED TO COME FROM THE FACT THAT IT BEARS A RESEMBLANCE TO ANTS CLIMBING TREES, WITH LITTLE PIECES OF MINCED PORK COATING LUSTROUS BEAN THREAD NOODLES.

125 g (4 oz) minced pork or beef
1/2 teaspoon light soy sauce
1/2 teaspoon Shaoxing rice wine
1/2 teaspoon roasted sesame oil
125 g (4 oz) bean thread noodles
1 tablespoon oil
2 spring onions (scallions), finely chopped
1 tablespoon finely chopped ginger
1 garlic clove, finely chopped
1 teaspoon chilli bean paste (toban jiang), or to taste
2 spring onions (scallions), green part only, finely chopped

SAUCE
1 tablespoon light soy sauce
1 tablespoon Shaoxing rice wine
1/2 teaspoon salt
1/2 teaspoon sugar
1/2 teaspoon roasted sesame oil
250 ml (1 cup) chicken stock (page 565)

SERVES 4

COMBINE the minced meat with the soy sauce, rice wine and sesame oil. Soak the bean thread noodles in hot water for 10 minutes, then drain.

HEAT a wok over high heat, add the oil and heat until very hot. Stir-fry the minced meat, mashing and separating it, until it changes colour and starts to brown. Push the meat to the side of the wok, add the spring onion, ginger, garlic and chilli paste and stir-fry for 5 seconds, or until fragrant. Return the meat to the centre of the pan.

TO MAKE the sauce, combine all the ingredients. Add the sauce to the meat mixture and toss lightly. Add the noodles and bring to the boil. Reduce the heat to low and cook for 8 minutes, or until almost all the liquid has evaporated. Sprinkle with the spring onion.

Stir the paste into the coconut cream before adding the chicken, soy sauce, sugar, stock and coconut milk.

CHIANG MAI NOODLES

ONE OF THAILAND'S WELL KNOWN DISHES, THIS IS FOUND ON CHIANG MAI'S RESTAURANT MENUS AND HAWKER STALLS, PARTICULARLY THOSE NEAR THE MOSQUE. SERVE WITH THE ACCOMPANIMENTS SUGGESTED AS THEY COMPLEMENT THE NOODLES PARTICULARLY WELL.

PASTE
3 dried long red chillies
4 Asian shallots, chopped
4 garlic cloves, crushed
2 cm (¾ inch) piece of turmeric, grated
5 cm (2 inch) piece of ginger, grated
4 tablespoons chopped coriander (cilantro) roots
1 teaspoon shrimp paste
1 teaspoon curry powder (page 563)

5 tablespoons coconut cream (page 551)
2 tablespoons palm sugar
2 tablespoons soy sauce
4 chicken drumsticks and 4 chicken thighs, with skin and bone
500 ml (2 cups) chicken stock or water
410 ml (1⅔ cups) coconut milk (page 551)
400 g (14 oz) fresh flat egg noodles
chopped or sliced spring onions (scallions), for garnish
a handful of coriander (cilantro) leaves, for garnish
lime wedges, to serve
pickled mustard greens or cucumber, to serve
roasted chilli sauce (page 561), to serve
Asian shallots, quartered, to serve

SERVES 4

TO MAKE the paste, soak the dried chillies in hot water for 10 minutes, then drain and chop the chillies into pieces, discarding the seeds. Put the chillies in a pestle and mortar with the shallots, garlic, turmeric, ginger, coriander roots and shrimp paste and pound to a fine paste. Add the curry powder and a pinch of salt and mix well.

PUT the coconut cream in a wok or saucepan and simmer over a medium heat for about 5 minutes, or until the cream separates and a layer of oil forms on the surface. Stir the cream if it starts to brown around the edges.

ADD the paste and stir until fragrant. Add the palm sugar, soy sauce and chicken and stir well, then add the stock and coconut milk and bring to the boil. Reduce the heat and simmer for 30 minutes or until the chicken is cooked and tender.

MEANWHILE, cook 100 g (3 oz) of the egg noodles by deep-frying them in very hot oil in a saucepan until they puff up. Drain on paper towels. Cook the remaining noodles in boiling water according to the packet instructions.

PUT the boiled noodles in a large bowl and spoon the chicken mixture over the top. Garnish with the crispy noodles, spring onions and coriander leaves. Serve the accompaniments alongside.

LAMB BIRYANI

IN THIS INDIAN RICE AND LAMB DISH BOTH INGREDIENTS ARE COOKED TOGETHER IN A SEALED CONTAINER. YOU CAN COOK THE LAMB WITHOUT BROWNING IT FIRST AND, IN FACT, THIS IS THE TRADITIONAL METHOD. HOWEVER, BROWNING THE MEAT ADDS EXTRA FLAVOUR.

Cook the meat and then put the rice and saffron mixture on top. Use a rope of dough to seal on the lid and keep in the flavours.

1 kg (2 lb 3 oz) boneless lamb leg or shoulder, cut into 3 cm (1¼ inch) cubes
7 cm (2¾ inch) piece of ginger, grated
2 garlic cloves, crushed
2 tablespoons garam masala (page 556)
½ teaspoon chilli powder
½ teaspoon ground turmeric
4 green chillies, finely chopped
20 g (⅔ oz) chopped coriander (cilantro) leaves
15 g (½ oz) chopped mint leaves
500 g (1 lb 2 oz) basmati rice
4 onions, thinly sliced
¼ teaspoon salt
120 ml (½ cup) oil
125 g (4 oz) unsalted butter, melted
250 ml (1 cup) thick natural yoghurt (page 554)
½ teaspoon saffron strands, soaked in 2 tablespoons hot milk
3 tablespoons lemon juice

SEALING DOUGH
200 g (7 oz) wholewheat flour
1 teaspoon salt

SERVES 6

MIX the lamb cubes in a bowl with the ginger, garlic, garam masala, chilli powder, turmeric, chilli, coriander and mint. Cover and marinate in the fridge overnight.

WASH the rice in a sieve under cold, running water until the water from the rice runs clear. Put the sliced onion in a sieve, sprinkle with the salt and leave for 10 minutes to drain off any liquid that oozes out. Rinse and pat dry.

HEAT the oil and butter in a large, heavy-based saucepan, add the onion and fry for about 10 minutes or until golden brown. Drain through a sieve, reserving the oil and butter.

REMOVE the lamb from the marinade, reserving the marinade, and fry in batches in a little of the oil and butter until the lamb is well browned all over. Transfer to a 'degchi' (thick-based pot) or heavy casserole and add the browned onion, any remaining marinade and the yoghurt, and cook everything over low heat for 30–40 minutes, or until the lamb is tender.

IN a separate saucepan, boil enough water to cover the rice. Add the rice to the pan. Return the water to the boil, cook the rice for 5 minutes, then drain well and spread the rice evenly over the meat. Pour 2 tablespoons of the leftover oil and ghee over the rice and drizzle with the saffron and milk.

TO MAKE the sealing dough, preheat the oven to 220°C (425°F/Gas 7). Make a dough by mixing the flour and salt with a little water. Roll the dough into a sausage shape and use to seal the lid onto the rim of the pot or casserole, pressing it along the rim where the lid meets the pot. Put the pot over high heat for 5 minutes to bring the contents to the boil, then transfer it to the oven for 40 minutes. Remove the pot and break the seal of dough.

THAI FRIED NOODLES WITH PRAWNS

THIS IS ONE OF THE MOST FAMOUS DISHES IN THAILAND. EVERYONE WHO VISITS SHOULD TRY IT, OTHERWISE THEY HAVE NOT REALLY BEEN THERE AT ALL. TO MAKE IT, YOU NEED TO USE SMALL WHITE NOODLES OF THE DRIED SEN LEK VARIETY. YOU CAN SUBSTITUTE MEAT FOR PRAWNS.

This melding of flavours with noodles is popular in Thailand.

150 g (5 oz) dried noodles *(sen lek)*
300 g (10 oz) raw large prawns
  (shrimp)
3 tablespoons tamarind purée
  (page 554)
2½ tablespoons fish sauce
2 tablespoons palm sugar
3 tablespoons vegetable oil
3–4 garlic cloves, finely chopped
2 eggs
85 g (3 oz) Chinese chives
  (1 bunch)
¼ teaspoon chilli powder,
  depending on taste
2 tablespoons dried shrimp, ground
  or pounded
2 tablespoons preserved turnip,
  finely chopped
2½–3 tablespoons chopped
  roasted peanuts
180 g (2 cups) bean sprouts
3 spring onions (scallions), slivered
1 long red chilli, seeded and
  shredded, for garnish
a few coriander (cilantro) leaves,
  for garnish
lime wedges, to serve

SERVES 4

SOAK the noodles in hot water for 1–2 minutes or until soft, then drain.

PEEL and devein the prawns and cut each prawn along the back so it opens like a butterfly (leave each prawn joined along the base and at the tail, leaving the tail attached).

COMBINE the tamarind with the fish sauce and palm sugar in a bowl.

HEAT 1½ tablespoons oil in a wok or frying pan and stir-fry the garlic over a medium heat until light brown. Add the prawns and cook for 2 minutes.

USING a spatula, move the prawns out from the middle of the wok. Add another 1½ tablespoons oil to the wok. Add the eggs and stir to scramble for 1 minute. Add the noodles and chives and stir-fry for a few seconds. Add the fish sauce mixture, chilli powder, dried shrimp, preserved turnip and half of the peanuts. Add half of the bean sprouts and spring onions. Test the noodles for tenderness and adjust the seasoning if necessary.

SPOON onto the serving plate and sprinkle the remaining peanuts over the top. Garnish with shredded chillies and a few coriander leaves. Place the lime wedges and remaining bean sprouts and spring onions at the side of the dish.

BREADS AND PIZZA

NAAN

PERHAPS THE MOST FAMOUS LEAVENED BREAD FROM NORTH INDIA, TRADITIONALLY THIS BREAD IS COOKED ON THE WALLS OF A TANDOOR (CLAY OVEN). IT IS NOT EASY TO RECREATE THE INTENSE HEAT IN A DOMESTIC OVEN SO THE TEXTURE IS SLIGHTLY DIFFERENT BUT THE TASTE IS DELICIOUS.

Make sure that the naan dough is very soft but not sticky. Shape it by pulling it into the right shape with your hands.

500 g (1 lb 2 oz) maida or plain flour
300 ml (1¼ cups) milk
2 teaspoons (7 g) easy-blend dried yeast or 15 g (½ oz) fresh yeast
2 teaspoons kalonji (nigella seeds), (optional)
½ teaspoon baking powder
½ teaspoon salt
1 egg, beaten
2 tablespoons oil or ghee
200 ml (¾ cups) thick natural yoghurt (page 554)

MAKES 10

SIFT the maida into a large bowl and make a well in the centre. Warm the milk over low heat in a saucepan until it is hand hot (the milk will feel the same temperature as your finger when you dip your finger into it). If you are using fresh yeast, mix it with a little milk and a pinch of maida and set it aside to activate and go frothy.

ADD the yeast, kalonji, baking powder and salt to the maida. In another bowl, mix the egg, oil and yoghurt. Pour into the maida with 250 ml (1 cup) of the milk and mix to form a soft dough. If the dough seems dry add the remaining 50 ml (¼ cup) of milk. Turn out onto a floured work surface and knead for 5 minutes, or until smooth and elastic. Put in an oiled bowl, cover and leave in a warm place to double in size. This will take several hours. Preheat the oven to 200°C (400°F/Gas 6). Place a roasting tin half-filled with water at the bottom of the oven. This provides moisture in the oven which prevents the naan from drying out too quickly.

PUNCH down the dough, knead it briefly and divide it into 10 portions. Using the tips of your fingers, spread out one portion of dough to the shape of a naan bread. They are traditionally tear-drop in shape, so pull the dough on one end. Put the naan on a greased baking tray. Bake on the top shelf for 7 minutes, then turn the naan over and cook for another 5 minutes. While the first naan is cooking, shape the next one. If your tray is big enough, you may be able to fit two naan at a time. Remove the cooked naan from the oven and cover with a cloth to keep it warm and soft.

REPEAT the cooking process until all the dough is used. You can only use the top shelf of the oven because the naan won't cook properly on the middle shelf. Refill the baking tray with boiling water when necessary.

415

PIZZA QUATTRO STAGIONI

1 x 30 cm (12 inch) pizza base
  (page 577)
cornmeal
1 quantity tomato sauce (page 569)
1 tablespoon grated Parmesan
60 g (2 oz) mozzarella, chopped
30 g (1 oz) thinly sliced prosciutto,
  cut into small pieces
1 plum tomato, thinly sliced
3 basil leaves, shredded
4 small artichoke hearts, marinated
  in oil, drained and quartered
4 button mushrooms, sliced
pinch of dried oregano
1 tablespoon olive oil

MAKES ONE 30 CM (12 INCH)
  PIZZA

PREHEAT the oven to 240°C (475°F/Gas 9). Place the pizza base on a baking tray dusted with cornmeal and spoon the tomato sauce onto the base, spreading it up to the rim. Sprinkle the Parmesan on top.

VISUALLY divide the pizza into quarters. Scatter the mozzarella over two opposite quarters. Spread the prosciutto over one of these, and arrange the tomato over the other. Lightly salt the tomato and sprinkle on the basil.

ARRANGE the artichoke over the third quarter, and the mushrooms over the final quarter. Sprinkle the oregano over both these sections.

DRIZZLE the oil over the pizza. Bake for 12–15 minutes, or until golden and puffed.

Italy is the world's largest producer of artichokes, with 98 per cent of the crop being grown for export. This beautiful vegetable, which varies in colour from green to vibrant purple, is actually a thistle.

PIZZA MELANZANA

220 g (8 oz) long thin eggplant
  (aubergine), thinly sliced
60 ml (¼ cup) olive oil
1 x 30 cm (12 inch) pizza base
  (page 577)
cornmeal
1 quantity tomato sauce
  (page 569), made with a pinch of
  chilli flakes
170 g (6 oz) mozzarella, chopped
15 black olives
1 tablespoon capers
4 tablespoons grated pecorino
1 tablespoon olive oil

MAKES ONE 30 CM (12 INCH)
  PIZZA

LAYER the eggplant in a colander, sprinkling salt on each layer. Leave to drain for 1 hour. Wipe off the salt with paper towels. Preheat the oven to 240°C (475°F/Gas 9).

HEAT the olive oil in a large frying pan and quickly brown the eggplant on both sides, cooking in batches. Drain on paper towels.

PLACE the pizza base on a baking tray dusted with cornmeal and spoon the tomato sauce onto the base, spreading it up to the rim. Arrange the eggplant in a circular pattern over the top, then scatter with mozzarella. Cover with the olives, capers and pecorino, then drizzle with the oil. Bake for 12–15 minutes, or until golden and puffed.

PIZZA MELANZANA

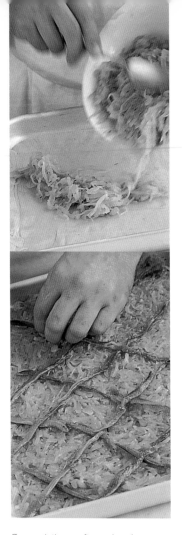

PISSALADIÈRE

PISSALADIÈRE TAKES ITS NAME FROM *PISSALAT*, PURÉED ANCHOVIES. IT CAN VARY IN ITS TOPPING FROM ONIONS AND ANCHOVIES TO ONIONS, TOMATOES AND ANCHOVIES OR SIMPLY ANCHOVIES PURÉED WITH GARLIC. TRADITIONAL TO NICE, IT CAN BE MADE WITH A BREAD OR PASTRY BASE.

40 g (1 oz) butter
1 tablespoon olive oil
1.5 kg (3 lb 5 oz) onions, thinly sliced
2 tablespoons thyme leaves
1 quantity bread dough (page 573)
1 tablespoon olive oil
16 anchovies, halved lengthways
24 pitted olives

SERVES 6

MELT the butter with the olive oil in a saucepan and add the onion and half the thyme. Cover the saucepan and cook over low heat for 45 minutes, stirring occasionally, until the onion is softened but not browned. Season and cool. Preheat the oven to 200°C (400°F/Gas 6).

ROLL OUT the bread dough to roughly fit an oiled 34 x 26 cm (13½ x 10¼ inch) shallow baking tray. Brush with the olive oil, then spread with the onion.

LAY the anchovies in a lattice pattern over the onion and arrange the olives in the lattice diamonds. Bake for 20 minutes, or until the dough is cooked and lightly browned. Sprinkle with the remaining thyme leaves and cut into squares. Serve hot or warm.

Spread the softened onion over the bread base and then arrange the anchovies over the top in the traditional lattice pattern.

TARTE FLAMBÉE

TARTE FLAMBÉE IS THE ALSATIAN VERSION OF THE PIZZA. IT IS COOKED QUICKLY AT A VERY HIGH TEMPERATURE IN A WOOD-FIRED OVEN AND TAKES ITS NAME FROM THE FACT THAT THE EDGE OF THE DOUGH OFTEN CAUGHT FIRE IN THE INTENSE HEAT OF THE OVEN.

TARTE FLAMBÉE

2 tablespoons olive oil
2 white onions, sliced
100 g (3 oz) cream cheese or curd cheese
185 ml (⅔ cup) fromage frais
200 g (7 oz) piece of bacon, cut into lardons
1 quantity bread dough (page 573)

SERVES 6

PREHEAT the oven to 230°C (450°F/Gas 8). Heat the olive oil in a saucepan and fry the onion until softened but not browned. Beat the cream or curd cheese with the fromage frais and then add the onion and bacon and season well.

ROLL OUT the bread dough into a rectangle about 3 mm (⅛ inch) thick—the dough needs to be quite thin, like a pizza—and place on an oiled baking tray. Fold the edge of the dough over to make a slight rim. Spread the topping over the dough, right up to the rim, and bake for 10–15 minutes, or until the dough is crisp and cooked and the topping browned. Cut into squares to serve.

STUFFED PARATHAS

STUFFED PARATHAS ARE VERY MUCH A FESTIVE FOOD. AFTER STUFFING THEM, ROLL THEM OUT CAREFULLY SO THE FILLING DOESN'T OOZE OUT. IF YOU CAN'T GET HOLD OF CHAPATI FLOUR YOU CAN USE EQUAL AMOUNTS OF WHOLEMEAL AND MAIDA.

400 g (14 oz) atta (chapati flour)
1 teaspoon salt
4 tablespoons oil or ghee
200 g (7 oz) potatoes, unpeeled
1/4 teaspoon mustard seeds
1/2 onion, finely chopped
pinch of ground turmeric
pinch of asafoetida
ghee or oil for shallow-frying
extra ghee or oil for brushing
  on the dough

MAKES 14

SIFT the atta and salt into a bowl and make a well in the centre. Add 2 tablespoons of the oil or ghee and about 290 ml (1¼ cup) tepid water and mix to a soft, pliable dough. Turn out onto a floured surface, knead for 5 minutes, then place in an oiled bowl. Cover and allow to rest for 30 minutes.

SIMMER the potatoes for 15–20 minutes or until cooked. Cool slightly, then peel and mash. Heat the remaining oil or ghee in a saucepan over medium heat, add the mustard seeds, cover and shake the pan until the seeds start to pop. Add the onion and fry for 1 minute. Stir in the turmeric and asafoetida. Mix in the potato and cook over low heat for 1–2 minutes, or until the mixture leaves the side of the pan. Season with salt, to taste, and leave to cool.

DIVIDE the dough into 14 portions and roll each into a 15 cm (6 inch) circle. Spread 1 teaspoon of the potato filling evenly over one half of each circle of dough and fold into a semicircle. Rub oil on half the surface area, then fold over into quarters. Roll out until doubled in size. Cover the parathas with a cloth, then cook them one at a time.

HEAT a tava, griddle or a heavy-based frying pan over medium heat. Brush the surface of the tava or griddle with oil. Remove the excess flour on each paratha prior to cooking by holding it in the palms of your hands and gently slapping it from one hand to the other. If you leave the flour on it may burn.

COOK each paratha for 2–3 minutes, then turn over and cook for 1 minute, or until the surface has brown flecks. Cooking should be quick to ensure the parathas remain soft. Cover the cooked parathas with a cloth. Parathas must be served warm. They can be reheated in a microwave, or wrapped in foil and heated in a conventional oven at 180°C (350°F/Gas 4) for 10 minutes.

Fold the filling into the parathas and then gently roll them out so that the filling doesn't ooze out.

421

STEAMED BREADS

THE BASIC YEAST DOUGH CAN BE USED TO MAKE LOTS OF DIFFERENT STEAMED BUNS, CALLED MANTOU IN CHINA. FLOWER ROLLS ARE ONE OF THE SIMPLEST SHAPES, WHILE SILVER THREAD ROLLS REQUIRE MORE DEXTERITY. THESE BREADS ARE DELICIOUS WITH RED-COOKED MEATS INSTEAD OF RICE.

1 quantity basic yeast dough
   (page 570)
3 tablespoons roasted sesame oil

MAKES 12 FLOWER ROLLS
OR 6 SILVER THREAD LOAVES

Folding sesame oil into the dough means that when the breads are steamed, the layers will spring open.

Steaming mantou being sold in the streets in Beijing.

CUT the dough in half and, on a lightly floured surface, roll out each half to form a 30 x 10 cm (12 x 4 inch) rectangle. Brush the surface of the rectangles liberally with the sesame oil. Place one rectangle directly on top of the other, with both oiled surfaces facing up. Starting with one of the long edges, roll up the dough swiss-roll style. Pinch the two ends to seal in the sesame oil.

LIGHTLY FLATTEN the roll with the heel of your hand and cut the roll into 5 cm (2 inch) pieces. Using a chopstick, press down on the centre of each roll, holding the chopstick parallel to the cut edges. (This will cause the ends to 'flower' when they are steamed.) Arrange the shaped rolls well apart in four steamers lined with greaseproof paper punched with holes. Cover and let rise for 15 minutes.

COVER and steam each steamer separately over simmering water in a wok for 15 minutes, or until the rolls are light and springy. Keep the rolls covered until you are about to eat them to make sure they stay soft.

THE DOUGH can also be shaped in other ways, one of the most popular being silver thread bread. Divide the dough in half and roll each half into a sausage about 3 cm (1¼ inches) in diameter, then cut each sausage into six pieces. Roll six of the pieces into rectangles 20 x 10 cm (8 x 4 inches) and set aside. Roll the remaining pieces into rectangles 20 x 10 cm (8 x 4 inches), brush each with a little sesame oil and fold in half to a 10 cm (4 inch) square. Brush with more sesame oil and fold in half again. Cut into thin strips crossways. Place one of the rectangles on the work surface and stretch the strips so they fit down the centre. Fold the ends and sides in to completely enclose the strips. Repeat with the remaining dough until you have six loaves. Steam as for the flower rolls for 20–25 minutes.

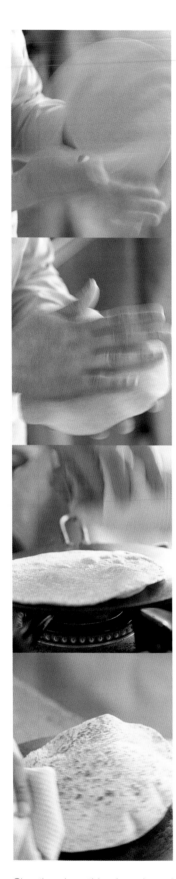

Slap the chapati backwards and forwards to get rid of any excess flour. Press it with a tea towel to make it puff up as it cooks.

CHAPATIS

CHAPATIS ARE THE MOST BASIC FORM OF UNLEAVENED BREAD. THEY SHOULD BE COOKED ON A HIGH HEAT TO PREVENT THEM BECOMING TOUGH. IF YOU CAN'T BUY CHAPATI FLOUR, USE 100 G (3 OZ) EACH OF WHOLEMEAL AND MAIDA (PLAIN FLOUR).

200 g (7 oz) atta (chapati flour)
1/2 teaspoon salt
100 g (3 oz) ghee or clarified butter

MAKES 8

SIFT the atta and salt into a bowl and make a well in the centre. Add about 150 ml (2/3 cup) tepid water, enough to mix to form a soft, pliable dough. Turn the dough out onto a floured work surface and knead for 5 minutes. Place in an oiled bowl, cover and allow to rest for 30 minutes.

PUT a tava or griddle, or a heavy-based frying pan over medium heat and leave it to heat up. Divide the dough into eight equal portions. Working with one portion at a time and keeping the rest covered, on a lightly floured surface roll out each portion to form a 15 cm (6 inch) diameter circle. Keep the rolled chapatis covered with a damp cloth while you roll them and cook them. Remove the excess surface flour on the chapati prior to cooking by holding the chapati in the palms of your hands and gently slapping it from one hand to the other. If you leave the flour on it may burn.

PLACE each chapati on the tava, leave it for 7–10 seconds to brown, then turn it over to brown on the other side. Depending on the hotness of the griddle, the second side should take about 15 seconds. Turn over the chapati again and, using a folded tea towel, apply gentle pressure to the chapati in several places to heat it and encourage it to puff up like a balloon. It is this puffing up process that gives the chapati its light texture. Smear the hot chapati with a little of the ghee or butter, and leave stacked and covered with a tea towel until all the chapatis are cooked.

BRIOCHE

BRIOCHE IS SO BUTTERY THAT YOU CAN SERVE IT UP FOR BREAKFAST WITH NOTHING MORE FANCY THAN A LITTLE GOOD-QUALITY JAM OR CURD. IF YOU HAVE ONE, USE A FLUTED BRIOCHE TIN. IF NOT, AN ORDINARY LOAF TIN WILL BE FINE.

Because brioche dough has so much butter in it, you will notice that it is heavier to knead than bread dough.

2 teaspoons dried yeast or 15 g (½ oz) fresh yeast
50 ml (¼ cup) warm milk
2 tablespoons caster sugar
225 g (8 oz) plain flour
pinch of salt
2 large eggs, lightly beaten
few drops vanilla extract
75 g (2½ oz) butter, cubed
lightly beaten egg, to glaze

MAKES 1 LOAF

MIX the yeast with the warm milk and 1 teaspoon of the sugar. Leave for 10 minutes in a warm place until the yeast becomes frothy. If the yeast does not bubble and foam in this time, throw it away and start again.

SIFT the flour into a large bowl and sprinkle with the salt and the rest of the sugar. Make a well in the centre and add the eggs, vanilla extract and yeast mixture. Use a wooden spoon to mix all the ingredients together, then use your hands to knead the dough for a minute to bring it together. Transfer to a lightly floured work surface and gradually knead in the butter, piece by piece. Knead for 5 minutes, then put the dough into a clean bowl and cover with oiled clingfilm. Leave to rise in a draught-free spot for 1–1½ hours or until the dough has doubled in size.

KNOCK BACK the dough by punching it with your fist several times to expel the air, and then lightly knead it again for a couple of minutes. Shape the dough into a rectangle and place in a 20 x 7 x 9 cm (8 x 2¾ x 3½ inch) buttered loaf tin. Cover with oiled clingfilm and leave to rise in a draught-free spot for 30–35 minutes, or until risen almost to the top of the tin. Preheat the oven to 200°C (400°F/Gas 6).

ONCE the brioche has risen, use a pair of scissors to carefully snip into the top of the dough at regular intervals. Snip three times on each side and twice at each end. The cuts should only be about 2.5 cm (1 inch) deep. This will give the top of the loaf its traditional bubble shape. Brush the top with egg to glaze and bake for 30–35 minutes, or until the top of the brioche is rich brown. Turn the hot brioche out of the tin and tap the bottom of the loaf—if it sounds hollow, it is cooked. Put the brioche back in the tin upside-down and return to the oven for 5 minutes to crisp the base of the loaf. Transfer to a wire rack and leave to cool.

CALZONE

CALZONE DIFFERS FROM A PIZZA IN THAT THE BASE IS FOLDED OVER THE TOPPING. THIS NEAPOLITAN SPECIALITY MEANS 'TROUSER LEG', PRESUMABLY BECAUSE THERE IS A RESEMBLANCE. EACH OF THE FOLLOWING FILLINGS MAKES ONE 25 CM (10 INCH) CALZONE—ENOUGH FOR ONE TO TWO PEOPLE.

cornmeal
1/2 quantity pizza dough (page 577)
　for each calzone
1 1/2 tablespoons olive oil

MOZZARELLA AND PROSCIUTTO
170 g (6 oz) mozzarella, cut into
　2 cm (3/4 inch) cubes
2 thin slices prosciutto, cut in half
1 artichoke heart, marinated in oil,
　drained and cut into 3 slices from
　top to bottom

POTATO, ONION AND SALAMI
2 tablespoons vegetable oil
1 small onion, very thinly sliced
75 g (2 1/2 oz) small red potatoes,
　unpeeled, very thinly sliced
75 g (2 1/2 oz) mozzarella, chopped
60 g (2 oz) sliced salami
2 tablespoons grated Parmesan

EACH RECIPE MAKES ONE 25 CM
(10 INCH) CALZONE

PREHEAT the oven to 230°C (450°F/Gas 8). Lightly oil a baking tray and dust with cornmeal.

ON a lightly floured surface roll out the dough into an 18 cm (7 inch) circle. Now, using the heels of your hands and working from the centre outwards, press the circle out to a diameter of about 30 cm (12 inches). Transfer to the baking tray. Brush the entire surface lightly with the oil.

TO MAKE the mozzarella and prosciutto calzone, spread the mozzarella cheese over one half of the pizza base, leaving a narrow border around the edge. Roll the half slices of prosciutto into little tubes and place on top of the cheese. Top with the artichoke slices, then season well.

TO MAKE the potato, onion and salami calzone, heat the oil in a frying pan and add the onion slices. Cook for 1 minute, then scatter the potato on top. Cook, stirring, for 3–4 minutes, until beginning to brown. Season with salt and pepper. Spread over one half of the pizza base, leaving a narrow border around the edge. Scatter the mozzarella on top, followed by the salami slices and Parmesan.

WHICHEVER calzone you are making, now fold the plain side of the base over the filling to make a half-moon shape. Match the cut edges and press them firmly together to seal. Fold them over and press into a scrolled pattern to thoroughly seal in the filling. Brush the surface with a little extra olive oil, then transfer to the oven. Bake for about 20 minutes, until the crust is golden.

POTATO, ONION AND
SALAMI CALZONE

MOZZARELLA AND PROSCIUTTO CALZONE

SAAG ROTI

A SIMPLE ROTI WITH A SPINACH BASE IS NOT ONLY INTERESTING AND TASTY, BUT NUTRITIOUS AS WELL. MAKE IT WITH SOME CHOPPED BROWNED ONION FOR AN AROMATIC ALTERNATIVE. YOU CAN USE EQUAL AMOUNTS OF WHOLEMEAL AND MAIDA IF YOU CAN'T BUY CHAPATI FLOUR.

200 g (7 oz) spinach leaves, stalks
  removed
500 g (1 lb 2 oz) atta (chapati flour)
1 teaspoon salt
1 teaspoon ghee or oil
ghee or oil for cooking

MAKES 20

COOK the spinach briefly in a little simmering water until it is just wilted, then refresh in cold water. Drain thoroughly, then finely chop. Squeeze out any extra water by putting the spinach between two plates and pushing them together.

SIFT the atta and salt into a bowl and make a well in the centre. Add the spinach, ghee and about 250 ml (1 cup) tepid water and mix to form a soft, pliable dough. Turn out the dough onto a floured work surface and knead for 5 minutes. Place in an oiled bowl, cover and allow to rest for 30 minutes.

DIVIDE the dough into 20 balls. Working with one portion at a time and keeping the rest covered, on a lightly floured surface evenly roll out each portion to a 12 cm (4¾ inch) circle about 1 mm (¹⁄₁₆ inch) thick.

HEAT a tava, griddle or heavy-based frying pan until hot, oil it lightly with ghee or oil and cook one roti at a time. Cook each on one side, covered with a saucepan lid (this will help keep them soft), for about 1 minute. Turn it over, cover again and cook the other side for 2 minutes. Check the roti a few times to make sure it doesn't overcook. The roti will blister a little and brown in some places. Remove the roti and keep it warm under a tea towel. Cook the remaining roti.

Make sure that the spinach is evenly distributed throughout the dough. Cover the roti with a lid to keep it soft as it cooks.

PROVENÇAL TART

PASTRY
250 g (9 oz) plain flour
150 g (5 oz) butter, diced
1 egg yolk, beaten

2 tablespoons olive oil
1 large white onion, finely chopped
10 tomatoes (or 2 x 400 g/14 oz
    tins chopped tomatoes)
1 teaspoon tomato purée
2 garlic cloves, finely chopped
1 tablespoon roughly chopped
    oregano, plus a few whole leaves
    to garnish
1 red capsicum (pepper)
1 yellow capsicum (pepper)
6 anchovies, halved
12 pitted olives
drizzle of olive oil

SERVES 6

TO MAKE the pastry, sift the flour into a bowl, add the butter and rub in with your fingertips until the mixture resembles breadcrumbs. Add the egg yolk and a little cold water (about 2–3 teaspoons) and mix with the blade of a palette knife until the dough just starts to come together. Bring the dough together with your hands and shape into a ball. Wrap in clingfilm and put in the fridge to rest for at least 30 minutes.

HEAT the oil in a frying pan, add the onion, cover and cook over very low heat for 20 minutes, stirring often, until softened but not browned.

SCORE a cross in the top of each tomato. Plunge into boiling water for 20 seconds, then drain and peel the skin away from the cross. Chop the tomatoes, discarding the cores. Add the tomato, tomato purée, garlic and oregano to the frying pan and simmer, uncovered, for 20 minutes, stirring occasionally. Once the tomato is soft and the mixture has become a paste, leave to cool.

ROLL OUT the pastry to fit a 34 x 26 cm (3½ x 10¼ inch) shallow baking tray. Prick the pastry gently all over, without piercing through. Cover with clingfilm and chill for 30 minutes. Preheat the oven to 200°C (400°F/Gas 6) and preheat the grill (broiler).

CUT the capsicums in half, remove the seeds and membrane and place, skin side up, under the hot grill until the skin blackens and blisters. Leave to cool before peeling away the skin. Cut the capsicums into thin strips.

LINE the pastry shell with a crumpled piece of greaseproof paper and fill with baking beads (use dried beans or rice if you don't have beads). Blind bake the pastry for 10 minutes, remove the paper and beads and bake for a further 3–5 minutes, or until the pastry is just cooked but still very pale. Reduce the oven to 180°C (350°F/Gas 4).

SPREAD the tomato over the pastry, then scatter with capsicums. Arrange the anchovies and olives over the top. Brush with olive oil and bake for 25 minutes. Scatter with oregano leaves to serve.

Simmer the filling until the tomato is so soft that it forms a paste.

ITALIAN COUNTRY-STYLE BREAD

THIS IS ONE OF THE BASIC LOAVES OF ITALY (ALTHOUGH NOT TUSCANY, WHERE THE REGIONAL *PANE TOSCANO* IS MADE WITHOUT SALT). IF YOU'RE SERVING IT FRESH WITH BUTTER, IT'S BEST EATEN ON BAKING DAY, BUT THE DAY-OLD BREAD IS EXCELLENT FOR MAKING BRUSCHETTA AND CROSTINI.

STARTER
185 ml (⅔ cup) milk, warmed
2 teaspoons honey
1 teaspoon dried yeast or
  7 g (¼ oz) fresh yeast
125 g (4 oz) plain flour

DOUGH
1 teaspoon dried yeast or
  7 g (¼ oz) fresh yeast
2½ teaspoons salt
500 g (1 lb 2 oz) plain flour

MAKES 2 LOAVES

TO MAKE the starter, mix the milk and honey in a large bowl with 3 tablespoons warm water. Sprinkle the yeast over the top and stir to dissolve. Leave in a draught-free spot to activate. If the yeast does not bubble and foam in 5 minutes, throw it away and start again. Add the flour and whisk to form a thick paste. Cover loosely with clingfilm and leave at room temperature overnight.

TO MAKE the dough, sprinkle the yeast over the starter. Break up the starter by squeezing it between your finger tips. Gradually add 250 ml (1 cup) water, combining it with the starter. Mix in the salt and flour with your fingers until the mixture comes together to form a soft dough.

TURN the dough out onto a lightly floured work surface and knead for 10 minutes or until smooth and elastic. Place the dough in a lightly oiled bowl and cover with a damp tea towel. Leave to rise in a draught-free place for 1–1½ hours or until doubled in size. Knock back, turn out onto a lightly floured surface and knead for 1–2 minutes until smooth.

DIVIDE the dough into two and shape into round loaves, then flatten them slightly. Lightly grease a large baking tray with oil and dust with flour. Put the loaves on the tray and score a criss-cross pattern about 5 mm (¼ inch) deep on top of each loaf. Dust lightly with more flour.

COVER with a damp tea towel and leave to rise in a draught-free place for about 40 minutes, or until doubled in size. Preheat the oven to 200°C (400°F/Gas 6). Bake for 30–35 minutes or until the bread sounds hollow when tapped underneath. Transfer to a wire rack to cool.

DOSAS

THESE ARE LARGE, SPONGY, RICE PANCAKES WITH A CRISP SURFACE. FOR THE BEST RESULT, RICE FLOUR THAT IS SPECIALLY MADE FOR MAKING DOSAS SHOULD BE SOUGHT OUT AS IT IS GROUND TO THE RIGHT CONSISTENCY.

110 g (4 oz) urad dal
1 teaspoon salt
300 g (10 oz) rice flour
oil for cooking

MAKES 20

PUT the dal in a bowl and cover with water. Soak for at least 4 hours or overnight.

DRAIN, then grind the dal with the salt and a little water in a food processor, blender or pestle and mortar to form a fine paste. Mix the paste with the rice flour, add 1 litre (4 cups) water and mix well. Cover with a cloth and leave in a warm place for 8 hours, or until the batter ferments and bubbles. The batter will double in volume.

HEAT a tava or a non-stick frying pan over medium heat and leave to heat up. Don't overheat it—the heat should always be medium. Lightly brush the surface of the tava or frying pan with oil. Stir the batter and pour a ladleful into the middle of the griddle and quickly spread it out with the back of the ladle or a palette knife, to form a thin pancake. Don't worry if the dosa is not perfect, they are very hard to get exactly right. Drizzle a little oil or ghee around the edge to help it crisp up. Cook until small holes appear on the surface and the edges start to curl. Turn over with a spatula and cook the other side. (The first dosa is often a disaster but it will season the pan for the following ones.)

REPEAT with the remaining mixture, oiling the pan between each dosa. Roll the dosas into big tubes and keep warm. Dosas are often filled with chutneys, or with curries.

Spread the dosa batter out as thinly as you can. This will take a little practice. Drizzle the edge with oil to help it crisp up.

PASTA
AND POLENTA

The fresh porcini is considered the king of mushrooms. Several different varieties are available and appear during the summer and autumn. Porcini are also dried and preserved in oil for the months they are not available.

POLENTA WITH WILD MUSHROOMS

POLENTA, MADE FROM COARSE-GROUND CORN, WAS KNOWN AS THE FOOD OF THE POOR IN ROMAN TIMES. TODAY, ESPECIALLY AMONG ITALIANS LIVING ABROAD, IT HAS A WIDE AND LOVING AUDIENCE. SOMETIMES POLENTA IS SO FINE IT IS ALMOST WHITE; MORE OFTEN IT IS GOLDEN YELLOW.

POLENTA
1 tablespoon salt
300 g (10 oz) coarse-grain polenta
50 g (2 oz) butter
75 g (2½ oz) Parmesan, grated

50 ml (¼ cup) olive oil
400 g (14 oz) selection of wild
    mushrooms, particularly fresh
    porcini, sliced if large, or chestnut
    mushrooms
2 garlic cloves, crushed
1 tablespoon chopped thyme
150 g (5 oz) mascarpone

SERVES 6

BRING 1.5 litres (6 cups) water to the boil in a heavy-based saucepan and add the salt. Add the polenta to the water in a gentle stream, whisking or stirring vigorously as you pour it in. Reduce the heat immediately so that the water is simmering. Stir continuously for the first 30 seconds to avoid any lumps appearing—the more you stir, the better the texture will be. Once you have stirred well at the beginning you can leave the polenta to mildly bubble away, stirring it every few minutes to prevent it sticking. Cook for 40 minutes.

MEANWHILE, prepare the mushrooms. Heat the olive oil in a large saucepan or frying pan. When the oil is hot, add just enough mushrooms to cover the base of the pan and cook at quite a high heat, stirring frequently. Season with salt and pepper. Sometimes the mushrooms can become watery when cooked: just keep cooking until all the liquid has evaporated. Add a little of the garlic at the last minute to prevent it burning and then add a little thyme.

REMOVE this batch of mushrooms from the pan and repeat the process until they are all cooked. Return all the mushrooms to the pan (if the polenta isn't yet cooked, leave all the mushrooms in the pan and then reheat gently). Add the mascarpone and let it melt into the mushrooms.

ADD the butter and 50 g (2 oz) of the Parmesan to the cooked polenta and season with pepper. Spoon the polenta onto plates and then spoon the mushrooms on top. Sprinkle with the remaining Parmesan and serve immediately.

Santa Maria della Salute, Venice.

TAGLIATELLE WITH TRUFFLES

IF YOU ARE GOING TO THE EXTRAVAGANCE OF USING TRUFFLES, DON'T SKIMP ON THE PARMESAN—
USE PARMIGIANO REGGIANO FOR THE BEST FLAVOUR. IF YOU CAN'T GET A FRESH TRUFFLE, USE ONE
FROM A JAR, PRESERVED IN BRINE.

135 g (4 oz) butter
1 garlic clove
400 g (14 oz) fresh tagliatelle
60 g (2 oz) Parmesan, grated
1 small white Alba truffle or black
   Norcia truffle

SERVES 4 AS A STARTER

MELT the butter in a saucepan over moderately
low heat. Add the garlic clove and heat until the
butter bubbles, separates and turns lightly golden.
Strain the butter.

MEANWHILE, cook the pasta in a large saucepan
of boiling salted water until *al dente*. Drain and
return to the saucepan. Add the browned butter
and the Parmesan. Season with salt and black
pepper and toss lightly.

PLACE on warmed plates and take to the table.
Using a mandolin or potato peeler, shave a few
very thin slices of the truffle onto each serving.

Black truffles are found around
Norcia in Umbria. When they're not
in season, use preserved truffles.

SPAGHETTI VONGOLE

2 tablespoons olive oil
3 cloves garlic, crushed
2 pinches of chilli flakes
1 teaspoon chopped parsley
125 ml (½ cup) dry white wine
2 x 400 g (14 oz) tins chopped
   tomatoes
1 kg (2 lb 3 oz) clams
3 tablespoons finely chopped
   parsley
400 g (14 oz) spaghetti or linguine
½ teaspoon grated lemon zest
lemon wedges

SERVES 4

HEAT the oil in a large deep frying pan. Add the
garlic and chilli and cook over low heat for
30 seconds. Add the parsley, wine and tomatoes.
Increase the heat and boil, stirring occasionally, for
8–10 minutes until the liquid is reduced by half.

CLEAN the clams by scrubbing them thoroughly.
Rinse well under running water. Discard any that
are broken or cracked or do not close when
tapped on the work surface. Add to the saucepan.
Cover the pan, increase the heat and cook for
3–5 minutes until the clams open. Shake the pan
often. Remove the clams from the pan, discarding
any that stay closed. Stir in the parsley and
season. Uncover the pan and boil until thick. Set
12 clams aside and extract the meat from the rest.

COOK the pasta in a large saucepan of boiling
salted water until *al dente*. Drain and stir through
the sauce. Add the lemon zest, reserved clams
and clam meat and toss well. Serve with the
lemon wedges.

SPAGHETTI VONGOLE

442

LA BANDIERA

LA BANDIERA IS THE NAME OF THE ITALIAN FLAG. THIS DISH, FROM PUGLIA IN ITALY'S SOUTH, CONTAINS TOMATOES, ROCKET AND PASTA—THE RED, GREEN AND WHITE INGREDIENTS MIMIC THE COLOURS OF THE FLAG.

The colours of the Italian flag are reflected in many dishes, as tomatoes, capsicums and green vegetables are often eaten with white mozzarella and pasta.

2 potatoes, cut into 2 cm (¾ inch) cubes
300 g (10 oz) ditali, pennette or maccheroncini rigati
4 tablespoons olive oil
3 garlic cloves, crushed
½ teaspoon minced anchovy fillets
2 x 400 g (14 oz) tins tomatoes, roughly chopped
¼ teaspoon sugar
2 tablespoons chopped basil leaves
45 g (1½ oz) rocket leaves, torn into small pieces if large
2 tablespoons grated pecorino, plus a little extra for serving

SERVES 4

PUT a large saucepan of water on to boil. Add the potato with 1 teaspoon salt. When the potato has been boiling for 3–4 minutes, stir the pasta into the water and cook until *al dente*.

MEANWHILE, heat the oil, garlic and anchovies in a large frying pan over low heat for about 30 seconds. Before the garlic colours, add the tomato, sugar and basil. Increase the heat, season with salt and pepper and simmer until the pasta in the other pan has finished cooking.

DRAIN the potato and pasta and add to the tomato sauce. Add the rocket and pecorino, toss to coat and serve at once, with a little extra grated pecorino over the top.

BEANS WITH RED PEPPER

200 g (7 oz) broad beans
300 g (10 oz) ditali, pennette or maccheroncini rigati
80 ml (⅓ cup) oil
2 garlic cloves, crushed
1 red capsicum (pepper), julienned
pinch of cayenne pepper
200 g (7 oz) mozzarella, diced
3 tablespoons grated pecorino

SERVES 4

BRING a large saucepan of water to the boil. Add the broad beans and cook for 2 minutes. Using a slotted spoon, transfer the beans to a bowl and cover with a plate. Stir the pasta into the boiling water with 1 teaspoon salt and cook until *al dente*. Meanwhile, peel off the broad bean skins.

HEAT the oil in a large frying pan and add the garlic and red capsicum. Cook over low heat, without browning, for 2–3 minutes then add the cayenne pepper.

DRAIN the pasta and add to the frying pan with the broad beans, mozzarella and pecorino. Toss to coat and heat until the mozzarella just begins to melt. Season and serve.

BEANS WITH RED PEPPER

TIMBALLO

THE ELABORATE BAKED PIES OF RENAISSANCE ITALY, CALLED *PASTICCI* OR *TORTE,* WERE EMBRACED BY FRENCH CUISINE AND RENAMED *TIMBALES*. TWO CENTURIES LATER, THE ITALIANS RECLAIMED THE TIMBALE AS THEIR OWN AND IT WAS CHRISTENED THE TIMBALLO.

6 tomatoes
2 tablespoons olive oil
1 large onion, finely chopped
2 garlic cloves, crushed
5 chicken breast fillets
4 chicken thighs
1 bay leaf
2 thyme sprigs
3 tablespoons white wine
175 g (6 oz) mushrooms, sliced
75 g (2½ oz) provolone, grated
9 eggs, beaten
2 tablespoons double cream
3 tablespoons chopped parsley
800 g (1 lb 12 oz) ziti

SERVES 6

SCORE a cross in the top of each tomato, plunge into boiling water for 20 seconds, then drain and peel the skin away from the cross. Dice the flesh.

HEAT the oil in a large saucepan, add the onion and garlic and cook, stirring, for 7 minutes or until softened. Add the tomato and cook for 5 minutes over low heat. Add the chicken breasts and thighs, the bay leaf and thyme and stir well. Add the wine, cover the pan and cook over moderate heat for 20 minutes.

ADD the mushrooms to the saucepan and cook for another 10–15 minutes, turning the chicken once or twice until it is cooked through. Remove the chicken from the saucepan and cook the sauce until it has reduced and thickened. Remove the bay leaf and thyme and leave the sauce to cool to room temperature.

REMOVE the chicken meat from the bones, shred the meat and return to the sauce. Stir in the cheese, eggs, cream and parsley. Season with salt and pepper.

PREHEAT the oven to 180°C (350°F/Gas 4) and grease a round 1.25 litre (5 cup) ovenproof dish with a little butter or oil.

COOK the pasta in a large saucepan of boiling salted water until *al dente*. Drain well and place in the dish, one by one, in a single layer, starting in the middle and spiralling outwards to cover the base and side. Make sure there are no gaps.

FILL the centre with the chicken sauce and bake for 1 hour. Leave to rest for a few minutes, then invert onto a plate to serve.

Start coiling the ziti in the centre of the base and work your way to the outer edge. Then build up the side, without leaving any gaps.

447

BAKED POLENTA WITH FOUR CHEESES

IF YOU HAVE TIME, USE 'PROPER' POLENTA INSTEAD OF THE QUICK-COOK VARIETY. IT MIGHT SEEM LABOUR INTENSIVE, AS YOU HAVE TO STIR CONSTANTLY, BUT THE FLAVOUR IS BETTER. IN ITALY THEY SOLVE THE PROBLEM BY HAVING SPECIAL 'SELF-STIRRING' POLENTA PANS WITH A REVOLVING SPOON.

POLENTA
1 tablespoon salt
300 g (10 oz) coarse-grain polenta
75 g (2½ oz) butter

TOMATO SAUCE
3 tablespoons olive oil
2 garlic cloves, thinly sliced
15 g (½ oz) rosemary or thyme,
  roughly chopped
800 g (1 lb 12 oz) tin tomatoes

200 g (7 oz) Gorgonzola, cubed
250 g (9 oz) Taleggio, cubed
250 g (9 oz) mascarpone
100 g (3 oz) Parmesan, grated

SERVES 6

BRING 1.5 litres (6 cups) water to the boil in a heavy-based saucepan and add the salt. Add the polenta to the water in a gentle stream, whisking or stirring vigorously as you pour it in. Reduce the heat immediately so that the water is simmering. Stir continuously for the first 30 seconds to avoid any lumps appearing—the more you stir, the better the texture will be. Once you have stirred well at the beginning you can leave the polenta to mildly bubble away, stirring it every few minutes to prevent it sticking. Cook for 40 minutes. Add the butter and mix well.

POUR the polenta into a shallow casserole or baking tray about 5 cm (2 inches) deep (the polenta should come no more than halfway up the side of the dish). Leave to cool completely.

TO MAKE the tomato sauce, heat the olive oil in a saucepan and cook the garlic gently until light brown. Add half the rosemary or thyme and then the tomatoes. Season with salt and pepper and cook gently, stirring occasionally, until reduced to a thick tomato sauce.

PREHEAT the oven to 180°C (350°F/Gas 4). Turn the polenta out of the dish and onto a board, then slice it horizontally in two. Pour half the tomato sauce into the bottom of the empty dish. Place the bottom slice of the polenta on top of the sauce and season. Scatter the Gorgonzola and Taleggio over the top. Dot the mascarpone over the polenta with a teaspoon, and sprinkle with half the Parmesan and the remaining herbs.

PUT the other layer of polenta on top and pour over the remaining tomato sauce. Sprinkle with the remaining Parmesan and bake for 30 minutes. Leave to rest for 10 minutes before serving with a simple rocket salad.

Arrange the first layer of polenta carefully in the dish but don't worry if you break it—it will seal again as it cooks. Lay the cheese in an even layer on top of the polenta before finishing with the final layers.

449

RAVIOLI APERTO

FILLING
30 g (1 oz) butter
1 small onion, finely chopped
85 g (3 oz) baby spinach leaves
250 g (9 oz) ricotta
3 tablespoons double cream

1 quantity pasta (page 578),
  rolled out
100 g (3 oz) frozen spinach, thawed
250 ml (1 cup) chicken stock

SERVES 4

TO MAKE the filling, melt the butter in a frying pan and add the onion. Cook, stirring, for 5 minutes, or until softened. Add the baby spinach leaves and cook for 4 minutes. Remove from the heat, cool to room temperature and then chop. Add the ricotta and 2 tablespoons of the cream and stir well. Season with salt and pepper.

TO MAKE the ravioli, cut the rolled out pasta into sixteen 8 cm (3¼ inch) squares and cook in a large saucepan of boiling salted water until *al dente*. Drain. Preheat the oven to 180°C (350°F/Gas 4).

LINE a baking tray with baking parchment and lay out half the pieces of pasta on the tray. Divide the filling into eight portions and spoon into the centre of each square. Place the other eight pasta sheets on top to enclose the filling and cover with a damp tea towel.

TO MAKE a sauce, blend the spinach with a little of the chicken stock until smooth. Transfer to a saucepan with the remaining stock and heat for 2 minutes. Add the remaining cream, stir well, season and remove from the heat.

HEAT the ravioli in the oven for 5 minutes, or until just warm. Place two ravioli on each plate, reheat the sauce gently, pour over the ravioli and serve immediately.

Take time to place the filling carefully in the middle of each pasta square, so it doesn't ooze out of the sides when it cooks.

POTATO GNOCCHI WITH PANCETTA AND SAGE

WHEN COOKING THE POTATOES FOR GNOCCHI YOU WANT TO KEEP THEM AS DRY AS POSSIBLE—TOO MUCH MOISTURE WILL RESULT IN A HEAVY DOUGH. FLOURY POTATOES HAVE A LOW MOISTURE CONTENT AND BAKING THE POTATOES IN THEIR SKINS KEEPS THEM DRIER THAN BOILING.

GNOCCHI
1 kg (2 lb 3 oz) floury potatoes, unpeeled
2 egg yolks
2 tablespoons grated Parmesan
125–185 g (4–6 oz) plain flour

SAUCE
1 tablespoon butter
75 g (2½ oz) pancetta or bacon, cut into thin strips
8 very small sage or basil leaves
150 ml (⅔ cup) double cream
50 g (2 oz) Parmesan, grated

SERVES 4

PRICK the potatoes all over, then bake for 1 hour, or until tender. Leave to cool for 15 minutes, then peel and mash, or put through a ricer or a food mill (do not use a blender or food processor).

MIX IN the egg yolks and Parmesan, then gradually stir in the flour. When the mixture gets too dry to use a spoon, work with your hands. Once a loose dough forms, transfer to a lightly floured surface and knead gently. Work in enough extra flour to give a soft, pliable dough that is damp to the touch but not sticky.

DIVIDE the dough into six portions. Working with one portion at a time, roll out on the floured surface to make a rope about 1.5 cm (½ inch) thick. Cut the rope into 1.5 cm (½ inch) lengths. Take one piece of dough and press your finger into it to form a concave shape, then roll the outer surface over the tines of a fork to make deep ridges. Fold the outer lips in towards each other to make a hollow in the middle. Continue with the remaining dough.

BRING a large saucepan of salted water to the boil. Add the gnocchi in batches, about 20 at a time. Stir gently and return to the boil. Cook for 1–2 minutes, or until they rise to the surface. Remove them with a slotted spoon, drain and put in a greased shallow casserole or baking tray. Preheat the oven to 200°C (400°F/Gas 6).

TO MAKE the sauce, melt the butter in a small frying pan and fry the pancetta until crisp. Stir in the sage leaves and cream. Season and simmer for 10 minutes, or until thickened.

POUR the sauce over the gnocchi, toss gently and sprinkle the Parmesan on top. Bake for 10–15 minutes, or until the Parmesan melts and turns golden. Serve hot.

Knead enough to just bring the dough together and make it smooth. Keep the work surface, your hands and any storage trays well floured. Roll and shape the dough quickly to stop it drying out.

TORTELLINI FILLED WITH PUMPKIN AND SAGE

LEGEND HAS IT THAT VENUS, BARRED FROM HEAVEN, SOUGHT REFUGE IN AN INN IN BOLOGNA INSTEAD. THE INNKEEPER, FILLED WITH LUST, SPIED ON HER THROUGH THE KEYHOLE, THEN RUSHED TO HIS KITCHEN TO CREATE PASTA IN THE SHAPE OF HER NAVEL—TORTELLINI.

Brushing the pasta with egg wash will make sure it holds together when filled and shaped. Don't overfill the tortellini or the filling will ooze out as it cooks. Pinching the edges together on the fat side of the pasta makes tortellini. Pinching them away from the fat side makes cappelletti (bishops' hats).

FILLING
900 g (2 lb) pumpkin or butternut
    squash, peeled and cubed
6 tablespoons olive oil
1 small red onion, finely chopped
100 g (3 oz) ricotta
1 egg yolk, beaten
25 g (1 oz) Parmesan, grated
1 teaspoon grated nutmeg
2 tablespoons chopped sage

1 quantity pasta (page 578),
    rolled out
1 egg
2 teaspoons milk

SAGE BUTTER
250 g (9 oz) butter
10 g (⅓ oz) sage leaves

grated Parmesan

SERVES 6

TO MAKE the filling, preheat the oven to 190°C (375°F/Gas 5). Put the pumpkin in a roasting tin with half the olive oil and lots of salt and pepper. Bake in the oven for 40 minutes, or until it is completely soft.

MEANWHILE, heat the remaining olive oil in a saucepan and gently cook the onion until soft. Put the onion and pumpkin in a bowl, draining off any excess oil, and mash well. Leave to cool, then crumble in the ricotta. Mix in the egg yolk, Parmesan, nutmeg and sage. Season well.

TO MAKE the tortellini, cut the rolled out pasta into 8 cm (3¼ inch) squares. Mix together the egg and milk to make an egg wash and brush lightly over the pasta just before you fill each one. Put a small teaspoon of filling in the middle of each square and fold it over diagonally to make a triangle, pressing down the corners. Pinch together the two corners on the longer side.

(IF YOU are not using the tortellini immediately, place them, well spaced out, on baking paper dusted with cornmeal and cover with a tea towel. They can be left for 1–2 hours before cooking— don't refrigerate or they will become damp.)

COOK the tortellini, in small batches, in a large saucepan of boiling salted water until *al dente*. Remove and drain with a slotted spoon.

TO MAKE the sage butter, melt the butter slowly with the sage and leave to infuse for at least 5 minutes. Drizzle over the tortellini and serve with a sprinkling of Parmesan.

SPAGHETTI ALLA PUTTANESCA

4 tablespoons olive oil
1 small onion, finely chopped
2 garlic cloves, finely sliced
1 small red chilli, cored, seeded
  and sliced
6 anchovy fillets, finely chopped
400 g (14 oz) tin chopped tomatoes
1 tablespoon finely chopped
  oregano or ¹/₄ teaspoon dried
  oregano
100 g (3 oz) pitted black olives,
  halved
1 tablespoon capers, chopped if
  large
400 g (14 oz) spaghetti

SERVES 4

HEAT the olive oil in a large saucepan and add the onion, garlic and chilli. Fry gently for about 6 minutes, or until the onion is soft. Add the anchovies and cook, stirring, until well mixed.

ADD the tomatoes, oregano, olives and capers and bring to the boil. Reduce the heat, season and leave to simmer.

MEANWHILE, cook the pasta in a large saucepan of boiling salted water until *al dente*. Drain, toss well with the sauce and serve at once.

BUCATINI ALL'AMATRICIANA

THIS DISH IS TRADITIONALLY MADE WITH GUANCIALE, CURED PIG'S CHEEK, BUT PANCETTA IS AN ACCEPTABLE SUBSTITUTE. PECORINO CAN BE USED INSTEAD OF PARMESAN.

1 tablespoon olive oil
150 g (5 oz) guanciale or pancetta,
  in 2 thick slices
1 small onion, finely chopped
2 garlic cloves, crushed
³/₄ teaspoon dried chilli flakes
600 g (1 lb 5 oz) tin chopped
  tomatoes
400 g (14 oz) bucatini
2 tablespoons finely chopped
  parsley
grated Parmesan

SERVES 4

HEAT the oil in a large saucepan. Trim the fat from the pancetta and add the fat to the pan. Cook the pancetta fat over medium-high heat until it is crisp to extract the liquid fat, then discard the rinds. Dice the pancetta, add to the saucepan and cook until lightly browned.

ADD the onion and fry gently for about 6 minutes, or until soft. Add the garlic and chilli flakes and cook, stirring, for 15–20 seconds then stir in the tomatoes. Season with salt and pepper.

SIMMER the sauce for about 15 minutes, or until it thickens and darkens.

MEANWHILE, cook the pasta in a large saucepan of boiling salted water until *al dente*. Stir the parsley into the sauce, drain the pasta, toss together well and serve with Parmesan.

BUCATINI ALL'AMATRICIANA

A biscuit cutter gives a good clean edge to the gnocchi. If you don't have one, use an upturned glass or teacup instead.

This cheesemaker has just opened a whole Parmesan. Traditionally Parmesan is 'flaked', as shown here, rather than cut.

ROMAN GNOCCHI

THESE GNOCCHI CAN BE PREPARED A DAY OR TWO IN ADVANCE, WRAPPED AND STORED IN THE REFRIGERATOR IN THE SLAB FORM OR AS CIRCLES. ROMAN GNOCCHI ARE MADE WITH SEMOLINA AND ARE QUITE DIFFERENT FROM THE MORE WELL-KNOWN POTATO GNOCCHI SERVED WITH PASTA SAUCE.

45 g (1½ oz) unsalted butter, melted
30 g (1 oz) Parmesan, grated
3 egg yolks
1 litre (4 cups) milk
pinch of nutmeg
200 g (7 oz) semolina flour

TOPPING
40 g (1⅓ oz) butter, melted
90 ml (⅓ cup) double cream
30 g (1 oz) Parmesan, grated

SERVES 4

LINE a 30 x 25 cm (12 x 10 inch) swiss roll tin with baking paper. Beat together the butter, Parmesan and egg yolks and season lightly. Set aside.

HEAT the milk in a large saucepan. Add the nutmeg, and season with salt and pepper. When the milk is just boiling, pour in the semolina in a steady stream, stirring as you pour. Reduce the heat and continue to cook, stirring, for about 10–12 minutes, or until all the milk has been absorbed and the mixture pulls away from the side of the pan in one mass.

REMOVE the pan from the heat and beat in the egg yolk mixture. When smooth, spoon quickly into the swiss roll tin. Smooth the surface to give an even thickness, using a knife dipped in cold water. Set aside to cool.

PREHEAT the oven to 180°C (350°F/Gas 4) and grease a 25 x 18 cm (10 x 7 inch) shallow casserole or baking tray.

LIFT the semolina slab out of the tin and peel off the baking paper. Cut the semolina into circles, using a 4 cm (1½ inch) biscuit cutter dipped in cold water. Arrange the circles, slightly overlapping, in the greased casserole.

TO MAKE the topping, blend together the butter and cream. Pour this over the gnocchi and sprinkle the Parmesan on top. Transfer to the oven and bake for about 25–30 minutes, or until golden. Serve at once.

DESSERTS AND BAKING

TARTE TATIN

THIS FAMOUS FRENCH DESSERT IS NAMED AFTER THE TATIN SISTERS WHO RAN A RESTAURANT NEAR ORLÉANS AT THE BEGINNING OF THE TWENTIETH CENTURY. THEY CERTAINLY POPULARIZED THE DISH, BUT MAY NOT HAVE INVENTED IT THEMSELVES.

1.5 kg (3 lb 5 oz) dessert apples
70 g (2½ oz) unsalted butter
185 g (6 oz) caster sugar
1 quantity tart pastry (page 572)

CRÈME CHANTILLY
200 ml (¾ cup) double cream
1 teaspoon icing sugar
½ teaspon vanilla extract

SERVES 8

PEEL, core and cut the apples into quarters. Put the butter and sugar in a deep 25 cm (10 inch) frying pan with an ovenproof handle. Heat until the butter and sugar have melted together. Arrange the apples tightly, one by one, in the frying pan, making sure there are no gaps. Remember that you will be turning the tart out the other way up, so arrange the apple pieces so that they are neat underneath.

COOK over low heat for 35–40 minutes, or until the apple is soft, the caramel lightly browned and any excess liquid has evaporated. Baste the apple with a pastry brush every so often, so that the top is caramelized as well. Preheat the oven to 190°C (375°F/Gas 5).

ROLL OUT the pastry on a lightly floured surface into a circle slightly larger than the frying pan and about 3 mm (⅛ inch) thick. Lay the pastry over the apple and press down around the edge to enclose it completely. Roughly trim the edge of the pastry and then fold the edge back on itself to give a neat finish.

BAKE for 25–30 minutes, or until the pastry is golden and cooked. Remove from the oven and leave to rest for 5 minutes before turning out. (If any apple sticks to the pan, just push it back into the hole in the tart.)

TO MAKE the crème chantilly, put the cream, icing sugar and vanilla extract in a chilled bowl. Whisk until soft peaks form and then serve with the hot tarte tatin.

Wedge the apples tightly into the pan—they shrink as they cook.

APRICOTS IN CARDAMOM SYRUP

A KASHMIRI SPECIALITY BEST MADE FROM DRIED KASHMIRI APRICOTS WHICH HAVE LOTS OF FLAVOUR. THE SILVER LEAF MAKES THIS A SPECIAL DESSERT BUT DOES NOT HAVE TO BE USED. IT CAN BE SERVED WITH THICK CREAM OR YOGHURT TO TEMPER THE SWEETNESS.

300 g (10 oz) dried apricots
3 tablespoons caster sugar
3 tablespoons slivered, blanched
  almonds
1 cm (½ inch) piece of ginger,
  sliced
4 cardamom pods
1 cinnamon stick
4 pieces edible silver leaf (varak),
  (optional)

SERVES 4

SOAK the apricots in 750 ml (3 cups) water in a large saucepan for 4 hours, or until plumped up.

ADD the sugar, almonds, ginger, cardamom and cinnamon to the apricots and bring slowly to the boil, stirring until the sugar has dissolved. Reduce the heat to a simmer and cook until the liquid has reduced by half and formed a thick syrup. Pour into a bowl, then refrigerate.

SERVE in small bowls with a piece of silver leaf for decoration. To do this, invert the piece of backing paper over each bowl. As soon as the silver leaf touches the apricots it will come away from the backing and stick to them.

KHEER

THIS IS THE INDIAN VERSION OF RICE PUDDING AND IS MADE ON THE STOVETOP INSTEAD OF IN THE OVEN. IT IS EXOTICALLY DELICIOUS, RICH AND CREAMY, WITH THE CARDAMOM AND ALMONDS GIVING IT A DISTINCTIVE TEXTURE AND FLAVOUR.

155 g (5 oz) basmati rice
20 cardamom pods
2.5 (10 cups) litres milk
30 g (1 oz) flaked almonds
175 g (6 oz) sugar
30 g (1 oz) sultanas

SERVES 6

WASH the rice, then soak for 30 minutes in cold water. Drain well. Remove the seeds from the cardamom pods and lightly crush them in a spice grinder or pestle and mortar.

BRING the milk to the boil in a large heavy-based saucepan and add the rice and cardamom. Reduce the heat and simmer for 1½–2 hours, or until the rice has a creamy consistency. Stir occasionally to stop the rice sticking to the pan.

DRY-FRY the almonds in a frying pan for a few minutes over medium heat. Add the sugar, almonds and sultanas to the rice, reserving some almonds and sultanas. Mix, then divide among bowls. Serve warm, garnished with almonds and sultanas.

KHEER

TIRAMISU

TIRA MI SU MEANS 'PICK ME UP' IN ITALIAN AND THIS IS HOW THE DESSERT STARTED LIFE—AS A NOURISHING DISH TO BE EATEN WHEN FEELING LOW. YOU CAN ALSO MAKE A FRUIT VERSION, USING FRAMBOISE AND PUREED RASPBERRIES INSTEAD OF BRANDY AND COFFEE.

5 eggs, separated
180 g (6 oz) caster sugar
300 g (10 oz) mascarpone
250 ml (1 cup) cold strong coffee
3 tablespoons brandy or sweet
  Marsala
36 small sponge fingers
80 g (3 oz) dark chocolate,
  finely grated

SERVES 4

BEAT the egg yolks with the sugar until the sugar has dissolved and the mixture is light and fluffy and leaves a ribbon trail when dropped from the whisk. Add the mascarpone and beat until the mixture is smooth.

WHISK the egg whites in a clean dry glass bowl, using a wire whisk or hand beaters, until soft peaks form. Fold into the mascarpone mixture.

POUR the coffee into a shallow dish and add the brandy. Dip enough biscuits to cover the base of a 25 cm (10 inch) square dish into the coffee. The biscuits should be fairly well soaked but not so much so that they break up. Arrange the biscuits in one tightly packed layer in the base of the dish.

SPREAD half the mascarpone mixture over the layer of biscuits. Add another layer of soaked biscuits and then another layer of mascarpone, smoothing the top layer neatly. Dust with the grated chocolate to serve. The flavours will be better developed if you can make the tiramisu a few hours in advance or even the night before. If you have time to do this, don't dust with the chocolate, but cover with clingfilm and chill. Dust with chocolate at the last minute or it will melt.

Made from cream rather than milk and a speciality of southern Lombardia, mascarpone is usually found as an ingredient in dishes rather than eaten as a cheese.

GINGER PUDDING

THIS DESSERT CAN ALSO BE EATEN AS A SNACK. THE GINGER JUICE CAUSES THE HOT MILK TO COAGULATE AND FORMS A GINGERY PUDDING WITH A SLIPPERY SMOOTH TEXTURE. IT IS IMPORTANT TO USE YOUNG, SWEET FRESH GINGER OR THE FLAVOUR WILL BE TOO HARSH.

200 g (7 oz) young ginger
1 tablespoon sugar
500 ml (2 cups) milk

SERVES 4

GRATE the ginger as finely as you can, collecting any juice. Place it in a piece of muslin, twist the top hard and squeeze out as much juice as possible. You will need 4 tablespoons. Alternatively, push the ginger through a juicer.

PUT 1 tablespoon of ginger juice and 1 teaspoon of sugar each into four bowls. Put the milk in a saucepan and bring to the boil, then divide among the bowls. Leave to set for 1 minute (the ginger juice will cause the milk to solidify). Serve warm.

Squeeze the juice out of the ginger by twisting it up in a piece of muslin.

ALMOND BEAN CURD WITH FRUIT

DURING HOT WEATHER IN CHINA, REFRESHING FRUIT SALADS MADE FROM PINEAPPLE, MANGO, PAPAYA, MELON, LYCHEE AND LOQUAT ARE POPULAR SNACKS. THE MILKY SQUARE OF ALMOND JELLY THAT GOES WITH THIS FRUIT SALAD IS SAID TO RESEMBLE BEAN CURD, HENCE THE TITLE.

2$\frac{1}{2}$ tablespoons powdered gelatine
    or 6 gelatine sheets
90 g (3 oz) caster sugar
2 teaspoons almond extract
125 ml ($\frac{1}{2}$ cup) condensed milk
400 g (14 oz) tin lychees in syrup
400 g (14 oz) tin loquats in syrup
$\frac{1}{2}$ papaya, cut into cubes
$\frac{1}{2}$ melon, cut into cubes

SERVES 6

PUT 125 ml water ($\frac{1}{2}$ cup) in a saucepan. If you are using powdered gelatine, sprinkle it on the water and leave to sponge for 1 minute. If you are using sheets, soak in the water until floppy. Heat the mixture slightly, stirring constantly to dissolve the gelatine. Place the sugar, almond extract and condensed milk in a bowl and stir to combine. Slowly add 625 ml (2$\frac{1}{2}$ cups) water, stirring to dissolve the sugar. Stir in the dissolved gelatine. Pour into a chilled 23 cm (9$\frac{1}{4}$ inch) square tin. Chill for at least 4 hours, or until set.

DRAIN half the syrup from the lychees and the loquats. Place the lychees and loquats with their remaining syrup in a large bowl. Add the cubed papaya and melon. Cut the almond bean curd into diamond-shaped pieces and arrange on plates, then spoon the fruit around the bean curd.

ALMOND BEAN CURD
WITH FRUIT

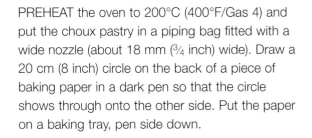

PARIS-BREST

THIS LARGE CHOUX PASTRY CAKE WAS NAMED AFTER THE PARIS-BREST BICYCLE RACE. IT WAS
INVENTED IN 1891 BY A CANNY PARISIAN PASTRY CHEF WHO OWNED A SHOP ALONG THE ROUTE AND
HAD THE IDEA OF PRODUCING THESE BICYCLE WHEEL-SHAPED CAKES.

1 quantity choux pastry (page 574)
1 egg, lightly beaten
15 g (½ oz) flaked almonds
1 quantity crème pâtissière
  (page 567)
icing sugar

PRALINE
100 g (3 oz) caster sugar
100 g (3 oz) flaked almonds

SERVES 6

PREHEAT the oven to 200°C (400°F/Gas 4) and
put the choux pastry in a piping bag fitted with a
wide nozzle (about 18 mm (¾ inch) wide). Draw a
20 cm (8 inch) circle on the back of a piece of
baking paper in a dark pen so that the circle
shows through onto the other side. Put the paper
on a baking tray, pen side down.

PIPE a ring of pastry over the guide you have
drawn. Now pipe another ring of pastry directly
inside this one so that you have one thick ring.
Pipe another two circles on top of the first two
and continue until all the choux pastry has been
used. Brush the choux ring with beaten egg and
sprinkle with the flaked almonds.

BAKE the choux ring for 20–30 minutes, then
reduce the oven to 180°C (350°F/Gas 4) and
bake for a further 20–25 minutes. Remove from
the baking tray and place on a wire rack.
Immediately slice the ring in half horizontally,
making the base twice as deep as the top. Lift off
the top and scoop out any uncooked pastry from
the base. Leave to cool completely.

TO MAKE the praline, grease a sheet of foil and
lay it out flat on the work surface. Put the sugar in
a small saucepan with 100 ml (⅓ cup) water and
heat gently until completely dissolved. Bring to the
boil and cook until deep golden, then quickly tip in
the flaked almonds and pour onto the oiled foil.
Spread a little and leave to cool. When the praline
has hardened, grind it to a fine powder in a food
processor or with a mortar and pestle. Mix into
the cold crème pâtissière.

SPOON the crème pâtissière into the base of the
choux pastry ring and cover with the top. Dust
with icing sugar to serve.

Pipe a double thickness ring of
choux pastry over the guide.

COCONUT ICE CREAM

400 ml (1⅔ cups) coconut milk
    (page 551)
250 ml (1 cup) thick (double/heavy)
    cream
2 eggs
4 egg yolks
160 g (⅔ cup) caster (superfine)
    sugar
¼ teaspoon salt

SERVES 10

POUR the coconut milk and cream into a medium saucepan. Stir over a gentle heat without boiling for 2–3 minutes. Remove from the heat, cover and keep warm over a bowl of boiling water.

PUT the eggs, egg yolks, sugar and salt in a large heatproof bowl. Beat the mixture with electric beaters for 3 minutes or until frothy and thickened.

PLACE the bowl over a pan of simmering water. Continue to beat the egg mixture, slowly adding all the coconut mixture until the custard thickens lightly. This process will take 8–10 minutes. The mixture should be a thin cream and easily coat the back of a spoon. Do not boil it or it will curdle. Set aside until cool. Stir the mixture occasionally while it is cooling. Pour into a freezer box or churn in an ice cream machine. If you are using a freezer box, take the mixture out of the freezer and beat it with electric beaters at least twice during the freezing. You want it to get plenty of air whipped into it. Cover and freeze completely. To serve, remove from the freezer for 10–15 minutes until slightly softened. Serve in scoops with slices of coconut.

MANGO SORBET

MANGO SORBET

3 ripe mangoes
150 g (5 oz) palm sugar
zest and juice from 1 lime

SERVES 4

PEEL the mangoes and cut the flesh off the stones. Chop into small pieces. Put the sugar and 185 ml (¾ cup) water in a saucepan and bring to the boil. Reduce the heat and simmer until the liquid reduces by half. Put the sugar syrup, mango and lime zest and juice in a food processor or blender and whiz until smooth.

POUR into a freezer box or churn in an ice cream machine. If you are using a freezer box, take the mixture out of the freezer and beat it with electric beaters at least twice during the freezing time. You want it to have plenty of air whipped into it or it will be too icy and hard. Cover and freeze completely.

PRALINE SEMIFREDDO

150 g (5 oz) croccante (praline)
600 ml (2½ cups) double cream
2 eggs, separated
100 g (3 oz) icing sugar
2 tablespoons Mandorla (almond-
   flavoured Marsala) or brandy

SERVES 6

FINELY CRUSH the almonds in a food processor or with a rolling pin. Pour the cream into a large bowl and whisk until soft peaks form. Beat the egg yolks with a quarter of the icing sugar until pale. Whisk the egg whites in a clean dry glass bowl until stiff peaks form, then gradually add the rest of the icing sugar and whisk until glossy stiff peaks form. Gently fold the egg yolks into the cream, then fold in the egg whites. Fold in the almonds and Mandorla.

LINE six 250 ml (1 cup) metal dariole moulds with two long strips of foil each. Spoon in the mixture, level the surface and tap each mould on the bench a few times. Cover the surface with more foil and freeze for at least 24 hours. To unmould, leave at room temperature for 5 minutes, then use the foil strips as handles to lift out the semifreddos. Serve with zabaione (page 524).

CHOCOLATE SEMIFREDDO

500 ml (2 cups) double cream
150 g (5 oz) caster sugar
50 g (2 oz) cocoa powder
4 eggs, separated
3 tablespoons brandy
3 tablespoons icing sugar
150 g (5 oz) skinned hazelnuts,
   roughly chopped

SERVES 10

LINE a 1.5 litre (6 cup) loaf tin with two long strips of foil. Heat 200 ml (¾ cup) of the cream in a small saucepan. Combine the caster sugar, cocoa powder and egg yolks in a bowl. Pour the hot cream on top and mix well. Pour back into the saucepan and cook over low heat, stirring continuously, until the mixture is thick enough to coat the back of a wooden spoon—do not allow the custard to boil. Stir in the brandy and remove from the heat. Cover the surface with clingfilm and cool for 30 minutes.

WHIP the egg whites in a clean dry glass bowl until stiff peaks form. Whip the remaining cream in a large bowl until soft peaks form. Add the icing sugar and continue whipping until stiff and glossy. Lightly fold the chocolate custard into the whipped cream, then fold in the egg whites. Gently fold through the hazelnuts. Spoon into the tin, smooth the surface and cover with foil. Freeze for at least 24 hours. Leave at room temperature for 5 minutes before serving in slices.

CHOCOLATE SEMIFREDDO

GULAB JAMUN

LITERALLY TRANSLATED TO MEAN ROSE-FLAVOURED PLUM, GULAB JAMUN IS AN EXTREMELY POPULAR INDIAN SWEET MADE BY SOAKING FRIED BALLS OF CHENNA IN SYRUP. A PINCH OF GROUND CARDAMOM CAN BE ADDED TO THE DOUGH FOR EXTRA FLAVOUR.

SYRUP
450 g (1 lb) sugar
4–5 drops rosewater

GULAB JAMUN
100 g (3 oz) low-fat powdered milk
2 tablespoons self-raising flour
2 teaspoons fine semolina
2 tablespoons ghee
4 tablespoons milk, to mix
24 pistachio nuts (optional)
oil for deep-frying

MAKES 24

TO MAKE the syrup, put the sugar in a large heavy-based saucepan with 850 ml (3½ cups) water. Stir over low heat to dissolve the sugar. Increase the heat and boil for 3 minutes to make a syrup. Stir in the rosewater and remove from the heat.

TO MAKE the gulab jamun, combine the powdered milk, flour, semolina and ghee in a bowl. Add enough milk to make a soft dough, mix until smooth, then divide into 24 portions. If using the pistachio nuts, press each piece of dough in the centre to make a hole, fill with a pistachio, then roll into a ball. If not using pistachios, just roll each piece into a ball.

FILL a karhai or deep saucepan one-third full with oil. Heat the oil to 150°C/300°F (a cube of bread will brown in 30 seconds) and fry the balls over low heat until golden brown all over. Remove with a slotted spoon and transfer to the syrup. When all the balls are in the syrup, bring the syrup to boiling point, then remove from the heat. Cool and serve the gulab jamun at room temperature.

Roll the gulab jamun into smooth balls. When they have fried to a deep golden brown, add them to the flavoured sugar syrup.

SHRIKHAND

½ teaspoon saffron strands
3 cardamom pods
275 ml (1 cup) thick natural yoghurt (page 554)
3 tablespoons caster sugar
a few toasted flaked almonds

SERVES 4

SOAK the saffron in 1 teaspoon boiling water. Remove the cardamom seeds from the pods and coarsely crush them in a spice grinder or pestle and mortar.

PUT the yoghurt, sugar, cardamom and saffron in a bowl and beat until well mixed. Divide among four bowls and refrigerate before serving. Serve with toasted almonds sprinkled on top.

SHRIKHAND

Ready-made eight-treasure rice.

Fresh longans.

Eight-treasure rice can be made in any round dish. If you want it to sit higher on the plate, then choose a deep bowl. Remember that the pattern you make on the bottom will come out on top.

EIGHT-TREASURE RICE

THIS CHINESE RICE PUDDING IS A FAVOURITE AT BANQUETS AND CHINESE NEW YEAR. THE EIGHT TREASURES VARY, BUT CAN ALSO INCLUDE OTHER PRESERVED FRUITS.

12 whole blanched lotus seeds
12 jujubes (dried Chinese dates)
20 fresh or tinned gingko nuts, shelled
225 g (8 oz) glutinous rice
2 tablespoons sugar
2 teaspoons oil
30 g (1 oz) slab sugar
8 glacé cherries
6 dried longans, pitted
4 almonds or walnuts
225 g (8 oz) red bean paste

SERVES 8

SOAK the lotus seeds and jujubes in bowls of cold water for 30 minutes, then drain. Remove the seeds from the jujubes. If using fresh gingko nuts, blanch in a pan of boiling water for 5 minutes, then refresh in cold water and dry thoroughly.

PUT the glutinous rice and 300 ml (1¼ cups) water in a heavy-based saucepan and bring to the boil. Reduce the heat to low and simmer for 10–15 minutes. Stir in the sugar and oil.

DISSOLVE the slab sugar in 200 ml (¾ cup) water and bring to the boil. Add the lotus seeds, jujubes and gingko nuts and simmer for 1 hour, or until the lotus seeds are soft. Drain, reserving the liquid.

GREASE a 1 litre (4 cup) heatproof bowl and decorate the base with the lotus seeds, jujubes, gingko nuts, cherries, longans and almonds. Smooth two thirds of the rice over this. Fill with the bean paste, cover with the remaining rice and smooth the surface.

COVER the rice with a piece of greased foil and put the bowl in a steamer. Cover and steam over simmering water in a wok for 1–1½ hours, replenishing with boiling water during cooking. Turn the pudding out onto a plate and pour the reserved sugar liquid over the top. Serve hot.

CINNAMON BAVAROIS

THE NAME OF THIS CREAMY DESSERT IS A PECULIARITY OF THE FRENCH LANGUAGE IN THAT IT CAN BE SPELT IN BOTH THE MASCULINE FORM, 'BAVAROIS' (FROM *FROMAGE BAVAROIS*), AND THE FEMININE 'BAVAROISE' (FROM *CRÈME BAVAROISE*). HOWEVER, ITS CONNECTION TO BAVARIA HAS BEEN LOST.

300 ml (1¼ cups) milk
1 teaspoon ground cinnamon
50 g (2 oz) sugar
3 egg yolks
3 gelatine leaves or 1½ teaspoons
  powdered gelatine
½ teaspoon vanilla extract
175 ml (⅔ cup) whipping cream
cinnamon, for dusting

SERVES 6

PUT the milk, cinnamon and half the sugar in a saucepan and bring to the boil. Whisk the egg yolks and remaining sugar until light and fluffy. Whisk the boiling milk into the yolks, then pour back into the saucepan and cook, stirring, until it is thick enough to coat the back of a wooden spoon. Do not let it boil or the custard will split.

SOAK the gelatine leaves in cold water until soft, drain and add to the hot custard with the vanilla. If using powdered gelatine, sprinkle it on to the hot custard, leave it to sponge for a minute, then stir it in. Strain the custard into a clean bowl and cool. Whip the cream, fold into the custard and pour into six 100 ml (⅓ cup) oiled bavarois moulds. Set in the fridge.

UNMOULD by holding the mould in a hot cloth and inverting it onto a plate with a quick shake. Dust with the extra cinnamon.

Drape the warm tuiles over a rolling pin so that they set in a curved shape.

TUILES

2 egg whites
60 g (2 oz) caster sugar
15 g (½ oz) plain flour
60 g (2 oz) ground almonds
2 teaspoons peanut oil

MAKES 12

BEAT the egg whites in a clean dry bowl until slightly frothy. Mix in the sugar, then the flour, ground almonds and oil. Preheat the oven to 200°C (400°F/Gas 6).

LINE a baking tray with baking paper. Place one heaped teaspoon of tuile mixture on the tray and use the back of the spoon to spread it into a thin round. Cover the tray with tuiles, leaving 2 cm (¾ inch) between them for spreading during cooking.

BAKE for 5–6 minutes or until lightly golden. Lift the tuiles off the tray with a metal spatula and drape over a rolling pin while still warm to make them curl (you can use bottles and glasses as well). Cool while you cook the rest of the tuiles. Serve with ice creams and other creamy desserts.

TUILES

CANNOLI

IDEALLY YOU SHOULD USE METAL CANNOLI TUBES FOR THIS RECIPE. YOU'LL FIND THESE IN MAJOR DEPARTMENT STORES AND SPECIALITY KITCHEN SHOPS. ALTERNATIVELY, YOU COULD USE 2 CM (¾ INCH)-WIDE WOODEN OR CANE DOWELING, CUT INTO 12 CM (4¾ INCH) LENGTHS.

PASTRY

150 g (5 oz) plain flour
2 teaspoons cocoa powder
1 teaspoon instant coffee
1 tablespoon caster sugar
20 g (⅔ oz) unsalted butter, chilled
    and cut into small cubes
3 tablespoons dry white wine
1 teaspoon dry Marsala

1 egg, beaten
oil for deep-frying

FILLING

300 g (10 oz) ricotta
150 g (5 oz) caster sugar
¼ teaspoon vanilla extract
½ teaspoon grated lemon zest
1 tablespoon candied peel, finely
    chopped
6 glacé cherries, chopped
15 g (½ oz) dark chocolate, grated
icing sugar

SERVES 6

TO MAKE the pastry, mix the flour, cocoa powder, coffee and sugar in a bowl. Rub in the butter, then add the wine and Marsala and mix until the dough gathers in a loose clump. Transfer to a lightly floured surface and knead until smooth (the dough will be quite stiff). Chill in a plastic bag for 30 minutes.

LIGHTLY DUST the work surface with flour and roll the pastry out to about 32 x 24 cm (12¾ x 9½ inches). Trim the edges, then cut the pastry into twelve 8 cm (3¼ inch) squares. Lightly oil the metal cannoli tubes. Wrap a pastry square diagonally around each tube, securing the overlapping corners with beaten egg and pressing them firmly together.

HEAT the oil in a deep-fat fryer or deep frying pan to about 180°C (350°F), or until a scrap of pastry dropped into the oil becomes crisp and golden, with a slightly blistered surface, in 15–20 seconds. If the oil starts to smoke it is too hot. Add the cannoli, a couple at a time, and deep-fry until golden and crisp. Remove with tongs and drain on paper towels. As soon as the tubes are cool enough to handle, slide them out and leave the pastries on a rack to cool.

TO MAKE the filling, mash the ricotta with a fork. Blend in the sugar and vanilla extract, then mix in the lemon zest, candied peel, glacé cherries and chocolate. Fill the pastries, either with a piping bag or a spoon. Arrange on a plate and dust with icing sugar for serving. The cannoli should be eaten soon after they are filled.

Traditional cannoli moulds need to be lightly greased before use. Wrap a pastry square around each tube, then deep-fry.

BLACK STICKY RICE WITH TARO

VEGETABLES LIKE TARO ARE OFTEN USED IN THAI DESSERTS. BLACK STICKY RICE IS SIMPLY WHITE RICE WITH THE BRAN LEFT ON AND IS ACTUALLY MORE PURPLE THAN BLACK. YOU MUST COOK THE RICE BEFORE ADDING ANY SUGAR OR IT WILL TOUGHEN AND NEVER BECOME TENDER.

175 g (6 oz) black sticky rice
(black glutinous)
280 g (10 oz) taro, cut into 1 cm
(½ inch) squares and soaked in
cold water
150 g (5 oz) palm sugar
1 teaspoon salt
185 ml (¾ cup) coconut milk
(page 551)

SERVES 6

PUT the rice in a bowl and pour in cold water to come 5 cm (2 inches) above the rice. Soak for at least 3 hours, or overnight if possible.

DRAIN the rice and add clean water. Scoop the rice through your fingers four or five times to clean it, then drain. Repeat two or three times with clean water to remove the unwanted starch. (The water will never be completely clear when using black rice, even when all the unwanted starch has gone.) Put the rice in a saucepan and add 625 ml (2½ cups) cold water.

BRING to the boil, stirring the rice frequently as it reaches boiling point. Reduce the heat to medium. Stir and simmer for 30–35 minutes or until nearly all the liquid has been absorbed. The rice should be very moist, but with hardly any water remaining in the bottom of the saucepan. (Taste a few grains to check whether the rice is cooked.)

MEANWHILE, drain the taro, spread it on a plate and transfer it to a bamboo steamer or other steamer. Taking care not to burn your hands, set the basket over a pan of boiling water over a high heat. Cover and steam for 8–10 minutes or until the taro is cooked and tender.

WHEN the rice is cooked, add the sugar and gently stir until the sugar has dissolved. Add the taro and gently mix.

MIX the salt into the coconut milk. Divide the pudding among individual bowls and drizzle coconut milk on top. Serve warm.

Black sticky rice is commonly used for desserts and, when cooked, is actually a dark purplish-red.

Akah bracelets for sale.

GÂTEAU BASQUE

THE BASQUE COUNTRY IS SQUEEZED INTO THE SOUTHWESTERN CORNER OF FRANCE, BORDERED BY THE SEA ON ONE SIDE AND SPAIN ON THE OTHER. JUST ABOUT EVERY BASQUE HOUSEHOLD HAS ITS OWN RECIPE FOR THIS BAKED TART, WHICH IS ALSO KNOWN AS *VÉRITABLE PASTIZA*.

Use the best-quality thick jam you can find to spread over the pastry shell. Spoon in the crème pâtissière over the top.

ALMOND PASTRY
400 g (14 oz) plain flour
1 teaspoon finely grated lemon zest
50 g (2 oz) ground almonds
150 g (5 oz) caster sugar
1 egg
1 egg yolk
1/4 teaspoon vanilla extract
150 g (5 oz) unsalted butter, softened

ALMOND CRÈME PÂTISSIÈRE
6 egg yolks
200 g (7 oz) caster sugar
60 g (2 oz) plain flour
60 g (2 oz) ground almonds
1 litre (4 cups) milk
4 vanilla pods

4 tablespoons thick black cherry or plum jam
1 egg, lightly beaten

SERVES 8

TO MAKE the pastry, mix the flour, lemon zest and almonds together, tip onto a work surface and make a well in the centre. Put the sugar, egg, egg yolk, vanilla extract and butter in the well.

MIX TOGETHER the sugar, eggs and butter, using a pecking action with your fingertips and thumb. Once they are mixed, use the edge of a palette knife to incorporate the flour, flicking it onto the dough and then chopping through it. Bring the dough together with your hands. Wrap in clingfilm and put in the fridge for at least 30 minutes.

ROLL OUT two-thirds of the pastry to fit a 25 cm (10 inch) tart ring. Trim the edge and chill in the fridge for another 30 minutes. Preheat the oven to 180°C (350°F/Gas 4).

TO MAKE the almond crème pâtissière, whisk together the egg yolks and sugar until pale and creamy. Sift in the flour and ground almonds and mix together well. Put the milk in a saucepan. Split the vanilla pods in two, scrape out the seeds and add the whole lot to the milk. Bring just to the boil and then strain over the egg yolk mixture, stirring continuously. Pour back into the clean saucepan and bring to the boil, stirring constantly—it will be lumpy at first but will become smooth as you stir. Boil for 2 minutes, then leave to cool.

SPREAD the jam over the base of the pastry case, then spread with the crème pâtissière. Roll out the remaining pastry to make a top for the pie. Brush the edge of the pastry case with beaten egg, put the pastry top over it and press together around the side. Trim the edge. Brush the top of the pie with beaten egg and gently score in a criss-cross pattern. Bake for 40 minutes, or until golden brown. Cool for at least 30 minutes before serving, either slightly warm or cold.

ZUCCOTTO

ZUCCOTTO IS A SPECIALITY OF THE CITY OF FLORENCE—ITS SHAPE PERHAPS INSPIRED BY THE ROUNDED ROOF OF THE LOCAL *DUOMO*. ZUCCOTTO IS ALSO A VARIANT OF *ZUCCHETTO*, THE NAME OF THE CARDINALS' SKULL-CAPS.

300 g (10 oz) Madeira or pound cake
3 tablespoons maraschino liqueur
3 tablespoons brandy
500 ml (2 cups) double cream
100 g (3 oz) icing sugar
150 g (5 oz) dark chocolate, roughly chopped
50 g (2 oz) blanched almonds
25 g (1 oz) skinned hazelnuts
25 g (1 oz) candied peel, chopped
cocoa powder, to dust
icing sugar, to dust

SERVES 6

CUT the cake into 1 cm (½ inch) slices and then cut each slice into two triangles. Combine the maraschino and brandy and sprinkle over the cake.

LINE a round 1.5 litre (6 cup) bowl with a layer of clingfilm and then with the cake slices. Arrange the slices with the narrow point of each triangle pointing into the bottom of the bowl to form a star pattern, fitting each piece snugly against the others so you don't have any gaps. Cut smaller triangles to fit the gaps along the top and keep the rest of the cake for the top.

WHIP the cream until soft peaks form and then whisk in the icing sugar until you have a stiff mixture. Add about a third of the chocolate and the almonds, hazelnuts and candied peel. Mix together thoroughly, then fill the cake-lined bowl with half the mixture, making a hollow in the middle and drawing the mixture up the sides. Leave in the fridge.

MELT the rest of the chocolate in a heatproof bowl over a saucepan of simmering water, or in a microwave, and fold it into the remaining cream mixture. Spoon this into the bowl and then cover the top with a layer of cake triangles, leaving no gaps. Cover the bowl with clingfilm and refrigerate overnight.

TO SERVE, unmould the zuccotto and use a triangular piece of cardboard as a template to dust the top with alternating segments of cocoa and icing sugar.

When filling the zuccotto, try not to disturb the pieces of cake you have arranged. The easiest way is to smooth the filling up the side and then fill the middle afterwards.

NEW YEAR SWEET DUMPLINGS

THESE GLUTINOUS SWEET DUMPLINGS ARE MADE AT CHINESE NEW YEAR AND ARE OFTEN EATEN IN A SWEET SOUP. THEY CAN BE FILLED WITH A NUT OR BEAN PASTE.

60 g (2 oz) black sesame paste, red bean paste or smooth peanut butter
4 tablespoons caster sugar
250 g (9 oz) glutinous rice flour
30 g (1 oz) rock sugar

MAKES 24

COMBINE the sesame paste with the sugar.

SIFT the rice flour into a bowl and stir in 200 ml (¾ cup) boiling water. Knead carefully (the dough will be very hot) to form a soft, slightly sticky dough. Dust your hands with extra rice flour, roll the dough into a cylinder, then divide it into cherry-size pieces. Cover the dough with a tea towel and, using one piece at a time, form each piece of dough into a flat round, then gather it into a cup shape. The dough should be fairly thin.

FILL each cup shape with 1 teaspoon of paste and fold the top over, smoothing the dough so you have a round ball with no visible joins.

BRING 1 litre (4 cups) water to the boil, add the rock sugar and stir until dissolved. Return to the boil, add the dumplings in batches and simmer for 5 minutes, or until they rise to the surface. Serve warm with a little of the syrup.

New Year dumplings are widely available in the markets and night markets of China during the New Year celebrations.

FRIED FRAGRANT BANANAS

125 g (4 oz) self-raising flour
2 tablespoons milk
20 g (⅔ oz) butter, melted
1 tablespoon caster sugar
4 apple or lady finger bananas, or 3 ordinary bananas
oil for deep-frying
honey (optional)

SERVES 4

COMBINE the flour, milk, butter and sugar, then add enough water to make a thick batter.

CUT the bananas into 3 cm (1¼ inch) chunks.

FILL a wok one quarter full of oil. Heat the oil to 180°C (350°F), or until a piece of bread fries golden brown in 15 seconds when dropped in the oil. Dip the banana pieces, a few at a time, into the batter and then fry them for 3 minutes, or until they are well browned on all sides. Drain on paper towels. Serve the bananas drizzled with honey for extra sweetness.

FRIED FRAGRANT BANANAS

APPLES AND PEARS IN PASTRY

IN LATE SUMMER AND AUTUMN, WHEN THE ORCHARDS ARE OVERFLOWING WITH FRUIT, THE NORMAN COOK MAKES *BOURDELOTS* OR *DOUILLONS*. THESE PASTRY-WRAPPED APPLES OR PEARS COULD ALSO CONTAIN A DRIZZLE OF CALVADOS.

Bring up the corners of the pastry square so they meet at the top of the fruit.

PASTRY
150 g (5 oz) unsalted butter
225 g (8 oz) plain flour
30 g (1 oz) caster sugar
1 egg yolk

HAZELNUT FILLING
30 g (1 oz) hazelnuts, finely chopped
60 g (2 oz) unsalted butter, softened
75 g (2½ oz) soft brown sugar
pinch of mixed spice

2 dessert apples
2 pears (ripe but still firm)
juice of 1 lemon
1 egg, lightly beaten

SERVES 4

TO MAKE the pastry, rub the butter into the flour until the mixture resembles fine breadcrumbs. Stir in the sugar. Add the egg yolk and 2 tablespoons water and stir with a knife to form a dough. Turn out and bring together with your hands. Wrap in clingfilm and refrigerate for at least 30 minutes. Preheat the oven to 200°C (400°F/Gas 6) and preheat the grill (broiler).

TO MAKE the hazelnut filling, toast the hazelnuts under the hot grill for 1–2 minutes or until browned, then cool. Mix the softened butter with the sugar, hazelnuts and mixed spice. Peel and core the apples and pears, leaving the stalks and trimming the bases of the pears if they are very big. Roll in the lemon juice and stuff with the hazelnut filling.

ROLL OUT the pastry to make a 32 cm (12¾ inch) square, trimming off any untidy edges. Cut into four equal squares and place an apple or pear in the centre of each. Brush the edges of the pastry with water and then bring them up so that the corners of each pastry square meet at the top of the fruit. Press the edges together so that the pastry follows the curve of the fruit.

CUT OFF the excess pastry and crimp the edges to seal the fruit parcels thoroughly. Use the pastry trimmings to cut out leaves, then stick these onto the fruit by brushing the backs with water.

BRUSH the pastry fruits with the beaten egg to glaze and bake on a lightly greased baking tray for 35–40 minutes or until the pastry is cooked and browned. Serve with cream.

Dinner in Saint Rémy.

The Writers building, Kolkata (Calcutta).

Make a dent in each ball and fill it with nuts before smoothing the balls into shape. Gently poach them in the sugar syrup.

ROSSOGOLLAS

KOLKATA (CALCUTTA) IS THE CITY WHERE THE BEST BENGALI SWEETS CAN BE FOUND. ROSSOGOLLAS OR RASGULLAS ARE SWEETENED MILK BALLS IN SYRUP, SAID TO HAVE BEEN INVENTED BY AN OLD FIRM, K.C. DAS, WHICH SPECIALIZES IN SWEETS. MAKE THE CHENNA BEFORE YOU START.

1 quantity chenna (page 553)
3 tablespoons chopped nuts
    (optional)

SYRUP
1 kg (2 lb 3 oz) sugar
3 tablespoons milk
rosewater (optional)

SERVES 6

DIVIDE the chenna dough into 30 portions and roll each into a ball. If you are using the nuts, make a hollow in each ball, add a few chopped nuts to the centre, then re-roll as a ball.

MAKE a thin syrup by combining the sugar with 1.5 litres (6 cups) of water in a heavy-based saucepan and simmering the mixture over low heat until it is slightly thickened. The syrup should feel sticky and greasy. Add the milk to the boiling syrup to clarify it—this will force any scum to rise to the surface. Skim off the scum with a spoon.

DROP the rossogollas into the clean boiling syrup, reduce the heat and simmer for 10 minutes, or until they float. Sprinkle a little water on the boiling syrup every 2 minutes to stop it reducing too much and foaming. When the rossogollas are cooked, they will float on the surface.

REMOVE from the heat and leave to cool in the syrup. If you would like a rose flavour, add a few drops of rosewater. Keep the rossogollas refrigerated until required. Serve with a little of the syrup poured over them.

CHOCOLATE SOUFFLÉS

SOUFFLÉS ARE RENOWNED FOR THEIR DIFFICULTY TO MAKE, BUT CAN IN FACT BE VERY EASY. IF YOU ARE FEELING PARTICULARLY DECADENT WHEN YOU SERVE THESE CHOCOLATE SOUFFLÉS, MAKE A HOLE IN THE TOP OF EACH ONE AND POUR IN A LITTLE CREAM.

40 g (1 oz) unsalted butter, softened
185 g (6 oz) caster sugar

SOUFFLÉS
1 quantity crème pâtissière (page 567)
90 g (3 oz) unsweetened cocoa powder
3 tablespoons chocolate or coffee liqueur
80 g (3 oz) dark chocolate, chopped
12 egg whites
3 tablespoons caster sugar
icing sugar

SERVES 8

TO PREPARE the dishes, brush the insides of eight 300 ml (1¼ cup) soufflé dishes with the softened butter. Pour a little caster sugar into each one, turn the dishes round to coat thoroughly and then tip out any excess sugar. Preheat the oven to 190ºC (375ºF/Gas 5) and put a large baking tray in the oven to heat up.

WARM the crème pâtissière in a bowl over a saucepan of simmering water, then remove from the heat. Whisk the cocoa powder, chocolate liqueur and chocolate into the crème pâtissière.

BEAT the egg whites in a clean dry bowl until firm peaks form. Whisk in the sugar gradually to make a stiff glossy mixture. Whisk half the egg white into the crème pâtissière to loosen it, and then fold in the remainder with a large metal spoon or spatula. Pour into the soufflé dishes and run your thumb around the inside rim of each dish, about 2 cm (¾ inch) into the soufflé mixture to help the soufflés rise without sticking.

PUT the dishes on the hot baking tray and bake for 15–18 minutes, or until the soufflés are well risen and wobble slightly when tapped. Test with a skewer through a crack in the side of a soufflé—the skewer should come out clean or slightly moist. If it is slightly moist, by the time you get the soufflés to the table, they will be cooked in the centre. Serve immediately, dusted with a little icing sugar.

Beat egg whites in a clean dry bowl—any hint of grease will prevent them aerating.

STICKY RICE WITH MANGO

IN THAILAND THE MANGO SEASON IS IN APRIL. SOME MANGOES TASTE BETTER WHEN GREEN, CRISP AND CRUNCHY, OTHERS WHEN THEY ARE RIPE. EITHER WAY, THERE IS A LOT OF VARIETY AND MANY DIFFERENT FLAVOURS. THIS STICKY RICE WITH MANGO IS ARGUABLY THE BEST THAI DESSERT.

4 large ripe mangoes
1 quantity of steamed sticky rice
  with coconut milk (page 550)
170 ml (⅔ cup) coconut cream
  (page 551) mixed with ¼ teaspoon
  salt, for garnish
2 tablespoons dry-fried mung beans
  (optional)

SERVES 4

PEEL the mangoes and slice off the two outside cheeks of each, removing as much flesh as you can in large pieces. Avoid cutting very close to the stone where the flesh is fibrous. Discard the stone. Slice each cheek lengthways into four or five pieces.

ARRANGE the mango pieces on a serving plate. Spoon a portion of steamed sticky rice with coconut milk near the mango slices. Spoon the coconut cream garnish on top and sprinkle with mung beans. Serve at room temperature.

BANANA IN COCONUT CREAM

BANANA IN COCONUT CREAM

THERE ARE MORE THAN 20 VARIETIES OF BANANA IN THAILAND, ALL OF WHICH ARE USED IN COOKING. USE NICE SWEET BANANAS FOR THIS RECIPE AND AVOID PARTICULARLY LARGE ONES.

400 ml (1⅔ cups) coconut milk
  (page 551)
4 tablespoons sugar
5 just-ripe bananas
½ teaspoon salt

SERVES 4

PUT the coconut milk, sugar and 125 ml (½ cup) water in a saucepan and bring to a boil. Reduce the heat and simmer until the sugar dissolves.

PEEL the bananas and cut them into 5 cm (2 inch) lengths. If you are using very small bananas, leave them whole.

WHEN the sugar in the coconut milk has dissolved, add the bananas and salt. Cook gently over a low to medium heat for 5 minutes or until the bananas are soft.

DIVIDE the bananas and coconut cream among four bowls. Serve warm or at room temperature.

PANFORTE

PANFORTE MEANS 'STRONG BREAD', AN APT DESCRIPTION FOR THIS DENSE, FRUITY ITILIAN LOAF THAT STILL RETAINS ITS MEDIEVAL FLAVOUR. PANFORTE IS ALSO KNOWN AS SIENA CAKE—SIENA POSSIBLY BEING THE FIRST ITALIAN CITY TO USE SUGAR AND SPICES SUCH AS WHITE PEPPER.

110 g (4 oz) hazelnuts
110 g (4 oz) almonds
125 g (4 oz) candied mixed peel, chopped
100 g (3 oz) candied pineapple, chopped
grated zest of 1 lemon
75 g (2½ oz) plain flour
1 teaspoon ground cinnamon
¼ teaspoon ground coriander
¼ teaspoon ground cloves
¼ teaspoon grated nutmeg
pinch of white pepper
150 g (5 oz) sugar
4 tablespoons honey
50 g (2 oz) unsalted butter
icing sugar

MAKES ONE 23 CM (9 INCH) CAKE

LINE a 23 cm (9 inch) springform tin with rice paper or baking parchment and grease well with butter. Toast the nuts under a hot grill (broiler), turning them so they brown on all sides, then leave to cool. Put the nuts in a bowl with the mixed peel, pineapple, lemon zest, flour and spices and toss together. Preheat the oven to 150°C (300°F/Gas 2).

PUT the sugar, honey and butter in a saucepan and melt them together. Cook the syrup until it reaches 120°C on a sugar thermometer, or a little of it dropped into cold water forms a soft ball when moulded between your finger and thumb.

POUR the syrup into the nut mixture and mix well, working fast before it stiffens too much. Pour straight into the tin, smooth the surface and bake for 35 minutes. (Unlike other cakes this will neither firm up as it cooks or colour at all so you need to time it carefully.)

COOL in the tin until the cake firms up enough to remove the side of the tin. Peel off the paper and leave to cool completely. Dust the top heavily with icing sugar.

The hills around Siena.

Dairy cows in Normandy.

Ladling the crème brûlée custard into the ramekins.

CRÈME BRÛLÉE

CRÈME CARAMEL

CARAMEL
100 g (3 oz) caster sugar

650 ml (2¾ cups) milk
1 vanilla pod
125 g (4 oz) caster sugar
3 eggs, beaten
3 egg yolks

SERVES 6

TO MAKE the caramel, put the sugar in a heavy-based saucepan and heat until it dissolves and starts to caramelize—tip the saucepan from side to side to keep the colouring even. Remove from the heat and carefully add 2 tablespoons water to stop the cooking process. Pour into six 125 ml (½ cup) ramekins and leave to cool.

PREHEAT the oven to 180°C (350°F/Gas 4). Put the milk and vanilla pod in a saucepan and bring just to the boil. Mix together the sugar, eggs and egg yolks. Strain the boiling milk over the egg mixture and stir well. Ladle into the ramekins and place in a roasting tin. Pour enough hot water into the tin to come halfway up the sides of the ramekins. Cook for 35–40 minutes, or until firm to the touch. Remove from the tin and leave for 15 minutes. Unmould onto plates and pour on any leftover caramel.

CRÈME BRÛLÉE

CRÈME BRÛLÉE HAS BEEN KNOWN IN ENGLAND SINCE THE SEVENTEENTH CENTURY BY THE NAME 'BURNT CREAM'. THE CREAMY CUSTARD IS SIMILAR TO THAT OF THE CRÈME CARAMEL, BUT THE TOPPING IS CARAMELIZED TO A HARD CRUST.

500 ml (2 cups) cream
200 ml (¾ cup) milk
125 g (4 oz) caster sugar
1 vanilla pod
5 egg yolks
1 egg white
1 tablespoon orange flower water
100 g (3 oz) demerara sugar

SERVES 8

PREHEAT the oven to 120°C (250°F/Gas ½). Put the cream, milk and half the sugar in a saucepan with the vanilla pod. Bring just to the boil.

MEANWHILE, mix together the remaining sugar, egg yolks and white. Strain the boiling milk over the egg mixture, whisking well. Stir in the orange flower water.

LADLE into eight 125 ml (½ cup) ramekins and place in a roasting tin. Pour enough hot water into the tin to come halfway up the sides of the ramekins. Cook for 1½ hours, or until set in the centre. Cool and refrigerate until ready to serve. Just before serving, sprinkle the tops with demerara sugar and caramelize under a very hot grill (broiler) or with a blowtorch. Serve immediately.

KULFI

YOUNG AND OLD TAKE GREAT DELIGHT IN THESE FLAVOURED ICES WHICH ARE SOLD IN INDIA AT ROADSIDE STALLS. THEY ARE NOT GENERALLY MADE IN HOUSEHOLDS AS THEY ARE TIME-CONSUMING.

2 litres (8 cups) milk
10 cardamom pods, lightly crushed
6 tablespoons sugar
15 g (½ oz) almonds, blanched and finely chopped
15 g (½ oz) unsalted pistachio nuts, skinned and finely chopped
edible silver leaf (varak), (optional)

MAKES 12

PUT the milk and cardamom pods in a heavy-based saucepan and bring to the boil. Reduce the heat to low and simmer, stirring frequently, for about 2 hours, until the milk has reduced to a third of the original amount, about 750 ml (3 cups). Whenever a thin skin forms on top, stir it back in. Add the sugar to the pan, simmer for 5 minutes, then strain into a shallow plastic freezer box. Add the almonds and half the pistachios, then cool. Put twelve 75 ml (¼ cup) kulfi moulds or dariole moulds in the freezer to chill.

PLACE the kulfi mixture in the freezer and every 20 minutes, using electric beaters or a fork, give the ice cream a good stir to break up the ice crystals. When the mixture is quite stiff, divide it among the moulds and freeze until hardened completely. Dip the moulds in hot water and turn out the kulfi. Sprinkle with the remaining pistachios and decorate with a piece of silver leaf.

Kulfi are flavoured ices made in specially shaped moulds. When the mixture has hardened, fill the conical moulds, then freeze.

CARROT HALVA

THIS IS A VERY SIMPLE INDIAN SWEET. THE ONLY SECRET TO MAKING IT LOOK AUTHENTIC IS TO USE REALLY BRIGHT-ORANGE CARROTS TO GIVE A GOOD COLOUR. CARROT HALVA IS TRADITIONALLY MADE IN THE WINTER MONTHS AND IS BEST EATEN HOT WITH A DOLLOP OF CREAM.

1 kg (2 lb 3 oz) carrots, coarsely grated
1 litre (4 cups) milk
100 g (3 oz) ghee
250 g (9 oz) caster sugar
80 g (3 oz) raisins
1 teaspoon cardamom seeds, finely ground
50 g (2 oz) slivered almonds
ground cardamom

SERVES 8

PUT the grated carrot and milk in a heavy-based saucepan over low heat and bring to a simmer. Cook, stirring until the carrot is tender and the milk evaporates. This must be done slowly or the mixture will burn. Add the ghee and cook until the carrot starts to brown.

ADD the sugar and cook until the mixture is thick and dry. Add the raisins, cardamom and almonds. Serve hot in small bowls, with double cream or ice cream, and sprinkle with a little ground cardamom.

CARROT HALVA

HAZELNUT AND CHOCOLATE CAKE

140 g (5 oz) skinned hazelnuts
3 tablespoons cocoa powder
60 g (2 oz) plain flour
30 g (1 oz) self-raising flour
185 g (6 oz) soft brown sugar
250 g (9 oz) unsalted butter,
   softened
4 eggs, separated
icing sugar

SERVES 8

TOAST the hazelnuts under a hot grill (broiler), turning them so they brown on all sides. Leave them to cool, then put in a food processor and process until fine (don't overprocess or they will become oily), or chop finely with a knife. Transfer to a bowl with the cocoa powder and sifted flours. Preheat the oven to 180°C (350°F/Gas 4).

BEAT TOGETHER the sugar and butter until very creamy. Add the egg yolks one at a time, mixing well after each addition. Add the hazelnut mixture and stir well. Whisk the egg whites in a clean dry glass bowl until stiff peaks form, then fold into the mixture. Pour into the tin and bake for 50 minutes or until a skewer inserted into the centre comes out clean. Rest for 15 minutes, then cool on a wire rack. Dust with icing sugar before serving.

In Tuscany chestnuts are grown in quantity. The season is short—early November until Christmas—so they are also dried for year-round use. The dried chestnuts are soaked in water, then boiled in milk for soups or sweet desserts.

CHESTNUT CAKE

400 g (14 oz) chestnuts or 250 g
   (9 oz) cooked peeled chestnuts
5 egg yolks
200 g (7 oz) sugar
100 g (3 oz) unsalted butter,
   softened
1 tablespoon grated lemon zest
150 g (5 oz) ground almonds
2 tablespoons plain flour
4 egg whites

SERVES 8

PREHEAT the oven to 180°C (350°F/Gas 4) and grease and flour a 20 cm (8 inch) cake tin.

BOIL the chestnuts in a saucepan of water for 25 minutes, or until they are tender. Drain, peel and, while still hot, purée and sieve. (If you are using the cooked chestnuts, simply purée them.)

WHISK the egg yolks and sugar until light and fluffy. Add the butter, lemon zest, chestnut purée, ground almonds and flour and stir well. Whisk the egg whites until soft peaks form and fold into the mixture. Pour into the tin and bake for 50–60 minutes. Cool on a wire rack and serve with whipped cream.

CHESTNUT CAKE

BLACKCURRANT SORBET

WE'VE USED GLUCOSE FOR THIS SORBET BECAUSE IT STOPS THE SUGAR CRYSTALLIZING AND GIVES A GOOD TEXTURE. TO WEIGH GLUCOSE WITHOUT IT RUNNING EVERYWHERE, MEASURE THE SUGAR INTO THE PAN OF THE SCALES, THEN MAKE A HOLLOW IN THE MIDDLE AND POUR IN THE GLUCOSE.

215 g (8 oz) caster sugar
30 g (1 oz) liquid glucose
350 g (12 oz) blackcurrants, stalks
　　removed
1 tablespoon lemon juice
2 tablespoons crème de cassis

SERVES 4

PUT the sugar and glucose in a saucepan with 225 ml (¾ cup) water. Heat gently to dissolve the sugar and then boil for 2–3 minutes. Leave to cool completely.

PUT the blackcurrants and lemon juice in a blender with half of the cooled syrup and mix to a thick purée. (Alternatively, push the fruit through a sieve to purée and then mix with the lemon juice and syrup.) Add the remaining syrup and the crème de cassis and mix well.

CHURN in an ice-cream maker following the manufacturer's instructions. Alternatively, pour into a plastic freezer box, cover and freeze. Stir every 30 minutes with a whisk during freezing to break up the ice crystals and give a better texture. Freeze overnight with a layer of clingfilm over the surface and the lid on the container. Keep in the freezer until ready to serve.

RED WINE SORBET

250 g (9 oz) caster sugar
100 ml (⅓ cup) orange juice
250 ml (1 cup) light red wine

SERVES 4

DISSOLVE the caster sugar in 250 ml (1 cup) boiling. Add the orange juice and red wine and stir well.

CHURN in an ice-cream maker following the manufacturer's instructions. Alternatively, pour into a plastic freezer box, cover and freeze. Stir every 30 minutes with a whisk during freezing to break up the ice crystals and give a better texture. Freeze overnight with a layer of clingfilm over the surface and the lid on the container. Keep in the freezer until ready to serve.

Stir the sugar until it is completely dissolved before adding the orange juice and wine.

STEAMED PEARS IN HONEY

THIS RECIPE COMBINES SWEET PEARS WITH JUJUBES, SMALL RED CHINESE DATES THAT ARE THOUGHT TO HAVE MEDICINAL BENEFITS. THEY CAN BE LEFT OUT IF THEY ARE UNAVAILABLE.

100 g (3 oz) jujubes (dried Chinese dates)
6 nearly ripe pears
6 tablespoons honey

SERVES 6

SOAK the jujubes in hot water for 1 hour, changing the water twice. Drain, stone and cut crosswise into strips.

SLICE the bottom off each pear so that it will sit flat. Cut a 2.5 cm (1 inch) piece off the top and set it aside. Using a fruit corer or knife, remove the cores without cutting right through to the bottom.

ARRANGE the pears upright on a heatproof plate. Place 1 tablespoon of honey and some jujubes into the cavity of each pear. Replace the tops and, if necessary, fasten with toothpicks.

PUT the plate in a steamer. Cover and steam over simmering water in a wok for 30 minutes, or until tender when pierced with a knife. Serve hot or cold.

STEAMED PEARS IN HONEY

ALMOND BISCUITS

ALMONDS ARE USED FOR SWEET RATHER THAN SAVOURY DISHES IN CHINA. THESE BISCUITS MAKE GREAT SNACKS AND CAN ALSO BE SERVED ALONGSIDE DESSERTS SUCH AS ALMOND BEAN CURD.

125 g (4 oz) unsalted butter, softened
185 g (6 oz) sugar
1 egg, lightly beaten
200 g (7 oz) plain flour
1/2 teaspoon baking powder
1/2 teaspoon salt
150 g (5 oz) finely chopped almonds
1 teaspoon almond extract
1 egg, lightly beaten, extra
25 whole blanched almonds

MAKES 25

PREHEAT the oven to 180°C (350°F/Gas 4). Lightly grease a baking tray. Cream the butter and sugar for 5 minutes. Add the egg and beat until smooth. Sift together the flour, baking powder and salt and slowly add to the butter, stirring until smooth. Add the almonds and extract and stir until smooth.

DROP tablespoons of the mixture onto the baking tray, spacing them about 3 cm (1¼ inches) apart. Dip your thumb into some flour and make an indentation in the centre of each biscuit. Brush each biscuit with the beaten egg and place an almond in the centre of each indentation. Bake for 10–12 minutes, or until the biscuits are golden and puffed. Cool slightly, then transfer to a rack to cool completely.

Dip your thumb in some flour and make an indent in each biscuit to hold the almonds.

ALMOND BISCUITS

LEMON GELATO

GELATO IS THE ITALIAN NAME FOR AN ICE CREAM BASED ON AN EGG CUSTARD MIXTURE, THOUGH IT HAS NOW COME TO MEAN ALL ICE CREAMS, INCLUDING SORBETS. ITALIANS ARE DISCERNING ABOUT ICE CREAM AND FLAVOURS TEND TO BE FRESH AND AROMATIC, OFTEN BASED ON FRUIT.

5 egg yolks
125 g (4 oz) sugar
500 ml (2 cups) milk
2 tablespoons grated lemon zest
185 ml (⅔ cup) lemon juice
3 tablespoons double cream

SERVES 6

WHISK the egg yolks and half the sugar together until pale and creamy. Place the milk, lemon zest and remaining sugar in a saucepan and bring to the boil. Pour over the egg mixture and whisk to combine. Pour the custard back into the saucepan and cook over low heat, stirring continuously until the mixture is thick enough to coat the back of a wooden spoon—do not allow the custard to boil.

STRAIN the custard into a bowl, add the lemon juice and cream and then cool over ice. Churn in an ice-cream maker following the manufacturer's instructions. Alternatively, pour into a plastic freezer box, cover and freeze. Stir every 30 minutes with a whisk during freezing to break up the ice crystals and give a better texture. Keep in the freezer until ready to serve.

COFFEE GELATO

5 egg yolks
125 g (4 oz) sugar
500 ml (2 cups) milk
120 ml (½ cup) freshly made espresso
1 tablespoon Tia Maria

SERVES 6

WHISK the egg yolks and half the sugar together until pale and creamy. Place the milk, coffee and remaining sugar in a saucepan and bring to the boil. Pour over the egg mixture and whisk to combine. Pour back into the saucepan and cook over low heat, stirring continuously until the mixture is thick enough to coat the back of a wooden spoon—do not allow the custard to boil.

STRAIN the custard into a bowl and cool over ice. Stir in the Tia Maria. Churn in an ice-cream maker following the manufacturer's instructions. Alternatively, pour into a plastic freezer box, cover and freeze. Stir every 30 minutes with a whisk during freezing to break up the ice crystals and give a better texture. Keep in the freezer until ready to serve.

COFFEE GELATO

LEMON GELATO

CASHEW NUT BARFI

500 g (1 lb 2 oz) cashew nuts
6 cardamom pods
200 g (7 oz) powdered milk
2 tablespoons ghee or butter
1/4 teaspoon ground cloves
200 g (7 oz) caster sugar
2 sheets edible silver leaf (varak),
    (optional)

SERVES 12

PLACE a small frying pan over low heat and dry-roast the cashew nuts until browned all over. Cool and chop in a food processor or with a knife. Remove the cardamom seeds from the pods and crush them in a spice grinder or pestle and mortar. Line a 26 x 17 cm (10 x 7 inch) baking tin with baking paper.

COMBINE the milk powder and cashew nuts in a large bowl and rub in the ghee until completely mixed in. Stir in the cardamom and cloves.

COMBINE the sugar and 250 ml (1 cup) water in a heavy-based saucepan and heat over low heat until the sugar melts. Bring to the boil and simmer for 5–7 minutes to make a sugar syrup. Quickly stir the sugar syrup into the cashew mixture—if you leave it too long it will stiffen—and spread the mixture into the baking tin (the mixture should be about 1.5 cm (3/4 inch) thick). Smooth with a buttered spatula. Place the silver leaf on top by inverting the sheets onto the surface and peeling off the paper backing. Leave to cool, then slice into diamond shapes. Serve cold.

Carefully lay sheets of silver on the barfi and pull off the backing paper. If you touch the silver with your hands it will stick to them.

PAYASAM

PAYASAM

100 g (3 oz) sago
2 tablespoons ghee
80 g (3 oz) chopped or slivered
    almonds
125 g (4 oz) sultanas
50 g (2 oz) sevian, broken into
    3 cm (1 1/4 inch) pieces
1 litre (4 cups) milk
185 g (6 oz) soft brown sugar
3 tablespoons golden syrup
1 teaspoon ground cardamom
1/4 teaspoon ground cloves
1 teaspoon rosewater (optional)
2 tablespoons grated coconut
    (page 555)

SERVES 6

SIMMER the sago in 1 litre (4 cups) simmering water, stirring occasionally, for 20–25 minutes, until the sago is clear, then drain. Rinse and drain the sago again.

HEAT the ghee in a heavy-based frying pan over low heat, brown the nuts and sultanas and remove from the pan. Fry the sevian in the same pan until light brown. Add most of the milk and simmer the sevian until soft, stirring as it cooks. Add the sago and remaining milk. Stir with a fork, add the sugar and golden syrup and simmer, stirring constantly.

ADD a little milk if necessary as the payasam thickens, then add the cardamom, cloves and rosewater and stir to a pourable consistency. Add two-thirds of the nuts and sultanas and stir. Serve immediately or chill. Garnish with the coconut and

Almonds are native to the Mediterranean. In Italy fresh almonds are picked while they still have their green coating and the kernel is soft and a bit wet. They are then eaten on their own or served with cheese.

BISCOTTI

380 g (13½ oz) plain flour
160 g (5 oz) caster sugar
3 eggs
½ teaspoon baking powder
½ teaspoon vanilla extract
150 g (5 oz) blanched almonds

MAKES 20

PREHEAT the oven to 180ºC (350ºF/Gas 4) and line two baking trays with baking parchment. Sieve the flour into a large bowl or food processor, add the sugar, eggs, baking powder, vanilla and a pinch of salt and mix or process until you have a smooth dough. Transfer to a floured surface and knead in the almonds.

DIVIDE the dough into two pieces and roll each one into a log about 20 cm (8 inches) long. Put on the baking trays and press down gently along the top to flatten the logs slightly. Bake for 25 minutes until the dough is golden. Take the logs out of the oven and leave to cool slightly while you turn the oven down to 170ºC (325ºF/Gas 3).

CUT each log into 1 cm (½ inch)-thick diagonal slices, lay these on the baking tray and return to the oven for 15 minutes until they start to brown and are dry to the touch. Store in an airtight container.

AMARETTI

125 g (4 oz) blanched almonds
125 g (4 oz) icing sugar
3 teaspoons plain flour
2 egg whites
75 g (2½ oz) caster sugar
1 teaspoon almond extract

MAKES 15

PREHEAT the oven to 180ºC (350ºF/Gas 4). Put the almonds, icing sugar and flour in a pestle and mortar or food processor and grind to a fine powder (be careful not to overwork the mixture or it will become oily).

WHISK the egg whites in a clean dry glass bowl until soft peaks form. Add the caster sugar a tablespoon at a time and beat continuously until you have a stiff shiny mixture. Fold in the almond mixture and the almond extract until just blended.

SPOON the mixture into a piping bag with a 1 cm (½ inch) plain nozzle and pipe 3 cm (1¼ inch)-wide mounds, well spaced, onto a baking tray. Smooth the top of each biscuit with a damp finger and bake for 40 minutes until light brown. Turn off the oven, leave the door ajar and let the biscuits cool and dry out. Store in an airtight container.

ÎLE FLOTTANTE

THIS ROUND ISLAND OF MERINGUE FLOATING ON A SEA OF CUSTARD IS OFTEN CONFUSED WITH ANOTHER FRENCH MERINGUE DESSERT, *OEUFS A LA NEIGE*. 'FLOATING ISLAND' IS ONE LARGE BAKED MERINGUE, WHILE 'EGGS IN THE SNOW' ARE SMALL POACHED MERINGUES ON CUSTARD.

MERINGUE
4 egg whites
110 g (4 oz) caster sugar
1/4 teaspoon vanilla extract

PRALINE
55 g (2 oz) sugar
55 g (2 oz) flaked almonds

2 quantities crème anglaise
  (page 567)

SERVES 6

PREHEAT the oven to 140°C (275°F/Gas 1) and put a roasting tin in the oven to heat up. Grease and line the base of a 1.5 litre (6 cup) charlotte mould with a circle of greaseproof paper and lightly grease the base and side.

TO MAKE the meringue, beat the egg whites in a clean dry bowl until very stiff peaks form. Whisk in the sugar gradually to make a very stiff glossy meringue. Whisk in the vanilla extract.

SPOON the meringue into the mould, smooth the surface and place a greased circle of greaseproof paper on top. Put the mould into the hot roasting tin and pour boiling water into the tin until it comes halfway up the side of the charlotte mould.

BAKE for 50–60 minutes, or until a knife poked into the centre of the meringue comes out clean. Remove the circle of paper, put a plate over the meringue and turn it over. Lift off the mould and the other circle of paper and leave to cool.

TO MAKE the praline, grease a sheet of foil and lay it out flat on the work surface. Put the sugar in a small saucepan with 3 tablespoons water and heat gently until completely dissolved. Bring to the boil and cook until deep golden, then quickly tip in the flaked almonds and pour onto the oiled foil. Spread a little and leave to cool. When the praline has hardened, grind it to a fine powder in a food processor or with a mortar and pestle.

SPRINKLE the praline over the meringue and pour a sea of warmed crème anglaise around its base. Serve in wedges with the remaining crème anglaise.

Grease and line the charlotte mould and place greased paper over the top after filling so that the meringue will not stick.

KARANJI

THESE MINI, COCONUT-FILLED, DEEP-FRIED SWEET PASTRIES ARE EATEN AT AFTERNOON TEA TIME IN INDIA. BECAUSE THEY CAN BE STORED FOR ABOUT A WEEK, THEY ARE GOOD TO HAVE ON HAND FOR SERVING TO HUNGRY, UNEXPECTED VISITORS AT ANY TIME OF THE DAY.

225 g (8 oz) maida or plain flour
4 tablespoons oil or ghee
oil for deep-frying

FILLING
10 cardamom pods
100 g (3 oz) sugar
5 cm (2 inch) piece of cinnamon
   stick
150 g (5 oz) grated coconut
   (page 555)

MAKES 30

SIFT the maida into a bowl. Add the oil or ghee and rub it in with your fingers until the mixture resembles breadcrumbs. Add 5 tablespoons lukewarm water, a little at a time, and, using a palette knife, blend the dough together. Turn out onto a floured surface and knead for 5 minutes, until smooth and pliable. Cover and leave at room temperature for 15 minutes. Don't refrigerate or the oil will congeal, making it difficult to roll.

TO MAKE the filling, remove the cardamom seeds from the pods and coarsely crush them in a pestle and mortar. In a heavy-based saucepan, combine the sugar, cinnamon and 200 ml (¾ cup) water. Heat gently until the sugar has dissolved. Bring to the boil, add the coconut, then stir over low heat until the liquid has evaporated and the mixture comes together. The mixture should not be bone dry. Remove from heat, add the cardamom and allow to cool.

ON a lightly floured surface, roll out one-third of the pastry to a 28 cm (11 inch) diameter circle. Using an 8 cm (3¼ inch) cutter, cut out 10 circles of pastry. Place ½ tablespoon of the filling in the centre of each circle, then moisten the edges with water. Seal into a semicircle and crimp the edge. Repeat until all the pastry and filling has been used. Cover until ready to fry.

FILL a karhai or deep, heavy-based saucepan one-third full with oil and heat. Add a small piece of pastry and if it rises to the surface in a couple of seconds the oil is ready for use. Put in a few karanjis at a time and fry for about 30–60 seconds, until lightly browned. Turn them over and brown them on the other side. Remove from the pan
and place on a cooling rack for 5 minutes before draining on paper towels. When cold, store in an airtight container for up to a week.

Cut circles from the pastry with a cutter and then fill them with the coconut mixture. Seal firmly so they don't leak when cooked.

521

CUSTARDS

THE CLASSIC CUSTARD COOKED IN A PUMPKIN IS JUST ONE OF MANY POPULAR CUSTARDS IN THAILAND. AS HERE, COCONUT, SWEET POTATO, JACKFRUIT AND TARO ARE ALSO USED AS FLAVOURINGS. SERVE IN BANANA CUPS, AS SHOWN, OR POUR THE MIXTURE INTO BABY PUMPKINS.

banana leaves
80 ml (⅓ cup) coconut milk
   (page 551)
7 eggs
275 g (10 oz) palm sugar, cut into
   very small pieces
¼ teaspoon salt
5–6 fresh pandanus leaves, dried
   and cut into small pieces, bruised,
   or 3 teaspoons vanilla essence
100 g (3 oz) young coconut meat,
   cut into small pieces, or orange
   sweet potato, jackfruit or taro,
   cut into matchsticks

MAKES 6

TO SOFTEN the banana leaves and prevent them from splitting, put them in a hot oven for about 10 seconds, or blanch them briefly. Cut the banana leaves into 12 circles about 13 cm (5 inches) in diameter with the fibre running lengthways. Place one piece with the fibre running lengthways and another on top of it with the fibre running across. Make a 1 cm (½ inches) tuck 4 cm (1½ inch) long (4 cm in from the edge and no further) and pin securely with a small sharp toothpick. Repeat this at the opposite point and at the two side points, making four tucks altogether. Flatten the base as best you can. Repeat to make 6 square-shaped cups. Alternatively, use a small shallow rectangular tin such as a brownie tin.

COMBINE the coconut milk, eggs, sugar, salt and pandanus leaves in a bowl, using a spoon, for 10 minutes or until the sugar has dissolved. Pour the custard through the sieve into a bowl to discard the pandanus leaves.

ADD the coconut, orange sweet potato, taro or jackfruit to the custard and lightly mix. Spoon the mixture into each banana cup, filling to within 1 cm (½ inch) from the top.

HALF FILL a wok or a steamer pan with water, cover and bring to a rolling boil over a high heat. Place the banana cups on a plate. Use a plate that will fit on the rack of a traditional bamboo steamer basket or on a steamer rack inside the wok or pan. Taking care not to burn your hands, place the plate on the bamboo steamer or steamer rack inside the wok or pan. Cover, reduce the heat to low and cook for 10–15 minutes. Check and replenish the water after 10 minutes. Serve at room temperature or chilled. The custards can be covered and refrigerated for up to 3–4 days.

Make and balance the cups carefully so none of the liquid spills out.

Preparing durian for sale.

BAKED PEACHES

THE PEACH IS ONE OF ITALY'S FAVOURITE FRUITS, WITH THE BEST BEING PRODUCED IN LE MARCHE, EMILIA-ROMAGNA AND CAMPANIA. THIS RECIPE ALSO WORKS WELL WITH FRESH APRICOTS. ALLOW THREE APRICOTS PER PERSON.

4 ripe peaches
45 g (1½ oz) amaretti biscuits
1 tablespoon sweet Marsala
20 g (⅔ oz) ground almonds
1 egg yolk
1 tablespoon sugar
25 g (1 oz) unsalted butter
icing sugar

SERVES 4

PREHEAT the oven to 180°C (350°F/Gas 4). Halve the peaches and remove the stones. Crush the amaretti biscuits in a food processor or with the end of a rolling pin and mix them with the Marsala, almonds, egg yolk and sugar.

FILL the peaches with the biscuit mixture, spreading the filling in an even layer over the entire surface. Dot each peach with butter and arrange in a shallow ovenproof dish or baking tray. Bake for 20–30 minutes or until the peaches are tender right through. Dust lightly with icing sugar before serving.

ZABAIONE

ZABAIONE IS ONE OF THOSE HAPPY OCCURRENCES, A DISH CREATED PURELY BY ACCIDENT WHEN, IN SEVENTEENTH CENTURY TURIN, A CHEF POURED FORTIFIED SWEET WINE INTO EGG CUSTARD. IN RURAL AREAS ZABAIONE (ALSO KNOWN AS ZABAGLIONE) IS EATEN HOT FOR BREAKFAST.

6 egg yolks
3 tablespoons caster sugar
125 ml (½ cup) sweet Marsala
250 ml (1 cup) double cream

SERVES 4

WHISK the egg yolks and sugar together in the top of a double boiler or in a heatproof bowl set over a saucepan of simmering water. When the mixture is tepid, add the Marsala and whisk for another 5 minutes, or until it has thickened.

WHIP the cream until soft peaks form. Gently fold in the egg yolk mixture. Cover and refrigerate for 3–4 hours before serving.

ZABAIONE

FOOD JOURNEYS

COMMERCIAL RICE GROWING Rather than investing in large expanses of land on which to grow rice, many rice companies buy unhusked rice from farmers surrounding their mills. Once harvested, the rice is bagged up and taken to the mill to be tested: if it is good quality it is bought by the mill and processed. At the Chia Meng rice mill it is tested for ripeness and for the percentage of jasmine or fragrant rice in the

RICE

RICE *(KHAO)* IS NOT ONLY THE STAPLE FOOD OF THAILAND, IT IS A FUNDAMENTAL PART OF THAI LIFE, INTEGRAL TO ITS CULTURE AND TRADITIONS. THE GREETING *KIN KHAO LAEW REU YANG* MEANS 'HOW ARE YOU' BUT IS TRANSLATED AS 'HAVE YOU EATEN RICE YET?'. RICE IS NOT JUST PART OF A MEAL, IT IS THE MEAL. OTHER DISHES ARE ACCOMPANIMENTS.

The cultivation of rice may have started in Thailand. Wild rice originated somewhere in an area that now runs through Upper Assam, Burma, northern Thailand, South-West China and northern Vietnam, a fertile belt that is given over to rice cultivation today. The indigenous inhabitants of the area, were cultivating rice in what would eventually become part of the kingdom of Thailand at a time when most of China was still eating millet. The cultivation of rice led to settlements of people as paddy fields needed supervising.

Rice became important to the Thai economy as it became a staple elsewhere. Arab and Indian traders took rice to India and the Middle East and the Chinese absorbed rice into the cuisine until it became their staple as well. Rice also travelled throughout South-East Asia. Thailand is one of the world's major rice exporters and is self sufficient in this staple food.

TYPES OF RICE
Most of the rice eaten in Thailand comes from local paddy. Originally, sticky rice was predominant but gradually long-grain rice became popular. The North and North-East still

RICE NOODLES Rice is also used to make *kuaytiaw* or rice noodles. Rice flour is mixed with water, then this paste is spread out in trays and steamed before being cut into different widths. Wide noodles are *sen yai* or wide line, medium are *sen lek* or small line, and thin noodles are *sen mii*, line noodles. Rice noodles are sold fresh in markets or dried in packets and are used in soups or stir-fried and eaten with sauces.

mix. The rice is dried by spreading it out in the sun and is then cleaned of impurities, husked, polished and sorted into broken and whole grains. It is finally sieved to sort it into different sizes before being bagged. Broken and smaller grained rices are sold locally. New crop rice is often exported to Singapore, and older, harder rice to Hong Kong. Local companies may mix new and old rice to give a 'perfect' mix.

prefer sticky rice but elsewhere long-grain is more common. Sticky rice is also used for desserts in both its white and 'black' forms. Long-grain rice is served with every meal except snacks. A spoonful is usually eaten by itself before any other dish is added to it and it is never swamped with other food. Sticky rice is eaten by rolling some rice into a ball with one hand. It is then used to pick up food or to dip into a sauce. It is always eaten using your hand.

QUALITY

The quality of rice is of paramount importance to the Thais. Jasmine rice, which has a flowery fragrance, is considered to be the best variety of long-grain. Like wine connoisseurs, some Thais can tell how old rice is, and how and where it was grown. Rice is generally eaten within 12 to 18 months of harvesting. It is at its best after three months because when it is very new and still high in moisture, it is stickier. The drier rice becomes, the more water it needs to be cooked in.

STICKY RICE Sticky rice is often cooked in a container or wrapping. It is soaked in water overnight and then pushed into lengths of bamboo that are plugged at one end. Coconut milk mixed with salt and sugar is added and the bamboo then grilled over coals. Little parcels of sticky rice are also steamed in leaves. Banana, coconut and lotus leaves are all used as wrappings.

HILL TRIBE RICE Rice is cut and threshed by hand by the hill tribes of northern Thailand. The harvested rice is gathered up between two sticks and threshed against the sides of a giant woven bowl until the rice grains are shaken loose from the stalks. The grains are then tossed in the air and fanned, to blow away as much chaff as possible, before being transferred to a flat area where it is raked out and dried in the sun.

CULTIVATION

Rice is cultivated in several different ways depending on the area in which it is grown. An average crop of rice takes between 100 and 200 days to mature depending on variety and growing climate. Quick-maturing crops give some areas two rice harvests a year and in other regions quick and slow growing crops are planted together to string out the harvest and make it more manageable.

Rice can be grown in paddy fields — that is, in water — or in fields that are dry except for rainfall. Rice that relies on rainfall is mainly grown by hill tribes in northern Thailand. These farmers rotate their fields as the land becomes exhausted, cutting down new areas of jungle as they need them.

Technology is relatively primitive in these areas and there are few labour-saving devices. Families within each tribal group help each other. Planting takes place in the monsoon season, July to October, and sometimes in November.

Paddy rice is either grown by sowing seed where it is to grow, a less labour intensive but less regular way of planting, or by initially growing the rice in small nursery fields, where it can be nurtured, and then transplanting it to larger fields. Paddy fields, which are sunken, with raised dams around them, are irrigated with water channels. The channels are filled by rainfall supplied by Thailand's monsoonal climate. Rice is harvested, dried and husked by the farmer or village collective, or taken to a rice mill to be sold as raw rice.

Paddy fields are a common sight in Thailand where farmers help each other with planting and harvesting by growing crops in rotation.

NAYA BAZAAR is Delhi's spice market. Here in a labyrinth of alleyways and staircases, chillies, turmeric, ginger and seed spices are sold in bulk. Porters stagger backwards and forwards, weighed down by huge sacks that are heaved on and off large scales. The covered buildings around the edges of the bazaar hold the godowns and offices of the traders and all available space is used to display wares.

SPICES

SPICES BECAME IMPORTANT ITEMS OF COMMERCE EARLY IN THE EVOLUTION OF TRADE. THEY WERE SMALL, EASILY TRANSPORTED AND OFTEN WORTH THEIR WEIGHT IN GOLD.

India was essentially 'discovered' by Vasco da Gama in May 1498 as he searched for the 'Indies', the origin of the spices which were arriving in Europe via Arab traders. It is said that he came ashore and shouted "for Christ and for spices". The discovery of the spice coast of India had a profound effect on the European spice trade as it broke the stranglehold of the Arabs and cut out the middlemen.

Cloves and nutmeg from the East Indies were taken by Muslim traders from Malacca to southern India where black pepper and cinnamon (from Kerala and Sri Lanka) were added to the cargo. The whole lot was then sold onwards to Europe from the spice ports on the west coast of India. The use of maritime trading routes meant that war, religious differences and other disruptions to the overland routes did not upset the flow of spices to Europe. This kept their prices relatively constant and affordable. The next logical step was to grow spices like cloves and nutmeg in southern India which had only previously been available from the Moluccas.

Kochi (Cochin) in Kerala became a bustling spice port in 1341 after a flood in the area created a natural harbour. The area around Mattancherry is still busy with major trading and carts of spices trundle back and forth between the wholesale dealers and their godowns (warehouses) all day.

CARDAMOMS are the world's third most expensive spice. They are native to south India and here are shown growing in the hills around Kumily in Kerala. The seed pods are picked by hand just before they ripen and split. They are dried for 24 hours before being polished to remove the flower husks. Cardamoms are graded by size. They are sorted by passing them through sieves and then picked over by hand.

Amongst the spices of India, pepper, cardamom, nutmeg, mace, ginger, vanilla and turmeric are grown in Kerala and Tamil Nadu, seed spices such as coriander, cumin, dill and fennel are found in Gujarat and Rajasthan, and chillies grow in every state and union territory in India. Saffron is cultivated in Kashmir, mustard in Andhra Pradesh and fenugreek in Uttar Pradesh.

Spices have a strong association with Indian food of all types and Indian cuisine is probably the most highly spiced in the world. In the North, spices are often dry-roasted and ground before use, warming mixtures such as garam masala are used as a seasoning and chillies are not always important. In the South, spices are ground with coconut or fresh herbs to make a wet paste and a seasoning (tarka) of mustard seeds, curry leaves and dried chilli, all fried in oil, may be stirred into the dish at the end of cooking.

JEW TOWN, the centre of India's spice trade, is built on a plot of land given to the Jewish community by the Raja of Kochi (Cochin) in the 16th century.

AMCHOOR or amchur powder is made from finely ground, dried green mangoes. It is used as a souring agent in northern dishes and is one of the main flavourings in chaat masala.

TAMARIND adds a sour flavour to dishes and is particularly popular in the South. The shells and seeds are removed and the surrounding pulp is compressed into a cake.

CLOVES are one of the spices brought to India from the Moluccas. Cloves are dried flower buds. They are widely used in Indian cooking and have a distinctive aroma and flavour.

BLACK PEPPER is native to Kerala on India's spice coast. Black pepper is made by fermenting and drying ripe peppercorns. It is very aromatic and is the original 'hot' flavour.

GINGER The rhizomes of a plant which are used both fresh and dried, ginger has a pungent, hot flavour which is sweeter in younger 'roots'. Ginger is used fresh in many Indian dishes.

FENUGREEK Known as methi, this spice has a curry aroma and slightly bitter flavour. Fenugreek is often dry-roasted to intensify its flavour and is used in many masala mixes.

KALONJI Also called nigella, these tiny black seeds have an onion flavour. They add a distinctive taste to breads, raitas and vegetable dishes and are used in Bengali panch phoron.

POMEGRANATE SEEDS are actually dried seeds and flesh which are used whole or ground as a souring agent. They are popular in the Punjab and are often used in chickpea dishes.

SAFFRON Made from the stigmas of a type of crocus, this is the world's most expensive spice. Saffron was introduced into Indian food by the Moghuls and it is grown in Kashmir.

KOKUM is the dried fruit of the gamboge tree. This adds a tart flavour and is often used in Kerala to flavour fish dishes. It also balances sweetness in coconut-based dishes.

CURRY LEAVES are aromatic leaves with a strong curry-like fragrance and flavour. They are used liberally in the South, either added to dishes during cooking or fried to use as a garnish.

TURMERIC Dried turmeric is one of the main ingredients of curry powders. It has both flavour and colour and is widely used. It is available as a fresh root, dried whole root, or a ground powder.

NUTMEG

NUTMEG grow on a tropical evergreen tree indigenous to the Moluccas. The inner nut is surrounded by a red lacy aril and a yellow nutmeg fruit. When the fruit is ripe, it splits to show the aril and nut. The nut and aril are separated and dried. As the aril dries, it loses its colour and becomes the spice known as mace. The nut inside is cracked open and the kernel, the nutmeg, is removed.

CHILLIES

CHILLIES give Indian food heat, colour and flavour. The heat factor depends on the variety and there is no rule as to what the hottest or mildest chillies look like. The most common Indian chillies are red or green finger-like ones *(left and centre left)*. They are used fresh or dried and usually have a medium heat. Mundu chillies *(centre right)* are quite hot but the hottest are the tiny dhani (bird's-eye) chillies *(right)*.

SUPARI MIXES

SUPARI mixes are another way in which spices are used. Eaten after a meal to aid digestion and freshen the breath they range from fennel seeds and cardamom pods coated in silver to colourful mixes of split, roasted coriander seeds, sugar balls, sesame seeds, sugar-coated fennel seeds, coconut shreds, bits of betel nut and aniseed. Look for plates of these beside the cash register and take a pinch as you leave.

PIZZA MARGHERITA has its birthplace at the famous Antica Pizzeria Brandi, still operating over 100 years later in Naples. Here pizza is made by hand, following the traditional methods. The kitchen is open so customers can see the work of the *pizzaiolo* and the brick-lined wood-fired pizza oven is kept at such a high temperature and is so thick that it retains its heat overnight. Each pizza takes only 1 or 2 minutes to brown and puff up.

PIZZA

PIZZA BEGAN LIFE AS A FAST FOOD, EATEN HOT ON THE BACKSTREETS OF NAPLES. TODAY IT IS FOUND ALL OVER THE WORLD, BUT IT IS STILL IN NAPLES THAT SKILLED *PIZZAIOLI* (PIZZA-MAKERS) USE WONDERFUL LOCAL TOMATOES, MOZZARELLA AND BASIL TO PRODUCE THE FINEST OF PIZZAS.

A pizza, in the sense of a flat bread covered with toppings, has probably been around since the Greeks and Romans, and many regions developed their own versions. However, it is the pizza of Naples that has come to be regarded as the true pizza. The first Neapolitan pizzas were white, made with garlic, lard, salt and anchovies. It was the tomato that was to transform pizza and the Neapolitans who were the first Europeans to embrace this new fruit, successfully growing them from seeds brought from the New World. The first tomato pizza was probably the classic *marinara*.

PIZZA MARGHERITA

By the mid-nineteenth century, pizzerias had opened in Naples and wandering vendors sold slices to people on the streets. A way of life was born for the Neapolitans and their pizza began to achieve wider notoriety, with visitors venturing into poor neighbourhoods to sample this new food. When Queen Margherita visited in 1889, she too wanted to try the famous pizza. A *pizzaiolo,* Raffaele Esposito, was summoned and created a pizza of mozzarella, tomatoes and basil based on the colours of the Italian flag—later to be named after her.

PIZZA IS THE CLASSIC fast food and in Naples traditional round pizzas are baked to order, then folded into quarters and wrapped in paper to take away. Elsewhere, it is more usual to find *pizza a tagglio,* pizza that has been baked in a large tray and then sold by the slice. Probably originating in Rome, *pizza a tagglio* can be ordered by weight in many places and is then reheated as a fast snack or lunch.

ASSOCIAZIONE VERA PIZZA NAPOLETANA

The True Neapolitan Pizza Association has been set up to safeguard the pizza. Their guidelines include that the dough must be made only from flour, yeast, salt and water and not be worked by machine. Pizzas are to be cooked directly on the floor of a brick or stone-lined wood-fired oven and the temperature must exceed 400°C (750°F). The *cornicione* (border) must be high and soft and the whole crust not too crisp. A pizza should take only 2 minutes to cook and be brown and crispy with all the ingredients melted together.

Emigrating Neapolitans took pizza with them to America and, by the 1950s, pizza could probably be found more easily in America than in the north of Italy. When the rest of Italy did finally take to pizza, they adapted it to their own tastes: the Roman pizza has more topping, is thinner and crisper and does not have a *cornicione.*

MAKING A PIZZA

THE DOUGH *(impasto)* for the Brandi pizza bases is made with 00 *(doppio zero)* flour, water, salt and a piece of the previous day's dough as a leavening agent. The dough is risen slowly over 12 hours before being shaped. Each piece of dough *(pagnotte)* is stretched and flattened by hand to a diameter not more than 30 cm across. A true Neapolitan pizza is never tossed or rolled with a rolling pin and needs to be shaped gently to retain more air so that it puffs up in the oven. As the dough sits on the surface, it shrinks back slightly.

The base of the pizza is spread with a fresh tomato sauce made from the pulp of tomatoes picked in the San Marzano region near Naples. The sauce is never cooked—like the rest of the ingredients it cooks only in the oven. The pizza is then scattered with shredded fresh buffalo mozzarella *(mozzarella di buffala)* or a cow's milk mozzarella called *fior di latte*. Salt is scattered over the surface, followed by a drizzle of extra virgin olive oil from a brass can and fresh basil leaves. This is the classic combination for a pizza Margherita or Napoletana.

The pizza base is then stretched out a little further as it is transferred onto the long-handled wooden paddle that places it inside the brick-lined, wood-burning oven. The pizza is slid off the paddle onto the floor of the oven and cooked for just 1 or 2 minutes at a red-hot temperature of about 400ºC (750ºF). The extreme heat of the oven melts together the ingredients and causes the pizza base to puff up and crispen. The pizza is then removed, sprinkled with a little more olive oil and served immediately.

PISSALADEIRA A Ligurian pizza that has a topping of onion, anchovy, tomato, garlic and black olives, it is also known as pizza all'Andrea.

PIZZETTE These miniature pizzas can often be found as part of an antipasto selection to be eaten with drinks in an Italian bar. They are also sold in bakeries as snacks.

BIANCA means 'white pizza' and is a pizza without a tomato base. Toppings vary from onions, peppers, olives, cheese and herbs to a simple garlic, rosemary and olive oil pizza.

ROMANA Similar to a Margherita but with added anchovies and oregano, romana is one of the classic pizzas that are recognized by the Associazione Vera Pizza Napoletana.

SPINACI often has a *bianca* base topped with spinach and garlic, though some varieties do include tomatoes or cheese as well.

QUATTRO FORMAGGIO Four cheeses are used on this pizza, usually a mixture of mozzarella, fontina, Parmesan, Gorgonzola or pecorino.

QUATTRO STAGIONI The name means 'four seasons', and the seasons are represented by ingredients in each quarter, from prosciutto, mushrooms and artichokes to clams or olives.

MARINARA is topped with tomato sauce, olive oil, garlic and oregano and sometimes other herbs. Despite its name, this pizza never has seafood— Marinara refers to the sauce.

PROSCIUTTO E RUCOLA A modern pizza topping where the base is baked with cream and Parma ham and then scattered with fresh rocket as soon as it comes out of the oven.

MARGHERITA The pizza invented for Queen Margherita. In Naples, it is made with San Marzano tomatoes topped with buffalo mozzarella or *fior di latte* and fresh basil.

CALZONE Also called a *pizza ripieno,* this classic pizza is made by folding the pizza base over the filling. The word *calzone* means trouser leg—supposedly a reflection of its shape.

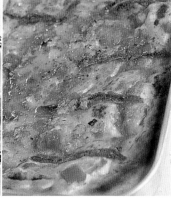

SICILIANA A pizza from Sicily that is baked in a rectangular tray and has a thicker base than a Neapolitan pizza. It is often topped with tomatoes and anchovies.

CHÂTEAU MARGAUX is one of Bordeaux's *grands crus classés*, a classification dating back to 1855 when wines from Médoc, Sauternes and one from Graves were classified according to the prices they fetched. The five-tier classification, from *premiers* down to *cinquièmes* (fifth) *crus* (growths), is still used today, with Châteaux Margaux, Haut-Brion, Latour, Lafite-Rothschild and Mouton-Rothschild (elevated to this level

WINE

FRANCE IS INDISPUTABLY THE CENTRE OF THE WINE WORLD, AND GREAT BORDEAUX, BURGUNDIES AND CHAMPAGNES CONTINUE TO SET THE STANDARDS ALL OTHERS ASPIRE TO.

The French were making wines from indigenous vines before even the Romans arrived. Over the centuries, wine-makers have cultivated an incredible number of grape varieties, eventually matching each one up to the right methods of production, the perfect climate and terrain, from the wet North to the cool mountains and the hot Mediterranean. This fact means that today France produces nearly every classic wine in the world.

CLASSIFYING FRENCH WINE

France's *appellation d'origine contrôlée* (AC) is the oldest and most precise wine governing body in the world. The French attach much importance to the notion of *terroir*, that there is a perfect environment in which to grow a wine and that every wine should demonstrate the character of that environment, so the smaller and more pinpointed an *appellation*, the more prestigious it is. Thus, within the broad Bordeaux AC, sub-regions, such as Médoc, and even individual communities within this, such as Pauillac, may gain their own *appellation*. The AC also defines grape varieties, yields and production methods.

Vin délimité de qualité supérieure (VDQS) classifies less distinguished regions standing between AC and *vins de pays* status. *Vins de pays* (country wines) can be great if they have a strong local character. *Vins de table* should be drinkable.

in 1973) all *premiers crus*. The fact that the classification remains in use reflects the suitability of the *terroir* for growing Cabernet Sauvignon, especially the mild climate and gravelly soil, and also the efforts of the châteaux to maintain standards. At Château Margaux, the land is still worked by hand and a cooper handcrafts the French oak barrels. The best of their elegant wines can be aged for at least 20 years.

READING FRENCH LABELS

CHÂTEAU a Bordeaux wine estate

CLOS on some Burgundies, meaning a walled vineyard

CRU meaning 'growth', it refers to wine from a single estate

CRU BOURGEOIS an unofficial level of classification just below Bordeaux's *crus classés*

GRAND CRU CLASSÉ/CRU CLASSÉ a Bordeaux classified in 1855 and usually of a very high quality. Also used in other regions to signify their most prestigious wines

CUVÉE a blended wine from different grapes or vineyards

CUVÉE PRESTIGE a special vintage or blend

MILLÉSIMÉ vintage

MIS EN BOUTEILLE AU CHÂTEAU/DOMAINE estate-bottled, rather than a merchant or cooperative blend

NÉGOCIANT-ÉLEVEUR a wine merchant, often an international firm, who buys grapes to blend and age and finished wines

PROPRIÉTAIRE-RÉCOLTANT growers who make their own wine

WINES can be bought from a *marchand de vin* (wine shop), *négociant* (specialized wine merchant) or *en vrac* (unbottled wine sold by the litre at markets). In wine areas you can also buy directly from the vineyards or from a *cave coopérative* (wine cooperative).

MINERVOIS Red and white wines from Languedoc, France's largest wine-growing area. Good value, the reds are fruity and light with a typical Mediterranean grape blend, including Grenache and Syrah.

CORBIÈRES An *appellation* in Languedoc making good dry white wines and reds—mixing Grenache and Carignan (used in mass-produced wines but here used to give character).

CHÂTEAUNEUF-DU-PAPE great red wines from the papal vineyards of Provence, mixing up to 13 different grape varieties to produce a full-bodied wine that usually needs ageing.

GRAVES Famed Bordeaux area producing dry Semillon/Sauvignon Blanc whites and rich Cabernet Sauvignon reds. Split in 1987, the outstanding *crus classés* are now in Pessac-Léognan AC.

ALSACE Dry white wines from the North. The area produces many varietal (single grape variety) wines that bear the name of the grape, here Pinot Blanc, rather than the region.

MÂCONNAIS A Burgundian district producing decent Gamay and Pinot Noir reds and white Chardonnays, especially the very good Pouilly-Fuissé. In Mâcon, Mâcon-Villages is a superior AC.

MÉDOC Bordeaux's outstanding wine area, producing Cabernet Sauvignon reds. Within Médoc, the greatest areas (Pauillac, Saint Julien and Estèphe and Margaux) have their own *appellations*.

SAUTERNES A Bordeaux region, classified in 1855 and producing the world's most prestigious dessert wines from Semillon, Sauvignon Blanc and Muscadelle grapes.

POUILLY FUMÉ One of the world's great Sauvignon wines, along with neighbouring Sancerre. Made in the Loire Valley, it has an elegant gooseberry character and should be drunk young.

NUITS-SAINT-GEORGES Situated in the Côte d'Or in the middle of Burgundy, this commune has a number of *premiers crus* producing classic Pinot Noir reds for ageing.

BERGERAC East of Bordeaux, this area has the same climate and grapes as its neighbour. Fine reds centering on Cabernet Sauvignon, Franc and Merlot; dry whites based around Sauvignon.

BEAUJOLAIS A Burgundian area producing fruity reds from Gamay grapes to be drunk chilled and young (within weeks for Nouveau). Beaujolais-Villages is a superior *appellation* within Beaujolais.

CHAMPAGNE

THE CELLARS AT TAITTINGER, one of Reim's world-famous champagne houses, date back to the Benedictine monks who first created champagne. Champagne is a mixture of red Pinot Noir and Pinot Meunier and white Chardonnay grapes, carefully picked and pressed to prevent any red skin colour leaking into the juice. First a *cuvée* is blended by adding previous years' harvests to the present one, creating a champagne in the house's style (their non-vintage brut; though a vintage may be made in exceptional years). A secondary fermentation is initiated by adding sugar and yeast *(liqueur de tirage)* before bottling, sealing with a cap and ageing slowly in the cold cellars. After a 3-month fermentation, ageing continues *sur lie* from one to several years, and a yeasty, less acid flavour develops. During this time, the upended bottles are turned periodically, called *remuage* (riddling), to slide the sediment into the neck. Finally, *dégorgement* takes place, with the sediment frozen into a plug and ejected when the bottle is opened. The plug is replaced by some sweet wine that determines the sweetness of the champagne.

TYPES OF CHAMPAGNES

VINTAGE This champagne is made only every 3 or 4 years, when an exceptional harvest produces a distinctive, fine wine that is not blended with previous vintages into a house style.

BRUT This is the most common champagne, a dry wine made every year from a mixture of Pinot and Chardonnay grapes, blended with a little wine from previous harvests to create a house style.

ROSÉ Usually made from normal white champagne blended with 15% red wine (produced from the same red pinot grapes), rosé is a fruity wine not made in large quantities and good with food.

BLANC DE BLANCS Meaning 'white of whites' and made just from white Chardonnay grapes, a blanc de blancs has a fine, delicate taste and makes a great apéritif.

TEA HOUSES are popular all over China. Some are a male domain where business is conducted, such as at this one in Yuyuan Bazaar, Shanghai *(top)*, while others, like this one at Wenshu Monastery, Chengdu *(bottom right)*, are family-orientated and allow patrons to sit all day over a constantly refilled cup of tea. Tea houses also offer snacks to accompany the tea, from melon seeds or oranges to more ornate sweet offerings *(bottom left)*.

TEA

TEA HAS BEEN POPULAR IN CHINA SINCE AT LEAST THE SIXTH CENTURY BC, AND IT WAS FROM CHINA THAT TEA TRAVELLED TO JAPAN, EUROPE AND INDIA. INTEGRAL TO FESTIVALS, A SIGN OF HOSPITALITY, A MEDICINE, AND STEEPED IN TRADITION, TEA IS BOTH A DRINK AND A PART OF CHINESE CULTURE ITSELF.

For the Chinese, tea is a drink to be savoured on its own or before or after a meal. The exception is tea with yum cha, which means to 'drink tea' and originated as a few snacks to complement the tea at tea houses, rather than the full meal it often is today. In China, hot water is provided in hotels, waiting rooms and on trains for people to make tea using their own screwtop jar or in a large cup with a lid that can be slid back just enough to drink the tea without the leaves coming too. Carrying a receptacle for tea is not a statement of class or rank, everyone does it.

ORIGINS OF TEA

Tea plants (*Camellia sinensis*) are native to the mountains of Southwest China, and are now grown all over the South, and in the East and North where conditions are favourable. Teas from Yunnan and Fujian are particularly treasured. Tea is made from the two top leaves and bud, picked every 7–10 days to gather the young shoots and to encourage more shoots to sprout, known as a flush. These small leaves are more prized than too large or broken leaves. Fannings (tea dust and broken leaves) are the lowest grades of all.

DRAGON WELL TEA is China's finest green tea, grown around the West Lake of Hangzhou, especially in the village of Longjing (Dragon Well). Here, the Wen family runs a small tea estate producing three pickings a year. The tea buds are hand-picked, then dried by rubbing the leaves around a heated metal basin to arrest any fermentation. The Wen family teas are sold by weight from their house in the village.

VARIETIES OF TEA

Tea is categorized by the different methods of its production:
GREEN an unfermented tea made by firing (drying) fresh leaves in a kind of wok to prevent them oxidizing (fermenting). The tea is usually rolled and twisted to uncurl in boiling water.
OOLONG the leaves are semi-fermented before firing to produce a tea halfway between green and black. The most famous oolong teas are from Fujian and Taiwan.
BLACK a fully fermented tea where the leaves are wilted and bruised by rolling, then fermented and dried.
WHITE a very rare, totally unfermented green tea from Fujian.

Chinese teas can also be categorized by other factors:
BRICK usually pu-er teas from Yunnan compressed into blocks. A piece is sliced off to make tea.
SCENTED tea leaves mixed with scented flowers.
FLOWER petal teas, which are not true teas but tisanes.

MAKING GREEN TEA

GREEN TEA is served in glasses so its colour and the leaves themselves can be appreciated. The glasses are warmed, then tea added with a little freshly boiled water (spring water is considered best). The glasses are topped up by pouring in more water from a height, known as flushing, to aerate the water for a better infusion. The tea is drunk very hot and the leaves briefly steeped compared to black teas.

MAKING OOLONG TEA

OOLONG is made here by the *gong fu* method. The cups and pot are warmed, then the leaves are rinsed with boiling water, strained into a jug and topped up with more water. Water is poured over the pot to keep it warm while the tea brews, then when dry, the tea is poured back and forth over tall smelling cups to ensure an even strength. The aroma is taken in from the tall cups after the tea is tipped into small cups to taste.

TEA SEASONS

TEA is seasonal: spring teas are the finest, while winter teas have an enticing aroma but are rare as there is little harvesting. For Dragon Well tea, the first and best quality picking of the year is the *nu'er* (daughter) tea *(left)*. The second is known as *Qing Ming (middle)* as it is picked around the time of that festival in April. The last picking is called *gu yu (right)* and is picked in the season of this name between spring and summer.

BRICK TEA A compressed tea, usually made from Yunnan pu'er, which was originally devised to carry tea easily and was even used as a form of currency. The character on the tea is for wealth.

CLOUD AND MIST (*Yun Wu*) A green tea grown on mountain sides and cliffs, appreciated for its colour and fine clear flavour. It is a legendary 'monkey pick' tea, said to be harvested by monkeys.

IRON GODDESS (*Tie Guan Yin*) A strong, bitter oolong tea, also called Iron Buddha, drunk before and after a meal from a tiny cup. It is often served with Chiu Chow cuisine to balance the rich food.

FLOWER TEA Made from chrysanthemum flowers, wolf berries and peppermint sugar, this is not strictly a tea, but is served in tea houses as a medicinal tonic.

QIMEN RED TEA This prized mild, sweet and aromatic black tea from the Huangshan mountains in Anhui is known in the West as Keemun. A gong fu tea, meaning that it is precisely prepared.

LYCHEE TEA Made from black tea leaves that are processed with lychee juice, this tea has a fragrant sweet flavour that is very palate cleansing. It is also called lychee red.

DRAGON WELL (*Long Jing*) This fragrant, sweet green tea from Hangzhou in the East is considered the best in China. The leaves are flat, not rolled, and stand up when infused.

WHITE TEA (*Chai Tou Yu Ming*) This fine white tea is named after a hair ornament. White tea is made from hand-picked buds, dried in the sun to create a silvery tea with a very pure taste.

JASMINE TEA A light, fragrant tea of green or black leaves mixed with jasmine flowers. Jasmine is renowned as a good digestive after a rich meal and contains little caffeine.

CHRYSANTHEMUM TEA A flower tea with a mixture of whole chrysanthemum and tea or just chrysanthemum. It is regarded as cooling and its mild flavour goes well with dim sum.

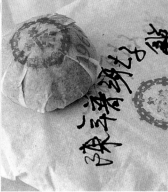

CAKE TEA Also known as bowl tea, this is the round form of compressed pu'er. The variety called gold melon symbolizes a blessing and is a gift for a couple's families after their wedding.

PU'ER, or Bou Lei, is a popular black tea from Yunnan that often accompanies dim sum as it is said to aid the digestion of fats (and ease hangovers). Pu'er is sold loose or as a cake or brick.

BASICS

STICKY RICE

STEAMED STICKY RICE WITH
COCONUT MILK

STEAMED RICE

400 g (2 cups) jasmine rice

SERVES 4

RINSE the rice until the water runs clear. Put the rice in a saucepan and add enough water to come an index-finger joint above the rice. Bring to the boil, cover and cook at a slow simmer for 10–15 minutes. Remove from the heat and leave it to rest for 10 minutes.

STICKY RICE

400 g (2 cups) sticky rice

SERVES 4

PUT the rice in a bowl and pour in cold water to come 5 cm (2 inches) above the rice. Soak for at least 3 hours, or overnight. Drain and transfer to a bamboo basket specially made for steaming sticky rice, or to a steamer lined with a double thickness of muslin. Spread the rice in the steamer. Bring the water in the bottom of the steamer to a rolling boil. Taking care, set the rice over the water. Lower the heat, cover and steam for 20–25 minutes or until the rice swells and is glistening and tender. The cooking time will vary depending on the soaking time. Check and replenish the water every 10 minutes or so.

WHEN the rice is cooked, tip it onto a large tray and spread it out to help it cool quickly. If it cools slowly it will be soggy rather than sticky. Serve warm or cold.

STEAMED STICKY RICE WITH COCONUT MILK

200 g (1 cup) sticky rice
170 ml (⅔ cup) coconut milk
  (page 551), well stirred
1 tablespoon palm sugar
  (not too brown)
½ teaspoon salt

SERVES 4

COOK the sticky rice according to the instructions in the recipe above.

WHILE the rice is cooking, stir the coconut milk, sugar and salt in a small saucepan over low heat until the sugar has dissolved. As soon as the rice is cooked, use a wooden spoon to gently mix it with the coconut milk. Set aside for 15 minutes.

COCONUT MILK AND CREAM

GRATED COCONUT IS BEST WHEN IT IS FRESH. DRIED OR DESICCATED COCONUT CAN ALSO BE USED TO MAKE COCONUT MILK BUT IT NEEDS TO BE SOAKED, THEN CHOPPED MORE FINELY OR GROUND TO A PASTE, OTHERWISE IT WILL BE FIBROUS. IF YOU CAN, BUY A PROPER COCONUT GRATER.

1 coconut
  (yields about 300 g/10 oz flesh)

MAKES 125 ML (½ CUP) COCONUT CREAM AND 250 ML (1 CUP) COCONUT MILK

DRAIN the coconut by punching a hole in two of the dark, coloured eyes. Drain out the liquid and use it as a refreshing drink. Holding the coconut in one hand, tap around the circumference firmly with a hammer or pestle. This should cause the coconut to split open evenly. (If the coconut doesn't crack easily, put it in a 150°C/300°F/ Gas 2 oven for 15 minutes. This may cause it to crack as it cools. If it doesn't, it will crack easily when hit with a hammer.)

IF YOU would like to use a coconut grater, the easiest ones to use are the ones that you sit on at one end, then scrape out the coconut from each half on the serrated edge, catching the grated coconut meat in a large bowl. If you don't have a coconut grater, prise the flesh out of the shell, trim off the hard, brown, outer skin and grate either by hand on a box grater or chop in a food processor. Grated coconut can be frozen in small portions until it is needed.

MIX the grated coconut with 125 ml (½ cup) hot water and leave to steep for 5 minutes. Pour the mixture into a container through a sieve lined with muslin, then gather the muslin into a ball to squeeze out any remaining liquid. This will make a thick coconut milk, which is usually called coconut cream.

REPEAT the process with another 250 ml (1 cup) water to make thinner coconut milk.

Tap the coconut until it splits open. Pull it apart, scrape out the coconut and soak it in hot water before draining in a sieve.

RICE

BASMATI IS A FRAGRANT, LONG-GRAIN RICE THAT GETS ITS UNIQUE FLAVOUR FROM THE SOIL IN WHICH IT IS GROWN. WE HAVE COOKED IT BY THE ABSORPTION METHOD BUT, IF YOU PREFER, YOU CAN ADD THE RICE TO A SAUCEPAN OF BOILING WATER AND BOIL THE RICE UNTIL READY.

400 g (2 cups) basmati rice

SERVES 6

RINSE the rice under cold running water until the water running away is clear, then drain well.

PUT the rice in a heavy-based saucepan and add enough water to come about 5 cm (2 inches) above the surface of the pan. (If you stick your index finger into the rice so it rests on the bottom of the pan, the water will come up to the 2nd joint.) Add 1 teaspoon of salt and bring the water quickly to the boil. When it boils, cover and reduce the heat to a simmer.

COOK for 15 minutes or until the rice is just tender, then remove the saucepan from the heat and rest the rice for 10 minutes without removing the lid. Fluff the rice with a fork before serving.

Rinse the rice very thoroughly under cold running water until the water running through it is completely clear.

BOILED ROSEMATTER OR PATNI RICE

ROSEMATTER IS EATEN IN SOUTHERN INDIA AND PATNI IN CENTRAL AND WESTERN INDIA. BOTH LOOK RED AND SPECKLED BECAUSE THE RICE HAS BEEN PRECOOKED IN ITS HUSK, LEAVING SOME BRAN AND HUSK STUCK TO THE GRAIN. COOK THEM AS WE HAVE, RATHER THAN BY THE ABSORPTION METHOD.

400 g (2 cups) rosematter or patni rice

SERVES 6

RINSE the rice under cold running water until the water running away is clear, then drain well.

BRING a large, heavy-based saucepan of water to the boil and add 1 teaspoon of salt. When the water is at a rolling boil, add the rice and bring back to the boil. Keep at a steady boil for 20 minutes, then test a grain to see if it is cooked. Drain the rice and serve.

ROSEMATTER RICE

PANEER

INDIAN CHEESE, CALLED PANEER OR CHENNA WHEN COMBINED WITH SUGAR, IS AN UNRIPENED CHEESE MADE BY COAGULATING MILK WITH LEMON JUICE, THEN LEAVING TO DRAIN TO ALLOW THE CURDS AND WHEY TO SEPARATE. IT IS THEN PRESSED INTO BLOCKS.

3 litres (12 cups) milk
6 tablespoons strained lemon juice, or vinegar

FOR THE CHENNA
1 teaspoon caster sugar
1 teaspoon maida or plain flour

MAKES 550 G (1 LB 4 OZ)

TO MAKE the paneer, pour the milk into a large heavy-based saucepan. Bring to the boil, stirring with a wooden spoon so that the milk doesn't stick to the base of the pan. Reduce the heat and stir in the lemon juice, then heat over low heat for a few more seconds before turning the heat off as large bits of curd start to form. Shake the pan slowly to allow the curds to form and release the yellow whey.

IF the curds are slow to form, put the pan over low heat again for a few seconds. This helps with the coagulation.

LINE a colander with muslin or cheesecloth so that it overlaps the sides. Pour off the whey, collecting the curds gently in the colander. Gently pull up the corners of the cheesecloth so that it hangs like a bag, twist the cloth so that the whey is released, then hold the "bag" under running water to wash off the remaining whey, twisting some more to remove the excess liquid.

LEAVE the bag to hang from your tap for several hours so the weight of the curds releases more liquid and the cheese compacts. To remove more liquid, press the bag under a heavy weight, such as a tray with some tinned food piled on top, for about 1 hour. This will form a firm block of paneer. When the block is firm enough to cut into cubes, the paneer is ready for use.

TO MAKE chenna, remove the cheese from the bag and knead the paneer well with the palms of your hands until it is very smooth. Combine the paneer with the sugar and maida, kneading the sugar in until it is fully incorporated.

Once curds have formed, drain everything through a muslin-lined sieve. Squeeze out any excess liquid and drain for several hours.

TAMARIND PUREE

150 g (5 oz) tamarind block, broken
  into small pieces

MAKES 300 ML (1⅓ CUPS)

PUT the tamarind in a bowl, pour in 250 ml (1 cup) very hot water and soak for 3 hours or until the tamarind is soft. (If you are in a hurry, simmer the tamarind in the water for 15 minutes. Although this is efficient, it doesn't give as good a result.) Mash the tamarind thoroughly with a fork.

PUT the mixture through a sieve and extract as much of the pulp as possible by pushing it against the sieve with the back of a spoon. Put the tamarind in the sieve back in the bowl with another 100 ml (½ cup) hot water and mash again. Strain again. Discard the fibres left in the sieve. The purée can be frozen in 1 tablespoon portions and defrosted as needed.

TAMARIND PUREE

YOGHURT

YOGHURT ACTS AS A TENDERIZER IN MARINADES, THICKENS SAUCES AND MAKES REFRESHING DRINKS.

600 ml (2½ cups) milk
2 tablespoons thick natural yoghurt

MAKES 600 ML (2½ CUPS)

BRING the milk to the boil in a heavy-based saucepan, then allow to cool to lukewarm. Stir in the yoghurt, cover and leave in a warm place for about 8 hours, or overnight. The yoghurt should be thick. If it is too runny, the milk was probably too hot for the starter yoghurt; if it is too milky, the yoghurt was probably not left in a warm enough place to ferment. From each batch, use 2 tablespoons to make the next batch.

WHEN the yoghurt is set, put it in a sieve lined with a piece of muslin and leave to drain overnight. This will give a thick yoghurt which does not contain too much moisture.

YOGHURT

GRATED COCONUT

GRATED COCONUT IS BEST WHEN IT IS FRESH. DRIED OR DESICCATED COCONUT CAN ALSO BE USED BUT IT NEEDS TO BE SOAKED, THEN CHOPPED MORE FINELY OR GROUND TO A PASTE, OTHERWISE IT WILL BE FIBROUS. IF YOU CAN BUY A PROPER COCONUT GRATER, YOUR LIFE WILL BE MUCH EASIER.

1 coconut

MAKES 300 G (10 OZ)

DRAIN the coconut by punching a hole in two of the dark, coloured eyes. Drain out the liquid and use it as a refreshing drink. Holding the coconut in one hand, tap around the circumference firmly with a hammer or pestle. This should cause the coconut to split open evenly. (If the coconut doesn't crack easily, put it in a 150°C (300°F/ Gas 2) oven for 15 minutes. This may cause it to crack as it cools. If it doesn't, it will crack easily when hit with a hammer.)

IF YOU would like to use a coconut grater (hiramne), the easiest ones to use are the ones that you sit on at one end, then scrape out the coconut from each half on the serrated edge, catching it in a large bowl. If you don't have a coconut grater, prise the flesh out of the shell, trim off the hard, brown, outer skin and grate either by hand on a box grater or chop in a food processor. Grated coconut can be frozen in small portions until it is needed.

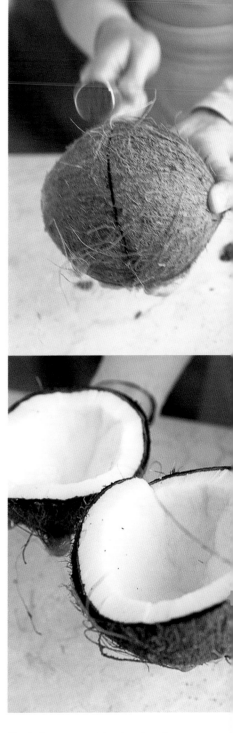

Crack the coconut by tapping it around the circumference with a heavy object. It will open neatly.

PANCH PHORON

PANCH PHORON IS A FIVE-SPICE MIX USED TO FLAVOUR VEGETABLES AND PULSES. THE MIX IS FRIED AT THE BEGINNING OF A DISH, OR FRIED AND ADDED AS A FINAL SEASONING (TARKA).

1 teaspoon cumin seeds
1 teaspoon fennel seeds
1 teaspoon fenugreek seeds
1 teaspoon brown mustard seeds
1 teaspoon kalonji (nigella seeds)

GRIND all the spices to a fine powder in a spice grinder, a pestle and mortar, or with a grinding stone. Store in a small airtight container until you need it.

MAKES 1 TABLESPOON

PANCH PHORON

GARAM MASALA

GARAM MASALA MEANS 'WARMING SPICE MIX'. IT CAN BE A MIXTURE OF WHOLE OR GROUND SPICES. RECIPES ARE NUMEROUS BUT THEY ARE ALL AROMATIC, RATHER THAN 'HOT' MIXES.

8 cardamom pods
2 Indian bay leaves (cassia leaves)
1 teaspoon black peppercorns
2 teaspoons cumin seeds
2 teaspoons coriander seeds
5 cm (2 inch) cinnamon stick
1 teaspoon cloves

REMOVE the seeds from the cardamom pods. Break the bay leaves into small pieces. Put them in a spice grinder or pestle and mortar with the remaining spices and grind to a fine powder. Store in a small airtight container until needed.

MAKES 3 TABLESPOONS

GARAM MASALA

CHAAT MASALA

CHAAT MASALA IS A SALTY, TANGY SEASONING USED IN POPULAR SNACKS SUCH AS BHEL PURI. IT CAN BE TOSSED THROUGH DRY SNACK MIXES OR SPRINKLED ONTO FRUIT AND VEGETABLES AS A SEASONING.

4 tablespoons coriander seeds
2 tablespoons cumin seeds
1 teaspoon ajowan
3 tablespoons black salt
1 tablespoon amchoor powder
2 dried chillies
1 teaspoon black peppercorns
1 teaspoon pomegranate seeds

PLACE a small frying pan over low heat and dry-roast the coriander seeds until aromatic. Remove from the pan and dry-roast the cumin seeds, then separately, the ajowan. Grind the roasted mixture to a fine powder with the other ingredients, using a spice grinder or pestle and mortar. Store in an airtight container.

MAKES 10 TABLESPOONS

SPICY SALT AND PEPPER

1 tablespoon salt
2 teaspoons ground Sichuan
   peppercorns
1 teaspoon five-spice powder

MAKES 2 TABLESPOONS

COMBINE the salt, Sichuan peppercorns and five-spice powder. Dry-fry over low heat, stirring constantly, for 2–3 minutes, or until aromatic. This mix can be used as an ingredient or as a dipping condiment for roast duck or chicken.

SPICY SALT AND PEPPER

CHILLI SAUCE

1 kg (2 lb 3 oz) red chillies, stalks
   removed
3 teaspoons salt
4 tablespoons sugar
160 ml (⅔ cup) clear rice vinegar

MAKES 400 ML (1½ CUPS)

PUT the chillies in a saucepan with 100 ml (⅓ cup) water, cover and bring to the boil. Cook until the chillies are tender, then add the salt, sugar and vinegar. Blend the chilli mixture to a paste in a blender or food processor, or push through a sieve. Store in the fridge for up to 1 month or freeze in small portions. Use as an ingredient or dipping sauce.

CHILLI OIL

50 g (2 oz) dried chilli flakes
125 (½ cup) ml oil
60 ml (¼ cup) roasted sesame oil

MAKES 200 ML (¾ CUP)

PUT the chilli in a heatproof bowl. Put the oils in a saucepan and heat until they are very hot but not smoking. Pour onto the chilli and leave to cool. Try not to breathe in the fumes. When cool, transfer to a jar. Store in the fridge for up to 6 months. The oil can be used as a flavouring, and the chilli at the bottom of the jar can be used instead of fresh chilli.

CHILLI OIL

GINGER JUICE

200 g (7 oz) young ginger

MAKES ABOUT 60 ML (¼ CUP)

GRATE the ginger as finely as you can, collecting any juice. Combine the ginger with an equal volume of cold water and place it in a piece of muslin, twist the top hard and squeeze out as much juice as possible. Alternatively, push the ginger through a juicer, then combine with an equal quantity of cold water. Use as an ingredient.

GINGER JUICE

RED CURRY PASTE

3–4 dried long red chillies, about 13 cm (5 inches) long
8–10 dried small red chillies, about 5 cm (2 inches) long, or 10 fresh small red chillies, seeded
2 lemon grass stalks, white part only, finely sliced
2.5 cm (1 inch) piece of galangal, finely sliced
1 teaspoon very finely chopped makrut (kaffir) lime skin or makrut lime leaves (about half the skin from a makrut lime or 4–5 leaves)
4–5 garlic cloves, finely chopped
3–4 Asian shallots, finely chopped
5–6 coriander (cilantro) roots, finely chopped
2 teaspoons shrimp paste
1 teaspoon ground coriander, dry-roasted

MAKES 125 G (½ CUP)

Before soaking the dried chillies in hot water, slit them lengthways and remove all the seeds.

REMOVE the stems from the dried chillies and slit the chillies lengthways with a sharp knife. Discard the seeds and soak the chillies in hot water for 1–2 minutes or until soft. Drain and roughly chop.

USING a pestle and mortar, pound the chillies, lemon grass, galangal and makrut lime skin or leaves into a paste. Add the remaining ingredients and pound together until the mixture forms a smooth paste.

ALTERNATIVELY, you can use a food processor or blender to blend all the ingredients into as smooth a paste as possible. Add cooking oil, as needed, to assist the blending.

USE as required or keep in an airtight jar. The paste will keep for at least two weeks in the refrigerator and for two months in a freezer.

MASSAMAN CURRY PASTE

MASSAMAN CURRY PASTE

2 dried long red chillies, about 13 cm (5 inches) long
1 lemon grass stalk, white part only, finely sliced
2.5 cm (1 inch) piece of galangal, finely chopped
5 cloves
10 cm (4 inch) piece of cinnamon stick, crushed
10 cardamom seeds
½ teaspoon freshly grated nutmeg
6 garlic cloves, finely chopped
4 Asian shallots, finely chopped
4–5 coriander (cilantro) roots, finely chopped
1 teaspoon shrimp paste

MAKES 250 G (1 CUP)

REMOVE the stems from the chillies and slit the chillies lengthways with a sharp knife. Discard the seeds and soak the chillies in hot water for 1–2 minutes or until soft. Drain and roughly chop.

USING a pestle and mortar, pound the chillies, lemon grass, galangal, cloves, cinnamon, cardamom seeds and nutmeg into a paste. Add the garlic, shallots and coriander roots. Pound and mix together. Add the shrimp paste and pound until the mixture is a smooth paste.

ALTERNATIVELY, use a food processor or blender to grind or blend all the ingredients into as smooth a paste as possible. Add cooking oil, as needed, to assist the blending. Use as required or keep in an airtight jar. The paste will keep for two weeks in the refrigerator and for two months in a freezer.

GREEN CURRY PASTE

1 teaspoon ground coriander

1 teaspoon ground cumin

8–10 small green chillies, seeded

2 lemon grass stalks, white part only, finely sliced

2.5 cm (1 inch) piece of galangal, finely chopped

1 teaspoon very finely chopped makrut (kaffir) lime skin or makrut lime leaves (about half the skin from a makrut lime or 4–5 leaves)

4–5 garlic cloves, finely chopped

3–4 Asian shallots, chopped

5–6 coriander (cilantro) roots, finely chopped

a handful of holy basil leaves, finely chopped

2 teaspoons shrimp paste

MAKES 125 G (½ CUP)

DRY-ROAST the coriander in a small frying pan for 1 minute until fragrant, then remove from the pan. Repeat with the cumin.

USING a pestle and mortar, pound the chillies, lemon grass, galangal and makrut lime skin or leaves into a paste. Add the garlic, shallots and coriander roots and pound together. Add the remaining ingredients and dry-roasted spices one at a time and pound until the mixture forms a smooth paste.

ALTERNATIVELY, you can use a food processor or blender to blend all the ingredients into as smooth a paste as possible. Add cooking oil as needed to assist the blending.

USE as required or keep in an airtight jar. The paste will keep for at least two weeks in the refrigerator and for two months in a freezer.

Whether using makrut lime skin or leaves, chop them very finely. Dry-roasting the ground spices helps to bring out the flavour.

YELLOW CURRY PASTE

3 teaspoons coriander seeds, dry-roasted

1 teaspoon cumin seeds, dry-roasted

2–3 dried long red chillies

2 lemon grass stalks, white part only, finely sliced

3 Asian shallots, finely chopped

2 garlic cloves, finely chopped

2 tablespoons grated turmeric or 1 teaspoon ground turmeric

1 teaspoon shrimp paste

MAKES 250 G (1 CUP)

GRIND the coriander seeds to a powder with a pestle and mortar. Grind the cumin seeds.

REMOVE the stems from the chillies and slit the chillies lengthways with a sharp knife. Discard the seeds and soak the chillies in hot water for 1–2 minutes or until soft. Drain and roughly chop.

USING a pestle and mortar, pound the chillies, lemon grass, shallots, garlic and turmeric to as smooth a paste as possible. Add the shrimp paste, ground coriander and ground cumin and pound until the mixture forms a smooth paste. Alternatively, using a small processor or blender, blend all the ingredients into a very smooth paste. Add cooking oil as needed to ease the grinding. Use as required or keep in an airtight jar. The paste will keep for at least two weeks in the refrigerator and for two months in a freezer.

YELLOW CURRY PASTE

DRY CURRY PASTE

2 dried long red chillies, about
    13 cm (5 inches) long
2 lemon grass stalks, white part
    only, finely sliced
2.5 cm (1 inch) piece of galangal,
    finely chopped
4–5 garlic cloves, finely chopped
3–4 Asian shallots, finely chopped
5–6 coriander (cilantro) roots,
    finely chopped
1 teaspoon shrimp paste
1 teaspoon ground cumin,
    dry-roasted
3 tablespoons unsalted peanuts,
    chopped

MAKES 80 G (⅓ CUP)

REMOVE the stems from the chillies and slit the chillies lengthways with a sharp knife. Discard the seeds and soak the chillies in hot water for 1–2 minutes or until soft. Drain and roughly chop.

USING a pestle and mortar, pound the chillies, lemon grass and galangal into a paste. Add the remaining ingredients one at a time and pound until the mixture forms a very smooth paste.

ALTERNATIVELY, you can use a food processor or blender to blend all the ingredients together into as smooth a paste as possible. Add cooking oil, as needed, to assist the blending.

USE as required or keep in an airtight jar. The paste will keep for at least two weeks in the refrigerator and for two months in a freezer.

Pound the chopped ingredients until a smooth paste is formed.

CHIANG MAI CURRY PASTE

1 tablespoon coriander seeds
2 teaspoons cumin seeds
2 dried long red chillies, about
    13 cm (5 inches) long
½ teaspoon salt
5 cm (2 inch) piece of galangal,
    grated
1 lemon grass stalk, white part only,
    finely chopped
2 Asian shallots, chopped
2 garlic cloves, chopped
1 teaspoon grated turmeric or
    a pinch of ground turmeric
1 teaspoon shrimp paste
½ teaspoon ground cassia
    or cinnamon

MAKES 185 G (¾ CUP)

DRY-ROAST the coriander seeds in a small frying pan for 1 minute until fragrant, then remove from the pan. Repeat with the cumin seeds. Grind them both to a powder with a pestle and mortar.

REMOVE the stems from the chillies and slit the chillies lengthways with a sharp knife. Discard the seeds. Soak the chillies in hot water for 1–2 minutes or until soft. Drain and roughly chop.

USING a pestle and mortar, pound the chillies, salt, galangal, lemon grass, shallots, garlic and turmeric to as smooth a paste as possible. Add the shrimp paste, ground coriander, cumin and cassia and mix until the mixture forms a smooth paste.

ALTERNATIVELY, use a small processor or blender to blend all the ingredients into a very smooth paste. Add a little cooking oil, as needed, to ease the grinding.

CHIANG MAI CURRY PASTE

CHILLI JAM

80 ml (⅓ cup) oil
2 Asian shallots, finely chopped
2 garlic cloves, finely chopped
40 g (1½ oz) dried chilli flakes
¼ teaspoon palm sugar

MAKES 185 G (¾ CUP)

HEAT the oil in a small saucepan and fry the shallots and garlic until brown. Add the chilli flakes and palm sugar and stir well. Season with a pinch of salt. Use as a dipping sauce or accompaniment. The sauce can be stored in a jar in the refrigerator for several weeks.

ROASTED CHILLI SAUCE

oil, for frying
20 Asian shallots, sliced
10 garlic cloves, sliced
3 tablespoons dried shrimp
7 dried long red chillies, chopped
3 tablespoons tamarind purée or
   3 tablespoons lime juice
6 tablespoons palm sugar
1 teaspoon shrimp paste

MAKES 250 G (1 CUP)

HEAT the oil in a wok or saucepan. Fry the shallots and garlic together until golden, then transfer from the wok to a blender or food processor.

FRY the dried shrimp and chillies for 1–2 minutes, then add these to the blender along with the remaining ingredients. Add as much of the frying oil as necessary to make a paste that you can pour. Put the paste back in the clean saucepan and bring to a boil. Reduce the heat and simmer until thick. Be careful because if you overcook this you will end up with a caramelized lump. Season the sauce with salt or fish sauce. Chilli jam is used as a base for recipes, especially stir-fries, as well as a seasoning or accompaniment. It will keep for several months in an airtight jar in the refrigerator.

ROASTED CHILLI SAUCE

GARLIC AND CHILLI SAUCE

4 garlic cloves, finely chopped
3 bird's eye chillies, mixed red and
   green, stems removed, lightly
   crushed
2 tablespoons lime juice
1 tablespoon fish sauce
1 teaspoon sugar

MAKES 125 ML (½ CUP)

MIX all the ingredients together in a small bowl. The sauce can be stored in a jar in the refrigerator for several weeks.

GARLIC AND CHILLI SAUCE

PLUM SAUCE

PEANUT SAUCE

SWEET CHILLI SAUCE

7 long red chillies, seeded and
    roughly chopped
185 ml (¾ cup) white vinegar
8 tablespoons sugar
½ teaspoon salt

MAKES 60 ML (¼ CUP)

USING a pestle and mortar or a small blender,
pound or blend the chillies into a rough paste.

IN a small saucepan, boil the vinegar, sugar and
salt over a high heat to boiling point, stirring
constantly. Reduce the heat to medium and
simmer for 15–20 minutes until the mixture forms
a thick syrup. Spoon the paste into the syrup,
cook for 1–2 minutes, then pour into a bowl ready
to serve.

PLUM SAUCE

185 ml (¾ cup) white vinegar
8 tablespoons sugar
1 preserved plum (available in jars)
    without liquid

MAKES 60 ML (¼ CUP)

IN a small saucepan, heat the vinegar and sugar
quickly, stirring constantly, until it reaches boiling
point. Lower the heat to medium and simmer for
15–20 minutes until it forms a thick syrup.

ADD the preserved plum and mash it with a spoon
or fork. Cook for 1–2 minutes to form a smooth
paste, then pour into a bowl ready to serve.

PEANUT SAUCE

2 garlic cloves, crushed
4 Asian shallots, finely chopped
1 lemon grass stalk, white part only,
    finely chopped
2 teaspoons Thai curry powder
    (page 563) or bought powder
1 tablespoon tamarind purée
1 tablespoon chilli paste
160 g (1 cup) unsalted roasted
    peanuts, roughly chopped
375 ml (1½ cups) coconut milk
    (page 551)
2 teaspoons palm sugar

MAKES 375 G (1½ CUPS)

HEAT 1 tablespoon vegetable oil in a saucepan
and fry the garlic, Asian shallots and lemon grass
for a minute. Add the Thai curry powder and stir
until fragrant.

ADD the remaining ingredients and bring slowly
to the boil. Add enough boiling water to make
a spoonable sauce and simmer for 2 minutes.
Season with salt to taste.

SALTED EGGS

10 fresh duck eggs (if available),
  or large chicken eggs, cleaned
175 g (6 oz) salt
a preserving jar, big enough to
  hold all the eggs

MAKES 10

IN a saucepan, heat 625 ml (2½ cups) water and the salt until the salt has dissolved. Allow to cool.

BEING very careful not to crack the shells, place the eggs into a large jar. Pour in the cool salt water. Seal the jar and leave for only three weeks. If you leave them any longer they will get too salty. Salted eggs will last for up to two months in their jar. Drain and use as required: boil the eggs, then scoop out the yolks and discard the whites.

CURRY POWDER

THAI CURRY POWDER

1 tablespoon black peppercorns
2 teaspoons white peppercorns
1 tablespoon cloves
3 tablespoons coriander seeds
3 tablespoons cumin seeds
1 tablespoon fennel seeds
seeds from 8 cardamom pods
3 tablespoons dried chilli flakes
2 tablespoons ground ginger
3 tablespoons ground turmeric

MAKES 125 G (½ CUP)

DRY-ROAST the peppercorns, cloves, coriander, cumin and fennel seeds, doing one ingredient at a time, in a frying pan over a low heat until fragrant.

TRANSFER to a spice grinder or pestle and mortar and grind to a powder. Add the remaining ingredients and grind together. Store in an airtight container.

CUCUMBER RELISH

CUCUMBER RELISH

4 tablespoons rice vinegar
125 g (½ cup) sugar
1 small red chilli, seeded and
  chopped
1 teaspoon fish sauce
80 g (½ cup) peanuts, lightly roasted
  and roughly chopped
1 Lebanese cucumber, unpeeled,
  seeded, finely diced

MAKES 185 G (¾ CUP)

PUT the vinegar and sugar in a small saucepan with 125 ml (½ cup) of water. Bring to the boil, then reduce the heat and simmer for 5 minutes.

ALLOW to cool before stirring in the chilli, fish sauce, peanuts and cucumber.

SOY AND VINEGAR

SOY AND VINEGAR DIPPING SAUCE

125 ml (½ cup) light soy sauce
3 tablespoons Chinese black rice
  vinegar

MAKES 225 ML (¾ CUP)

COMBINE the soy sauce and vinegar with
2 tablespoons water in a small bowl, then
divide among individual dipping bowls.

SOY, VINEGAR AND CHILLI

SOY, VINEGAR AND CHILLI DIPPING SAUCE

125 ml (½ cup) light soy sauce
2 tablespoons black rice vinegar
2 red chillies, thinly sliced

MAKES 200 ML (¾ CUP)

COMBINE the soy sauce, vinegar and chilli in a
small bowl, then divide among individual dipping
bowls. This dipping sauce goes well with dim sum
like har gau (page 29) or bean curd rolls
(page 47).

RED VINEGAR DIPPING SAUCE

125 ml (½ cup) red rice vinegar
3 tablespoons shredded ginger

MAKES 225 ML (¾ CUP)

COMBINE the rice vinegar, 2½ tablespoons
water and the ginger in a small bowl, then divide
among individual dipping bowls.

SOY, CHILLI AND SESAME

SOY, CHILLI AND SESAME DIPPING SAUCE

125 ml (½ cup) light soy sauce
1½ tablespoons chilli oil
1 tablespoon roasted sesame oil
1 spring onion (scallion), finely
  chopped

MAKES 200 ML (¾ CUP)

COMBINE the soy sauce, chilli oil, sesame oil
and spring onion in a small bowl, then divide
among individual dipping bowls. This dipping
sauce goes well with steamed breads (page 422).

CHINESE CHICKEN STOCK

1.5 kg (3 lb 5 oz) chicken
   carcasses, necks, pinions and
   feet
250 ml (1 cup) Shaoxing rice wine
6 slices ginger, smashed with the
   flat side of a cleaver
6 spring onions (scallions), ends
   trimmed, smashed with the flat
   side of a cleaver
4 litres (16 cups) water

MAKES 3 LITRES (12 CUPS)

REMOVE any excess fat from the chicken, then
chop into large pieces and place in a stockpot
with the rice wine, ginger, spring onions and water
and bring to the boil. Reduce the heat and
simmer gently for 3 hours, skimming the surface
to remove any impurities.

STRAIN through a fine strainer, removing the
solids, and skim the surface to remove any fat. If
the stock is too weak, reduce it further. Store in the
fridge for up to 3 days or freeze in small portions.

CHICKEN AND MEAT STOCK

CHINESE CHICKEN AND MEAT STOCK

650 g (1 lb 6 oz) chicken
   carcasses, necks, pinions and
   feet
650 g (1 lb 6 oz) pork spareribs or
   veal bones
4 spring onions (scallions), each tied
   into a knot
12 slices ginger, smashed with the
   flat side of a cleaver
4 litres (16 cups) water
80 ml (1/3 cup) Shaoxing rice wine
2 teaspoons salt

MAKES 3 LITRES (12 CUPS)

REMOVE any excess fat from the chicken and
meat, then chop into large pieces and place in a
stockpot with the spring onions, ginger and water
and bring to the boil. Reduce the heat and
simmer gently for 3 1/2–4 hours, skimming the
surface to remove any impurities.

STRAIN through a fine strainer, removing the
solids, and skim the surface to remove any fat.
Return to the pot with the rice wine and salt. Bring
to the boil and simmer for 3–4 minutes. Store in the
fridge for up to 3 days or freeze in small portions.

VEGETABLE STOCK

CHINESE VEGETABLE STOCK

500 g (1 lb 2 oz) fresh soya bean
   sprouts
10 dried Chinese mushrooms
6 spring onions (scallions), each
   tied into a knot (optional)
4 litres (16 cups) water
3 tablespoons Shaoxing rice wine
2 teaspoons salt

MAKES 3 LITRES (12 CUPS)

DRY-FRY the sprouts in a wok for 3–4 minutes.
Place the sprouts, mushrooms, spring onions and
water in a stockpot and bring to the boil. Reduce
the heat and simmer for 1 hour.

STRAIN through a fine strainer, removing the
solids (keep the mushrooms for another use).
Return to the pot with the rice wine and salt. Bring
to the boil and simmer for 3–4 minutes. Store in the
fridge for up to 3 days or freeze in small portions.

MAYONNAISE

4 egg yolks
1/2 teaspoon white wine vinegar
1 teaspoon lemon juice
500 ml (2 cups) groundnut oil

MAKES 500 ML (2 CUPS)

PUT the egg yolks, vinegar and lemon juice in a bowl or food processor and whisk or mix until light and creamy. Add the oil, drop by drop from the tip of a teaspoon, mixing constantly until the mixture begins to thicken, then add the oil in a very thin stream. (If you're using a processor, pour in the oil in a thin stream with the motor running.) Season well.

MAYONNAISE

VINAIGRETTE

1 garlic clove, crushed
1/2 teaspoon Dijon mustard
1 tablespoon white wine vinegar
90 ml (1/3 cup) olive oil

MAKES 100 ML (1/3 CUP)

MIX TOGETHER the garlic, mustard and vinegar. Add the oil in a thin stream, whisking continuously to form an emulsion. Season with salt and pepper. Store in a screw-top jar in the fridge and shake well before use. You can also add some chopped herbs such as chives or chervil.

BÉCHAMEL SAUCE

100 g (3 oz) butter
1 onion, finely chopped
100 g (3 oz) plain flour
1 litre (4 cups) milk
pinch of nutmeg
bouquet garni

MAKES 750 ML (3 CUPS)

MELT the butter in a saucepan, add the onion and cook, stirring, for 3 minutes. Stir in the flour to make a roux and cook, stirring, for 3 minutes over low heat without allowing the roux to brown.

REMOVE from the heat and add the milk gradually, stirring after each addition until smooth. Return to the heat, add the nutmeg and bouquet garni and cook for 5 minutes. Strain through a fine sieve into a clean pan and lay a buttered piece of baking paper on the surface to prevent a skin forming.

VINAIGRETTE

VELOUTÉ SAUCE

70 g (2½ oz) butter
75 g (2½ oz) plain flour
1 litre (4 cups) hot chicken stock

MAKES 500 ML (2 CUPS)

MELT the butter in a saucepan. Stir in the flour to make a roux and cook, stirring, for 3 minutes over low heat without allowing the roux to brown. Cool to room temperature. Add the hot stock and mix well. Return to the heat and simmer very gently for 10 minutes or until thick. Strain through a fine sieve, cover and refrigerate until needed.

BÉCHAMEL SAUCE

CRÈME PÂTISSIÈRE

6 egg yolks
125 g (4 oz) caster sugar
30 g (1 oz) cornflour
10 g (⅓ oz) plain flour
550 ml (2 cups) milk
1 vanilla pod
15 g (½ oz) butter

MAKES 500 G (1 LB 2 OZ)

WHISK together the egg yolks and half the sugar until pale and creamy. Sift in the cornflour and flour and mix together well.

PUT the milk, remaining sugar and vanilla pod in a saucepan. Bring just to the boil and then strain over the egg yolk mixture, stirring continuously. Pour back into a clean saucepan and bring to the boil, stirring constantly—it will be lumpy at first but will become smooth as you stir. Boil for 2 minutes, then stir in the butter and leave to cool. Transfer to a clean bowl, lay clingfilm on the surface to prevent a skin forming and refrigerate for up to 2 days.

CRÈME PÂTISSIÈRE

CRÈME ANGLAISE

300 ml (1¼ cups) milk
1 vanilla pod
2 egg yolks
2 tablespoons caster sugar

MAKES 300 ML (1¼ CUPS)

PUT the milk in a saucepan. Split the vanilla pod in two, scrape out the seeds and add the whole lot to the milk. (This will give small black spots in the custard—if you don't want them, you can leave the vanilla pod whole.) Bring just to the boil. Whisk the egg yolks and sugar until light and fluffy. Strain the milk over the egg mixture, whisking continuously.

POUR the custard back into the saucepan and cook, stirring, until it is thick enough to coat the back of a wooden spoon. Do not let it boil or the custard will split. Strain into a clean bowl, lay clingfilm on the surface to prevent a skin forming and refrigerate for up to 2 days.

FRANGIPANE

FRANGIPANE

250 g (9 oz) unsalted butter,
    softened
250 g (9 oz) icing sugar
250 g (9 oz) ground almonds
40 g (1 oz) plain flour
5 eggs, lightly beaten

MAKES 800 G (1 LB 12 OZ)

BEAT the butter until very soft. Add the icing sugar, ground almonds and flour and beat well. Add the egg gradually, beating until fully incorporated. Transfer to a clean bowl, cover with clingfilm and refrigerate for up to 24 hours.

OVEN-DRIED TOMATOES

GIARDINIERA

VINAIGRETTE

2 tablespoons lemon juice
4 tablespoons olive oil
2 teaspoons finely chopped onion
   or 1 finely chopped shallot
1 tablespoon chopped parsley

MAKES 180 ML (²/₃ CUP)

MAKE the dressing by combining all the ingredients. Season with salt and pepper.

OVEN-DRIED TOMATOES

24 plum tomatoes
sea salt
4 garlic cloves, crushed
¹/₂ tablespoon extra virgin olive oil
24 basil leaves
1 mild red chilli, cut into 24 small
   pieces
¹/₂ tablespoon dried oregano
750 ml (3 cups) olive oil

FILLS A 2 LITRE (8 CUP) JAR

PREHEAT the oven to 75°C (150°F/Gas ¹/₄). Core each tomato and slice almost in half along its length, with just the skin keeping it together. Open out butterfly-fashion and space out, cut side up, on wire racks. Sprinkle with sea salt and bake for about 8 hours, until dark and almost leathery, but not crisp. Cool and store in sterilized jars for up to six months, or preserve as below.

MIX the garlic with the extra virgin olive oil. Brush one half of each tomato, then place a basil leaf, piece of chilli and sprinkling of oregano on top. Fold the other half over to enclose and place in a sterilized jar. Pour in the olive oil to cover the tomatoes and push down firmly to expel any air. Seal and refrigerate for up to two months.

GIARDINIERA (GARDEN PICKLES)

280 g (10 oz) carrots, cut into short
   lengths
280 g (10 oz) pearl onions
220 g (8 oz) small fresh gherkins
875 ml (3¹/₂ cups) white wine
   vinegar
1 tablespoon sea salt
2 tablespoons honey
220 g (8 oz) stringless green beans,
   cut into short lengths
10 black peppercorns
6 whole cloves
5 juniper berries
2 bay leaves

FILLS A 1.25 LITRE (5 CUP) JAR

PREHEAT the oven to 120°C (250°F/Gas ¹/₂). Put the carrot, onions, gherkins, vinegar, salt and honey in a saucepan with 600 ml (2¹/₂ cups) water and bring to the boil. Reduce the heat and simmer for 20 minutes. Add the beans and simmer for 5 minutes, or until the vegetables are tender but still slightly crisp.

DRAIN the vegetables, reserving the liquid. Arrange the vegetables in a sterilized 1.25 litre (5 cup) jar and add the peppercorns, cloves, juniper berries and bay leaves. Pour in the liquid to cover the vegetables. Seal and refrigerate for 24 hours before use. Will keep for up to two months.

ITALIAN-STYLE BECHAMEL SAUCE

65 g (2 oz) butter
40 g (1 oz) plain flour
pinch of grated nutmeg
600 ml (2½ cups) milk
1 bay leaf

MAKES 800 ML (3 CUPS)

HEAT the butter in a saucepan over low heat. Add the flour and nutmeg and cook, stirring, for 1 minute. Remove from the heat and gradually stir in the milk. Add the bay leaf, return to the heat and simmer, stirring often, until the sauce thickens. Season, cover with clingfilm to prevent a skin forming, and cool. Discard the bay leaf.

BECHAMEL SAUCE

TOMATO SAUCE

120 g (4 oz) plum tomatoes
3 basil leaves
2 garlic cloves, crushed
1 tablespoon tomato passata
2 teaspoons extra virgin olive oil

MAKES 200 ML (¾ CUP)

CORE the tomatoes and purée in a food processor with the basil leaves (or chop the tomatoes and basil very finely and stir together). Stir in the garlic, passata and olive oil and season well. Leave for at least 30 minutes before serving to allow the flavours to blend. Use on pizzas, toss through pasta or serve with arancini or suppli.

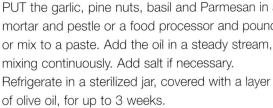

PESTO

2 garlic cloves
50 g (2 oz) pine nuts
80 g (3 oz) basil leaves
4 tablespoons grated Parmesan
150 ml (⅔ cup) extra virgin olive oil

MAKES 200 ML (¾ CUP)

PUT the garlic, pine nuts, basil and Parmesan in a mortar and pestle or a food processor and pound or mix to a paste. Add the oil in a steady stream, mixing continuously. Add salt if necessary. Refrigerate in a sterilized jar, covered with a layer of olive oil, for up to 3 weeks.

TOMATO SAUCE

SALSA VERDE

1½ tablespoons fresh white
    breadcrumbs
1 tablespoon milk
1 hard-boiled egg yolk
2 anchovy fillets
1 tablespoon capers
5 tablespoons finely chopped
    parsley, mint and basil
1 garlic clove, crushed
75 ml (⅓ cup) extra virgin olive oil

MAKES 200 ML (¾ CUP)

SOAK the breadcrumbs in the milk for 10 minutes. Finely chop together the egg yolk, anchovy and capers. Add the herbs, garlic and soaked breadcrumbs and mix with a fork. Slowly blend in the olive oil until the sauce is smooth and thick. Season with pepper, then set aside for at least 1 hour before using.

SALSA VERDE

BASIC CHINESE YEAST DOUGH

CHINESE CHEFS USE TWO TYPES OF BREAD DOUGH FOR MAKING STEAMED BREADS, ONE MADE WITH YEAST AS HERE, THE OTHER MADE WITH A YEAST STARTER DOUGH.

3 tablespoons sugar
250 ml (1 cup) warm water
1¹/₂ teaspoons (5 g) dried yeast
   or 10 g (¹/₃ oz) fresh yeast
400 g (14 oz) plain flour
2 tablespoons oil
1¹/₂ teaspoons baking powder

MAKES 1 QUANTITY (400 G)

DISSOLVE the sugar in the water, then add the yeast. Stir lightly, then set aside for 10 minutes, or until foamy.

SIFT the flour into a bowl and add the yeast mixture and the oil. Using a wooden spoon, mix the ingredients to a rough dough. Turn the mixture out onto a lightly floured surface and knead for 8–10 minutes, or until the dough is smooth and elastic. If it is very sticky, knead in a little more flour—the dough should be soft. Lightly grease a bowl with the oil. Place the dough in the bowl and turn it so that all sides of the dough are coated. Cover the bowl with a damp cloth and set aside to rise in a draught-free place for 3 hours.

UNCOVER the dough, punch it down, and turn it out onto a lightly floured surface. If you are not using the dough straight away, cover it with clingfilm and refrigerate.

WHEN YOU are ready to use the dough, flatten it and make a well in the centre. Place the baking powder in the well and gather up the edges to enclose the baking powder. Pinch the edges to seal. Lightly knead the dough for several minutes to evenly incorporate the baking powder, which will activate immediately.

USE the prepared dough as directed.

This bread dough is double risen, first with yeast and then with baking powder, which is kneaded into the dough, making it very light and fluffy.

MANDARIN PANCAKES

THESE THIN PANCAKES ARE ALSO CALLED DUCK PANCAKES AND ARE USED FOR WRAPPING PEKING

DUCK (PAGE 208) AND OTHER NORTHERN CHINESE DISHES.

450 g (1 lb) plain flour
300 ml (1¼ cups) boiling water
1 teaspoon oil
roasted sesame oil

MAKES 24–30

SIFT the flour into a bowl, slowly pour in the boiling water, stirring as you pour, then add the oil and knead into a firm dough. Cover with a damp tea towel and set aside for 30 minutes.

TURN the dough out onto a lightly floured surface and knead for 8–10 minutes, or until smooth. Divide the dough into three equal portions, roll each portion into a long cylinder, then cut each cylinder into 8 to 10 pieces.

ROLL each piece of dough into a ball and press into a flat disc with the palm of your hand. Brush one disc with a little sesame oil and put another disc on top. Using a rolling pin, flatten each pair of discs into a 15 cm (6 inch) pancake.

HEAT an ungreased wok or frying pan over high heat, then reduce the heat to low and place the pairs of pancakes, one at a time, in the pan. Turn over when brown spots appear on the underside. When the second side is cooked, lift the pancakes out and carefully peel them apart. Fold each pancake in half with the cooked side facing inwards, and set aside under a damp cloth.

JUST BEFORE serving, put the pancakes on a plate in a steamer. Cover and steam over simmering water in a wok for 10 minutes.

TO STORE the pancakes, put them in the fridge for 2 days or in the freezer for several months. Reheat the pancakes either in a steamer for 4–5 minutes or a microwave for 30–40 seconds.

Mandarin pancakes are always rolled and cooked as a pair; the two pancakes are separated by a layer of sesame oil.

TART PASTRY

220 g (8 oz) plain flour
pinch of salt
150 g (5 oz) unsalted butter, chilled
    and diced
1 egg yolk

MAKES 450 G (1 LB)

SIFT the flour and salt into a large bowl, add the butter and rub in with your fingertips until the mixture resembles breadcrumbs. Add the egg yolk and a little cold water (about 2–3 teaspoons) and mix with the blade of a palette knife until the dough just starts to come together. Bring the dough together with your hands and shape into a ball. Wrap in clingfilm and put in the fridge to rest for at least 30 minutes. You can also make the dough in a food processor, using the pulse button.

ROLL OUT the pastry into a circle on a lightly floured surface and use to line a tart tin, as directed in the recipe. Trim the edge and pinch up the pastry edge to make an even border raised slightly above the rim of the tin. Slide onto a baking tray and rest in the fridge for 10 minutes.

When making the sweet pastry it is easiest to work directly on the work surface.

SWEET PASTRY

350 g (12 oz) plain flour
small pinch of salt
150 g (5 oz) unsalted butter
100 g (3 oz) icing sugar
2 eggs, beaten

MAKES 700 G (1 LB 9 OZ)

SIFT the flour and salt onto a work surface and make a well in the centre. Put the butter into the well and work, using a pecking action with your fingertips and thumb, until it is very soft. Add the sugar to the butter and mix together. Add the eggs to the butter and mix together.

GRADUALLY incorporate the flour, flicking it onto the mixture and then chopping through it until you have a rough dough. Bring together with your hands and then knead a few times to make a smooth dough. Roll into a ball, wrap in clingfilm and put in the fridge for at least 1 hour.

ROLL OUT the pastry into a circle on a lightly floured surface and use to line a tart tin, as directed in the recipe. Trim the edge and pinch up the pastry edge to make an even border raised slightly above the rim of the tin. Slide onto a baking tray and rest in the fridge for 10 minutes.

SWEET PASTRY

BREAD DOUGH

LUNCH ON THICK SLICES OF THIS RUSTIC BREAD WITH UNSALTED BUTTER AND A GOOD CHEESE. THIS IS A BASIC BREAD DOUGH AND IS EASILY FLAVOURED—YOU COULD ADD CHOPPED WALNUTS, FRESH HERBS, OLIVES OR CHEESE.

2 teaspoons dried yeast or 15 g
   (1/2 oz) fresh yeast
250 g (9 oz) strong plain flour
1/2 teaspoon salt
3 tablespoons olive oil

MAKES 1 LOAF

MIX the yeast with 120 ml (1/2 cup) warm water. Leave for 10 minutes in a warm place until the yeast becomes frothy. If it does not bubble and foam in this time, throw it away and start again.

SIFT the flour into a large bowl and add the salt, olive oil and the yeast mixture. Mix until the dough clumps together and forms a ball.

TURN OUT onto a lightly floured work surface. Knead the dough, adding a little more flour or a few drops of warm water if necessary, until you have a soft dough that is not sticky but is dry to the touch. Knead for 10 minutes, or until smooth, and the impression made by a finger springs back immediately.

RUB the inside of a large bowl with olive oil. Roll the ball of dough around in the bowl to coat it with oil, then cut a shallow cross on the top of the ball with a sharp knife. Leave the dough in the bowl, cover with a tea towel or put in a plastic bag and leave in a draught-free spot for 1–11/2 hours or until the dough has doubled in size (or leave in the fridge for 8 hours to rise slowly).

KNOCK BACK the dough by punching it with your fist several times to expel the air and then knead it again for a couple of minutes. (At this stage the dough can be stored in the fridge for 4 hours, or frozen. Bring back to room temperature before continuing.) Leave in a warm place to rise until doubled in size. Place in a tin, on a baking tray or use as directed in the recipe, then bake at 230°C (450°F/Gas 8) for 30 minutes. When cooked, the base of the bread will sound hollow when tapped.

Use flour that is packaged as 'strong' or 'bread' flour. You can use plain flour or a mixture of plain and wholemeal, but the results won't be quite as good.

Sift in the flour and stir until the choux dough comes away from the side of the pan.

CHOUX PASTRY

CHOUX PASTRY

150 g (5 oz) unsalted butter
225 g (8 oz) plain flour, sifted twice
7 eggs
1 tablespoon caster sugar

MAKES 500 G (1 LB 2 OZ)

MELT the butter with 375 ml (1½ cups) water in a saucepan, then bring it to a rolling boil. Remove from the heat and add all the flour at once and a pinch of salt. Return to the heat and beat continuously with a wooden spoon to make a smooth shiny paste that comes away from the side of the pan. Cool for a few minutes.

BEAT IN the eggs one at a time, until shiny and smooth—the mixture should drop off the spoon but not be too runny. Beat in the sugar. Store in a pastry bag in the fridge for up to 2 days.

CRÊPES

250 g (9 oz) plain flour
pinch of salt
1 teaspoon sugar
2 eggs, lightly beaten
400 ml (1½ cups) milk
1 tablespoon melted butter
butter or oil, for frying

MAKES 12 SMALL OR
6 LARGE CRÊPES

SIFT the flour, salt and sugar into a bowl and make a well in the centre. Mix the eggs and milk together with 100 ml (⅓ cup) water and pour slowly into the well, whisking all the time to incorporate the flour until you have a smooth batter. Stir in the melted butter. Cover and refrigerate for 20 minutes.

HEAT a crêpe pan or a deep non-stick frying pan and grease with a little butter or oil. Pour in enough batter to coat the base of the pan in a thin even layer and tip out any excess. Cook over moderate heat for about a minute, or until the crêpe starts to come away from the side of the pan. Turn the crêpe and cook on the other side for 1 minute or until lightly golden. Stack the crêpes on a plate with pieces of greaseproof paper between them and cover with foil while you cook the rest of the batter.

PUFF PASTRY

LIGHTNESS IS THE HALLMARK OF GOOD PUFF PASTRY AND THE MANY LAYERS SHOULD RISE WITHOUT STICKING. THE KEY IS TO HAVE THE BUTTER AND PASTRY AT THE SAME CONSISTENCY WHEN YOU ROLL THEM OUT, AND TO KEEP THE ROLLING AND FOLDING AS NEAT AS YOU CAN.

250 g (9 oz) plain flour
1 teaspoon lemon juice
1 teaspoon salt
25 g (1 oz) butter, melted
200 g (7 oz) butter, chilled

MAKES 650 G (1 lb 6 oz)

SIFT the flour into a bowl and make a well in the centre. Pour in 125 ml (½ cup) water, the lemon juice, salt and melted butter. Draw in the flour with your fingertips, little by little, until you have a rough dough. Turn out onto a work surface and knead with the heel of your hand until the dough is smooth. Shape into a ball and cut a cross on the top. Wrap with clingfilm and refrigerate for 1–2 hours.

PLACE the chilled butter between two pieces of greaseproof paper and beat with a rolling pin to make a square 1–2 cm thick. Keep the butter cool so that it doesn't harden again or melt any further—it needs to be about the same softness as the pastry or it will break up when you roll it.

ON A LIGHTLY floured surface, roll out the dough in four different directions to form a cross large enough to hold the square of butter in its centre. Put the butter in the centre and fold the four arms of dough over it, one by one, to enclose the butter completely. Position the dough so that it looks like a book with the spine to the left and the open piece of dough to the right. Roll the pastry away from you into a rectangle, keeping the corners as square as you can, then fold the top third down and the bottom third up to make a parcel of three even layers. Turn the pastry 90 degrees to the right and repeat the rolling, folding and turning, trying to keep the corners neat and square—this will help make the pastry layers even. Wrap in clingfilm and chill for 30 minutes. (You can mark the pastry with finger indents each time you refrigerate so you remember how many turns you have made.)

REPOSITION the pastry as before, with the hinge to your left, then roll out, fold, turn and chill twice more. Rest for 30 minutes, then make two more turns as before. The pastry is now ready to use.

Although it can be time-consuming to make, home-made puff pastry that uses butter will always taste better than commercial pastry, which is often made with vegetable fat.

FOCACCIA DOUGH

Make the dough in a large bowl so you have enough room to bring it together. Knead on a well-floured surface until the dough is really elastic. Use the heel of your hand to stretch it into a rectangle.

$^{1}/_{2}$ teaspoon caster sugar
2 teaspoons dried yeast or
   15 g ($^{1}/_{2}$ oz) fresh yeast
800 ml (3 cups) lukewarm water
1 kg (2 lb 3 oz) plain flour
2 teaspoons salt
2 tablespoons olive oil
cornmeal

MAKES 2 FOCACCIA

PUT the sugar and yeast in a small bowl and stir in 60 ml ($^{1}/_{4}$ cup) of the water. Leave in a draught-free spot to activate. If the yeast does not bubble and foam in 5 minutes, throw it away and start again.

MIX the flour and salt in a bowl or in a food processor fitted with a plastic blade. Add the olive oil, the yeast mixture and three-quarters of the remaining water. Mix, then add the rest of the water, a little at a time, until the dough loosely clumps together. Transfer to a lightly floured surface and knead for 8 minutes until smooth, or until the impression made by a finger springs back immediately.

RUB the inside of a large bowl with olive oil. Roll the ball of dough around in the bowl to coat it with oil, then cut a shallow cross on the top of the ball with a sharp knife. Leave the dough in the bowl, cover with a tea towel or put in a plastic bag and leave in a draught-free spot for 1–1$^{1}/_{2}$ hours until doubled in size (or leave in the fridge for 8 hours to rise slowly).

PUNCH DOWN the dough to its original size, then divide into two portions. (At this stage the dough can be stored in the fridge for 4 hours, or frozen. Bring back to room temperature before continuing.) Roll each portion of dough out to a 28 x 20 cm (11$^{1}/_{4}$ x 8 inch) rectangle, then use the heels of your hands, working from the centre of the dough outwards, to make a 38 x 28 cm (15$^{1}/_{4}$ x 11$^{1}/$ inch) rectangle.

LIGHTLY OIL 2 baking trays and dust with cornmeal. Put a portion of dough in the centre of each tray and press out to fill the tray. Slide the trays inside a plastic bag. Seal and leave in a draught-free spot for 2 hours to rise again. The focaccia dough is now ready to use, as instructed in the recipe.

PIZZA DOUGH

1 tablespoon caster sugar
2 teaspoons dried yeast or
   15 g (½ oz) fresh yeast
215 ml (¾ cup) lukewarm water
450 g (1 lb) plain flour
½ teaspoon salt
3 tablespoons olive oil
cornmeal

MAKES TWO 30 CM (12 INCH)
PIZZA BASES

PUT the sugar and yeast in a small bowl and stir in 90 ml (⅓ cup) of the water. Leave in a draught-free spot to activate. If the yeast does not bubble and foam in 5 minutes, throw it away and start again.

MIX the flour and salt in a bowl or in a food processor fitted with a plastic blade. Add the olive oil, remaining water and the yeast mixture. Mix until the dough loosely clumps together. Transfer to a lightly floured surface and knead for 8 minutes, adding a little flour or a few drops of warm water if necessary, until you have a soft dough that is not sticky but is dry to the touch.

RUB the inside of a large bowl with olive oil. Roll the ball of dough around in the bowl to coat it with oil, then cut a shallow cross on the top of the ball with a sharp knife. Leave the dough in the bowl, cover with a tea towel or put in a plastic bag and leave in a draught-free spot for 1–1½ hours until doubled in size (or leave in the fridge for 8 hours to rise slowly).

PUNCH DOWN the dough to its original size, then divide into two portions. (At this stage the dough can be stored in the fridge for up to 4 hours, or frozen. Bring back to room temperature before continuing.)

WORKING with one portion at a time, push the dough out to make a thick circle. Use the heels of your hands and work from the centre of the circle outwards, to flatten the dough into a 30 cm (12 inch) circle with a slightly raised rim. (If you find it difficult to push the dough out by hand you can use a rolling pin.) The pizza dough is now ready to use, as instructed in the recipe. Cook on a lightly oiled tray, dusted with cornmeal, and get it into the oven as quickly as possible.

Knead the dough by stretching it away from you and then folding it back on itself. Use your fist to squash it into a flat circle. You will need to push quite hard.

PASTA

500 g (1 lb 2 oz) 00 *(doppio zero)*
    or plain flour
4 eggs
chilled water

MAKES 700 G (1 LB 9 OZ)

MOUND the flour on a work surface or in a large bowl. Make a well in the centre. Break the eggs into the well and whisk with a fork, incorporating the flour as you whisk. You may need to add a little chilled water (1/4 teaspoon at a time) to make a loosely massed dough. Turn the dough onto a lightly floured surface—it should be soft, pliable and dry to the touch. Knead for 6–8 minutes, or until smooth and elastic with a slightly glossy appearance. Cover with a tea towel and leave for 30 minutes. The dough is then ready to roll out.

TO MAKE the dough in a processor, mix the flour for 2–3 seconds, then add the eggs with the motor running. Mix again for 5 seconds, or until the mixture looks like coarse meal. Mix until a loose ball forms, then continue for 4–5 seconds until the machine slows and stops. If the dough seems too sticky to form a smooth ball, add 2 teaspoons flour, mix briefly and continue adding small amounts of flour until the ball forms. If the mixture is too dry, add chilled water, a teaspoon at a time. Transfer to a lightly floured surface and knead for 2–3 minutes until smooth and elastic. Cover with a tea towel and leave for 30 minutes.

TO ROLL OUT the dough, divide into two or three manageable portions. Work with one portion at a time, keeping the rest covered. Flatten the dough onto a lightly floured surface and roll out from the centre to the outer edge, rotating the dough often. When you have a 5 mm (1/4 inch) thick circle of dough, fold it in half and roll it out again. Do this eight times to give a smooth circle of pasta, then roll to a thickness of 2.5 mm (1/8 inch). Mend any tears with a little pasta from the outside of the circle and a little water. Transfer to a lightly floured tea towel. If the pasta is to be filled, keep it covered and don't allow it to dry out. If the sheets are to be cut into lengths or shapes, leave them uncovered so that the surface moisture will dry slightly before cutting.

IF YOU have a pasta machine, work the dough through the rollers, making the setting smaller each time until the dough is the correct thickness.

Pasta is traditionally made on the work surface and not in a bowl. Roll it by hand or with a pasta machine—whichever method you choose, it must be thin enough to read a newspaper through.

GLOSSARY OF FOOD AND COOKING

GLOSSARY OF FOOD AND COOKING

abalone A single-shelled mollusc that is a delicacy in China. Sometimes available fresh from specialist fish shops, but more often used dried or tinned. Dried abalone, bought from dried goods shops, needs to be soaked for 6 hours, then simmered for 4. Tinned can be used as it is.

agar-agar Also known as China grass, this is a setting agent made from certain types of seaweed. It is sold as strips, sheets, flakes or powder, dissolves in boiling water, and unlike gelatine will set at room temperature. Available from supermarkets, health food shops and Indian food shops.

ajowan A spice that looks like miniature cumin seeds and has a similar aroma but stronger flavor. Use sparingly.

al dente Meaning 'to the tooth'. Pasta and risotto rice are cooked until they are *al dente*—the outside is tender but the centre still has a little resistance or 'bite'. Pasta cooked beyond this point becomes soggy.

amaranth A leafy green, or green and dark red vegetable. It has a peppery flavorand can be substituted with spinach in recipes. Available at Indian food shops.

amaretti Small biscuits like macaroons, made from sweet and bitter almonds. They vary in size, but are usually 2–3 cm (1 inch) wide.

amchoor/amchur powder A fine beige powder made by drying green mangoes. It is used as a souring agent or meat tenderizer in Indian cooking. It is an essential flavorin chaat masala. Available at Indian food shops.

andouillette A sausage made from pork or veal chitterlings or tripe. Andouillettes are usually broiled and often served with mustard, potatoes or cabbage. Some have an outer layer of lard that melts as they cook.

artichoke The edible flower of a member of the thistle family. Some have thorns and the types vary greatly in size. The largest are usually boiled, but the smallest and most tender can be eaten raw as antipasto. Most common varieties include Romanesco (large and purple), Precoce di Chioggia (large and green), Violetto Toscano (small and tender enough to eat raw) and Spinoso di Palermo (a purple variety from Sicily).

asafoetida This yellowish powder or lump of resin is made from the dried latex of a type of fennel. Asafoetida has an extremely pungent smell which has earned it the name 'devil's dung'. It is used to make pulses and legumes more digestible and Hindu Brahmins and Jains use it instead of garlic and onions which are forbidden to them. Asafoetida is always fried to calm its aroma. It comes in small airtight containers and is available from Indian food shops.

Asian shallots Small reddish-purple shallots used in South-East Asia. French shallots can be used instead.

atta Sometimes called chapati flour, this is made from finely ground whole durum wheat. Some have a proportion of white flour added, labelled as 80/20 or 60/40. Atta is much finer and softer than wholemeal flour so if you can't find it, use half wholemeal and half maida or plain flour instead.

bain-marie Literally a water bath for gentle oven-cooking of delicate terrines and desserts. Usually the dish is placed in a roasting pan, which is half-filled with water.

bamboo shoots The edible shoots of bamboo. Available fresh when in season, otherwise preserved in jars or canned. Fresh shoots should be blanched (possibly more than once) if they are bitter.

bamboo shoots A bamboo is a giant grass and its shoots are a common vegetable in China. Fresh shoots are cone-shaped and can contain a toxin called hydrocyanic acid, which is removed by boiling for 5 minutes. The more readily available tinned ones are usually cut into strips and need to be rinsed. Dried or preserved bamboo shoots may also be available. Dried ones should be soaked. Winter shoots are more highly prized than spring shoots as they are more tender. Bamboo is known as 'winter' in many dishes.

banana chillies are large fat yellow/green (almost fluorescent) chillies with a mild flavor. They are used in stir-fries as well as in salads.

banana flower This is the purple, teardrop-shaped flower of the banana plant.The purple leaves and pale yellow buds which grow between them are discarded. Only the inner pale core is eaten. This needs to be blanched in boiling water to remove any bitterness. Wear rubber gloves to prepare banana flower as it has a gummy substance, which can stain your fingers. Available from Indian food shops.

banana leaves Large green leaves, which can be used as a wrapping (dip briefly in boiling water or put in a hot oven for 10 seconds to soften them before use) for foods, or to line plates. Young leaves are preferable. Available from Asian food shops.

bananas There are more than 20 different types of banana available in Thailand, all of which are used in cooking and are very popular. Varieties differ in flavor, with the small sugar bananas being the sweetest.

barbecue pork A Cantonese speciality, these pork pieces are coated in maltose or honey and roasted until they have a red, lacquered appearance. Available at Chinese roast meat restaurants.

basil seeds These tiny black seeds of a type of wild Indian basil are soaked in water until they swell. When soaked, they are surrounded by clear jelly. They have no flavorand are used for texture in drinks like falooda. Buy at Indian food shops.

bean curd *see tofu.*

bean curd Called doufu in China and made by coagulating soya bean milk. The curds are sold in blocks, either soft, firm or pressed, depending on their water content. Keep the blocks in water in the fridge, changing the water frequently, for up to 2 to 3 days. Japanese tofu can be used but the silken variety is softer than Chinese soft bean curd. Available at supermarkets.

bean curd puffs Deep-fried squares of bean curd, crispy on the outside and spongy in the middle. Frying your own bean curd will not be the same, but can be substituted. Puffs, sold in Chinese shops, can be frozen.

bean curd skins Made by scooping the layer of skin off the top of boiling soya milk and drying it. Bean curd skins come either as dried sheets, which need to be soaked in water, or already softened in vacuum packs. The skins are used as a wrapper or split into sticks and added to stir-fries and soups.

bean sprouts These can be sprouted mung or soya beans. Soya bean sprouts are bigger and more robust, but the two are usually interchangeable. Recipes may tell you to remove the straggly ends, but this is not necessary and is for aesthetic reasons. You can keep the sprouts in water in the fridge for several days. Change the water daily.

bean thread noodles Not true noodles, these are made from mung bean starch and are also labelled as cellophane or glass noodles. They come as vermicelli or slightly thicker strands and need to be soaked. They have no flavorof their own but soak up flavorings they are cooked with.

besan flour Also known as gram flour, this is a yellow flour made from ground Bengal gram or chickpeas. It has a nutty flavorand is used as a thickener in curries, as well as in batters, dumplings, sweets and breads.

betel leaves Known also as piper leaves or wild tea leaves, these are not true betel but are a close relative. They are used to wrap some snacks. Use baby spinach leaves if you can't get betel leaves.

beurre manié A paste made by mixing together butter and flour. Stirred into sauces at the end of cooking to thicken them.

beurre noisette A simple sauce made by cooking butter until it is brown and nutty.

Bird's eye or mouse dropping chillies (phrik khii nuu) are the smallest and hottest. Most commonly green, but red can be used in most recipes.

bitter melon Also known as bitter gourd, karela or warty melon, this looks like a pale cucumber with a warty skin. The flesh is bitter and needs to be blanched or degorged, then married with strong flavors.

black fungus Also known as wood or cloud ears, this is a cultivated wood fungus, which is dried in pieces and can be found in bags in Chinese shops. When reconstituted, it expands to up to five times its original size. It is used in recipes for both its color and slightly crunchy, rubbery texture.

black salt (kala namak) A rock salt mined in central India. Available as black or dark brown lumps, or ground to a pinkish grey powder. Unlike white salt, it has a tangy, smoky flavor. Buy at Indian food shops.

black-eyed beans (lobhia) Also called black-eyed peas, these are actually dried cow peas and are also known as chowli dal when split. They are buff-colored beans with a small dark eye on one side. They need to be soaked overnight or pre-cooked before use. Avoid dark or wrinkled beans as they are old.

bocconcini Means literally 'small mouthful' and is used to describe various foods, but generally refers to small balls of mozzarella, about the size of walnuts.

bok choy Also called a little Chinese white cabbage, this is a mild, open-leaved cabbage with a fat white or pale-green stem and dark-green leaves. A smaller variety is called Shanghai or baby bok choy. Bok choy is widely available.

bouquet garni A bundle of herbs used to flavordishes. Made by tying sprigs of parsley, thyme, celery leaves and a bay leaf in either a piece of muslin or portion of leek.

bresaola Lean beef that is cured and air-dried for 2–3 months—a speciality of the Valtellina Valley in Lombardia, Italy. Has a dark red color and stronger flavorthan prosciutto. Serve thinly sliced.

brown stock Stock made from browned beef or veal bones. As beef and veal stock are usually interchangeable, the term brown stock is used.

butter Butter is flavored both by the lactic fermentation of cream and the diet of the cows from whose milk it is made. Butter from Normandy and the Alps region in France is high quality and has a sweet flavor. French butter tends not to be heavily salted, with the amount varying between regions—Isigny butter from Normandy is unsalted, while next door in Brittany, butter from Poitou-Charentes is salted. Both butters have AOC status. Use either salted or unsalted butter for savory dishes, but unsalted in sweet recipes.

buttermilk (chaas) The mildly sour liquid left when milk is churned to butter. Commercial buttermilk is made from fermented skim milk and is not 'live' as real buttermilk would be.

cantucci Tuscan almond biscuits, also known as biscotti di Prato. These hard, double-baked biscuits often contain whole almonds. They are usually eaten dipped into a dessert wine such as vin santo.

caperberries The fruit of the caper bush, which appear after the flowers. They are usually preserved in brine and served as an accompaniment, like olives.

capers The pickled flowers of the caper bush. These are available preserved in brine, vinegar or salt and should be rinsed well and squeezed dry before use.

cardamom Dry green pods full of sticky, tiny brown or black seeds which have a sweet flavorand pungent aroma. If you need ground cardamom, open the pods and grind the seeds. Ready-ground cardamom quickly loses flavor. Use pods whole or crushed. Brown cardamom has a peppery flavornot suitable for sweet dishes.

cardoons Similar to the artichoke plant, cardoons have large leaves and long stems. Unlike artichokes, it is the stems that are eaten rather than the flowers. The stalks are usually blanched like celery.

casalinga Means 'home-made' or 'homely'. When attributed to sausages or salami, it generally means having a coarse texture and earthy flavor.

cassia The bark of the cassia tree is similar to cinnamon, which can be used instead, though cassia has a more woody flavor. It is used as a flavoring, especially in braises, and is a component of five-spice powder.

cavolo nero Cabbage with long leaves that are so dark green they appear to be almost black. Used mainly in Tuscan cooking. If unavailable, Savoy cabbage can be used.

cayenne pepper A very hot red chilli powder made from sun-dried red chillies.

cervelas A long, fat pork sausage, often flavored with garlic, pistachios or truffles. It is a boiling sausage (saucisse à cuire) and should be poached before browning under the broiler. Ordinary pork sausages flavored with pistachios can be used instead if cervelas are unavailable.

cetriolini Small gherkins. If unavailable, use cornichons or small cocktail gherkins.

cha om A bitter green vegetable resembling a fern. Cha om is used in omelette-style dishes and in stir-fries.

chaat masala Seasoning used for various snacks known as chaat (which means 'to lick' in Hindi). The spice blend uses a variety of flavorings including asafoetida, amchoor, black salt, cumin, cayenne, ajowan and pepper.

chana dal These are husked, split, polished, yellow Bengal gram, the most common type of gram lentil in India. They are often cooked

with a pinch of asafoetida to make them more easy to digest.

chenna Sweetened Indian cheese, used in sweet dishes. Found in the refrigerated section in supermarkets and Indian food shops.

chickpeas Chickpeas come white (kabuli/kubli) or black (kala). The white chickpeas are actually a tan color and the black ones are dark brown. Usually sold whole, but also sold split, dried chickpeas need to be soaked for 8 hours in cold water before use. They will double in size. Tinned ones can be used but need to be added at the end of the cooking time as they are already very soft.

chilli bean paste Made from broad beans fermented with chillies and salt to give a browny-red sauce, this is an important ingredient in Chinese cooking, but is never served as a dipping sauce. Other pastes, called hot or Sichuan bean pastes, can be substituted. These are made of fermented soya beans and sometimes other ingredients such as garlic. It is hard to judge their heat, so take care when adding a new one to a recipe. Chinese shops usually have a large number to choose from.

chilli flakes Dried, coarsely ground chillies with the seeds included; usually hot.

chilli jam A thick, sweet chilli relish that can also be used as a sauce. Make it yourself or buy it ready-made.

chilli oil A condiment made by pouring smoking hot oil over chilli flakes and seeds. Ready-made versions can be bought as chilli oil or Sichuan red oil.

chilli powder A wide variety of chillies are dried and crushed to make chilli powders. Some, such as Kashmiri chilli powder and paprika, are used for color, whereas others like cayenne are used for heat. Don't use chilli powder indiscriminately. The amount used can be varied, to taste, so start with a small amount and determine how hot it is.

chilli sauce The common name for siracha chilli sauce (naam phrik sii raachaa), this is used more than any of the many other types of chilli sauce. Usually served alongside

grilled fish, this thick orange sauce is named after the seaside town famous for its production. Made from fresh chillies and a variety of other ingredients, such as garlic and vinegar, the thicker version is good for cooking and the thinner for a dipping sauce.

chillies Red and green chillies are widely used in Indian cuisine. Recipes generally give a color, rather than a variety. Many varieties are grown in India and are used in a regional or seasonal context. Kashmiri chillies are dark red and mild, Goan chillies are short and stubby and mundu chillies are round. Small dhani (bird's eye chillies) are the hottest.

chillies Red and green chillies are widely used in Thai cuisine. Recipes usually give a variety, rather than a color. Generally, with Thai chillies, the smaller they are the hotter they are.

chillies, dried Dried whole chillies of various shapes, sizes and heat levels. Sometimes soaked to soften them. Remove the seeds if they are very hot.

Chinese broccoli This has dark-green stalks and leaves and tiny florets. It is widely available.

Chinese cabbage A white cabbage also known as Chinese leaf; Tianjin, Beijing or napa cabbage; or wong bok. There are two main types: one is long with pale-green leaves and a thick white stem, while the other is pale yellow with curlier leaves and a rounder shape. Both are widely available.

Chinese chives Garlic chives have a long, flat leaf and are green and very garlicky, or yellow with a milder taste. Flowering chives are round-stemmed with a flower at the top, which can be eaten. Both are used as a vegetable rather than as a herb.

Chinese curry powder A strong and spicy version of five-spice powder, with additional spices including turmeric and coriander, which lend the curry flavor.

Chinese ham A salted and smoked ham with a strong flavorand dryish flesh. Yunnan and Jinhua hams are the best known, and outside China, Yunnan ham can be bought in tins. You can substitute prosciutto if you can't find it.

Chinese kale Known as gai laan in Chinese food shops.

Chinese keys A rhizome with skinny fingers that hang down like a bunch of keys. Has a peppery flavor. Available tinned, or preserved in jars, from Asian food shops.

Chinese mushrooms The fresh version, found as shiitake mushrooms, is cultivated by the Japanese. The Chinese, however, usually use dried ones, which have a strong flavor and aroma and need to be soaked to reconstitute them before they are used. The soaking liquid can be used to add flavor to dishes. These are widely available.

Chinese pickles These can be made from several types of vegetables, preserved in a clear brine solution or in a soy-based solution, which is called jiang cai. Both can be used where Chinese pickles are called for in a recipe. They are available in packets and jars from Chinese shops.

Chinese sausage There are two kinds of Chinese sausage: a red variety, lap cheong or la chang, which is made from pork and pork fat and dried; and a brown variety, yun cheung or xiang chang, which is made from liver and pork and also dried. Chinese sausages have to be cooked before eating.

Chinese shrimp paste Very pungent pulverized shrimp. Refrigerate after opening.

Chinese spirits Distilled from grains, these vary in strength but generally are stronger than Western spirits. Spirits are used for drinking and cooking and Mou Tai is a common brand. Brandy can be substituted.

Chinese turnip Looking like a huge white carrot, this is actually a type of radish and is also called Chinese white radish. It has a crisp, juicy flesh and mild radish flavor. It is also known as mooli, or by the Japanese name daikon, and is widely available.

Chinese-style pork spareribs These are the shorter, fatter ribs known as pai gwat and are cut into short lengths. If unavailable, use any spareribs but trim off any excess fat.

chipolata In France, a chipolata can be as long as an ordinary sausage but is always much thinner. Usually made from pork and pork fat, chipolatas are used as a garnish in French cooking.

choy sum A green vegetable with tender pale-green stalks, small yellow flowers and dark-green leaves. It has a mild flavor and is often just blanched and eaten with a simple flavoring like garlic or oyster sauce.

ciabatta Slipper-shaped Italian bread with a rough, open texture. They are made from a very wet dough, which allows large bubbles to form and gives a thin crust. Ciabatta quickly goes stale and is best eaten on the day it is bought or made.

cipolline Small white onions, usually flattened in appearance rather than round.

clarified butter Made by melting butter so that the fat separates out from the impurities and water. The fat is then either spooned off or the water poured away and the butter allowed to reset. Clarified butter keeps longer than ordinary butter because all the water has been removed and it can be used for cooking at higher temperatures because it has a higher burning point.

clay pot Also known as a sand pot, these earthenware, lidded pots are used for braises, soups and rice dishes that need to be cooked slowly on the stove. The pots come in different shapes: the squatter ones are for braising and the taller ones for soups and rice. The pots can be fragile and should be heated slowly, preferably with a liquid inside.

cleaver A large, oblong, flat-bladed knife. In China, different cleavers are used for all chopping and cutting, but heavy-duty ones are good for chopping through bones as they are very robust. They can be bought in shops and at kitchenware shops.

cloves The dried, unopened flower buds of the clove tree. Brown and nail-shaped, they have a pungent flavor and so should be used in moderation. Use cloves whole or ground.

coconut The fruit of a coconut palm. The inner nut is encased in a husk which has to be removed. The hard shell can then be drained of juice before being cracked open to extract the white meat. Coconut meat is jellyish in younger nuts and harder in older ones. Medium-hard coconuts, which are perfect for desserts, are sold as grating coconuts in Thailand.

coconut cream This is made by soaking freshly grated coconut in boiling water and then squeezing out a thick, sweet coconut-flavored liquid. It is available tinned but if you can make your own. Coconut cream is sometimes 'cracked' in order to fry curry pastes. This means it is boiled until the water evaporates out and it separates into oil and solids.

coconut milk A thinner version of coconut cream, made as above but with more water or from a second pressing. Available tinned.

coconut milk powder A powdered form of coconut which when mixed with water makes coconut milk or cream. Sold in supermarkets or Indian food shops.

coconut sugar This sugar is made from the sap from coconut trees. Dark brown in color, it is mainly used in sweet dishes. Palm sugar or unrefined soft brown sugar can be used instead.

confit From the French word for preserve, confit is usually made from goose or duck meat, cooked in its own fat and then preserved in a jar or pot. It is eaten on its own or added to dishes such as cassoulet for extra flavor.

coppa A type of cured pork made from half pork fat and half pig's neck and shoulder. It is rolled and cured in a casing and, when sliced, resembles a fatty sausage.

coriander The round seeds of the coriander plant. The seeds have a spicy aroma, are widely used in Indian cooking and are common in spice mixes such as garam masala. To intensify the flavor, dry-roast the seeds until aromatic, before crushing them. Best freshly ground for each dish. Available whole or ground.

coriander Fresh coriander leaves are used both as an ingredient and as a colorful garnish. The roots (raak phak chii) are chopped or ground and used in curry pastes and sauces. Buy bunches that have healthy green leaves and avoid any that are yellowing.

corn Now commonly grown in northern Thailand, corn is eaten freshly grilled as a healthy snack. Baby corn (khao phoht awn) is often used in stir-fries and curries.

cornichon The French term for a small gherkin. It you can't find cornichons, use cocktail gherkins instead.

cotechino A sausage made from pork and pork rind, giving it a gelatinous texture. Cotechino is flavored with cloves and cinnamon and needs to be cooked before eating.

country-style bread Any bread that is bought as a whole loaf and has a rough texture. Pugliese, ciabatta and pane Toscano are all examples. Other white bread is not a suitable substitute.

court bouillon A flavored poaching liquid, usually for cooking fish.

couscous Made from very tiny balls of dough, couscous is usually steamed and served like rice with a main meal. Couscous was traditionally made by hand from freshly milled flour and came in different sizes of grain. Now that it is commercially produced, the grains tend to be uniformly quite tiny.

creamed coconut A solid block of coconut cream which needs to be reconstituted with water, or can be added straight to a dish to give a strong coconut flavor. Slice pieces off the block as required.

crème de cassis Originating near Dijon in Burgundy, France, crème de cassis is a black currant liqueur used in desserts and also to flavor the drink kir.

crème fraîche Often used in place of cream in the French kitchen. Lightly fermented, it has a slightly tart taste. Crème fraîche from Isigny has AOC status.

croccante Caramelized nuts, usually almonds but sometimes hazelnuts (these are also known as pralines).

cumin seeds The green or ochre, elongated ridged seeds of a plant of the parsley family. It has a peppery, slightly bitter flavorand is very aromatic.To intensify the flavor, dry-roast the seeds before crushing them. Best freshly ground for each dish. Available whole or ground. Kala jeera are a black variety.

curd cheese A smooth soft cheese made from curds that have not undergone lactic fermentation. Curd cheese is lower in fat than cream cheese but higher in fat than cottage cheese.

curry leaves Smallish green aromatic leaves of a tree native to India and Sri Lanka. These give a distinctive flavorto south Indian dishes. They are usually fried and added to the dish or used as a garnish at the end.

curry pastes Most often homemade in Thailand, though they can be bought freshly made in markets, and packaged in supermarkets. All curry pastes are ground and pounded together in a pestle and mortar until they are very smooth. The most common ones are red or hot (kaeng phet), green (kaeng khiaw-waan), panaeng or dry (kaeng phanaeng), matsaman or massaman (kaeng matsaman), sour orange (kaeng som), yellow (kaeng leuang), Chiang Mai or hangleh (kaeng hangleh) and jungle or forest (kaeng paa).

curry powder Usually bought ready-made. Widely used in stir-fries, marinades, sauces and in curry puffs.

dal is used to describe not only an ingredient but a dish made from it. In India, dal relates to any type of dried split pea, bean or lentil. The cooking times vary as do the texture and flavor. A dal dish can be a thin soup or more like a stew. All dal should be rinsed before use.

dang gui A bitter Chinese herb that is a relation of European Angelica and is valued for its medicinal properties. It can be found in Chinese shops or herbalists and looks like small bleached pieces of wood. It is generally added to braises or soups.

degchi A cooking pot, often brass lined with tin, which has no handle. It has a thick base and straight sides like a saucepan.

Dijon mustard A pale yellow mustard, made from verjuice or white wine and mustard seeds that have been ground to a flour. Originating in Dijon, this style of mustard is now made all over France.

doppio zero (00) flour The finest grade of flour, made from soft wheat (grano tenero) and mainly used for making cakes and fresh egg pasta.

Dragon's eye chillies Chillies which are slightly larger than normal and less hot.

dried chillies Dried red chillies are either long chillies or bird's eye. They are sometimes soaked in hot water to soften them. Remove the seeds if you prefer less heat.

dried fish Used extensively in Thai cuisine and a common roadside sight near the coast, dried fish is usually fried and crumbled and used in dips, salads and pastes.

dried scallops Scallops dried to thick amber discs. They need to be soaked or steamed until soft and are often shredded before use. They have a strong flavorso you don't need many, and as they are expensive they are mostly eaten at banquets.

dried shrimps These are tiny, orange, saltwater shrimps that have been dried in the sun. They come in different sizes and the really small ones have their heads and shells still attached. Dried shrimp need to be soaked in water or rice wine to soften them before use and are used as a seasoning, not as a main ingredient.

drumsticks Long, dark green, ridged fibrous pods from the horseradish tree. Drumsticks, so called because of their rigidity, need to be cut into lengths before being cooked. The inner pulp, the only part eaten, is scooped out with a spoon or scraped out with your teeth. Buy uniformly slim pods.

dumpling wrappers Used for jiaozi, wheat wrappers, also called Shanghai wrappers or wheat dumpling skins, are white and can be round or square. Egg wrappers for siu mai are yellow and may also be round or square. They are sometimes labelled gow gee wrappers or egg dumpling skins. All are found in the refrigerated cabinets in Chinese shops and good supermarkets and can be frozen until needed.

durian The most infamous of fruit with a notoriously noxious aroma and sweet, creamy flavorand texture. It is banned from airlines and hotels.

eggplant There are lots of varieties of eggplant (aubergine). In Thailand, bitterness is a prized quality. Common eggplants include Thai eggplant (ma-kheua phraw) which are pale green, orange, purple, yellow or white and golf-ball sized. Long eggplant (ma-kheua yao) are long, skinny and green. Pea eggplant (ma-kheau phuang) are tiny, bitter and look like large peas. Cut eggplant using a stainless steel knife and store in salted water to prevent them from turning black.

farro A type of spelt grain, farro is used in soups and stews in a similar way to barley. If farro is unavailable, spelt or barley can be used. Farro is most commonly used in the cuisines of the areas where it is grown—Tuscany, Umbria and Lazio.

fennel seeds The dried seeds of a Mediterranean plant, fennel seeds are oval, greenish yellow, with ridges running along them, and look like large cumin. Used as an aromatic and a digestive. To intensify the flavor, dry-roast the seeds before crushing them. Available whole or ground. Best freshly ground.

fenugreek seeds Not a true seed, but a dried legume. Ochre in color and almost square, with a groove down one side, fenugreek has a curry aroma (it is a major ingredient in commercial curry powders) and is best dry-roasted for a few seconds before use. Don't brown them too much or they will be bitter.

fermented bean curd A marinated bean curd that is either red, colored with red rice, or white, and may also be flavored with chilli. It is sometimes called preserved bean curd or bean curd cheese and is used as a condiment or flavoring. It can be found in jars in Chinese shops.

finocchiona A type of salami from Itlay, flavored with wild fennel seeds. The salami is very often large and is aged for up to a year before use. It also comes in a more crumbly version called sbriciolona.

fish sauce Made from salted anchovy-like fish that are left to break down naturally in the heat, fish sauce is literally the liquid that is drained off. It is the main source of salt flavoring in Thai cooking and is also used as a condiment. It varies in quality. Look for Tiparos or Golden Boy brands. A fermented version (naam plaa raa) is also available.

five-spice powder A Chinese mixed spice generally made with star anise, cassia, Sichuan pepper, fennel seeds and cloves, which gives a balance of sweet, hot and aromatic flavors. Five-spice may also include cardamom, coriander, dried orange peel and ginger. Used ground together as a powder or as whole spices tied in muslin.

flat cabbage Also known as a rosette cabbage, this is a type of bok choy. It looks like a giant flower with pretty, shiny, dark-green leaves that grow out flat.

flat-leaf parsley Also known as Italian or continental parsley. Used as an ingredient rather than a garnish, unlike curly parsley.

foie gras The enlarged livers of fattened geese or ducks. Regarded as a delicacy, with foie gras from Strasbourg and southwest France both highly regarded.

fontina A traditional mountain cheese from the Valle d'Aosta in Piemonte, Italy. Full-fat and semi-soft with a sweetish flavor, fontina melts evenly and well and so is particularly good for cooking.

fromage frais A fresh white cheese with a smooth creamy consistency. There are a number of varieties, many artisan-produced. Fromage blanc is traditionally used in Lyon's cervelle de canut. The fat content of fromage frais varies, which may affect its cooking qualities, but generally it makes a good low-fat alternative to cream.

galangal or galingale A rhizome, similar to ginger, used extensively in Thai cooking, usually in place of ginger. It is most famously used in tom khaa kai.

garam masala A northern Indian spice mix which means 'warming spice mix', it mostly contains coriander, cumin, cardamom, black pepper, cloves, cinnamon and nutmeg. There are many versions and you can buy ready-ground mixes or make your own. Garam masala is usually added to meat dishes as a final seasoning.

garlic Thai garlic has tiny cloves and is usually smashed with the side of a cleaver rather than being crushed before use. Deep-fried garlic is used as a garnish as is garlic oil. Deep-fried garlic can be bought in jars.

ghee A highly clarified butter made from cow or water buffalo milk. Ghee can be heated to a high temperature without burning and has an aromatic flavor. Vegetable ghees are also available but don't have the same aromatic qualities. You can substitute clarified butter, or make your own ghee by melting unsalted butter in a saucepan, bringing to a simmer and cooking for about 30 minutes to evaporate out any water. Skim any scum off the surface, then drain the ghee off, leaving the white sediment behind. Leave to cool.

ginger The rhizome of a tropical plant which is sometimes referred to as a 'root'. It is sold in 'hands'. Fresh young ginger should have a smooth, pinkish beige skin and be firm and juicy. As it ages, the skin toughens and the flesh becomes more fibrous. Avoid old ginger which is wrinkled as it will be tough. Choose pieces you can snap easily. Ginger is measured in centimetre pieces and this means pieces with an average-sized width. Variations in size will not adversely affect the flavorof the dish. Ginger is also available dried and ground.

gingko nuts These are the nuts of the maidenhair tree. The hard shells are cracked open and the inner nuts soaked to loosen their skins. The nuts are known for their medicinal properties and are one of the eight treasures in dishes like eight-treasure rice. Shelled nuts can be bought in tins in Chinese shops and are easier to use.

glutinous rice A short-grain rice that, unlike other rice, cooks to a sticky mass and so is used in dishes where the rice is required to hold together. Glutinous rice is labelled as such and has plump, highly polished and shiny grains. Black or red glutinous rice, used mainly in desserts, is slightly different.

goose fat A soft fat that melts at a low temperature and is used a lot in the cooking of southwest France to give a rich texture to dishes. Duck fat can be substituted, although it needs to be heated to a higher temperature.

Gorgonzola A blue cheese, originally made in Gorgonzola in Lombardia, Itlay, but now produced in other regions as well. It melts well and is often used in sauces. If not available, use another full-fat blue cheese.

green banana Cooking banana, also known as plantain, which looks like a large, unripe green banana.

green unripe mango A variety of mango widely used for cooking in Asian countries. Available from Indian food shops.

Gruyère A pressed hard cheese with a nutty flavor. French Gruyère is available as Gruyère de Comté, which can have large holes, and Gruyère de Beaufort, which has virtually no holes. Although French Gruyére does have a different flavor than Swiss, the two are interchangeable in recipes.

Guilin chilli sauce From the southwest of China, this sauce is made from salted, fermented yellow soya beans and chillies. It is used as an ingredient in cooking. If it is unavailable, use a thick chilli sauce instead.

haricot beans The general French name for beans, though the term is also used just to mean a kind of small, dried bean. Dried haricot beans come in many different varieties, including cannellini, flageolet (white or pale green beans) and navy beans. When slow-cooked in stews such as cassoulet they become tender. They also break down very well when mashed to make a smooth purée.

hilsa A much-prized fish, this is a type of shad with sweet flesh and lots of tiny bones. Hilsa are caught when they enter fresh water to spawn. Large herrings or firm white fish can be used instead.

hoisin sauce This sauce is made from salted, yellow soya beans, sugar, vinegar, sesame oil, red rice for coloring and spices such as five-spice or star anise. It is generally used as a dipping sauce, for meat glazes or in barbecue marinades.

Holy basil is either red or green with slightly pointed, variegated leaves. Holy basil is used in stir-fries and fish dishes.

Indian bay leaves These are the dried leaves of the cassia tree. They look somewhat like dried European bay leaves but they have a cinnamon flavor. They are used mainly in Bengali cuisine and cuisine of the north of India and are available from Indian food shops.

jackfruit A large spiky fruit with segmented flesh enclosing large stones. It tastes like fruit salad and is used unripe in curries.

jaggery Made from sugar cane, this is a raw sugar with a caramel flavor and alcoholic aroma. Jaggery, which is sold in lumps, is slightly sticky and varies in color depending on the juice from which it is made. Jaggery can also refer to palm sugar. Soft brown sugar can be used as a substitute.

jujubes Also known as Chinese or red dates, jujubes are an olive-sized dried fruit with a red, wrinkled skin, which are thought to build strength. They need to be soaked and are used in eight-treasure or tonic-type dishes. They are also thought to be lucky because of their red color.

julienne To cut a vegetable or citrus rind into short, thin julienne strips. Vegetables used as a garnish are often julienned for decorative purposes and to ensure quick even cooking.

juniper berries Blackish-purple berries with a resinous flavor. Used in stews and robust game dishes. Use the back of a knife to crush the berries lightly before use to release their flavor.

kalonji Small teardrop-shaped black seeds with an onion flavor, used both as a spice in northern India and as a decoration for breads such as naan. It is used in panch phoron.

karhai/kadhai A deep wok-shaped cooking dish. Heavy cast iron ones are best for talawa (deep-frying) and carbon steel ones for bhoona (frying). There are decorative ones which are best for serving, not cooking.

Kashmiri chilli powder Made from ground red Kashmiri chillies which have a deep red color but little heat. A mild, dark red chilli powder can be substituted.

ketchap manis A thick, sweet soy sauce used as a flavoring.

kokum The dried purple fruit of the gamboge tree which is used in southern Indian, Gujarati and Maharashtran cuisine to impart an acid fruity flavor. Kokum looks like dried pieces of purple/black rind and is quite sticky. It can be bought from Indian food shops and is sometimes called cocumful. A smoked version which is called kodampodli is also available. Kokum needs to be briefly soaked before use.

lemon basil is also called mint basil. It is less common and is used in curries and stir-fries and as a condiment with rice noodles.

lemon grass This ingredient is used in many Thai dishes. The fibrous stalk of a citrus perfumed grass, it is finely chopped or sliced or cut into chunks. Discard the outer layers until you reach a softer purple layer.

limes Limes and lime juice are used extensively in Thai cuisine. Lime juice is a souring agent though Thai limes are sweeter than their Western counterparts. Lemon juice is not a particularly good substitute but can be used. Limes are often cut into cheeks rather than wedges.

longans From the same family as lychees, these are round with smooth, buff-colored skins, translucent sweet flesh and large brown pips. Available fresh, tinned or dried.

lotus leaves The dried leaves of the lotus, they need to be soaked before use and are used for wrapping up food like sticky rice to hold it together while it is cooking. They are sold in packets in Asian shops.

lotus root The rhizome of the Chinese lotus, the root looks like a string of three cream-colored sausages, but when cut into it has a beautifully lacy pattern. Available fresh, which must be washed, tinned or dried. Use the fresh or tinned version as a fresh vegetable and the dried version in braises.

lotus seeds These seeds from the lotus are considered medicinal and are used in eight-treasure dishes as well as being roasted, salted or candied and eaten as a snack. Lotus seeds are also made into a sweet paste to fill buns and pancakes. Fresh and dried lotus seeds are both available and dried seeds need to be soaked before use.

lychees Small round fruit with a red leathery skin and translucent white flesh surrounding a brown stone. Very perfumed and often available peeled and seeded in a syrup as a dessert.

Madeira A type of fortified wine from the Portuguese island of Madeira. There are a number of different varieties of Madeira, from sweet (Malmsey or Malvasia and Bual), to medium (Verdelho) and dry (Sercial).

maida Plain white flour used for making naan and other Indian recipes. Plain flour is a suitable substitute.

makrut limes These knobbly skinned fruit are used for their zest rather than their bitter juice. Leaves (bai makrut) are double leaves with a fragrant citrus oil. They are used very finely shredded or torn into large pieces. Frozen leaves are available but less fragrant than fresh ones.

maltose A sweet liquid of malted grains used to coat Peking duck and barbecued meats. It is sold in Chinese shops, but honey can be used instead.

mangoes Green unripe mangoes are used in relishes, curries, soups and salads, or preserved in brine. Ripe mangoes are eaten out of the hand or alongside sticky rice as a dessert.

Maroilles A square soft cheese with an orange washed-rind and a strong smell but sweet flavor. As an alternative, you could use other washed-rind varieties, such as Livarot, or a cheese with a white-molded rind, such as Camembert.

Marsala A fortified wine from Marsala in Itlay that comes in varying degrees of dryness

and sweetness. Dry Marsalas are used in savoury dishes, and sweet ones in desserts such as zabaione. Do not try to use sweet Marsala in savoury dishes.

mascarpone A cream cheese originally from Itlay. Made with cream rather than milk, it is very high in fat. Mascarpone is generally used in desserts such as tiramisu or instead of cream in sauces.

masoor dal (red lentils) When whole (known as matki or bagali) these are dark brown or green. When split, they are salmon in color. The split ones are the most common as they cook more easily and do not usually need soaking as the whole ones do.

master sauce This is a basic stock of soy sauce, rice wine, rock sugar, spring onions, ginger and star anise. Additional ingredients vary according to individual chefs. Meat, poultry or fish is cooked in the stock, then the stock is reserved so it matures, taking on the flavors of everything that is cooked in it. The spices are replenished every few times the sauce is used. Master sauce spices can be bought as a mix, or a ready-made liquid version. Freeze between uses.

Mei Kuei Lu Chiew A fragrant spirit known as Rose Dew Liqueur. Made from sorghum and rose petals. It is used in marinades, but brandy can be used instead.

Mesclun A salad mix containing young lettuce leaves and herbs such as arugula, mâche, dandelion leaves, basil, chervil and endive.

methi The leaves of young fenugreek plants, these are used as a vegetable and treated much like spinach. They have a mildly bitter flavor. Strip the leaves off the stalks as the stalks are often tough. Spinach leaves can be used but will not give the same flavor. Available fresh or dried, from Indian food shops.

mint Mint is used in salads such as laap as well as being served alongside salads and rice-noodle soups.

misticanza A Roman salad that was once made of wild greens. Today it is generally a mixture of rocket, purslane, sorrel, mint, dandelion, wild fennel and endive with some

lettuce. In Italy it also refers to a mixture of dried beans used for soups.

moong dal Split and skinned mung beans, which are pale yellow. The dal does not always need to be soaked. Whole mung beans (sabat moong), also called green gram, must be soaked before use.

mortadella A large, finely textured pork sausage, with lengths of lard running through it. Some versions contain pistachio nuts and all should be eaten thinly sliced or in cubes and very fresh. Traditionally made in Bologna, Italy, the sausage is also known as bologna or boloney in the USA.

mung bean sprouts These are used in stir-fries, soups and salads. Keep them in a bowl of cold water in the fridge to prolong their life.

mung beans Whole beans are puréed or ground and used in desserts. Also used to make a type of noodle.

mushrooms Straw mushrooms (het faang) are usually found tinned except in Asia. Replace them with oyster mushrooms if you need to. Shiitake (het hawm) are used both fresh and dried. Dried ones need to be soaked in boiling water before they are used.

mussels Grown commercially around the coast on bouchots (poles) driven into mud flats or in beds in estuaries, mussels can be eaten raw but are usually cooked in dishes such as moules à la marinière. French mussels have blue-black shells and vary slightly in size and flavor according to the waters in which they are grown. The mussels grown around Boulogne in northern France are of a very high quality.

mustard oil Made from pressed brown mustard seeds, this is a strongly flavored oil which is used in Bengali and Punjabi cooking. The oil is usually preheated to smoking point and then cooled to temper its strong aroma.

mustard seeds Yellow, brown and black mustard seeds are used in Indian cooking, especially in Bengal. Brown and black are interchangeable. The seeds are either added to hot oil to pop, to make them taste nutty rather than hot, or are ground to a

589

paste before use in which case they are still hot. Split mustard seeds are called mustard dal.

noodles Rice noodles (kuaytiaw) are made of rice flour and water and steamed in sheets before being cut into widths. Wide line or sen yai noodles are about 2.5 cm (1 inch) wide, small line (sen lek) are 5 mm (1/4 inch) in width and line noodles (sen mii) are 1–2 mm. Rice noodles are sold fresh and dried. The widths can be used interchangeably. Wheat noodles (ba-mii) are usually made with egg. Mung bean starch noodles (wun sen) are very thin white translucent noodles that go clear when soaked. They are much tougher than rice noodles. Both wun sen and sen mii are referred to as vermicelli. Egg noodles come fresh and dried in varying thicknesses. In recipes they are interchangeable, so choose a brand that you like and buy the thickness appropriate to the dish you are making. Wheat noodles are also available fresh and dried and are interchangeable in recipes. Rice noodles are made from a paste of ground rice and water and can be bought fresh or as dried rice sticks or vermicelli. The fresh noodles are white and can be bought in a roll.

oil Several types of oil are used in Indian cuisine, depending on where the dish comes from. An Indian pantry should contain several oils for different uses. Cold-pressed or refined peanut (groundnut) oil is used in northern and central India and is a good all-purpose oil (use only the refined version for deep-frying). Sesame oil made from raw sesame seeds is used in the South, and mustard oil in the Punjab and Bengal. These oils impart flavor to the dishes in which they are used. Coconut oil is also used in the South where coconut is a major flavoring. It fries well but is very high in saturated fats.

okra Also known as ladies' fingers, these are green, fuzzy, tapered pods with ridges running down them. When cut they give off a mucilaginous substance which disappears during cooking.

olive Eating olives can be named after where they come from, such as Ligurian; their curing style, such as Sicilian; or their variety, such as Cerignola. Though green

and black olives have a different flavor, they can be used interchangeably in recipes unless the final color is a factor.

olive oil Extra-virgin and virgin olive oils are pressed without any heat or chemicals and are best used in simple uncooked dishes and for salads. Pure olive oil can be used for cooking or deep-frying. Different varieties of olives are grown all over the Mediterranean and the oil of each region has a distinctive taste. Tuscan oil tends to be full-bodied and peppery; Ligurian oil pale and subtle; and Pugliese and Sicilian oil fruity and sharp.

one-thousand-year old eggs Also known as one-hundred-year old or century eggs, these are eggs that have been preserved by coating them in a layer of wood ash, slaked lime and then rice husks. The eggs are left to mature for 40 days to give them a blackish-green yolk and amber white. To eat, the coating is scraped off and the shell peeled. These eggs are eaten as an hors d'oeuvre or used to garnish congee.

Orange chillies are hot but not as hot as bird's eye chillies.

orange flower water Produced when the flower of the bitter orange is distilled. Orange flower water is a delicate flavoring used in dessert recipes.

oyster sauce Use the Thai version of the Chinese sauce if you can. It has a stronger oyster flavor. A fairly recent invention, add to dishes at the end of cooking or use as a dipping sauce or marinade.

oyster Huîtres plates are European oysters, or natives. They have a flat round shell and are better in the winter months when they are not spawning. The most famous are the belons from Brittany. Huîtres creuses are the much more common Portuguese (or Pacific) oysters, with deep, bumpy and flaky shells. Some of the best Portuguese oysters are grown in Marennes. Fines de claires are oysters grown in water full of algae, giving them a green color and a distinct, iodine flavor.

palm sugar Palm sugar is made by boiling sugar palm sap until it turns into a granular paste. Sold in hard cakes of varying sizes or as a slightly softer version in tubs. Malaysian

and Indonesian brands of palm sugar are darker in color and stronger in flavor. Unrefined, soft light brown sugar can be used instead.

pancetta Cured belly of pork, somewhat like streaky bacon. Available in flat pieces or rolled up (arrotolata), and both smoked and unsmoked. Generally used, either sliced or cut into cubes, as an ingredient in dishes like spaghetti carbonara.

panch phoron Meaning five spices, this mix is used in Bengali and Bangladeshi cuisine. It contains fennel, brown mustard, kalonji, fenugreek, and cumin seeds in equal amounts. It can be used whole or ground.

pandanus leaves These long green leaves are shaped like blades and are used as a flavoring in desserts and sweets, as well as a wrapping for small parcels of food. Pandanus are also called screwpine. Essence can be bought in small bottles from speciality Asian food shops. Pandanus leaves are often sold frozen.

paneer A fresh cheese made by coagulating milk with lemon juice and leaving it to drain. Paneer is usually pressed into a block and can be found in the refrigerated section in supermarkets and Indian food shops.

paprika A reddish orange powder made from ground sweet peppers grown in Kashmir. Usually sweet rather than hot, paprika is used for color. It needs to be fried to get rid of any raw flavor. Spanish or Hungarian paprika can be substituted.

Parma ham This prosciutto comes from traditionally reared pigs fed on the whey from making Parmigiano Reggiano. It has a sweet taste and is only flavored with salt. Parma hams can be identified by the stamp on the skin showing the five-pointed star of the Dukes of Parma. Other prosciutto can be used if Parma ham is unavailable.

passata Meaning 'puréed', this most commonly refers to a smooth uncooked tomato pulp bought in tins or jars. Best without added herbs and flavorings.

peanuts Peanuts are used raw in some curries, deep-fried as a garnish, or in dipping sauces. Buy raw peanuts and fry them yourself for the best results.

pecorino One of Italy's most popular cheeses, virtually every region produces a version. Made from sheep's milk and always by the same method, although the result varies according to the milk and ageing process used. Pecorino Romano is a well-known hard variety from Lazio and Sardinia.

peperoncini The Italian name for chillies, these are popular in the cooking of the South, and are also served there as a condiment. The smallest are called diavolilli.

pepper Used as an ingredient rather than as a condiment, most hot dishes were originally flavored with copious quantities of pepper rather than the chillies used now. White pepper is used rather than black.

peppercorns Green peppercorns are used fresh in curries. Dried white peppercorns are used as a seasoning in dishes and as a garnish but black pepper is seldom used.

pickled garlic Eaten as an accompaniment, pickled garlic has a sweet/sour flavor. Preserved as whole heads that can be used as they are. Available at Chinese food shops.

pickled ginger Eaten as an accompaniment to curries and snacks. Buy ready-made from Asian food shops.

pine nuts Small cream-colored seeds from Neosia pine cones which grow in the Himalayas. In Kashmir, they are a staple and are used both whole and ground. Any pine nut may be used.

plum sauce This comes in several varieties, with some brands sweeter than others and some adding chilli, ginger or garlic. It is often served with Peking duck rather than the true sauce and is a good dipping sauce.

polenta The name of the dish and also the ingredient itself, which is ground corn. The cornmeal comes in different grades of coarseness. Finer varieties are better in cakes and coarse ones to accompany stews. A white cornmeal is also available.

pomegranate seeds Sun-dried whole or ground sour pomegranate seeds, used to add a sour, tangy flavor to north Indian dishes. They are also used as a garnish. Available from Indian food shops.

pomfret A silvery seawater fish with tiny black spots. Pomfret is expensive and hard to find outside India, although it is sometimes available frozen. Sole, flounder, leatherjacket or John Dory fillets can be substituted.

poppadom These are quite thin wafers made from a paste of lentil (gram) flours, rice flour or even tapioca or sago flour, which is rolled out very thin and then sun-dried. Poppadoms come in different sizes and flavors. Northern Indian ones often have chilli flakes or spices added. To fry poppadoms, heat oil in a frying pan until very hot, add the poppadoms one at a time and press them down into the oil with a spatula until they expand and lighten in color. To flame-roast them, hold a poppadom in some tongs above a gas flame until it expands in size, curls and gets flecked with bubbles (toast both sides). Fried poppadoms will stay crisp for about two hours.

poppy seeds In India, white poppy seeds are used rather than the European black or grey ones. They are used either whole or ground. The ground poppy seeds are used to thicken dishes like korma. Whole ones are often roasted and used in spice mixes. Don't use black poppy seeds as a thickener or the color of your dish will be greyish.

porcini The Italian name for a cep or boletus mushroom. Usually bought dried and reconstituted in boiling water, but available fresh in the spring and autumn.

poussin A baby chicken weighing about 13 oz–1 lb. Poussin are often butterflied and broiled or stuffed. Usually one poussin is served per person, though slightly bigger ones are adequate for two people.

preserved cabbage Salted and preserved cabbage is usually sold shredded. It sometimes comes in eathenware pots and is labelled Tianjin preserved vegetables. Available at Asian food shops.

preserved ginger Ginger pickled in rice vinegar and sugar, which is typically used for sweet-and-sour dishes. Japanese pickled ginger could be used as a substitute.

preserved mustard cabbage Also called Sichuan pickle or preserved vegetables, this is the root of the mustard cabbage preserved in chilli and salt. It is available whole and shredded in jars or tins from Chinese shops.

preserved plums Salty, sour, preserved plums are used in sweet/sour dishes, to make plum sauce, and with steamed fish. Can be bought at Asian food shops.

preserved radish Salted and preserved radish is sold shredded or as strips. It is also referred to by the Japanese name, daikon, or the Indian, mooli. Comes salty and sweet/salty. Buy from Asian food shops.

preserved turnip This is Chinese turnip, sliced, shredded or grated, and usually preserved in brine. It has a crunchy texture and needs to be rinsed before using so it is less salty.

prosciutto Italian name for ham. Prosciutto crudo is cured ham and includes Parma ham and San Daniele. Prosciutto cotto is cooked ham.

provolone Curd cheese made from cows' milk. The curds are spun and worked into large pear- or tube-shaped cheeses, then immersed in brine and bound with string. Available fresh or matured and eaten as a table cheese or used in cooking.

puffed rice Rather like popcorn, puffed rice is made by exploding dried rice out of its husks by dropping the grains onto hot sand. It is used in snacks such as bhel puri, or rolled in jaggery to make sweets. Available from Indian food shops.

Puy lentils Tiny green lentils from Puy in central France that are AOC graded. Puy lentils do not need to be presoaked and do not break down when cooked. They have a firm texture and go very well with both meat and fish. Traditionally they are cooked and served with a mustard vinaigrette.

radicchio A salad leaf of the chicory family with slightly bitter red leaves. There are several varieties: radicchio di Castelfranco, di Chioggia and rosso di Verona are similar to a red cabbage with round leaves; radicchio di Treviso has longer, pointed leaves.

rambutan A small round fruit with a red skin covered in soft, fine red spikes. Buy rambutan when they are vibrant in color.

red bean paste Made from crushed adzuki beans and sugar, this sweet paste is used in soups and to fill dumplings and pancakes. There is a richer black version and this can be used instead.

rice Rice grain types and sizes vary greatly. In India much of the rice is grown locally and it is nearly always white and polished. Popular long-grained rices include basmati, a particularly fragrant rice used for special occasions (it is expensive); patna, with a more rounded grain, is eaten in the North; and gobindavog is used in Bengal. Rices with some husk left on, which gives them some red coloration, include red patni, grown in central and western India, and rosematter, grown in southern India. You can use whichever variety you like best. Jasmine (long-grain) and sticky rice are the two main varieties eaten in Thailand. Sticky rice comes in white and black, which is quite purple in reality. Much of the rice that is eaten is grown locally and it is nearly always white and polished. Jasmine rice is steamed, boiled or, more traditionally, cooked in a clay pot. Sticky rice is soaked and then steamed, either in a steamer or packed into lengths of bamboo.

rice flour This is finely ground rice, often used to make rice noodles. Glutinous rice flour, used for making sweet things, makes a chewier dough. Obtainable from Chinese shops or supermarkets.

rice sticks Made from rice flour, these noodles are very thin. They are used for sweets or savoury snacks and need to be softened in boiling water. Other Asian rice vermicelli can be used as a substitute.

rice vinegar Made from fermented rice, Chinese vinegars are milder than Western ones. Clear rice vinegar is mainly used for pickles and sweet-and-sour dishes. Red rice vinegar is a mild liquid used as a dipping sauce and served with shark's fin soup. Black rice vinegar is used in braises, especially in northern recipes—Chinkiang (Zhenjiang) vinegar is a good label. Rice vinegars can last indefinitely but may lose their aroma, so buy small bottles. If you can't find them, use cider vinegar instead of clear and balsamic instead of black.

risotto rice Round-grained, very absorbent rice, cultivated in northern Italy. Risotto rice comes in four categories, classified not by quality but by the size of each grain. The smallest, Riso Comune (common rice) is very quick to cook (12–13 minutes), and is ideal for rice pudding. Semifino rice includes varieties like vialone nano and cooks in about 15 minutes. Fino takes a minute longer and has more bite. The largest, Superfino, includes arborio and carnaroli and takes about 20 minutes.

roasted chana dal Bengal gram which have been roasted so they puff up and get a porous, crunchy texture. Used in snacks. Buy in bags from Indian food shops.

roasted chilli powder Both bird's eye and sky-pointing chilies are used to make chilli powder. Buy from Asian food shops or make your own by roasting and grinding whole chillies.

roasted chilli sauce This sauce is made from dried red chillies roasted in oil, hence the name. It usually includes shrimp paste and palm sugar. Roasted chilli sauce comes in mild, medium and hot and is sold in jars and plastic pouches. Use as a flavoring and as a relish.

roasted sesame oil Chinese sesame oil is made from roasted white sesame seeds and is a rich amber liquid, unlike the pale unroasted Middle Eastern sesame oil. Buy small bottles as it loses its aroma quickly. It does not fry well as it smokes at a low temperature, but sprinkle it on food as a seasoning or use it mixed with another oil for stir-frying.

rock sugar Yellow rock sugar comes as uneven lumps of sugar, which may need to be further crushed before use if very big. It is a pure sugar that gives a clear syrup and makes sauces it is added to shiny and clear. You can use sugar lumps instead.

rohu A black, silvery carp with one central bone and firm flesh. It cuts into steaks very well. Any firm-fleshed fish can be substituted.

rose apple A crisp, watery fruit with no overwhelming taste, except for sweetness. Eaten on its own as a fruit and sometimes as an accompaniment to dips such as naam phrik.

rosewater Made from rose essence and water, this is used to perfume sweets, desserts and drinks. It has aroma but no flavor. Use sparingly.

saag A generic term for leafy greens.

saffron strands The dried stigmas of a crocus flower. The strands give an intense yellow color and musky aroma. Only a few threads are needed for each recipe as they are very pungent (and expensive). Indian saffron grows in Kashmir. It needs to be soaked in liquid before use.

sago Small dried balls of sago palm sap which are used for milky desserts and savoury dishes. Cooked sago is transparent and soft with a silky texture.

salt cod Brought to Europe as long ago as the fifteenth century, salt cod's popularity in France is a legacy of the religious need to eat fish on Fridays and feast days. Salt cod is cod that has been gutted, salted and dried, and is different from stockfish (dried cod), which is just dried but not salted. A center-cut fillet of salt cod tends to be meatier than the thinner tail end, and some varieties are drier than others so the soaking time varies.

salted, fermented black beans Very salty black soya beans that are fermented using the same moulds as are used for making soy sauce. Added to dishes as a flavoring, they must be rinsed before use and are often mashed or crushed. They are available in jars or bags from specialist shops. You can also use a black bean sauce made with black beans and garlic.

saucisse à cuire A cooking, or specifically boiling, sausage that is usually larger than an ordinary sausage. Saucisses à cuire are poached in liquid, either as part of a dish like choucroute garnie or just with red wine.

sea cucumber A slug-like sea creature related to the starfish. Always sold dried, it needs to be reconstituted by soaking. It has a gelatinous texture and no flavor.

semolina A fine, coarse or medium grain made from processed wheat with the wheat germ removed. It swells when cooked to give a creamy, textured effect. Used for sweets and upama.

sesame paste Made from ground, roasted white sesame seeds, this is a fairly dry paste. It is more aromatic than tahini, which can be used instead by mixing it with a little Chinese sesame oil. Black sesame paste is used for sweets like New Year dumplings.

sevian These are very fine noodles made from wheat flour. They have a biscuity flavor. Sold at Indian food shops.

Shaoxing rice wine Made from rice, millet, yeast and Shaoxing's local water, this is aged for at least 3 years, then bottled either in glass or decorative earthenware bottles. Several varieties are available. As a drink, rice wine is served warm in small cups. Dry sherry is the best substitute.

shark's fin Prized for its texture more than for its flavor, shark's fin is very expensive. Preparing a dried fin takes several days, so using the ready-prepared version is much easier as it just needs soaking and then cooking. It looks like very thin dried noodles.

shrimp paste A strong smelling dark brownish-pink paste sold in small tubs that are usually sealed with wax. It is made from salted, fermented and dried shrimp. Buy a Thai version as those from other Asian countries vary. Used as it is or roasted first and refrigerated. This is very strong smelling and is a main ingredient in dips such as naam phrik.

Sichuan peppercorns Not a true pepper, but the berries of a shrub called the prickly ash. Sichuan pepper, unlike ordinary pepper, has a pungent flavor and the aftertaste, rather than being simply hot, is numbing. The peppercorns should be crushed and dry-roasted to bring out their full flavor.

silver leaf Very thin, edible sheets of silver. They have no flavor or aroma and come in boxes or books between sheets of tissue paper. Always apply the silver to the food from the backing sheet and then pull off the backing sheet. If you touch the foil it will stick to you. Silver leaf does not go on in an even layer because it is so fragile.

Sky-pointing or long chillies are about 5 cm (2 inches) in length and milder than the smaller ones. Used in stir-fries, salads and curry pastes.

slab sugar Dark brown sugar with a caramel flavor sold in a slab. Soft brown sugar can be used instead.

snake beans Also called long beans or yard-long beans, these are sold in coils or tied together in bunches. Eaten fresh and cooked. Green beans can be used instead.

soffritto The flavor base for many soups, stews and risottos. Soffritto is a mixture of fried ingredients like onion, celery, carrot, garlic, pancetta and herbs. It means literally to 'under-fry' and the mixture should be sweated rather than colored.

sour sausage Thai sausages can be bought ready-made or you can make them yourself. They sometimes come wrapped in cellophane or banana leaves, or are strung together. Chinese sausages can be used instead.

soy sauce Made from fermented soya beans, soy sauce comes in two styles: light soy sauce, which is also known as just soy sauce or superior soy sauce, and is used with fish, poultry and vegetables, and dark soy sauce, which is more commonly used with meats. Chinese soy sauce, unlike Japanese, is not used as a condiment except with Cantonese cuisine. As it is not meant to be a dipping sauce, it is best to mix a tablespoon of dark with two tablespoons of light to get a good flavor for a condiment. It does not last forever so buy small bottles and store it in the fridge.

soya beans These are oval, pale-green beans. The fresh beans are cooked in their fuzzy pods and served as a snack. The dried beans can be yellow or black, and the yellow ones are used to make soy milk by boiling and then puréeing the beans with water before straining off the milk. Dried beans need to be soaked overnight.

split peas Split dried peas which need to be soaked before they are cooked and have a slightly chewy texture. Green and yellow ones are available.

spring roll wrappers Also called spring roll skins, these wrappers are made with egg and are a pale or dark yellow. They are found in the refrigerated cabinets of Chinese shops and supermarkets and can be frozen until needed.

squid/cuttlefish ink Used to color and flavor pasta and risotto. The ink is stored in a sac that can be removed from whole squid and cuttlefish or bought in sachets from fishmongers or delicatessens.

star anise An aromatic ingredient in Chinese cooking, this is a star-shaped dried seed pod containing a flat seed in each point. It has a similar flavor and aroma to fennel seed and aniseed. It is used whole in braises or ground into five-spice powder.

steaming A method of cooking food in a moist heat to keep it tender and preserve its flavor. Bamboo steamers fit above a saucepan or wok and a 25 cm (10 inch) steamer is the most useful, although you will need a bigger one for whole fish. Use as many as you need, stacked on top of each other, and reverse them halfway through cooking to ensure the cooking is even. Metal steamers are available, but bamboo ones are preferred in China as they absorb the steam, making the food a little drier.

stir-frying A method of cooking in a wok that only uses a little oil and cooks the food evenly and quickly, retaining its color and texture. Everything to be cooked needs to be prepared beforehand, cut to roughly the same shape, dry and at room temperature. The wok is heated, then the oil added and heated before the ingredients are thrown in. Stir-frying should only take a couple of minutes, the heat should be high and the ingredients continually tossed.

sweetbreads The pancreas and thymus glands of calves or lambs, sweetbreads are white in color, soft in texture and have an irregular shape. Sweetbreads should be soaked in cold water to remove any blood before they are cooked.

Taleggio A mountain cheese originally from the Italian Alps near Bergamo, but now also made in other regions. Taleggio is a very good table and cooking cheese and should be eaten young—its flavor becomes more acidic with age. It is made in squares and has a pink-yellow crust and creamy centre.

tamarind (ma-khaam) A fruit whose flesh is used as a souring agent. Usually bought as a dried cake or prepared as a purée, tamarind is actually a pod filled with seeds and a fibrous flesh. If you buy tamarind cake, then it must be soaked in hot water and then rubbed and squeezed to dissolve the pulp around the fibres. The fibres are then sieved out. Pulp is sold as purée or concentrate but is sometimes referred to as tamarind water in recipes. Freshly made tamarind water has a fresher, stronger flavor.

tandoori food coloring A bright red powder which is used to color tandoori dishes. Add to tandoori pastes to color them.

tangerine peel Dried tangerine or orange peel is used as a seasoning. It looks like dark-brown strips of leather with a white underside, and is used mostly in braised dishes or master sauces. It is not soaked first but is added straight to the liquid in the dish. Sold in bags in Chinese shops.

tapioca flour Made from ground, dried cassava root, this flour is used in desserts, dumpling wrappers and as a thickener. It is sold in small plastic bags in Asian food shops.

tarka A seasoning process, either the first or last step, used in Indian cookery. Spices and aromatics are fried in oil to flavor the oil, then the oil is stirred into the dish, most commonly at the end of cooking.

tava A specially shaped hotplate used in India to cook breads. Some are flat, others are slightly convex or concave. Keep oiled to stop them going rusty. Non-stick ones are also available.

Thai sweet basil is the most common. This has purplish stems, green leaves and an aniseed aroma and flavor. It is aromatic and is used in curries, soups and stir-fries, as well as sometimes being served as an accompaniment to naam phrik.

tiger lily buds Sometimes called golden needles, these aren't from tiger lilies but are the unopened flowers from another type of lily. The buds are bought dried and then soaked. They have an earthy flavor and are used mainly in vegetarian dishes.

tofu Also called bean curd, this can be firm or silken (soft).

toor dal Also called yellow lentils, these come oiled and plain. Oiled ones look slightly greasy and need to be soaked in hot water to remove the oil. Soak the dal for a few hours before cooking.

Toulouse sausage A general term for meaty pork broiling sausages, usually sold in a coil.

truffles Considered an expensive delicacy, truffles are a type of fungus and have an earthy smell. The black truffles found in France, specifically around Périgord, are often considered the best black truffles in the world. Both black and white truffles can be found in Italy. The black ones come from Umbria (especially around Norcia), Piemonte and Emilia-Romagna. The white ones come from Alba (considered the best), Emilia-Romagna, Le Marche, Tuscany and Umbria. Truffles are best eaten fresh, but can also be bought preserved in jars, and only need to be used in small amounts to flavor dishes.

turmeric A rhizome like ginger and galangal. In Thailand turmeric comes in white and yellow varieties. The yellow type is often referred to as red and is used fresh in curry pastes. Dried, it adds a yellow color to curries, particularly Northern khao sawy. The white type is often eaten raw as a vegetable accompaniment to naam phrik.

urad dal The split variety (chilke urad) is a cream color with black skin. The skinned variety is cream. Urad dal does not usually need to be soaked. The dal is used when making dosa and idli batters and it becomes glutinous and creamy when cooked.

vanilla extract Made by using alcohol to extract the vanilla flavor from beans and not to be confused with artificial vanilla essence made with synthetic vanillin. Vanilla extract is very strong and should be used sparingly.

vin santo A golden dessert wine eaten with cantucci biscuits. Now made all over Italy, but the best known is made in Tuscany.

vinegar White coconut vinegar is the most common. Any mild white vinegar or better still, rice vinegar, can be used as a substitute.

vinegar Made from fermented alcohol, vinegars based on sugar cane molasses (dark) and coconut (clear) are used, mainly in Parsi, Anglo-Indian and Goan food. If unavailable, substitute balsamic or white vinegar.

water chestnuts These are the rhizomes of a plant that grows in paddy fields in China. The nut has a dark-brown shell and a crisp white interior. The raw nuts need to be peeled with a knife and blanched, then stored in water. Tinned ones need to be drained and rinsed. Freshly peeled nuts are sometimes available from Chinese shops.

water spinach Called ong choy in Chinese, this vegetable has long, dark-green pointed leaves and long hollow stems. Often cooked with shrimp paste.

wheat starch A powder-like flour made by removing the protein from wheat flour. It is used to make dumpling wrappers.

whole black gram (sabat urad) This whole urad dal has a black skin. Usually it has to be soaked or precooked before use.

wing beans (thua phuu) Also called angle beans, these have four frilly edges. Used cut into cross sections in salads and stir-fries. Buy as fresh as you can.

winter melon A very large dark-green gourd or squash that looks like a watermelon. The skin is dark green, often with a white waxy bloom, and the flesh is pale green. You can usually buy pieces of it in Chinese shops.

wok A bowl-shaped cooking vessel that acts as both a frying pan and a saucepan in the Chinese kitchen. Choose one made from carbon steel about 35 cm (13 inch) in diameter. To season it, scrub off the layer of machine oil, then heat with 2 tablespoons of oil over low heat for several minutes. Rub the inside with paper towels, changing the paper until it comes out clean. The inside will continue to darken as it is used and only water should be used for cleaning. Use a different wok for steaming, as boiling water will strip off the seasoning. A metal spatula (charn) is perfect for moving ingredients around the wok.

won ton wrappers Also called won ton skins, these are square and yellow and slightly larger than dumpling wrappers. They can be found in the refrigerated cabinets in Chinese shops and good supermarkets and can be frozen until needed. Gow gee and gyoza wrappers can also be used.

yard-long beans Also called snake or long beans, these are about 40 cm (16 inch) long. The darker green variety has a firmer texture.

yellow bean sauce This is actually brown in color and made from fermented yellow soya beans, which are sweeter and less salty than black beans, mixed with rice wine and dark brown sugar. It varies in flavor and texture (some have whole beans in them) and is sold under different names—crushed yellow beans, brown bean sauce, ground bean sauce and bean sauce. It is mainly used in Sichuan and Hunan cuisine.

yoghurt Yoghurt is made with whole milk and is a thick, set yoghurt. If you use commercial yoghurt, you may need to drain it in muslin first to remove any excess liquid.

zucchini The Italian name for courgettes.

RECIPE INDEX